EARLY ROMANTICISM AND RELIGIOUS DISSENT

Religious diversity and ferment characterize the period that gave rise to Romanticism in England. It is generally known that many individuals who contributed to the new literatures of the late eighteenth century came from Dissenting backgrounds, but we nonetheless often underestimate the full significance of nonconformist beliefs and practices during this period. Daniel White provides a clear and useful introduction to Dissenting communities, focusing on Anna Barbauld and her familial network of heterodox "liberal" Dissenters whose religious, literary, educational, political, and economic activities shaped the public culture of early Romanticism in England. He goes on to analyze the roles of nonconformity within the lives and writings of William Godwin, Mary Wollstonecraft, Samuel Taylor Coleridge, and Robert Southey, offering a Dissenting genealogy of the Romantic movement.

DANIEL E. WHITE is Assistant Professor of English at the University of Toronto.

CAMBRIDGE STUDIES IN ROMANTICISM

General editors

Professor Marilyn Butler, *University of Oxford*
Professor James Chandler, *University of Chicago*

Editorial Board

John Barrell, *University of York*
Paul Hamilton, *University of London*
Mary Jacobus, *University of Cambridge*
Claudia Johnson, *Princeton University*
Alan Liu, *University of California, Santa Barbara*
Jerome McGann, *University of Virginia*
Susan Manning, *University of Edinburgh*
David Simpson, *University of California, Davis*

This series aims to foster the best new work in one of the most challenging fields within English literary studies. From the early 1780s to the early 1830s a formidable array of talented men and women took to literary composition, not just in poetry, which some of them famously transformed, but in many modes of writing. The expansion of publishing created new opportunities for writers, and the political stakes of what they wrote were raised again by what Wordsworth called those "great national events" that were "almost daily taking place": the French Revolution, the Napoleonic and American wars, urbanization, industrialization, religious revival, an expanded empire abroad and the reform movement at home. This was an enormous ambition, even when it pretended otherwise. The relations between science, philosophy, religion, and literature were reworked in texts such as *Frankenstein* and *Biographia Literaria*; gender relations in *A Vindication of the Rights of Woman* and *Don Juan*; journalism by Cobbett and Hazlitt; poetic form, content, and style by the Lake School and the Cockney School. Outside Shakespeare studies, probably no body of writing has produced such a wealth of comment or done so much to shape the responses of modern criticism. This indeed is the period that saw the emergence of those notions of "literature" and of literary history, especially national literary history, on which modern scholarship in English has been founded.

The categories produced by Romanticism have also been challenged by recent historicist arguments. The task of the series is to engage both with a challenging corpus of Romantic writings and with the changing field of criticism they have helped to shape. As with other literary series published by Cambridge, this one will represent the work of both younger and more established scholars, on either side of the Atlantic and elsewhere.

For a complete list of titles published see end of book.

EARLY ROMANTICISM AND RELIGIOUS DISSENT

DANIEL E. WHITE

CAMBRIDGE
UNIVERSITY PRESS

CAMBRIDGE UNIVERSITY PRESS
Cambridge, New York, Melbourne, Madrid, Cape Town, Singapore, São Paulo

Cambridge University Press
The Edinburgh Building, Cambridge CB2 2RU, UK

Published in the United States of America by Cambridge University Press, New York

www.cambridge.org
Information on this title: www.cambridge.org/9780521858953

First published 2006
Printed in the United Kingdom at the University Press, Cambridge

A catalogue record for this publication is available from the British Library

ISBN-13 978-0-521-85895-3 hardback
ISBN-10 0-521-85895-x hardback

Contents

Illustrations

Acknowledgments

At the University of Pennsylvania, where this book began to take shape in the form of my doctoral dissertation, I was fortunate to find a remarkable group of mentors and fellow graduate students. Among those whose examples meant and continue to mean more to me than they could know, I would like to thank Stuart Curran, Toni Bowers, David DeLaura, Michael Gamer, Joe Farrell, Margreta deGrazia, and Peter Stallybrass for their generosity, spirit, and guidance. I have benefited greatly from the readings and suggestions of Alan Bewell, Pamela Clemit, Jeannine DeLombard, Markman Ellis, Tim Fulford, Gary Handwerk, Anne Janowitz, Jack Lynch, Jon Mee, and Anne Mellor, as well as Barbara Taylor and the members of the Gender and Enlightenment Collaborative Research Project. In the early stages of my research at the British Museum, I discovered a remarkable group of minds and friends in Sophie Carter, Will Fisher, Andrea Mackenzie, Phil Coogan, Frans De Bruyn, and Oz Frankl. With each passing year my admiration for the individuals who make up the Romanticist community deepens, and I would like to take this opportunity to express my love and esteem for Jeff Cox, Julie Kipp, Greg Kucich, Mark Lussier, Tilar Mazzeo, and Paul Youngquist. At the University of Toronto I am grateful for the support I consistently receive from my colleagues, especially Alan Bewell, Heather and Robin Jackson, Karen Weisman, Jeannine DeLombard, and Mark Levene. I have received material assistance from the University of Pennsylvania, the University of Puget Sound, the University of Toronto, the Connaught Fund, the Social Sciences and Humanities Research Council of Canada, and the Huntington Library and Andrew W. Mellon Foundation. Linda Bree and Maartje Scheltens of Cambridge University Press have been extremely supportive and helpful. I am indebted as well to the staffs of the British Library; Dr. Williams' Library; the Senate House Library at the University of London; the Thomas Fisher Rare Book Library, the E. J. Pratt Library, and Robarts Library at the University of Toronto; the

Huntington Library; the New York Public Library; the Van Pelt Library, especially the Annenberg Rare Book and Manuscript Library, at the University of Pennsylvania; and the Library Company of Philadelphia.

Material from several chapters has appeared in print in earlier versions: "The 'Joineriana': Anna Barbauld, the Aikin Family Circle, and the Dissenting Public Sphere," *Eighteenth-Century Studies* 32 (Summer 1999): 511–33; "'Properer for a Sermon': Particularities of Dissent and Coleridge's Conversational Mode," *Studies in Romanticism* 40 (Summer 2001): 175–98 (by permission of the Trustees of Boston University); "'With Mrs Barbauld it is different': Dissenting Heritage and the Devotional Taste," in *Women, Gender and Enlightenment*, edited by Sarah Knott and Barbara Taylor (London: Palgrave, 2005), pp. 474–92. I am grateful for permission to reprint these materials here. Every effort has been made to secure necessary permissions to reproduce copyright material in this work, though in some cases it has proved impossible to trace copyright holders. If any omissions are brought to our notice, we will be happy to include appropriate acknowledgments in any subsequent edition.

The special place in my heart, and in these acknowledgments, is reserved for my exquisite Jeannine, who has read every word and remains my collaborator, competitor, colleague, and consummate companion.

This book is dedicated to my family of writers, musicians, and talkers.

Frequently cited texts

The following texts are commonly cited in the abbreviated form shown below:

CL   Samuel Taylor Coleridge, *The Collected Letters of Samuel Taylor Coleridge*, ed. Earl Leslie Griggs, 6 vols. (Oxford: Clarendon Press, 1956–71).

CN   William Godwin, *The Collected Novels and Memoirs of William Godwin*, gen. ed. Mark Philp, 8 vols. (London: William Pickering, 1992).

CPB   Robert Southey, *Southey's Common-Place Book*, ed. John Wood Warter, 4 vols. (London, 1849–51).

CW   S. T. Coleridge, *The Collected Works of Samuel Taylor Coleridge*, gen. ed. Kathleen Coburn, 16 vols. (Princeton University Press, 1971–).

Evenings Anna Letitia Barbauld and John Aikin, *Evenings at Home*, 6 vols. (London, 1792–96).

LC   R. Southey, *The Life and Correspondence of Robert Southey*, ed. Charles Cuthbert Southey, 6 vols. (London, 1849–50).

NL   R. Southey, *New Letters of Robert Southey*, ed. Kenneth Curry, 2 vols. (New York: Columbia University Press, 1965).

PALB   A. L. Barbauld, *The Poems of Anna Letitia Barbauld*, ed. William McCarthy and Elizabeth Kraft (Athens: University of Georgia Press, 1994).

PPW   W. Godwin, *Political and Philosophical Writings of William Godwin*, gen. ed. Mark Philp, 7 vols. (London: William Pickering, 1993).

Selections R. Southey, *Selections from the Letters of Robert Southey*, ed. John Wood Warter, 4 vols. (London, 1856).

SPP   A. L. Barbauld, *Anna Letitia Barbauld: Selected Poetry and Prose*, ed. William McCarthy and Elizabeth Kraft (Peterborough: Broadview, 2002).

STC   S. T. Coleridge, *Samuel Taylor Coleridge: The Complete Poems*, ed. William Keach (London: Penguin, 1997).

Taylor   William Taylor, *A Memoir of the Life and Writings of the Late William Taylor of Norwich . . . Containing his Correspondence of Many Years with the late Robert Southey, Esq.*, ed. J. W. Robberds, 2 vols. (London, 1843).

Works   A. L. Barbauld, *The Works of Anna Laetitia Barbauld. With a Memoir by Lucy Aikin*, ed. Lucy Aikin, 2 vols. (London, 1825).

WMW   Mary Wollstonecraft, *The Works of Mary Wollstonecraft*, gen. ed. Janet Todd and Marilyn Butler, 7 vols. (London: William Pickering, 1989).

Epigraph

You have refused us; and by so doing, you keep us under the eye of the public, in the interesting point of view of men who suffer under a deprivation of their rights. You have set a mark of separation upon us, and it is not in our power to take it off, but it is in our power to determine whether it shall be a disgraceful stigma or an honourable distinction. If, by the continued peaceableness of our demeanour, and the superior sobriety of our conversation, a sobriety for which we have not quite ceased to be distinguished; if, by our attention to literature, and that ardent love of liberty which you are pretty ready to allow us, we deserve esteem, we shall enjoy it. If our rising seminaries should excel in wholesome discipline and regularity, if *they* should be the schools of morality, and yours, unhappily, should be corrupted into schools of immorality, you will entrust us with the education of your youth, when the parent, trembling at the profligacy of the times, wishes to preserve the blooming and ingenuous child from the degrading taint of early licentiousness. If our writers are solid, elegant, or nervous, you will read our books and imbibe our sentiments, and even your Preachers will not disdain, occasionally, to *illustrate* our morality. If we enlighten the world by philosophical discoveries, you will pay the involuntary homage due to genius, and boast of our names when, amongst foreign societies, you are inclined to do credit to your country. If your restraints operate towards keeping us in that middle rank of life where industry and virtue most abound, we shall have the honour to count ourselves among that class of the community which has ever been the source of manners, of population and wealth. If we seek for fortune in the track which you have left most open to us, we shall increase your commercial importance. If, in short, we render ourselves worthy of respect, you cannot hinder us from being respected – you cannot help respecting us – and in spite of all names of opprobrious separation, we shall be bound together by mutual esteem and the mutual reciprocation of good offices.

"A DISSENTER" (Anna Barbauld), from *An Address to the Opposers of the Repeal of the Corporation and Test Acts.* London, Printed for J. Johnson, No. 72, St. Paul's Church-Yard. 1790. [Price One Shilling.]

Introduction

The religious dispositions, political aspirations, economic interests, and literary tastes of Dissenting communities impelled the genesis of Romanticism in England. During the late eighteenth century, theological and denominational distinctions inhabited individual manners, shaped political organizations, fueled commercial endeavors, and informed cultural programs. Although there may have been some truth to William Hazlitt's claim in his essay of 1815, "On the Tendency of Sects," that "It would be vain to strew the flowers of poetry round the borders of the Unitarian controversy," in another light Hazlitt's seemingly withering conclusion could not be more misleading.[1] The Romantic Imagination itself, as articulated by the still Unitarian Samuel Taylor Coleridge as early as 1802, long before the *Biographia Literaria*, evolved from an opposition between the "poor stuff" of Greek pantheism – "All natural objects were *dead* . . . but there was a Godkin or Goddesling *included* in each" – and the "*Imagination*, or the modifying, and *co-adunating* Faculty" of the Hebrew poets, for whom "each Thing has a life of it's [*sic*] own, & yet they are all one Life" (*CL*, II, pp. 865–66). If the vast expanse of sermons, pamphlets, tracts, and periodical polemics produced by Hazlitt's "controversial cabal" of Dissenters may in retrospect have appeared a desert in contrast to the blooming, more secular fields of "taste and genius," it is equally clear that nonconformist identities, beliefs, and debates energized and molded much of the cultural achievement that we now associate with the early Romantic movement.[2] It would certainly be insufficient to say that the early Romantic lyrics of Anna Barbauld or Coleridge, to name two of the poets whose works will be discussed in this study, were merely flowers strewn "round the borders of the Unitarian controversy," but it would be even more so to imagine that we can understand late-eighteenth-century taste and genius, including the development of the Romantic lyric, without attending to the myriad thoughts and feelings produced and structured by religious Dissenting publics.

I

Historicist critics have indelibly redrawn the literary terrain of the period by mapping relations between gender, politics, landscapes, technology, science, and empire, to list a few major subjects of recent revisionary investigation. The sphere in which early Romantic writers imagined and produced new combinations of language and articulated and lived new and often untenable political selves, however, was almost always religious. Literary creation and political expression in late-eighteenth-century England were inextricable from religious discourse and practice, yet the interpenetration of religious, political, and artistic life during the period nonetheless remains insufficiently understood. It is in this area, as an account of the Dissenting genealogy of Romanticism, that this book should make a meaningful contribution to Romantic studies.

Specifically, I hope to provide a nuanced examination of religion in the early Romantic period, applying a detailed understanding of denominational and sectarian cultures.[3] Although my chapters generally focus on one or two authors, methodologically this book differs from other studies of Romantic religion in that my primary concern is with these writers' engagements with and participation in public religious communities, institutions, discourses, and practices, rather than with the influence of religious ideas on their writings. Because of my emphasis on public religion in the late eighteenth century, I have confined my study to authors who were viewed by others, and who viewed themselves, as representing religious beliefs, practices, values, and tastes from within Dissenting communities to various reading publics, including the national "republic of letters." Although William Blake and, to an extent, William Wordsworth could be treated in this manner, they are less obvious candidates than Barbauld, her family circle, and William Godwin, who were born Dissenters, or Mary Wollstonecraft, Coleridge, and Robert Southey, who were deeply and publicly involved in Dissenting life.

In spite of the recent burst of social-historical writings on eighteenth-century religion,[4] few literary studies have appeared that treat Romantic religion as more than an imaginative reaction against a mechanistic and Godless world – Romanticism as "natural supernaturalism," as M. H. Abrams called it, or "spilt religion," in the famous formulation of T. E. Hulme.[5] Robert M. Ryan's *The Romantic Reformation: Religious Politics in English Literature, 1789–1824* (1997) argues for a Romantic movement unified by progressive energies directed not primarily at the political sphere but toward religious reform.[6] His argument is salutary, but by "the Romantics" Ryan means Blake, Wordsworth, Coleridge, Byron, Percy Bysshe Shelley, John Keats, and Mary Shelley.[7] My discussion of Barbauld and the influential Aikin family circle along with Godwin, Wollstonecraft, Coleridge, and Southey will lay the groundwork for the necessary extension of criticism sensitive to religion beyond the traditionally canonical Romantics and back into the mid to late eighteenth century, the period during which the redefinition of Christianity dominated cultural and political life. Ryan, furthermore, understands the Romantic poets "as participants in a single literary movement" unfolding in a "historical milieu" that was "at least as intensely religious in character as it was political," a milieu in which "religion was perceived . . . to function as an ideology of liberation rather than one of repression."[8] To a greater extent than Ryan, I will seek to reveal the tensions and contradictions within the liberatory roles played by religion for the writers under consideration, all of whom thought of themselves as progressive advocates of reform, in both the political and religious senses of the word. Similarly, although this study will return to a specific set of "early Romantic" developments, and the term will prove to be more than just a periodic description for the last thirty or so years of the eighteenth century, I will be less invested in demonstrating the kinds of continuities suggested by the phrase "Romantic movement" than in discovering the diverse and often conflicting ways in which the intellectual, political, and creative world of the late eighteenth century both incorporated and resisted particular and public Dissenting dispositions, assumptions, and interests. Romantic narratives of lyric spontaneity and particularity, political dissidence and apostasy, and creative autonomy emerged out of conversation as well as contestation with Dissenting cultures.

In *Romantic Atheism: Poetry and Freethought, 1780–1830* (1999), Martin Priestman provides a necessary supplement to Ryan's examination of the religious ideologies of the major Romantic writers.[9] Although a book on atheism would seem to suggest a different set of concerns from other studies of religion, Priestman's insightful analysis foregrounds the fact that throughout the Romantic period infidelity was almost always a position assumed within, not outside, the sphere of religious debate. At times my readings of Barbauld and Joseph Priestley will differ from Priestman's, but his careful consideration of a wide range of literary and religious texts within specific theological and denominational contexts serves as a model for the kind of attention I wish to pay to early Romantic Dissent. Whereas Ryan, then, describes the progressive attempts of

Romantic writers to reform the political world by reforming the religious world, and whereas Priestman addresses a range of properly religious beliefs that were conceived as atheistic, including the Socinian denial of Christ's divinity, this study seeks to present the all-important middle ground, so to speak, of religious Dissenting life. Unlike many of Priestman's infidels, and unlike the variously nonsectarian yet heterodox major authors to whom Ryan dedicates his chapters, none of whom (with the exception of Blake) was a Dissenter, the subjects of the present study were either born into Dissenting denominations or participated in Dissenting life during periods of lapsed Anglicanism.

Most recently, Mark Canuel's *Religion, Toleration, and British Writing, 1790–1830* (2002) offers an illuminating and expansive discussion of religious discourses as central to a process by which Romantic writers came to envision the establishment in church and state as a national community that would tolerate and sustain divergent kinds of religious belief.[10] The Gothic genre and the later writings of Coleridge and Wordsworth, especially, depict nonconformist positions and beliefs in relation to political institutions and establishments in order to "embrace nonconformity within newly broadened and invigorated structures of social cooperation."[11] Distinct from Canuel's method and focusing on an earlier era in which heterodox nonconformist networks in particular were still actively defining themselves within and playing a prominent role throughout the public sphere, my approach will be to look squarely at Dissenting communities, beliefs, and practices themselves with a greater degree of specificity than is commonly found in literary-historical accounts of Romantic religion.

Early Romanticism and Religious Dissent, then, will make accessible and meaningful the theologies and cultures that accompanied nonconformist religious life, from the Arminian[12] and Arian[13] tradition of Anna Barbauld's Presbyterianism[14] and the ultra-Calvinism[15] of the Sandemanian[16] sect with which the young William Godwin was affiliated to the Socinianism of Coleridge's Unitarian[17] phase and the anti-dogmatic "Quakerism" that attracted Robert Southey around the turn of the century. In so doing, the book will provide a reflection on the status of religious division itself during the period (see Figure 1). Coleridge's "*co-adunating* Faculty," indeed, would be sorely strained in an age in which beliefs, practices, ideologies, and communities seemed to be proliferating with a dizzying dynamism. When Robert Southey sent his fictitious Spaniard, Don Manuel Alvarez Espriella, off to England in 1807, he reported back a "curious list!" of the "heretical sects in this country":

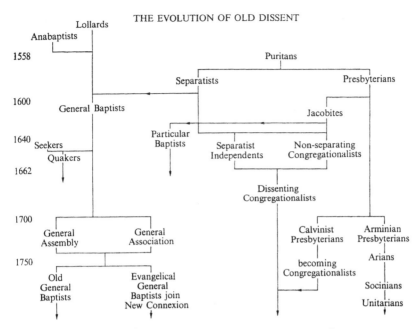

Figure 1. "The Evolution of Old Dissent," from Michael R. Watts, *The Dissenters: From the Reformation to the French Revolution*. Reproduced by permission of Oxford University Press.

Arminians, Socinians, Baxterians, Presbyterians, New Americans, Sabellians, Lutherans, Moravians, Swedenborgians, Athanasians, Episcopalians, Arians, Sabbatarians, Trinitarians, Unitarians, Millenarians, Necessarians, Sublapsarians, Supralapsarians, Antinomians, Hutchinsonians, Sandemonians [*sic*], Muggletonians, Baptists, Anabaptists, Paedobaptists, Methodists, Papists, Universalists, Calvinists, Materialists, Destructionists, Brownists, Independants, Protestants, Hugonots, Non-jurors, Seceders, Herhutters [*sic*], Dunkers, Jumpers, Shakers, and Quakers, &c.&c.&c. A precious nomenclature![18]

Simultaneously aided by and in spite of the joke – the "ignorant or insolent manner" in which the "popish author" classes "synonymous appellations . . . as different sects" (II, p. 28) – this "precious nomenclature" signifies what I will propose to be a defining feature of the early Romantic period, its encounter with the seemingly endless variety of religious beliefs and communities, with religious nonconformity.

Especially following the emergence of comparative religion and the revival of Orientalist scholarship (to be discussed in the final chapter), the religious world appeared to many as C. F. Volney described it in an

important passage of *Les Ruines* (1791).[19] When the Lawgiver addresses
the nations of the world, he arranges "chaque système de religion, chaque
secte" (p. 156) behind its chiefs and doctors: next to the Arabian Prophet
and the seventy-two sects of Mahometans stand the "adorateurs de *Jesus*"
(p. 160), including Luther and Calvin, behind whom are arrayed

les sectes subalternes qui subdivisent encore tous ces grand partis: les *Nestoriens*,
les *Eutychéens*, les *Jacobites*, les *Iconoclastes*, les *Anabaptistes*, les *Presbytériens*, les
Viclefites, les *Osiandrins*, les *Manichéens*, les *Piétistes*, les *Adamites*, les *Contempla-
tifs*, les *Trembleurs*, les *Pleureurs*, et cent autres semblables; tous partis distincts, se
persécutant quand ils sont forts, se tolérant quand ils sont foibles [*sic*], se haïssant
au nom d'un Dieu de paix. (p. 163)[20]

Such divisions and subdivisions could as easily be satirized in Swiftian lists
like these by a still moderately heterodox Southey in 1807 as an infidel
Volney in 1791, but for many of the figures this book will examine,
including old Dissenters such as Barbauld, Priestley, and Godwin as well
as lapsed Anglicans such as Wollstonecraft, Coleridge, and Southey
himself during the 1790s, denominational distinctions and identities
mattered.

    This is not to say that the early Romantic period was a "sectarian" age,
as the term is helpfully defined by Bryan Wilson in *Patterns of Sectarianism* (1967). Like Peter L. Berger, Wilson qualifies earlier definitions of
denominations and sects provided by Max Weber and H. Richard
Niebuhr.[21] For Wilson, sects are characterized by exclusive membership
through proof of personal merit, moral rigorism enforced by expulsion, a
self-conception of the sect as an elect community, personal perfection as
the standard of aspiration, the practice or at least the ideal of a priesthood
of all believers, a high level of spontaneous lay participation in public
worship, opportunity for the spontaneous expression of commitment to
the sect, and hostility or indifference to secular society and the state.[22] If
anything, the late eighteenth century witnessed a flourishing not of
sectarianism but of denominationalism, with its characteristics of inclusive membership without the imposition of traditional prerequisites,
breadth and tolerance combined with infrequent expulsion, an unclear
self-conception and unstressed doctrinal positions, the acceptance of
conventional standards of morality, a trained professional ministry, re-
striction of lay participation in formalized services from which spontaneity is largely absent, education of the young instead of evangelism of
non-believers, and acceptance of the values of secular society and the
state.[23] It is the very openness and fluidity of this denominationalism,

I will propose, that allowed religious thinkers and writers of the period to shape and reshape their aesthetic, political, and moral values through encounters with the range of theologies, habits, and manners accompanying the various communities of English nonconformity.

Although most late-eighteenth-century Dissenters thought of their religious communities in denominational rather than sectarian terms and were not openly hostile to the state, they of course remained opposed in fundamental ways to secular morality and the Established Church. The idea of opposition itself provided a challenge to Dissenters, whose very identity was based on difference: by definition one cannot be a Dissenter without dissenting *from* something else. Faced with the enduring Pauline ideal of a unified Church as well as the persistent early-eighteenth-century disdain for "sects" and "sectaries," Dissenters were forced to articulate the virtues of religious division precisely as a means toward political and social unity, or at least harmony. At stake in such struggles to claim and define unity was a radical schism between conflicting views of the individual, the nation, and God. Thus on Sunday, 17 April 1774, in his opening sermon at the first Unitarian chapel, in Essex Street, London, Theophilus Lindsey chose for his text Ephesians 4:3, "*Endeavouring to keep the unity of the Spirit in the bond of peace*": "God never designed that Christians should be all of one sentiment, or formed into one great church," Lindsey preached (to an audience including Priestley, Benjamin Franklin, and a government agent), "but that there should be different sects of Christians, and different churches."[24] In denominational division, Lindsey and others saw God's plan for a distinct kind of Christian unity: "in the midst of these differences and varieties, *the unity of the spirit was still to be kept in the bond of peace*, by a brotherly affection, and friendly correspondence one with another."[25] Five years later the Particular Baptist minister Robert Robinson posed the question, in more combative terms, "What if we could shew, that religious uniformity was an illegitimate brat of the mother of harlots?"[26] By disinheriting the "illegitimate brat," Robinson is able to envision a return to the union originally enabled by that "PRIMITIVE RELIGIOUS LIBERTY, which the Saviour of the world bestowed on his followers":

So many congregations, so many little states, each governed by its own laws, and all independent on [*sic*] one another. Like confederate states they assembled by deputies in one large ecclesiastical body, and deliberated about the common interests of the whole. The whole was unconnected with secular affairs, and all their opinions amounted to no more than advice devoid of coercion.

(I, p. xxviii)

"Here was an union," Robinson concludes, but "This is not the union intended by many" (I, pp. xxviii–xxix). It is a union based on different beliefs and practices, on a variety of independent communities equally acceptable in the eyes of a common God. For Richard Price, similarly, in *A Discourse on the Love of Our Country* (1789), human beings follow the will of God by following their own individual consciences rather than "public authority," in consequence of which the proliferation of forms of religious worship must necessarily keep pace with the number of individuals dissatisfied with the existing established and denominational churches. Among the passages singled out by Edmund Burke for particularly vehement censure is the following: "those who dislike that mode of worship which is prescribed by public authority, ought (if they can find no worship out of the church which they approve) to set up a separate worship for themselves; and by doing this, and giving an example of a rational and manly worship, men of weight, from their rank or literature, may do the greatest service to society and the world."[27] Dissenters thus felt at home with pluralism, and in a description of "experimental preaching," a method to be discussed in Chapters 2 and 4, Evangelical ministers could read that "Men may glory in uniformity. Variety, in all his ways, is the glory of the Deity."[28]

At the same time as some Dissenters upheld the virtues of religious division or variety, the peculiar legal status of Dissent often served to unify a wide range of theologically, economically, and culturally discordant groups into what seemed to both Dissenters and Anglicans alike to be one coherent oppositionist body.[29] The oppositionist identity of nonconformists cannot be separated from their largely shared legal status following the legislative inception of Dissent at the Act of Uniformity (1662) and the ensuing ejection of the nonconformist clergy.[30] Although the four major acts of post-Restoration anti-nonconformist legislation, passed between 1661 and 1665 under Charles II, and the Test Act of 1672, did initiate a policy persisting until 1828 that placed legal barriers between Dissenters and participation in the educational, clerical, civil, and political institutions of the English establishment, after the Toleration Act of 1689 legal proscription only applied to Socinian and Arian Dissenters who denied the Trinity.[31] Occasional conformity remained an option, and from 1727 almost annual Indemnity Acts gave Dissenters in practice a significant measure of access to local and even parliamentary power: between 1759 and 1790, thirty-nine Dissenters became Members of Parliament, constituting, however, only one percent of the membership of the House of Commons during that period.[32] Furthermore, after weathering the threats posed during the latter years of the reign of Queen Anne by the Occasional Conformity Act of 1711 and the Schism Act of 1714, the effects of the latter of which were only arrested by its subsequent repeal under George I, Dissenters publicly identified themselves as anti-Jacobite and firmly faithful to the Hanoverian succession.[33] Thus in the years following Anne's death in 1714, when the Tory backlash against nonconformity following Dr. Sacheverell's trial and the ensuing riots of 1710 had subsided, Dissenters, though still legislatively "marginalized," as we might say, would hardly have thought of themselves in terms of such a category under the Hanoverian regime they ardently supported. Consequently, Dissent did not represent itself as marginal to the main currents of English culture, but rather as a purer form of the English Protestant inheritance. At the same time, however, as heterodox Dissenters painted themselves in patriotic colors as stewards of England's Protestant and Hanoverian legacy, their theological and political rhetoric had to remain oppositional insofar as throughout the eighteenth century the official status of the establishment was theologically Trinitarian: the Athanasian Creed, to which many Presbyterians and General Baptists could not conscientiously subscribe, was part of the Book of Common Prayer and the basis of the first five Articles of the Church of England, and without at least occasional conformity to these Articles, Dissenters were in principle barred from careers in the Church, army, navy, and magistracy, from taking degrees at Oxford and Cambridge, and from parliamentary participation.[34]

While disparate beliefs, practices, and interests divided Dissent into numerous distinct entities, Dissenters were expected by themselves and their opponents to share a commitment to liberty consistent with their arguments against their own legal proscription. In spite of different levels of political commitment among Dissenters, religious nonconformity in the late eighteenth century was associated with a broad and fairly consistent political identity beyond the specifically partisan issue of the Corporation and Test Acts: parliamentary reform for a more equal representation, "Wilkes and Liberty" in the late 1760s, support for Corsican independence and the American colonies in the 1760s and '70s, "Wyvill and Reform" in the early 1780s, abolition of the slave trade and the boycott on sugar in the 1780s and '90s, and opposition to the war with revolutionary France in the mid 1790s. Over four decades these positions, actual or assumed, contributed to the broad association of Dissent with political dissidence, and, as Charles James Fox among others pointed out, in the heated atmosphere of the early 1790s this dissidence could all too easily be branded sedition. In a popular pamphlet of 1793, Fox sought to restrain the spirit of intolerance directed against Dissenters especially following the Birmingham Riots of July 1791:

In such a state . . . we extend the prejudices which we have conceived against individuals to the political party or even to the religious sect of which they are members. In this spirit a judge declared from the bench, in the last century, that poisoning was a Popish trick, and I should not be surprised if Bishops were not to preach from the pulpit that sedition is a Presbyterian or a Unitarian vice.[35]

Poison here has as little to do with the Trinity as sedition does with its denial, but in a heightened state of anti-sectarian retrenchment Dissenters could, by mere dint of verbal association, become the "friends of dissention," as in Haddon Smith's *The Church-Man's Answer to the Protestant-Dissenter's Catechism* (1795).[36]

Dissenters themselves frequently elided their radical differences as well in order to present a unified front, not as friends of dissention but as "friends to the civil liberty, and all the essential interests of our fellow citizens," as Priestley characterized them in his carefully titled *A Free Address to Protestant Dissenters, As Such, By a Dissenter* (1769).[37] Although one's belief or disbelief in the Athanasian Creed, or the staunchness with which one defended orthodox Calvinism from the encroachments of Arminianism, or vice versa, could play a significant role in shaping one's values, manners, and tastes, these differences could also be overshadowed by "the broad and liberal principles of a *Protestant Dissenter*," in the representative words of the General Baptist minister John Evans. These "broad and liberal principles," according to Evans' popular *A Sketch of the Several Denominations into which the Christian World is Divided*, published in 1795 and in its fourteenth edition by the time of his death in 1827, could be reduced to three fundamental and common beliefs: "The principles on which the Dissenters separate from the church of England . . . may be summarily comprehended in these three; 1. The right of private judgment. 2. Liberty of Conscience, and 3. The perfection of scripture as a Christian's *only* rule of faith and practice" (p. 73).[38] Similarly, Samuel Palmer's *The Protestant-Dissenter's Catechism* (1773; in its tenth edition by 1794) – to which Burke referred in the parliamentary debate over the repeal of the Corporation and Test Acts in 1790 – opens its second part, "The Reasons of the Protestant Dissent from the Established Church," with the following exchange:

Q.I.   *What are the* grand principles *on which the Protestant Dissenters* ground their separation *from the church by law established?*

A.   The right of private judgment and liberty of conscience, in opposition to
all human authority in matters of religion; the supremacy of Christ as the
only head of his church, and the sufficiency of holy scriptures as the rule of
faith and practice.[39]

Dissenting culture, then, was organized by dual and conflicting models of
self-understanding: on the one hand, Dissenters were divided by their
characteristic differences of faith and practice, but on the other, they were
united by their self-defined, libertarian principles of separation. "You have
refused us," Barbauld writes in *An Address to the Opposers of the Repeal of
the Corporation and Test Acts* (1790), "and by so doing, you keep us under
the eye of the public, in the interesting point of view of men who suffer
under a deprivation of their rights. You have set a mark of separation
upon us, and it is not in our power to take it off, but it is in our power to
determine whether it shall be a disgraceful stigma or an honourable
distinction" (*SPP*, p. 272).

The first three chapters of this book describe how, "under the eye of the
public," an extensive network of nonconformist writers, educators, reviewers, and publishers attempted to define and publicize their marks of
separation, giving rise to a new language of opposition, a dissident
middle-class language that suggests an influential and distinct fragment
of the bourgeois public sphere. I examine the collaborative literary and
religious conversations of Anna Barbauld – a prolific woman of letters
who is now the first poet commonly included in anthologies of Romanticism[40] – and her family circle associated with the Warrington Academy
(Barbauld, her brother John Aikin, Joseph and Mary Priestley, the publisher Joseph Johnson, the prison reformer John Howard, and others).[41]
The familial form of literary production characteristic of this Dissenting
public sphere, I contend, gave rise to a realized poetics of nonconformity,
which was both a method and an ideal, a practice and a representation, of
creativity. Conceived of explicitly as nonconformist, this cultural force
worked through collaborative literary production to associate Dissent's
austere and "enlightened" civil values, such as liberty, free and rational
enquiry, virtue, self-discipline, and a middle-class mercantile ethos, with
the sensibility and domesticity of both the family and the private literary
community. Subsequent chapters then reevaluate the early Romantic
literary and political writings of Godwin, Wollstonecraft, Coleridge,
and Southey in relation to religious heterodoxy and nonconformity in
general and to the Dissenting public sphere in particular. Relying at times
on the theories of Jürgen Habermas, Pierre Bourdieu, Antonio Gramsci,

and Mikhail Bakhtin, my readings of Godwin's *Political Justice*, his religious and polemical works, and his *Memoirs* of Wollstonecraft in relation to Wollstonecraft's own religious thought; Coleridge's conversation poems, Bristol lectures, and religious oratory; and Southey's "Arabian poem" *Thalaba* (1801) return the continuities and contradictions between Dissenting and dissident languages to the history of early Romanticism.

Chapter 1 provides a brief introduction to the book's main topic, the "liberal" or "free" heterodox Dissenters who, in their preaching and writings, did more than any other community both to produce and represent a Dissenting form of public life. By focusing on one of the more prestigious nonconformist educational institutions of the eighteenth century, the Warrington Academy (1757–86), I show that the oppositional but nonetheless patriotic rhetoric of moderate to radical middle-class Dissenters such as the Aikins, Joseph Priestley, and the affiliates of the Academy associated English liberty, and thus to a great extent "Britishness" itself, with a series of values resulting from the theological positions, religious and educational institutions, and economic interests of the heterodox Dissenting community. In the broadest sense, the rest of this book is concerned with the far-reaching consequences of this association.

Chapter 2 then demonstrates how a member of this community of liberal Dissenters, Anna Barbauld, developed a distinctive, early Romantic voice out of a complex and revisionary response to the terms of Dissenting devotion produced by her Presbyterian heritage. Barbauld's relation to "rational" Dissent, as William McCarthy has displayed, was a fraught one, and her devotional writings and early poetry represent a strategic attempt to recover forms of Dissenting spontaneity and particularity that seemed absent from her own religious culture.[42]

The result of this attempt can be seen as part of a larger movement among heterodox Dissenters to articulate a reformist, Dissenting public voice that would speak effectively and persuasively to nonconformists as well as to the nation at large. Chapter 3 accordingly locates a discrete fragment of the bourgeois public sphere in the extensive literary networks forged by nonconformist religious affiliations. As described in Chapter 1, the legally disenfranchised minority community of middle-class Dissent paradoxically represented itself as producer and keeper of the national public's imagined cultural, political, and economic heritage. We now see that the collaborative literary production of Barbauld and her brother John Aikin transformed this self-representation into a significant cultural force by tempering and domesticating Dissenting civil and religious characteristics. The intimate sphere, of the Aikin family circle and the

Warrington community in particular, produces literary commodities in which the competitive values of the market and the heterodox and dissident dispositions of Presbyterian Dissent are celebrated yet softened by association with the sensibility and conversation of the family within the home.

Chapters 4, 5, and 6 then address four early Romantic figures who, in various and conflicted ways, engaged with the legacy of the Dissenting public sphere. Like many writers of the 1790s, Godwin, Wollstonecraft, Coleridge, and Southey were dramatically affected by the fact that at the end of the century the Dissenting public sphere was rapidly disintegrating. Although orthodox Dissent was experiencing the remarkable revival that would make nonconformity such a powerful political force throughout the nineteenth century – the Particular Baptists, most notably, were optimistically launching the missionary activities which, especially after the Charter Act of 1813, would bring Protestant Christianity to every part of the world – the early Romantic literary culture of Dissent was dominated by the heterodox, and it is this culture which provided many of the public terms in and against which Romantic writers defined themselves and their work. The dissolution of public liberal Dissent reflected long-term demographic shifts within nonconformity: in England in 1715–18 there were approximately 179,350 Presbyterians, constituting 3.3 percent of the population, whereas in 1851 there were 84,190 Presbyterians and Unitarians, constituting only 0.5 percent of the population.[43] In addition to diminishing numbers, the impact of individual mortality and exile, and the institutional failure of many liberal nonconformist academies, in the mid 1790s the Dissenting public sphere was subject to the same forces which, according to Jon Klancher, were transforming the classical public sphere into "a representation instead of a practice."[44] As reading audiences fractured into numerous publics, it became increasingly difficult to project and sustain the idealized set of shared tastes and codes essential to classical publicity. But I think the same qualification can be made with respect to Dissenting publicity as Kevin Gilmartin suggests we need to apply to the popular radical public sphere of the early nineteenth century, which he describes as "both representation *and* practice, both an elusive phantom *and* a material body."[45] According to Klancher, the public sphere became "an image losing much of its force";[46] for the writers I will discuss, this is certainly the case, but at the same time we will need to attend to the different kinds of forces made possible by the shift from practice to representation – for example, from Dissenting conversation to the *idea* of conversation. Radical in their politics and heterodox in religion, Godwin, Wollstonecraft, Coleridge, and Southey in different ways and for different reasons develop literary and political programs that simultaneously depend on yet resist the conversational, collaborative, and rational-critical modes of Dissenting publicity, which for all of them, to varying degrees, was both lived experience and abstract idea. This strained engagement, I show, led all four to conceive and articulate different forms of subjectivity and models of creativity, and to modify their early radic-alisms into oppositionist aesthetic programs – novelistic for Godwin and Wollstonecraft, lyric for Coleridge, and mythopoetic for Southey – which have too often been dismissed in a generalized way as proto-reactionary or at least quietist.

In light of my dual interpretation of the revolutionary decade as both the so-called "English Terror" and the evening of the Dissenting public sphere, Chapter 4 examines Godwin's career during the 1780s and '90s as he encountered different Dissenting cultures, the dissolution of Dissent-ing sociability, and the rise of new types of corporate communication – those practiced by the popular political societies which, in place of the culture of liberal Dissent, came to dominate moderate to radical political life after 1792. Discussing aspects of *Sketches of History, Political Justice, Considerations on Lord Grenville's and Mr. Pitt's Bills, The Enquirer,* and the *Memoirs* of Wollstonecraft in the context of radical pamphlet culture, I suggest that his turn away from reason to sensibility in the *Memoirs* represents a political and aesthetic response to a "plebeian" public sphere that threatened Godwin's Calvinist investment in private judgment re-fined through individual conversation. Under the new and rapidly changing political circumstances of the mid 1790s, Godwin turns away from the tones of his own political philosophy, on the one hand, and the pamphlet culture of the radical societies, on the other, to those of narrative literary forms, especially the polite forms of fiction, biography, autobiography, and the essay. By comparing Godwin's representation of Wollstonecraft's nonconformity with her own writings on religion, I find an important articulation of this development in the *Memoirs.* Under-standably censured for the damage it did to Wollstonecraft's positions, to her memory, and to the cause of equality for women, Godwin's biograph-ical analysis is nonetheless based on an insightful interpretation of the anti-sectarian religious sensibility that informed Wollstonecraft's political and aesthetic theory. Often attributed to "retreatism" or "apostasy," to the early Romantic withdrawal from the political into the private, interior, and domestic, Godwin's development in fact reveals a difficult attempt to conceive of a cooperative form of discourse that will, in the absence of the emphatic sociability of Dissenting public life, maintain the integrity of the individual private judgment and marry rational and affective strategies.

Chapter 5 proposes that Coleridge's radical opposition to commerce and property in the 1790s leads him to reject the collaborative poetics of nonconformity for a different kind of religious conversation, that of his political lectures, Unitarian preaching, and meditative poems in blank verse. Before reading "Reflections on Having Left a Place of Retirement," "The Eolian Harp," and "Frost at Midnight," I consider Coleridge's Bristol lectures and Unitarian sermons both as texts and performances in order to show that although his Socinian beliefs and oppositionist politics during his Unitarian period placed him in line with many liberal Dissenters, he remained ideologically and, what is more interesting, "habitually" opposed to the economic and devotional culture of rational Dissent. Whereas many critics discuss Coleridge's nonconformist religion in the 1790s, they frequently fail to distinguish between Unitarianism, to which Coleridge came from the Church of England at age twenty-one, and the old Dissent of Presbyterian and General Baptist families, especially in Bristol, the Midlands, and the North of England. A clear distinction between the Dissenting beliefs of Coleridge and the Dissenting culture of provincial nonconformity explains how the disinterested and propertyless communities imagined by Coleridge in his political and religious writings of the mid 1790s inform the conversation poems of 1796–1802. The Coleridgean "conversational" subjectivity articulated by the early Romantic lyric, I conclude, emerges not from a latent German idealism awaiting the discovery of Kant, Fichte, and Schelling after 1801, but from Coleridge's Socinian rejection of the "habitus" of values, interests, manners, and beliefs that structured the Dissenting public sphere.[47]

The final chapter then turns to Robert Southey and the contexts of his "Mahometan" poem, *Thalaba the Destroyer, a Metrical Romance* (1801), thus broadening the scope of the study to examine relations between Dissenting sectarianism and representations of Islam in the eighteenth century. While Southey was actively pursuing an extensive program of Orientalist research, he was a heterodox radical whose anti-sectarian religious affinities led him to identify with an idealized form of Quakerism. By examining a strain of defensive Anglican Orientalism which portrayed the "Mahometan imposture" as homologous to antitrinitarian Dissenting sects within the British polity, I suggest that Southey's Islamic frame enables a mythopoetic synthesis of his religious and political dispositions at the end of the century. Simultaneously, the poem's largely unappreciated parodic elements express the anxieties and tensions concerning enthusiasm that underlie Southey's hybrid depiction of Islam as a monotheistic and dissident yet intuitive and fatalistic faith. Read in this manner, Southey's generically experimental "Mahometan" romance reaffirms his once prominent place among a generation of Romantic writers who were publicly and powerfully (mis)represented as, to borrow a phrase from Francis Jeffrey's review of *Thalaba*, a "*sect* of . . . *dissenters.*"[48]

By now it will be apparent that religious Dissent offers a complex field of study as both early Romantic experience and abstraction, as an internally divided yet definable range of lived forms of personal and public engagement in addition to a set of meanings and expectations that could be appropriated or rejected, by Dissenters and non-Dissenters alike, for specific creative and political ends. In order to trace the features of this simultaneously diffuse and coherent culture as well as its role in early Romantic literary history, we will need to approach Dissent both on its own terms – those of its theologies, denominations, and interests – and as it was represented in the larger public sphere, sometimes sympathetically, often defensively. The late eighteenth century was a period in which the political and cultural associations of religious communities and beliefs were strong and pervasive, and Dissent needs to be understood with a particularity seldom afforded in critical treatments of religion in Romantic literature. Like many eras of rapid and dramatic change, the early Romantic period witnessed an intense struggle concerning one of the most persistent dilemmas of personal and collective existence within the Judeo–Christian–Islamic tradition, the enduring dialectical conflict between impulses toward unity and plurality, synthesis and analysis, resolution and proliferation. If new forms of philosophy and literature emerged that attempted to reunite the individual with nature, to bridge the gaps opened by the analytical capacities of Enlightenment reason, and to express the autonomous mind in the unified work of art, they often did so by representing and engaging with the creeds and practices according to which individuals and groups worshipped the Deity, conceived models of community, and regulated human conduct.

CHAPTER I

"True Principles of Religion and Liberty": liberal Dissent and the Warrington Academy

From the subsiding of the Jacobite threat after 1745 to the movement to repeal the Corporation and Test Acts at the onset of the French Revolution, a network of Dissenting educators and writers publicly associated the religious, political, and economic features of their nonconformity with deeply nationalistic definitions of British liberty.[1] In a memorable assessment of the early eighteenth century by G. M. Trevelyan, "While religion divided, trade united the nation, and trade was gaining in relative importance. The Bible had now a rival in the ledger. The Puritan, sixty years back, had been Cromwell, sword in hand; thirty years back, Bunyan, singing hymns in gaol, but now the Puritan was to be found in the tradesman-journalist Defoe."[2] It is frequently asserted that by the late eighteenth century Dissenters dominated commercial life. Isaac Kramnick writes that although Dissenters "made up 7% of the population (90% were Anglican) these nonconformists contributed some 41% of the important entrepreneurs between 1760 and 1830."[3] Although it seems unlikely that Dissenters did in fact account for such a vastly disproportionate number of leading entrepreneurs and inventors,[4] they nonetheless accurately saw and represented themselves as publicly dedicated to promoting religion, liberty, and trade, and their educational institutions followed suit. After Defoe, and especially after the growth of the Dissenting academies in the 1740s and '50s, the Bible and the ledger, the Christian and the tradesman, ceased to be rivals and indeed seemed to cooperate in realizing a progressive vision of Protestant and national history. For Dissenters, liberty of conscience and advancement by merit came to define their nonconformity against liberty of subordination and advancement by patronage, against the "old society" which J. C. D. Clark has characterized as aristocratic, Anglican, and monarchical.[5]

Over the course of the eighteenth century, religious debates were also political debates concerning the spirit of Britain itself, and they therefore remained relevant in the minds of critics and supporters of the establishment alike. In 1787, for instance, readers could purchase *Bishop Sherlock's Arguments against a repeal of the Corporation and Test Acts* and *Bishop Hoadly's Refutation of Bishop Sherlock's Arguments*, both of which were reprints of pamphlets originally published in 1718. Whereas Benjamin Hoadly, bishop of Bangor, had triggered what came to be known as the Bangorian controversy by writing and preaching against either ecclesiastical or civil authority over individual conscience and salvation, Thomas Sherlock, bishop of London, and others upheld the high church position that authority resided in the naturally indivisible union of church and state. During a period of renewed energy against the old acts of anti-nonconformist legislation, such pamphlets again had currency almost seventy years after their initial appearance: the 1787 edition of *Bishop Sherlock's Arguments* was dedicated to William Pitt, and the editor concluded his dedication, "Let the Throne support the Church, and the Church support the Throne, and God will support both."[6] Having previously thought Pitt sympathetic, Dissenters had voted heavily in his favor during the 1784 general election, but this reprint was thought by many, including Theophilus Lindsey, the founder in 1774 of the first Unitarian church, to have turned Pitt against the cause of the repeal in 1787. The opposition immediately countered with a republication of *Bishop Hoadly's Refutation*, also dedicated to Pitt, proposing that "A Repeal of the Test and Corporation Acts would be a wise, just, and patriotic measure."[7]

Against the establishment position, critics of the constitution frequently questioned the assumption that Episcopacy was suited to the limited monarchy of the British throne whereas Catholicism was appropriate to absolutism. As Dissenters typically pointed out, a bishop was a bishop no matter whether he owed his allegiance to the Pope or the King of England, Scotland, and Wales. In *The Spirit of the Constitution and that of the Church of England, Compared* (1790), John Aikin repeats this common association of civil with religious governments: "A comparison has more than once been made between the three principal forms of church government, as they naturally allied themselves with different civil governments; and it has been said, that popery is particularly suited to the genius of absolute monarchy, the English church to that of mixed monarchy, and the presbyterian to that of a republic."[8] According to Aikin, this scale is formed "upon a very trifling analogy," however, for at issue is not ecclesiastical allegiance to a foreign or domestic temporal sovereign, but to any temporal sovereign at all. For Aikin the "spirit" or "genius" of the British constitution demands a religious structure separate from the political establishment and governed by dispersed religious bodies for reasons explicitly associated with his definition of what is appropriately or naturally British. Presbyterianism, in fact, would not be appropriate to a republic; instead, the Independent churches logically fill that role.[9] Aikin here aligns Presbyterianism with the "natural" "spirit" of the state, treating the Church of England as a remnant of Popery and maintaining a moderate posture by describing the Independent churches as representative of a more radical republicanism.

Moderate Dissenters such as Aikin, who commonly published with Joseph Johnson, were not the only ones to make the point that an established church was at odds with the spirit of the nation.[10] Even secular radicals like John Thelwall incorporated the structural arguments of moderate Dissent in the reformist strategies of 1790s constitutionalism. Thelwall, in his 1795 *Political Lectures*, published by the gutsy extremist Daniel Isaac Eaton, would conflate Catholicism and the Church of England by insisting that

Bishops are convenient tools to mould mankind to subordination and monarchic government: – necessary steps in the ladder of despotism: while Presbytery has a greater tendency to inspire ideas of liberty and equality. It is, therefore, also, that succeeding monarchs . . . have regarded with so jealous an eye the encroachments of the Dissenters, the very foundation of whose faith ha[s] a tendency to provoke enquiry.[11]

For an outspoken critic of the government and campaigner for the London Corresponding Society in favor of parliamentary reform, "liberty," "equality," and "enquiry" could still be identified with the "tendencies" of Presbyterianism, whereas "Bishops" of the Churches of England or Rome could rhetorically stand for anti-British absolutism.

The free enquiry of rational Christianity repeatedly came together with liberty in both the pulpit and the press. By the beginning of the nineteenth century, David Bogue and James Bennett's four-volume *History of Dissenters, from the Revolution in 1688, to the Year 1808* (1808–12) could treat the Dissenting Christian as the natural guardian of libertarian principles: "If there be an individual in the whole family of man who is warranted to be strongly attached to the cause of liberty, it is the disciple of Jesus Christ."[12] By "the disciple of Jesus Christ," these two Independent ministers, tutors, Calvinist theologians, and evangelicals mean those whose religion "is founded solely upon principles, and stands unsupported by secular policy or power."[13] For Bogue and Bennett, as for most Dissenters, political liberty was inseparable from the freedom of

conscience traditionally fought for against public doctrines of subscription. If the defining tenets of nonconformist religion from Arian Arminians among the liberal Presbyterians to orthodox Calvinists among the
Independents were that faith be founded on private judgment, personal
conscience, and free interpretation of scripture, then Dissent could be
represented as naturally and increasingly appropriate to a civil order
grounded in the preservation of individual liberties central to constitutional history: protection of private property, habeas corpus, trial by jury,
freedom of election, and liberty of the press.[14]

Public perceptions of both British liberty and Dissent were clarified in
debates over the American war. In the 1770s, supporters and opponents of
colonial independence interwove with the canonical definitions of liberty
from John Locke and Bishop Butler two opposing series of values and
interests between which liberty was negotiated as a counter of national
definition. For those who advocated the cause of the Colonies, the
theological value placed on free enquiry tended to coincide with the
standard libertarian definition of liberty from Locke's *Essay on Human
Understanding*: "a Power . . . to do or forbear any particular Action,
according to the determination or thought of the mind, whereby either of
them is preferr'd to the other."[15] In Richard Price's *Observations on the
Nature of Civil Liberty, the Principles of Government, and the Justice and
Policy of the War with America* (1776), of which several thousand copies
were sold within a few days, Lockean liberty of self-determination accords
with civil rule by the will of "the people": "all civil government, as far as it
can be denominated *free*, is the creature of the people. It originates with
them. It is conducted under their direction; and has in view nothing but
their happiness . . . In every free state every man is his own Legislator."[16]
Government by the direction of the people allied liberty with the
"bottom-up" ideology – generally a moderate, qualified form of populism –
identified with the values of middle-class rational Dissent, for which Price
came to stand. Against Dissent's embrace of Locke, defenders of the
establishment traditionally opposed the following position from Bishop
Butler's 30 January sermon (for the fast day in memory of the execution of
Charles I) before the House of Lords in 1741: "Civil liberty, the liberty of a
community, is a severe and restrained thing; implies in the notion of it,
authority, settled subordinations, subjection, and obedience; and is altogether as much hurt by too little of this kind, as by too much of it."[17]
Thus those who supported the war against the Colonies maintained, in
accord with the argument of John Wesley's immediate response to Price,
Some Observations on Liberty: Occasioned by a Late Tract (1776), that the

Americans could not have been seeking "liberty," for they were already in full possession of it; rather, they were fighting an unjust war for an unjustifiable "independency" from subjection to the rightful authority from which their actual civil and religious liberties flowed.[18]

During the 1770s this liberty of subjection became integrated with establishmentarian opposition to unbounded free enquiry. Two years later Alexander Gerard (1728–95), Professor of Divinity at King's College, Aberdeen, and associate of James Beattie, entered the dialogue with his published sermon, *Liberty The Cloke of Maliciousness, Both in the American Rebellion, and in the Manners of the Times* (1778), which took for its text 1 Peter 2:16, "As free, and not using your liberty for a cloke of maliciousness, but as the servants of God," part of the 30 January morning prayer. In the sermon, Gerard attacked the morals of the age through the "national" propensity to unbounded enquiry or free "examination."[19] For Gerard, "liberty" has been perverted by an equally perverted national spirit of excessive skepticism – a spirit implicitly associated with Dissenters – into libertinism and licentiousness, thus becoming a "cloke of maliciousness":

Many of the vices which stain our national character, and pollute individuals, spring from our indulging ourselves in what is wrong, under the colour of liberty. The faulty part of the British character, in the present age, cannot be more precisely defined, than by a reigning propensity to libertinism and licentiousness. The leading feature in the prevailing manners of the times, is a daring freedom in disdaining all restraints of laws human and divine, and in despising all that order and decorum which compliance with them would establish.[20]

"Liberty" becomes "libertinism" and "licentiousness" through the extreme value placed by the "national character" on free enquiry in matters of religion: "The liberty of examining every religious principle with impartiality, many abuse into a license of rejecting all religious principles without examination, and of treating all religion with scurrilous abuse or sneering ridicule."[21] For Price, on the other hand, "Licentiousness, which has been commonly mentioned, as an extreme of liberty, is indeed its opposite. It is government by the will of rapacious individuals, in opposition to the will of the community, made known and declared in the laws."[22] Thus unbounded enquiry and the "will of the community" (even if, as critics such as Wesley frequently pointed out, the community or "the people" in practice meant male Protestant adults with freeholds worth forty shillings *p.a.*) merged with Locke's "bottom-up" liberty of self-determination while limited enquiry, confined by respect for doctrine, and subordination through divine right to God's delegated civil authorities converged with Butler's "top-down" liberty of subjection. In opposition to Price's populism, Wesley responded, "The greater share *the people* have in the government, the less liberty, either civil or religious, does the nation in general enjoy."[23]

If Dissenters could integrate libertarian principles and ideals of free enquiry with their own nonconformity, so too did they seek to represent Dissenting practices as suited to a commercial economy. While over the first half of the century a dynamic if still limited middle class was beginning to refashion British economic identity in its own Whiggish image, the Church of England retained a clerisy and hierarchy associated with and dependent on landed interests: Anglican advowsons remained articles of property to be negotiated between the squire and the pastor to whom he chose to give the benefice tied to his estate. Nonconformist ministers, on the contrary, would be invited by a congregation or congregational board to assume a living, and would then be evaluated on grounds of performance and doctrinal compatibility. In numerous cases, resignations were requested and proffered over matters of individual effectiveness. Whether emphasis was placed on the self-sufficiency of the individual congregation, as among the Independents, or on the self-sufficiency of the network of assemblies, as with the Presbyterians and Baptists, the system of granting and maintaining ministries relied, in theory, on a free market of supply and demand, of "merit" and capital.[24] Dissenters' idealizations of their own systems produced rhetorically powerful arguments in favor of advancement by merit, and Joseph Priestley, who knew the Presbyterian system from firsthand experience, describes its ideal form in *An Essay on the First Principles of Government* (1768): "Among the Dissenters, if a minister introduce principles and practices which the people condemn, they dismiss him from their service, and chuse another more agreeable to them. If his difference of sentiment occasion any debate, the subject of the debate is thereby more thoroughly understood."[25] By the end of the eighteenth century, Dissenters were thus able to project the economic and political values associated with their own commercial interests and practices of church governance as corresponding to nascent ideologies of bourgeois liberalism, in spite of and in opposition to the continued hegemony of "a nexus of doctrines and practices which," Clark writes, "might be called, in its political aspect, the 'dynastic idiom'; in its social aspect, the 'aristocratic ethic'; in its structural aspect, 'patriarchalism'."[26]

The Warrington Academy was one of the foremost educational institutions that publicized nonconformity to the nation in this manner, and its history provides a socio-historical introduction to the community of heterodox Dissenters whose networks will be discussed in the following pages. In 1758, Dr. John Aikin (1713–80), the father of Anna Letitia Aikin (1743–1825, later Barbauld) and John Aikin (1747–1822),[27] accepted the post of tutor in Classics at the newly opened academy, which became a leading college for Dissenters.[28] Among the tutors were Joseph Priestley, Gilbert Wakefield, and William Enfield, and among the graduates of Warrington were a remarkable number of eminent ministers and doctors, as well as three Members of Parliament.[29]

It is, of course, difficult to assess with precision the impact of what I have described as the association of nonconformist interests and values with national identity. Although the Dissenting academies maintained modest enrollments and were for the most part geographically marginal, we should be cautious about assuming that cultural insignificance followed upon separation from the mainstream. A leading historian of Dissent, David Wykes, has proposed that "The isolation of Warrington and nonconformist academies . . . suggests that the direct influence of their ideas and methods was probably minor, particularly as the number of students educated there was too small to have had any significant impact on society."[30] Gregory Claeys, however, writes that the academies "compensated for their small numbers . . . with a rigour, breadth and enthusiasm which profoundly impressed generations of Dissenting as well as Anglican students . . . [who] went on to make considerable contributions to virtually every area of eighteenth- and nineteenth-century life,"[31] and a number of facts indicate that in spite of their isolation the academies did play a vital role in the image of the nation. When Benjamin Vaughan, a Warrington graduate and MP for Bristol, stood up on the floor of the House of Commons on 2 April 1792 to deliver a speech on the abolition of the slave trade, he reportedly began by disclosing that he had been educated by Dr. Priestley and "the father of Mrs. Barbauld": "Their sentiments I had imbibed," he announced, without choosing or needing to qualify what those sentiments were.[32] Indeed, the first two motions to repeal the Corporation and Test Acts, in 1787 and 1789, were both brought forward by Henry Beaufoy, MP for Minehead and later Yarmouth, and a Warrington graduate. The impact of the academies, furthermore, extended well beyond the ranks of Dissent. Beaufoy himself was not a Dissenter, and Warrington, like other nonconformist academies, did not just draw its enrollment from among the sons of Dissenters; according to Gilbert Wakefield, during his time at the Academy (1779–82) at least one third of the students were sent there from families of the establishment.[33] Additionally, the number of eminent figures who visited Warrington during the period suggests an influence beyond what might be assumed given the size of the town and the institution.[34] And finally, the academies produced a steady stream of publications by Dissenting tutors, many of whom were ministers as well, thus disseminating nonconformist educational, religious, and political positions beyond their provincial outposts. Warrington, for one, was fortunate in having an excellent local printer in William Eyres (1734–1809), recalled in 1853 as having been "One of the best printers of his day, not excepting the metropolitan press."[35] Eyres, the official printer of the Academy, put out numerous works by tutors and affiliates for Warrington's London agent, the publisher Joseph Johnson. By printing and publishing nationally recognized works by John Aikin and Anna Barbauld, Joseph Priestley, William Enfield, Thomas Pennant, William Roscoe,[36] and the prison reformer John Howard, Eyres and Johnson provided a coherent identity for the network of authors associated with Warrington.

Like so many aspects of mid-eighteenth-century Dissent, the Warrington Academy involves the story of a familial network within which an inherited Dissenting habitus incorporated and was transformed by contemporary religious and economic dispositions. Although the Academy is frequently described as innovative, in many ways it combined a specific nonconformist legacy with a moderate, heterodox perspective and a new emphasis on commercial progress. The Academy's lineage cannot be stressed enough: it runs through a succession of Dissenting educators beginning with Anna Barbauld's maternal grandfather John Jennings (1687–1723) – an Independent minister and tutor of the Kibworth Academy in Leicestershire – and continuing through Philip Doddridge (1702–51), who studied under Jennings from 1719–23. This lineage, in fact, demonstrates the degree to which Dissenting networks were shaped and interconnected by familial ties. After Jennings' death his school lapsed until 1729, when it was reopened in Harborough by his former student Doddridge, who almost immediately moved the Academy from Harborough to Northampton. Dr. John Aikin was one of Doddridge's original four students at Northampton and briefly served as his assistant there in the late 1730s, and Aikin would later marry the daughter of John Jennings, Jane Jennings, to whom Doddridge had already unsuccessfully proposed. In the 1740s, Aikin was tutor of his own school at Kibworth, where he educated Doddridge's son as well as the sons of other prominent Dissenters. After Doddridge's death, his student Caleb Ashworth carried on the Academy at Daventry, where Joseph Priestley and William Enfield both studied in the 1750s. In 1757, Aikin was chosen as tutor of Classics at the newly established academy in Warrington, and he remained at the head of the Academy from 1761 until his death in 1780.[37] Priestley and Enfield would both join Aikin at Warrington, where the two served from 1761–67 and from 1770–83, respectively.

When tutors and graduates of Warrington recalled the institution's educational methods, their descriptions always returned to the three principles of nonconformist identity – private judgment, personal conscience, and free interpretation of scripture. Jennings and Doddridge, however, were largely responsible for the new style of education subsequently associated with Aikin and Warrington. As Doddridge's letters indicate, for him the origins of these modern pedagogical ideals of discursive interchange and free discovery lay with his tutor, Jennings, who always encouraged "the greatest freedom of inquiry" and "inculcate[d] it as a law, that the scriptures [were] the only genuine standard of faith."[38] Although orthodox, Jennings demonstrated the same insistence on free enquiry that would come to characterize the succeeding generations of liberal or free Dissenters. As Doddridge recalled, Jennings "did not follow the doctrines or phrases of any particular party; but is sometimes a Calvinist, sometimes an Arminian, and sometimes a Baxterian, as truth and evidence determine him."[39] Andrew Kippis describes Doddridge's own lecturing in similar terms: Doddridge, a Baxterian and thus a more moderate Calvinist than Jennings, "never assumed the character of a dogmatist. He represented the arguments, and referred to the authorities on both sides. The students were left to judge for themselves; and they did judge for themselves, with his perfect concurrence and approbation."[40] The logical outcome of this inherited style was the innovation for which Doddridge is generally remembered: he was among the first to replace Latin with English as the appropriate language for modern science, philosophy, and theology.[41] Furthermore, Doddridge's students were allowed to interrupt his lectures in order to pose questions or objections.[42] Doddridge placed great emphasis on dialogue not just between student and tutor, however, but also between divergent ideas or beliefs within individual minds: as Isabel Rivers writes, "That the student should be familiar with opposing views and arrive at the truth by considering the arguments against it was one of Doddridge's favourite principles . . . Doddridge inherited it from his own tutor, John Jennings, and passed it on to his students."[43] One of these students was John Aikin, who in turn so encouraged free discussion along the lines laid down by Doddridge and Jennings before him that he can be credited with having presided over the first class we could properly call a seminar.[44] This openness, in fact, came to be the defining feature of a Warrington education. Aikin's fellow tutor, the Arian John Taylor, for instance, would begin his Divinity lectures with a remarkable four-part "Charge" to his students: first, that "you do constantly, carefully, impartially, and conscientiously attend to evidence as it lies in the Holy Scriptures, or in the nature of things and the dictates of reason"; second, that "you admit, embrace or assent to no principle or sentiment by me taught or advanced, but only so far as it shall appear to you to be supported and justified by proper evidence from revelation or the reason of things"; third, that if "any principle or sentiment by me taught or advanced, or by you admitted and embraced, shall upon impartial and faithful examination appear to you to be dubious and false, you either suspect or totally reject such principle or sentiment"; and fourth, that "you labour to banish from your breast all prejudices, prepossession, and party zeal . . . and that you steadily assert for yourself and freely allow to others, the inalienable rights of judgment and conscience."[45]

The Academy did more than just continue the legacy of Jennings and Doddridge, however, and in order to understand its role within the formation of late-eighteenth-century Dissenting publicity it will be necessary to consider the context of the town itself. According to an enumeration made in 1781, Warrington and its vicinity comprised 1,941 houses and 8,791 inhabitants.[46] Nonetheless, for a stretch of time in the 1760s and '70s coinciding with the period in which the Academy flourished, this township on the Mersey between Manchester and Liverpool assumed an enhanced cultural importance of national scope. During these years the extraordinary group of tutors and students at the Academy earned Warrington the title, the "Athens" of the North.[47] Because Warrington possessed the only bridge over the Mersey between the sea at Liverpool and just south of Manchester, the town served as an important gateway to North West England. The origin of Warrington's magnified role in provincial history begins with its gradual development into a commercial center. Long noted for its weekly linen markets, Warrington became one of the earliest manufacturing centers in Lancashire.[48] By the eighteenth century, Warrington could be considered a small port city with the development of Bankquay, a little below the town, where cranes and warehouses were assembled to unload vessels of up to eighty tons. In addition, Warrington was connected by frequent coaches to Liverpool, Manchester, and London, and after 1761 Lancashire boasted one of Britain's wonders of engineering, the Duke of Bridgewater's canal, which connected Manchester and Liverpool and allowed packet-boats to make the journey twice daily between Warrington and Manchester (see Figures 2 and 5).[49] The combination of communication, manufacturing, and trade turned Warrington into a typical and thriving provincial commercial center, and this pattern was reflected in the finances and enrollment of the young Academy.

By 1800 approximately 70 percent of all English peers were educated at the four public schools, Eton, Westminster, Winchester, and Harrow.[50] By contrast, even an important academy such as Warrington would accept on average only fourteen students per year: unlike young Anglican males, sons of Dissenters were educated through a network of institutions scattered throughout the country, loosely connected by religious organizations such as the Common, Presbyterian, and Congregational Fund Boards, through which subscriptions were gathered.[51] As with all institutions, the development of the Warrington Academy reflected the sources of its funding: Dissenting, provincial, and middle-class. Lancashire's status as the center of northern nonconformity and the stronghold of Presbyterianism outside London dating back to the Commonwealth period would have aided John Seddon, the Presbyterian minister of Warrington's Cairo Street congregation and later tutor and rector at the Academy, in his requests for support from Dissenting families and organizations around the country. By 1754 he had received pledges from churches as far away as Bristol, Exeter, and Birmingham, and from more local benefactors in Liverpool, Manchester, and Warrington itself. In 1754, the lion's share of contributions came from the commercial hubs of Liverpool, Manchester, Birmingham, and Warrington, amounting to £215, and these came almost exclusively from laymen with middle-class interests.[52]

When Seddon set about collecting subscriptions for the newly conceived Academy in 1753, the institution naturally sought prospective students who would be educated to become Dissenting ministers. A circular issued on 11 July 1754, however, further described the education offered by the proposed Academy as "well calculated for those that are to be engag'd in a commercial Life, as well as the Learned Professions."[53] Thus when we look at the breakdown of students educated at the Academy from 1757–83, reported in the *Monthly Repository* in 1813, we see that at this institution for the education of ministers, of 393 students enrolled, only 52 entered with the intention to study divinity; 22 entered for law, 24 for medicine, 98 for commerce, and 197 entered without any specified course.[54] Those entered for commerce would have been educated to become merchants or bankers, or to hold leading positions in large commercial companies. Those who entered without any specified course would have been expected to become shopkeepers and tradesmen. Only a handful of these would have entered the army or inherited the rank of "country gentlemen." In effect, almost 75 percent of the Academy's enrollment did sustain that British mercantile spirit reflected in the economy of Warrington and the finances of the institution.

Seeking students to be trained for the Dissenting ministry, Seddon's circular anticipated their future careers in telling terms: they were to become "ministers free to follow the dictates of their own judgments in the inquiries after truth, without any undue bias imposed on their understandings."[55] Significantly, when the circular reassured prospective donors that the education offered at the Academy would be suitable for those expected to follow commercial callings, it went on to claim that such practical education would also lead students "to an early Acquaintance with, and just concern for, the true Principles of Religion and Liberty: of which great Interests they must in future Life be the Supporters."[56] The importance of this distinctive association of commerce with "the true Principles of Religion and Liberty" is that Enlightenment values of free enquiry, rational Christianity, and free-market economics were imagined as naturally consonant interests: their cooperation would now lead the children of all Britons, regardless of class or religious denomination, in the path of British "truth." The tactic is similar to the one Priestley employs in the Preface to the third edition of *A Free Address to Protestant Dissenters, as Such* (1788), in which he coopts an ideologically specific model of national progress in normative terms, claiming that "The author of this work is not much concerned about the *civil privileges* of the dissenters . . . as a separate body in the state; but he most earnestly wishes that their liberal and generous views, with respect to civil and religious liberty, may be so fully imbibed by themselves, and so far diffused among others, as that all their countrymen . . . may reap the benefit of them" (p. viii). Here, as in most mid-eighteenth-century Dissenting descriptions of nonconformist educational institutions, a minority community defined by its opposition and heterodoxy represents itself to the nation as both parent and guardian of the nation's own libertarian and commercial spirit.[57]

After the Academy took its last students in 1783, Dissenters affiliated with the Literary and Philosophical Society of Manchester met to plan a new institution, the Manchester New College, in the hopes that "the happy art might be learned, of CONNECTING TOGETHER, LIBERAL SCIENCE AND COMMERCIAL INDUSTRY!"[58] "A Plan for the Improvement and

Extension of Liberal Education in Manchester" having been read to the society on 9 April 1783 by Thomas Barnes, the Warrington graduate who would become the new academy's co-director (with Ralph Harrison), the Society approved the plan. The first report of the new academy, published along with the Society's minutes by Eyres in Warrington and sold by Thomas Cadell in London, begins,

THIS INSTITUTION is intended to provide a course of LIBERAL INSTRUCTION, compatible with the engagements of commercial life, favourable to all its higher interests, and, at the same time, preparatory to the systematic studies of the UNIVERSITY. To unite *philosophy* with *art*, the moral and intellectual culture of the *mind*, with the pursuits of *fortune*, and to superadd the noblest powers of enjoyment to the acquisition of wealth, are the great objects which it professes to hold in view.[59]

Lectures would accordingly be held in the evenings, from six to nine o'clock, "so as not to interfere with the regular hours of business" (p. 41), and the course for the first term, as advertised, would include practical mathematics, chemistry, fine arts, moral philosophy, and "the *origin*, *history*, and *progress* of ARTS, MANUFACTURES, and COMMERCE, – the COMMERCIAL LAWS and REGULATIONS of different COUNTRIES, – the nature of COMMUTATIVE JUSTICE; of OATHS, CONTRACTS, and other branches of COMMERCIAL ETHICS" (p. 45).[60] Such a curriculum, it was assumed, would provide the soundest basis for training young tradesmen to lives of Christian virtue, industry, and science, but behind these broad terms lay an ideologically specific program of liberty and toleration. In *A Sermon Preached at the Dissenting Chapel in Cross-Street, Manchester, . . . on occasion of the Establishment of an Academy in that Town*, Ralph Harrison proposed that the foundational principle of both Dissent itself as well as the new Academy was "that of *equal* and *common* liberty . . . for all that name the name of Christ to worship God according to the dictates of their consciences":

We stand not forth as advocates for the doctrine of Calvin, nor for the Westminster confession, nor for any of the leaders of a sect or party. We . . . contend for the unalienable right, and indispensable duty of *all men* to judge and act for themselves in religious matters . . . We are not afraid nor ashamed to assert, that the members of the Established Church, that Protestant-dissenters, that every denomination of Christians have a right to the free exercise of their religion . . . [T]his Christian liberty universally allowed . . . what happy consequences would take place![61]

As we will hear repeatedly, mid- to late-eighteenth-century liberal Dissenting rhetoric found a new kind of energy in the latitudinarian spirit of denominationalism as opposed to sectarianism; commerce and liberty will provide all Christians with the (implicitly nonconformist) means of progressing toward a millenarian future, and the achievement of this progress will come when it is acknowledged "That Christ is the only king in his church, . . . That no profession, rank, or number of men has dominion over the conscience – That the scripture is a complete rule of faith, and . . . That to inflict penalties of any kind whatever for nonconformity to human systems . . . is a violation of men's natural and Christian privileges."[62]

Joseph Priestley's reflections on the Warrington curriculum consolidated this teleological model of progressive history appropriated by Dissenters through the interplay between their institutional structures, theological tenets, oppositional politics, and economic interests. Whereas Dr. Aikin's role was to associate a Warrington education with the Dissenting tradition of free enquiry and personal conscience inherited from Jennings and Doddridge, it was Priestley (tutor in Languages and Letters) who modernized the curriculum.[63] He was almost certainly the first to introduce the systematic study of English grammar, his pedagogical views on which he outlined in *Rudiments of English Grammar, Adapted to the Use of Schools, with Observations on Style* (1761, 1769). The result of his time at the Academy was his *Essay on a Course of Liberal Education for Civil and Active Life* (1765), in which he formally described a middle-class curriculum and pedagogy suitable for laymen outside the learned professions.[64] Although this work, dedicated to "the Trustees of the Academy at Warrington," characterizes an education distinctly fashioned according to a nexus of nonconformist practices and interests, it does so by proposing this education as naturally suited to and required by both the present and future of a universalized "Britain."

Priestley begins his discussion of contemporary educational needs by contrasting the present with the past. Formerly, clerical education was limited to the classical scholasticism of Oxford and Cambridge: "Time was, when scholars might, with a good grace, disclaim all pretensions to any branch of knowledge but what was taught in the universities."[65] Then, "none but the clergy were thought to have any occasion for learning," for "Few persons imagined what were the true sources of wealth, power, and happiness in a nation. Commerce was little understood, or even attended to" (pp. 2–3). In Priestley's assessment, the scholasticism of the Universities continues to exclude the new subjects taught at the nonconformist academies and is thus explicitly associated with an older British society, currently surviving only as an anachronism:

those times of revived antiquity have had their use, and are now no more . . . The politeness of the [present] times has brought the learned and the unlearned into more familiar intercourse than they had together before. They find themselves obliged to converse upon the same topics. The subjects of modern history, policy, arts, manufactures, commerce, &c. are the general topics of all sensible conversation . . . The topics of sensible conversation are likewise the favourite subjects of the present age, which are read with equal avidity by Gentlemen, Merchants, Lawyers, Physicians, and Divines. (pp. 22–23)

Discussions of the "true sources of wealth, power, and happiness in a nation" bring together members of the middle and upper social orders, to the exclusion of "low mechanics," in an educated or "sensible" discourse that does not distinguish between the interests of commercial and patriarchal classes. Rather, the course of lectures presented in the work offers the subjects of Priestley's Warrington curriculum as containing the normative body of knowledge required by all Britons of the "present age" who will participate in the political community: "That an acquaintance with the subjects of these lectures is calculated to form the statesman, the military commander, the lawyer, the merchant, and the accomplished country gentleman cannot be disputed" (p. 13). The "same topics" unite middling and elite Britons, Dissenters and Anglicans, provincial and metropolitan – in effect, the communities represented by the enrollment at Warrington. But these subjects, first of academic lectures within the classroom and then of conversations within the public sphere, are distinctly calculated to facilitate the progress of British culture away from a patriarchal past and toward a mercantile future, a future for which young men are to be prepared by studying "modern history, policy, arts, manufactures, commerce, &c."

The success of this progress rests on an all-encompassing anti-establishmentarianism. The *Essay on a Course of Liberal Education* ends with Priestley's response to a recent tract on education by John Brown (1715–66), *Thoughts on Civil Liberty, on Licentiousness and Faction* (1765).[66] Brown recommended, as Priestley summarized, the "interference of the civil magistrate in the business of education" (p. 137), calling for an educational establishment that would provide national definition and stability through uniformity in education as the Church provided definition and stability through uniformity in religion. In responding to this specific call for an educational establishment and cultural uniformity, Priestley writes a broad defense of British society against establishmentarian values of education, religion, and, perhaps most revealingly, national culture.

Progress comes to depend not just on the actual and ideological dispersal of economic, political, and religious capital, but finally on the diffusion of something as vague, and discursively powerful, as national "character." Brown holds up ancient Sparta as the model of a society in which uniformity of education provided young men with "all the mental and bodily Acquirements and Habits, which *corresponded* with the *Genius* of the *State*."[67] By contrast, "The first and ruling Defect" of the Athenian republic "seems to have been the total Want of an established Education, suitable to the Genius of the State."[68] The crucial matter in the dialogue between Brown, formerly chaplain to the Bishop of Carlisle, and the Dissenting tutor Priestley is that education conform to the "genius" of Britain. Furthermore, the definition of that genius hinges on the broad cultural alignments of establishmentarian and oppositional interests and values. For Brown the genius of Britain demands establishments in religion and education; for Priestley that same genius requires the opposite. Education, then, the building of political and religious subjects through familiarization with specific subjects of study, is the field on which the national character will be determined. Priestley writes,

EDUCATION . . . is properly that which makes the man. One method of education, therefore, would only produce one kind of men; but the great excellence of human nature consists in the variety of which it is capable. Instead then of endeavouring, by uniform and fixed systems of education, to keep mankind always the same, let us give free scope to every thing which may bid fair for introducing more variety among us . . .

Is it not universally considered as an advantage to England, that it contains so great a variety of original characters? And is it not, on this account, preferred to France, Spain, or Italy? (p. 149)

Protestant England is superior to Catholic France, Spain, and Italy for the same reason that the Athenian character was superior to the "savage uniformity of Sparta" (p. 163). As the "various character of the Athenians" (p. 149) produced the imaginary and dynamic origin of libertarian history in Attic democracy, the heterogeneous character of Britain, left unimpeded by national establishments, will expedite British progress according to Priestley's nonconformist, necessarian, and commercial vision of the nation's natural future. For the most part, the association between theoretical opposition to a proposed educational establishment and concrete opposition to the actual religious establishment remains subtextual, but toward the end of the argument Priestley insists "that an established code of education, such as this writer contends for, allowing its tendency to perpetuate the present constitution of this country in church and state, tends to interrupt its progress to a state of greater perfection than it has yet attained" (p. 160). British liberty will approximate its teleological culmination only when "the present constitution of this country in church and state" comes into accord with the imagined spirit or genius of the nation's common and various character.

In *The Rudiments of English Grammar, Adapted to the Use of Schools* (1761), Priestley had broadened such connections between Dissenting religion, commerce, and education to incorporate language itself. Like the Athenian and, by extension, the British character, language needs no uniform institutional power to direct its natural progress:

> As to a public *Academy*, invested with authority to ascertain the use of words, which is a project that some persons are very sanguine in their expectations from, I think it not only unsuitable to the genius of a *free nation*, but in itself ill calculated to reform and fix a language. We need make no doubt but that the best forms of speech will, in time, establish themselves by their own superior excellence: and, in all controversies, it is better to wait the decisions of *Time*, which are slow and sure, than to take those of *Synods*, which are often hasty and injudicious.[69]

As we will see throughout this study, middle-class Dissenters repeatedly express their most basic cultural hopes and values in terms of the market economy: "A *manufacture* for which there is a great demand, and a *language* which many persons have leisure to read and write, are both sure to be brought, in time, to all the perfection of which they are capable."[70] As Claeys writes, "The real advantages of free commerce . . . lay in other consequences besides the prospect of economic improvement."[71] In Priestley's dissident argument against forms of established control, the same market forces guide both language and commerce according to the natural definition of Athenian/British identity. The "best forms of speech" will establish themselves, just as the demands of the market will necessarily bring a manufacture to its highest "perfection." "It seems to be the uniform intention of divine providence to lead mankind to happiness in a progressive, which is the surest, though the slowest method" (*Essay*, p. 169), and Dissenters saw this progress, along with the "various character" of Britain, Britons, and the English language, reflected in their own nonconformist interests, beliefs, and practices.

CHAPTER 2

Anna Barbauld and devotional tastes: extempore, particular, experimental

"Mrs. Barbauld," remembered until recently as the writer for children who criticized *The Rime of the Ancient Mariner* for being improbable and having no moral, was in the late eighteenth and early nineteenth centuries a prominent poet, essayist, hymnist, pamphleteer, reviewer, editor, educator, and children's writer.[1] With the publication of William McCarthy and Elizabeth Kraft's *The Poems of Anna Letitia Barbauld* (1994) and *Anna Letitia Barbauld: Selected Poetry and Prose* (2002), the continuing reevaluation of her work has led critics to place her among the foremost poets of a revised late-eighteenth-century canon.[2] The most intensely productive period of her poetic career, between the ages of twenty-two and thirty-one (from 1765–74), took place at Warrington, in the environment provided by the town and the Academy, culminating in her influential *Poems* published by Joseph Johnson in 1773 and reissued in expanded form in 1792. After her marriage in 1774 to Rochemont Barbauld, a French Protestant who had come to be educated at Warrington, the couple moved to Palgrave, where Rochemont had been offered the ministry of a Dissenting congregation. They remained there until 1785, sharing the management of a boarding school for boys. Following their resignation of the school and a tour of France, the Barbaulds settled in Hampstead, where they would remain until 1802. These years saw Anna Barbauld take part in the movement to repeal the Corporation and Test Acts, the attempt to abolish the slave trade, and the debate over the French Revolution. The remainder of her life was spent in Stoke Newington, where her professional work continued unabated as she employed her pen in a variety of venues: she wrote for the new *Annual Review*; edited Richardson's *Correspondence* (1804), *Selections from the Spectator, Tatler, Guardian, and Freeholder* (1805), and *The Poetical Works of Mark Akenside* (1807); edited and produced prefaces for the fifty-volume collection *The British Novelists* (1810); and published her last major poem, *Eighteen Hundred and Eleven* (1812).

In August 1804, Barbauld received an interesting offer from Maria Edgeworth. Her father, Richard Lovell Edgeworth, had proposed a plan for a "periodical paper, to be written entirely by ladies," and Barbauld, naturally, was among "the literary ladies . . . invited to take a share in it."[3] In her reply, Barbauld foresaw the problem of division between different groups of women writers: "There is no bond of union among literary women, any more than among literary men; different sentiments and different connections separate them much more than the joint interest of their sex would unite them. Mrs. Hannah More would not write along with you or me, and we should probably hesitate at joining Miss Hays, or if she were living, Mrs. Godwin."[4] Barbauld's refusal to see gender as the primary determinant of literary or political affinity, as well as her rejection in 1774 of a proposal that she become principal of a Ladies' College, has confirmed her in the eyes of some as an anti-feminist.[5] William McCarthy, on the other hand, has analyzed the ways in which feminist "desire takes the form of compensatory fantasy" in her poetry, thus helpfully critiquing the "cardboard anti-feminist image of Barbauld."[6] By the same token, we need to be careful not to go to the opposite extreme and create a cardboard feminist image of Barbauld. Enlightenment feminism, in fact, in the sense of an overt, active, and conscious effort to theorize and realize educational, social, economic, and (to a lesser extent) political equality for women in the modes of Mary Wollstonecraft, Mary Hays, and later Harriet Martineau, was not a central element of Barbauld's literary work. As an agile thinker, an often daring poet, and a consistently commanding prose stylist, Barbauld did produce in her religious writings a noteworthy analysis and manipulation of eighteenth-century devotional theory and denominational cultures, elements of which at times involved deep-seated gendered associations.

Having placed herself and Edgeworth between female radicals and conservatives, Barbauld goes on to explain her response as follows: "There is a great difference between a paper written *by* a lady, and *as* a lady. To write professedly as a female junto seems in some measure to suggest a certain cast of sentiment, and you would write in trammels. If a number of clergymen were to join in writing a paper, I think they should not call it 'The Clergymen's Paper,' except they meant to make it chiefly theological."[7] Barbauld's simultaneous resistance to participating in a "female junto" and her acute awareness of gender politics indicate that the binary terms of feminist/anti-feminist may not be sufficient to a contemporary understanding of her literary, political, and religious writings. The best recent work on Barbauld has consistently emphasized the extent to which she reflected on and dialectically critiqued her own positions over the course of her career.[8] Along with this capacity came a general impetus to criticize and manipulate various identities usually seen as natural and innate, or at least as fixed and established. In keeping with the fluid and self-reflexive aspects of Barbauld's writing, in this chapter I propose that an important strain of Barbauld's religious thought is produced by a daring analysis and reconfiguration of powerful associations between denominational cultures and devotional practices, associations that were inextricable from the complexly gendered movement away from cold abstraction and rationalism and toward a morality of the senses and passions during the mid- to late-eighteenth-century Enlightenment.

As Deirdre Coleman rightly points out, "Barbauld's experience and understanding of knowledge as a gendered issue" and her expressions of "longing for equal participation in the world of knowledge and learning" at times produced a strong critique of "public/private distinctions."[9] Knowledge and learning, like religious devotion itself, were indeed gendered issues, and Barbauld's "dexterous negotiations"[10] should neither be tamed nor obscured by a reading sensitive to her articulations of religious moderation. Especially during the 1770s and '80s, such negotiations were a direct consequence of her strategic attempts to domesticate and concretize Dissenting values and cultural definitions. For in late-eighteenth-century religious terms, Barbauld's was a controversial yet still essentially a moderate position, tempering the enthusiasm of Puritan devotion and Calvinist rigorism in order to produce an open and warm religion that would be more endearing and personal than Socinian Dissent and both more demanding and less indifferent than the Church. One further consequence of Barbauld's analogy is thus worth noting: just as "different sentiments and different connections separate [women] much more than the joint interest of their sex would unite them," so would the different sentiments and connections of clergymen separate them more than the joint interests of their theological profession would unite them. Women have sentiments and connections beyond their gender, and clergymen have sentiments and connections beyond their vocation; the analogy alerts us to the need not to reduce the thought of a female religionist such as Barbauld either to questions of gender or religious belief. Nor, of course, can we ignore them. One way to understand Barbauld's contribution to the early Romantic discourse of devotion without either reducing it to or ignoring the nexus of gender and religion is to attend to the specific sentiments and connections – or, more broadly, the habitus – that Barbauld inherited as a late-eighteenth-century English Presbyterian.

THE DAUGHTER OF A PRESBYTERIAN CLERGYMAN

Although Barbauld is frequently, and with some truth, labeled a Unitarian, her Dissenting affiliations are more complex. As I will discuss below, she should properly be considered a liberal (i.e., Arminian and Arian) Presbyterian with Unitarian ties. She was descended from perhaps the single most influential family of eighteenth-century Calvinist Independents and Presbyterians, including her maternal grandfather John Jennings and his brother David Jennings (1691–1762). Among their students were Philip Doddridge, Joshua Toulmin, Abraham Rees, and many others. As we have seen, it is through Doddridge, the tutor of Barbauld's father, that the academic lineage most notably continues: among the numerous institutions overseen by Dissenters either taught or directly influenced by Doddridge were Caleb Evans' academy at Bristol, Andrew Kippis' at Hoxton and Hackney, Caleb Ashworth's at Daventry, Samuel Merivale's at Exeter, and John Aikin's at Warrington.[11] Barbauld's heritage was thus a powerful one, for both directly and indirectly her forebears were responsible for educating an astonishing proportion of the Dissenting elite. Too often references to her Unitarianism, or to her Dissenting background more generally understood, overlook this heritage and thus fail to grasp the nuances of her particular position within late-eighteenth-century nonconformity.

In order to understand the nature of her Dissent, we will need briefly to consider the history and historiography of Unitarianism.[12] Whereas the Socinian doctrine survives from the sixteenth century, the English denomination in its Enlightenment form begins to become recognizable only in the 1770s, with Priestley's defenses of Socinianism in pamphlets and sermons and with the foundation of the Essex Street congregation by Theophilus Lindsey in 1774.[13] Although late-eighteenth-century Unitarianism represents a discrete phenomenon, it has often been indiscriminately described along with the other branches of Dissent. Part of the reason for this slippage is that until the early nineteenth century no adults existed who had been born "Unitarians" in a *denominational* sense: "In the 1770s," writes Stuart Andrews, Unitarianism "was still a theological tendency, in one of its main variant forms of Socinianism or Arianism."[14] Even after 1774, the vast majority of Unitarians remained members of old Dissenting congregations (usually Presbyterian or General Baptist). Richard Price and Priestley himself ministered to Presbyterian meetings while Joshua Toulmin ministered to a General Baptist meeting, though all of their congregations were also Unitarian. Converts to Unitarianism in the late eighteenth century generally either descended or ascended, depending on one's perspective, from Calvinist Dissent (usually Presbyterian or Independent) through the Arminian and Arian heresies to Unitarianism, or they came directly from the Church of England. Price and Priestley, for instance, were born and raised as Independents but were acculturated by the Arminian communities of middle-class Dissent and the nonconformist academies – Price attended John Eames' Moorfields Academy, while Priestley studied at Caleb Ashworth's Daventry Academy – through which they passed to Arianism (and, in Priestley's case, Socinianism). Some members of the Church of England, such as John Prior Estlin and Gilbert Wakefield, became Unitarians after a similarly long process of affiliation with one of the academies.[15] Others, like Theophilus Lindsey, John Disney, William Frend, and Thomas Fyshe Palmer – as well as Coleridge and Southey in the 1790s – left the Church of England directly for the more rational and politically appealing religion of Unitarian Dissent.[16]

In Russell Richey's important essay "Did the English Presbyterians Become Unitarian?" (1973), Richey contrasts "the orthodox analysis" with the "Unitarian self-understanding" of how Unitarianism emerged from English Presbyterianism over the course of the eighteenth century. According to the former, "The evolution from Presbyterianism to Unitarianism is typified as a process of decline, decay or dry rot."[17] Unitarians themselves, on the other hand, embrace a Whiggish progressive refinement of liberty "from Calvinism, through Arminianism, through Arianism, to Unitarianism in gradual acceptance of humanitarian principles and the freedom of conscience" (p. 61). Richey proposes a third interpretation, an alternative to the two models by which Presbyterianism devolved or evolved, respectively, into Unitarianism – that the "Middle Way" of Baxterians or "Middle Way Men," such as Edmund Calamy, Isaac Watts, and Philip Doddridge, who dominated Dissenting culture and theology during the first half of the eighteenth century, successfully transformed the sectarian factionalism of Dissent's Puritan inheritance into a unified "community of Dissent" (p. 69). It is out of this community, Richey argues, that Unitarianism emerged. Dissenting families such as the Aikins and the Belshams, the direct inheritors of the tradition of Watts, Doddridge, and Jennings, typify the identification with the community of Dissent that superseded Presbyterian affiliation during the middle years of the century.

Here it is necessary to pose an important question: *was* Anna Barbauld a Unitarian, even accepting Richey's argument? Theologically she was an Arian, not a Socinian, and although there were Arians among the

Unitarians, the most famous being Richard Price, Barbauld was deeply suspicious of the Socinianism that dominated Unitarian thought, allegedly calling it "Christianity in the Frigid Zone."[18] She necessarily would have considered herself a Presbyterian, not a Unitarian, during her twenties and thirties (in the 1760s and '70s), and when William Woodfall reviewed her *Poems* (1773) in the *Monthly Review*, he informed his readers simply that "Miss Aikin is the daughter of a Presbyterian clergyman."[19] From 1787 to 1802 her husband was the Presbyterian minister of the old chapel on Red Lion Hill in Hampstead, where Barbauld herself of course worshipped.[20] (Joanna Baillie worshipped there too, as Barbauld put it "with as innocent a face as if she had never written a line.")[21] After 1802 Rochemont held the ministry at Newington Green, where the Unitarian Presbyterian Price had formerly presided, and the Barbaulds, like other Arminian Presbyterians, General Baptists, and, to a lesser extent, heterodox members of the Established Church, could thus move fluidly between the home denomination and Unitarianism. The Warrington Academy itself, although instituted by Presbyterians, was essentially non-denominational; of the more than fifty students educated there specifically for divinity, seventeen ultimately entered the Church, and the remainder would be divided between the Presbyterian, Baptist, and Independent ministries.[22] In 1786, as described in Chapter 1, three years after the academy took its last students a committee of Dissenters affiliated with the Literary and Philosophical Society of Manchester organized a new academy, declaring in their mission statement that "This Institution will be opened to young men of every religious denomination, from whom no test, or confession of faith, will be required."[23] Before printing its annual fees for tuition, the committee affirmed, "This Academy, like that of Warrington, is founded upon the most Liberal Principles, and will be open to young men of all Denominations and Professions."[24] In some respects, then, institutions and individuals understood themselves in denominational terms, but in other respects Dissenters saw themselves simply as Dissenting.

Late-eighteenth-century Presbyterians therefore could not be described as a "sect" in either Weber's, Niebuhr's, or Wilson's senses of the term; in fact, their openness and emphasis on education characterize them not just as a "denomination," but also as part of a larger community, precisely the kind of community identified by Richey. John Aikin, Barbauld's brother, in fact made this same distinction in 1794, describing the contemporary relationship between nonconformity and the establishment as conducive to what he called "religious societies" as opposed to sects:

By a *religious society*, in contradistinction to a *sect*, I understand simply this – that a number of persons of a similar way of thinking, for no other purpose than merely to enjoy to the greatest advantage their own tastes and opin[i]ons in religion, associate to form a congregation . . . Religion is to them merely a personal affair . . . and their only motive for associating in it at all, is that they find a duty or advantage in social worship . . . They have nothing to do either with attack or defence, unless the grand and universal principle of the right of private judgment in matters of religion be called in question.[25]

Barbauld thus did come out of that side of Presbyterianism which had retained the name, but had divided from the Calvinist Presbyterians (many of whom became Independents) and developed into the "free" community of "liberal" Dissent. And many members of this community, Barbauld included, worshipped and thought of themselves still as Presbyterians, while others, such as the Presbyterians Price and John Taylor (of Norwich), accepted the identity of Unitarians. As an emblem of this latitudinarian culture we might take two funereal requests, the first by the Independent and Baxterian Isaac Watts, that Dissent be represented at his funeral by two Independent, two Presbyterian, and two Baptist ministers, and the second by the General Baptist and Unitarian Joshua Toulmin, that his pall be borne by six ministers of different denominations.[26] Richey's argument is then carried out by the fluidity with which many Dissenters, especially ministers, thought of their denominational identities and could move between denominations within the Arian and Arminian side of nonconformity.

Nonetheless, I want to propose here that even in the case of a free Dissenter such as Barbauld we can and should trace the very real ideological and cultural inheritance of the various threads – from Puritan Calvinism to liberal and heterodox Unitarianism – that had become woven into the community of Dissent by the late eighteenth century. Barbauld's Presbyterianism, in short, demands that we consider her associations with Unitarian Dissent in a very different light than we will Coleridge's. Even when one inhabits, as did Barbauld, a denominational (Presbyterian) culture that has lost characteristics which formerly gave it a stronger, more exclusive and sectarian quality, those characteristics leave significant traces, for individuals as well as groups. Furthermore, the traces they leave can serve new purposes, can be reworked into different cultural forms or expressions which provide opportunities for new identities and definitions. Perhaps nowhere can the manifestations of Barbauld's Dissenting heritage be understood more clearly than in the role played by moral sensibility in her religious thought, particularly in how she understood and responded to the roles of particularity (as opposed to abstraction) and spontaneity in the cultivation of devotional feelings.

DENOMINATIONS AND DEVOTION: EXTEMPORE, PARTICULAR, AND EXPERIMENTAL

The specific elements of Dissenting denominationalism that mattered above all to a young Presbyterian poet such as Barbauld took the shape of devotional theory and practice.[27] Like many writers of the period, Dissenters did not always make a firm distinction between forms of polite literature and the more specifically devotional forms of hymns, prayers, and sermons. Barbauld herself proposes, in an important essay of 1775 to be discussed in this and the next chapter, that the "seat" of devotion is in the same imaginative faculty "by which we taste the charms of poetry and other compositions, that address our finer feelings."[28] Similarly, George Gregory, evening preacher at the Foundling Hospital and later chaplain to the Bishop of Llandaff, suggests in his "Thoughts on the Composition and Delivery of a Sermon" (1787) that "The utility of these remarks . . . may possibly not be altogether confined to one species of composition. What I have to advance . . . will, I flatter myself, not be unacceptable to young writers in general."[29] The eighteenth-century debate concerning how sermons should be written and delivered offers an opportunity to consider the range of public discourse enabled by Dissenting denominationalism and to see precisely what was at stake, culturally, in identifying with and inhabiting particular Dissenting communities.

Barbauld's attempts to theorize and foster a devotional *taste* clearly owe much to Isaac Watts' emphasis on "practical theology" and his introduction of hymns into nonconformist services: as Samuel Johnson put it, Watts was "one of the first authors that taught the Dissenters to court attention by the graces of language."[30] But beyond Watts' affective religion, his expressions of "the central tenets of the Christian faith in simple, direct, and often beautiful language which the ordinary believer could apply to his own experience,"[31] Barbauld's writings are also responding to and shaping a specifically early Romantic discourse of sensibility. Barbara Taylor has written of "underlying shifts of attitude in the late eighteenth century, as religious belief became increasingly aligned with the feminine and as both came under the rule of sentiment."[32] As Taylor proposes elsewhere, "From the mid-century on preachers of all stripes could be heard arguing that female religious feeling was intrinsically more powerful than that of men."[33] Looking back on the works of Barbauld and Hannah

More, Harriet Martineau began her first contribution to the Unitarian *Monthly Repository*, "Female Writers on Practical Divinity," by claiming that "some of the finest and most useful English works on the subject of Practical Divinity are by female authors," suggesting that their success could be attributed to "the peculiar susceptibility of the female mind, and its consequent warmth of feeling": the "productions" of the female mind, accordingly, "find a more ready way to the heart than those of the other sex."[34] A wide range of related cultural forces – especially Christian Platonism, Rousseauism, and the cult of sensibility – combined to strengthen the alignment of religious experience with feminized or domestic traits and qualities. In Platonic terms, the private language of love and the affections, of unity between individual human beings, could lead to love for and unity with God, and in the second preface to *Julie ou La Nouvelle Héloïse* Rousseau famously suggested that "comme l'enthousiasme de la dévotion emprunte le langage de l'amour, l'enthousiasme de l'amour emprunte aussi le langage de la dévotion."[35] The female mind, it seemed, was peculiarly susceptible to the warmth of both languages.

Passionate enthusiasm, however, posed a problem for middle-class Dissenters such as Barbauld. Concerned to distance their religious experience from what they perceived as the vulgar zealotry of Methodism – Barbauld memorably describes a Methodist preacher as a "florid declaimer who professes to work on the passions of the lower class" (*SPP*, p. 212) – many liberal Dissenters nonetheless sought new ways simultaneously to regulate and invigorate devotion.[36] Although their present religious taste may have tended to the "philosophical" and "abstract," their Puritan past embodied a very different devotional spirit. Geoffrey Nuttall does well to remind us that our "popular notion of a Puritan" as "a stiff surly, censorious and self-righteous person, priggish and prudish, too tightly wrapped up in himself to expand into passion or compassion or to be carried into tender intimacy or genuinely personal intercourse with God or man" – in short, as Malvolio – remains blind to a form of "Christian faith and experience . . . so alive and intense that at times it overflows in tender lyricism barely controllable."[37] As an Arminian and Arian Presbyterian, at the center yet also critical of the rational Dissenting Unitarian culture presided over by Priestley, Barbauld appropriated and revised two chief elements of her Puritan inheritance, the enthusiastic devotional methods of particularity and spontaneity, which were theorized by eighteenth-century religious writers as "particular and experimental" and "extempore" manners of preaching. As we shall see, these methods were consistently coded according to the aesthetic category of the sublime; were firmly associated with a violent, sectarian religious history; and were thus both alien and alienating to middle-class Dissenters in the late eighteenth century, who sought to represent themselves as embracing and sustaining the spirit of 1688–89 rather than 1649. In the tradition of Watts, then, yet distinct from it, Barbauld's attempts to describe and popularize an affective form of Dissent involved a strategic, revisionary, and regulatory association of these two elements of Puritan devotion with sensibility, that essence of humanity inherent in idealized social (especially familial) relationships and carefully modulated emotional responses to aesthetic experiences.

Two questions, for the most part, dominated discussions of sermon composition and preaching style throughout the century, and both offer insight into the transition of Dissenting sects into denominations as well as the specific character of late-eighteenth-century Unitarianism. First, devotional writers debated whether or not sermons should be preached entirely extempore, whether they should be unwritten and preached from notes, written and preached from memory, written and read, or even read from a printed text by another hand. The other issue concerned what was called "particular" and "experimental" preaching, which involved the relation both of the preacher to his audience and the sermon to its scriptural text. All sermons required explication as well as application – the preacher would both attempt to "remove the difficulties, and elucidate the obscurities of the Scriptures"[38] and to offer an "application of the doctrine to the conscience."[39] But against the seemingly abstract morality of the Church and the reputedly tedious, scholarly disquisitions of rational Dissent, Calvinist Dissenters hearkened back to Puritan preaching in order to propose a different style. "Particular" and "experimental" preaching would apply doctrine not to a general audience of Christians but to the particular members of the congregation, basing the application not on abstract morality but on the concrete experiences (thus "experimental") of individual congregants.

Whereas on the Continent sermons were seldom read, the practice was more or less the rule in England both in the Established Church and the heterodox Dissenting denominations of Arminian Presbyterians, General Baptists, and Unitarians. Orthodox Dissenters (Independents, Particular Baptists, some Presbyterians), Quakers, and "new" Dissenters (Methodists), however, often did practice extempore preaching, and for that reason they were repeatedly assaulted as zealous enthusiasts. James Glazebrook, an Anglican minister in the rational Dissenting stronghold of Warrington and one of the few voices from within the Church to endorse the practice, affirms these divisions. In *What is called Extempore Preaching Recommended* (1794), Glazebrook begins, "I enter with fear and trembling upon the support of an opinion so very unpopular": outside "the orthodox dissenters in this nation" (and "those few of our own church who follow that method of preaching"), in England "An extempore preacher . . . is by most looked upon as a kind of monster."[40] For the few Anglicans and rational Dissenters who supported the practice, an extempore sermon was generally not completely spontaneous; for them, most commonly extempore preaching meant that a minister would memorize the subject heads for each part of the sermon and then preach without notes. As Glazebrook puts it, "the question is . . . whether [the message] should be *read* from a written preparation, or whether it should be delivered in, what is *improperly* called, the *extempore* way? I say *improperly* . . . because the term, as it is generally understood . . . is only applicable to the *random, rhapsodical effusions* . . . of the wild enthusiast."[41] Thus Gregory writes, "It has been frequently debated, whether a sermon may be delivered to most advantage, perfectly extempore, from memory, or from written notes," giving his personal preference to the last method.[42] Nonetheless, others did espouse "perfectly extempore" preaching, running the risk of "being looked upon as a kind of monster" or a "wild enthusiast," and indeed the idea played a powerful and enduring role in Protestant self-understanding.

At the Reformation preaching was usually extempore, but by the 1540s the licensing of preachers along with the tenor of the new Church had produced an atmosphere in which the writing and reading of sermons became commonplace. As summarized by Gilbert Burnet in *The History of the Reformation of the Church of England* (1679), the last two injunctions of Bishop Bonner to the clergy in 1542 were "That there should be no railing in Sermons; but the Preacher should calmly and discreetly set forth the excellencies of Vertue, and the vileness of Sin" and "That none be suffered to Preach under the degree of a Bishop, who had not obtained a License, either from the King, or him their Ordinary."[43] According to Burnet, "From thence the reading of Sermons grew into a practise in this Church: in which, if there was not that heat, and fire . . . yet it has produced the greatest Treasure of weighty, grave and solid Sermons, that ever the Church of God had; which does in a great measure compensate that seeming flatness to vulgar ears, that is in the delivery of them."[44] The history of extempore preaching is a long one, but especially since the civil wars the practice had been thought of as meant for the "vulgar ears" of a subversive and unruly multitude. A typical anti-Puritan pamphlet, for instance, *A Discovery of 29, Sects here in London, all of which, except the first, are most Divelish and Damnable* (1641), describes a "Brownist" (i.e., a separatist, follower of Robert browne [ca. 1550–1633]) as a fellow who "had rather heare a Cobler, or a feltmaker preach, so hee doth it *extempore*, then heare a premeditated Sermon, pend, and preach'd by a Scholler who can distinguish, and unloke the secrets of the Scripture."[45] Thereafter, extempore preaching became associated not just with Puritan enthusiasm but with the cobblers and feltmakers of the urban working classes, and, along with the later advent of Methodism, with rural laborers as well. Against such unlettered religion the Church held up premeditated sermons, not only premeditated in the mind and heart but written with a pen and preached by a scholar whose main task would be to explicate his text, to "unloke the secrets of the Scripture."

In the eighteenth century, rational Dissenters seeking to distance themselves from Puritanism, which continued to be associated both with king-killing and a vulgar, overheated populace or crowd, found the written sermon to be most congenial to a learned ministry. Unitarians, famously (and not wholly accurately) stereotyped for their rational, scholarly sermons and cold preaching style – a sermon, indeed, was often called a "discourse," and preaching was often called "instruction" – generally shunned extempore preaching, though they were more sympathetic to extempore prayer.[46] Although Priestley himself had claimed in his Warrington lectures that "the perfection of speaking is, certainly, to speak extempore," attributing the success of the "primitive christians" and "the founders of our modern sects, such as the Independants, Quakers, and Methodists" to "the talent of haranguing extempore," he held that "the refinement of modern times requires that we speak, upon all occasions, with more temper, and use more address in raising the passions": "The English pulpit, the English bar, and the English senate, require an eloquence more addressed to the reason, and less directly to the passions."[47] It was not until the early nineteenth century that extempore preaching would regularly be found in Unitarian meetings. Following the establishment of the Unitarian Fund in 1806 to reverse the declining numbers of Unitarians by fostering a more popular preaching ministry, itinerant and missionary preachers began to expand Unitarianism into the less educated classes; in 1815, writing of the invitation to William Johnson Fox from the New Meeting in Birmingham, one member noted, "It will be a new era amongst us, to have extempore preaching in one of our leading congregations."[48]

Throughout the eighteenth century, extempore preaching was accordingly viewed by all sides primarily as the legacy of the Puritans. As early as

1712, in *The Present State of the Parties in Great Britain*, Daniel Defoe could look back to "The last Age of *Dissenters*," by which he meant "those who, upon the Restoration of the *Church Discipline*, and the *Act of Uniformity, Anno* 1661, found themselves straightned [*sic*] in their Consciences," and could claim that their ministers "preach'd their Sermons, rather than read them in the Pulpit; they spoke from the Heart to the Heart, nothing like our cold Declaiming Way, entertain'd now as a Mode, and read with a Flourish, under the ridiculous Notion of being Methodical."[49] Defoe then asks, "How has the Preaching sunk among the *Dissenters*, into all manner of Coldness, Meanness, Dull Fashionable Reading, &c. instead of Preaching?"[50] If by 1712 Defoe could already admonish Dissenters for their diminishing zeal, throughout the century the Church would be seen as the primary sufferer from a cold and dry preaching style. According to Hugh Blair in his *Lectures on Rhetoric and Belles Lettres* (1790), Puritan preaching could be faulted for its "minute divisions and subdivisions . . . but to these were joined very warm pathetic addresses to the consciences of the Hearers, in the applicatory part of the Sermon."[51] After the Restoration, preaching within the Church

became disencumbered from the pedantry and scholastic divisions of the sectaries; but it threw out also their warm and pathetic Addresses, and established itself wholly upon the model of cool reasoning, and rational instruction. As the Dissenters from the Church continued to preserve somewhat of the old strain of preaching, this led the established Clergy to depart the farther from it. Whatever was earnest and passionate, either in the composition or delivery of Sermons, was reckoned enthusiastic and fanatical; and hence that argumentative manner, bordering on the dry and unpersuasive, which is too generally the character of English Sermons.[52]

As Defoe made clear as early as 1712, however, not all Dissenters "continued to preserve somewhat of the old strain of preaching"; indeed fewer and fewer did as Presbyterians tended increasingly to Arminianism and Arianism, to rational Dissent, distancing themselves from their Puritan past.

It was accordingly the Calvinist Dissenters, and foremost among them the Particular Baptist Robert Robinson, who led the way in calling for a return to the sublime style of extempore preaching.[53] Probably the most important late-eighteenth-century work on sermon composition in England was written in the seventeenth century by a French Protestant, Jean Claude (1618–87). Claude's *An Essay on the Composition of a Sermon* (1688) took on new life in two competing translations, one Dissenting, by Robinson (1778–79), and one Church of England, by Charles Simeon

(1796), becoming the closest thing that English preachers had to a text book.[54] In 1796, for instance, ministers could purchase Simeon's *A Sermon . . . to which are Annexed Four Skeletons . . . with a View to Illustrate all Mr. Claude's Rules of Composition*, and as late as 1828 texts such as *The Preacher's Manual; . . . in which Claude's Principles . . . are More Fully Developed* were still appearing regularly. "Skeletons" – outlines – like Simeon's were commonly published to suggest the proper matter and structure for sermons on various texts, giving appropriate sketches for each of the five parts of the sermon (the exordium, the connection, the division, the discussion/explication, and the application), and Claude's *Essay* often provided the advice with which a young minister would add flesh to the bare bones.[55]

Robinson, raised to the Church of England in Norfolk but drawn by the preaching of Whitefield to the Calvinistic Methodists in 1752, seceded from Methodism in the late 1750s and would spend most of his career as an orthodox Baptist minister in Cambridge.[56] In his translation he makes Claude into one of his own contemporaries, and into one of his own: "Had Mr. Claude lived a hundred years longer, he would have been more non-conformable than ever" (I, p. lxviii). Simeon, a defender of the Church, took it upon himself to reclaim Claude, but in order to do so he needed to divest the text of Robinson's copious notes. Accordingly Simeon's Preface announces that Robinson's "notes, which . . . are at least four times as large as the original work," are to be omitted, and the reason assigned is that "they were compiled for '*dissenting* ministers,' and . . . they are indeed 'AN ODD FARRAGO.'" But a far more serious ground of objection against them is, that they are replete with levity, and teeming with acrimony against the established Church" (Preface). Simeon was right on both counts: at one point Robinson compares "A good sermon" to "a good peach" (I, p. 43), and in the Index the pious reader could find "Articles of the established church, some unintelligible," and "Laud, Archbishop, a worthless state-tool" (I, p. 460). It is in his notes that Robinson sets forth his arguments for extempore preaching. Having lamented the "dry lifeless way of preaching" from memory that "brought on the *reading* of sermons" (I, p. 84), Robinson asks, "Would you affect your auditors? be affected yourself. Would you excite their grief? weep yourself . . . These emotions must not be acted, they must be free and natural" (II, p. 466). The "best method" of "the most popular and pious preachers" is thus, "They study till they thoroughly understand the subject. They habitually feel it. They retire ten minutes before preaching, and in fervent prayer to God, possess their souls with a full idea of the importance of the matter . . . They go from prayer to the pulpit, as Moses went down from the mount from God to speak to the people" (II, pp. 466–67). As Moses bears not just the words but the sublime voice of God, so should the preacher spontaneously and immediately·communicate the fervor of religious inspiration. Like other devotional writers who describe the preacher's communicable inspiration in terms of the sublime, Robinson emphasizes the effect the preacher should have on the physical senses as well as the intellect: "the preacher should address the eyes, and ears of his auditors, as well as their reason" (II, p. 334).

Along with these arguments for spontaneity went a movement among orthodox Dissenters to make preaching "particular" and "experimental," as in the title of John Jennings' influential *Two Discourses: The First, Of Preaching Christ; the Second, Of Particular and Experimental Preaching* (1723). As Isaac Watts succinctly puts it in his preface to Jennings' work, particular and experimental preaching involves "distinguishing the Characters of our Hearers."[57] Watts asks, "Have we not been too often tempted to follow the Modish Way, and speak to our Hearers in general Terms . . . ? . . . Do we lead them constantly to enquire into the inward State of their Souls, the special Tempers and Circumstances of their Spirits, their peculiar Difficulties, Dangers and Temptations, and give them peculiar Assistance in all this Variety of the Christian Life?" (p. xi). The particular and experimental preacher, in other words, would not simply offer an abstract or philosophical explication of the text, but rather would attune his application to the individual hearts, to the specific experiences, sins, hopes, and fears, of the particular auditors he addresses. Watts would again argue for experimental preaching in *An Humble Attempt toward the Revival of Practical Religion among Christians, And particularly the Protestant Dissenters* (1731), where he instructs, "take heed that dry Speculations and mere Schemes of Orthodoxy do not take up too large a part of your Composures . . . And among the practical Parts of Christianity sometimes make it your Business to insist on those Subjects which are Inward and Spiritual, and which go by the Name of *Experimental Religion.*"[58] Doddridge in turn elaborates on the following instruction in his own *Lectures on Preaching*, transcribed around 1740: "make your sermons addresses to your hearers, rather than general essays or speculative harangues."[59] In their history of nonconformity the Independent ministers David Bogue and James Bennett would describe the scriptures as most effectively preached "with ability, with simplicity, with affection, and in an experimental manner; that is, when their influence on the hearts and lives of men is delineated with sacred skill and holy fervour."[60] Lastly, an extreme lampoon of particular and experimental preaching appears in one of the more rabid anti-nonconformist publications of the eighteenth century, *Scotch Presbyterian Eloquence Display'd* (1692, but republished often, well into the nineteenth century). In one of its many assaults on Puritanical zeal, a Presbyterian minister brings his message home to the individual members of his congregation, telling them that there are several sorts of drunkenness: "1. To be drunk like a sow, tumbling in the mire, *like many of this parish.* 2. There is to be drunk like a dog. The dog fills the stomach of him, and spues all out again; and *thou, John Jamison,* wast this way drunk the other day . . ." (my emphasis).[61]

Like extempore preaching, then, the particular and experimental method was associated in the minds of conformists with heated, unlettered, and unruly religion; by the opposite side of the same coin, in the mid eighteenth century particular and experimental preaching was thought of by Dissenters themselves as the peculiar strength of their seventeenth-century Puritan forebears. Thus Jennings asserts, "if you peruse the Writings of the most powerful and successful Preachers, particularly the *Puritan* Divines, you'll see that they . . . suit[ed] their Discourses to all the Variety of the Hearts of Men . . . In this Way they found their own Hearts warmed, and thus they reached the Hearts of their Hearers; whilst many were imagining the Minister had been told of their Case, and made the Sermon for them."[62] Beyond explication of revealed religion, Richard Baxter's sermons seemed to communicate actual experience of revelation itself: according to Edmund Calamy, "he talked in the pulpit with great freedom about another world . . . like one that had been there, and was come as a sort of an express from thence to make a report concerning it."[63] And looking back to "the old puritan mode" of experimental preaching, Bogue and Bennett describe it as "like an arrow shot at the heart, and piercing it to the core . . . The general way of preaching used by the ablest divines in the establishment, at the time, was in comparison as to effects, but like a pointless arrow."[64]

As this overview illustrates, spontaneity and particularity in preaching corresponded to denominational divides.[65] Orthodox nonconformists, especially, who sought to reinstill immediacy and spontaneity in religious devotion used the language of the sublime to refer to Puritan preaching, a language we have heard in the passages I have quoted, in their fervency and power – Moses coming down from the mount, the arrow that pierces the heart to the core. In the words of an anonymous pamphlet, *The Fashionable Preacher: or, Modern Pulpit Eloquence Displayed* (1773), which inveighs against both "abstract discourses from the pulpit" and the "absurdity . . . that is the *reading of sermons*," "A sublime eloquence is the offspring of nature, not of art."[66]

DEVOTIONAL TASTE

Because of the denominational divisions and cultural associations with which Barbauld lived as a liberal Dissenter from a Presbyterian family, she was able to appropriate and domesticate Puritan elements of her Dissenting heritage for a revisionary devotional theory. From the 1770s through '90s, Barbauld writes from a perspective that does not easily reside within "rational" Dissent in general or Unitarianism in particular: through careful manipulations of moral sensibility, she dialectically reclaims but tempers both the spontaneity and particularity of Puritan devotion, and then sets up this revised inheritance – the legacy of Isaac Watts, of her grandfather John Jennings, of Jennings' student and Watts' disciple Philip Doddridge, and of Doddridge's student and Barbauld's father, John Aikin – as the oppositional counterweight to "rational" (or as she often calls it, "philosophical") Dissent.

Barbauld's single most coherent theological position was Arminian, or more properly anti-Calvinist.[67] In her 1792 response to Gilbert Wakefield's *An Enquiry into the Expediency and Propriety of Public or Social Worship*, Barbauld is at once amusing and completely serious in her attack on Calvinism and its consequences on "manners":

> Above all, it would be desirable to separate from religion that idea of gloom which in this country has but too generally accompanied it . . . No one who embraces the common idea of future torments, together with the doctrine of election and reprobation, the insufficiency of virtue to escape the *wrath* of God, and the strange absurdity which, it should seem, through similarity of sound alone has been admitted as an axiom, that sins committed against an Infinite Being do therefore deserve infinite punishment – no one, I will venture to assert, can believe such tenets, and have them often in his thoughts, and yet be cheerful.[68]

She more often wrote, therefore, against "the gloomy perplexities of Calvinism, and the heart-withering prospective of cruel and never-ending punishments," than for Arminianism.[69] In spite of this opposition to "all the tremendous horrors of the Calvinistic faith,"[70] her devotional theory bears witness to a strong and enduring Puritan inheritance, with an important distinction. Although she attempts to instill contemporary religion with the very same qualities associated by both Dissenters and members of the Church with seventeenth-century Puritanism, her goal is never to return to such a sectarian world. Rather, she seeks to take up the spontaneous, particular, and experimental qualities of Puritan preaching espoused by her two preceding generations of Presbyterians and Independents, and to integrate them into the culture of a more latitudinarian and denominational age – an age, in fact, not of sectarian fervor but rather of sensibility and accommodation.

In this sense, Barbauld's innovative writings suggest that the early Romantic engagement with the minute particulars of both the internal and external worlds, the spontaneous feelings of the individual heart as well as the fine distinctions of specific and local nature, can be understood in terms of the religious and devotional culture from which that engagement emerged, rather than merely as the logical outcome of an inevitable and progressive secularism. Nor were Romantic particularity and spontaneity just the offspring of a reaction against eighteenth-century universal nature, poetic diction, and neoclassical form; by the 1780s, an entire critical vocabulary had developed with which to theorize and realize new relations among individuals, communities, and nature, and these relations depended not solely on a philosophical transformation of religious belief into "natural supernaturalism" but also on the lived religion of mid- to late-eighteenth-century denominational Protestants.

For Barbauld, this early Romantic program received its clearest articulation in her "Thoughts on the Devotional Taste, on Sects, and on Establishments," an essay first published in *Devotional Pieces* (1775) and republished in the third edition of *Miscellaneous Pieces in Prose* (1792). In this essay, Barbauld's application of religious sensibility serves as the basis for her controversial program to reform the character of Dissent itself. "Thoughts" begins by considering religion in three different aspects: one, "as a system of opinions," for which the correspondent faculty is "Reason, exerted in the freest and most dispassionate enquiry"; two, "as a habit" that "regulate[s] our conduct," strengthened "by repeated exertions"; and three, "as a taste . . . and in this sense it may properly be called Devotion" (*SPP*, p. 211). The first part of "Thoughts" is dedicated to analyzing this taste, after which the essay moves on to a historical survey of sects and establishments, to be discussed in Chapter 3. Barbauld draws an analogy between the material and immaterial worlds: "As . . . the process of vegetation restores and purifies vitiated air; so does that moral and political ferment which accompanies the growth of new sects, communicate a kind of spirit and elasticity necessary to the vigour and health of the soul" (*SPP*, p. 231). If sensibility was represented within the new bourgeois culture of the late eighteenth century as a civilizing force of sympathy that would emerge from private households to reform the corrupt, masculine world of public power, then Barbauld saw a similar role for religious sects. Yet in order to theorize and popularize this role, she needed to domesticate the extremely virile and austere set of dispositions associated with both rational Dissent and its Puritan past. This was no small task, but the two areas of orthodox Dissenting preaching that I have been discussing offered an opportunity. Although she writes that "prayer and praise" are "the more genuine and indispensible parts of public worship" (*SPP*, p. 224), she is consistently concerned with the different forms of preaching that distinguish sects (in their various phases) and establishments. Thus "In an infant sect . . . A strain of eloquence, often coarse, but strong and persuasive, works like leaven in the heart of the people," whereas among mature sects "pulpit discourses are studied and judicious," while establishments "aim at elegance and show in . . . the appearance of their preachers" (*SPP*, pp. 223–25). Barbauld's striking intervention is to vitalize devotional experience by taking a strong component of her Puritan inheritance – the particular, spontaneous, and affective direct appeal to the individual heart typical of devotion in the "infant sect" – and aligning it with the warmth of communal or familial life in the more settled denomination. She accomplishes this alignment by revising the sublimity inherited from Puritan devotion in one of two ways, either by coding devotional experience instead according to the aesthetic category of the beautiful or, in her later response to Gilbert Wakefield, by regulating the sublime by means of the sensibility and sociability of public worship.

In her analysis of religion in its third aspect, she writes that devotion may be "considered as a taste, an affair of sentiment and feeling"; the "seat" of this devotional taste "is in the imagination and the passions, and it has its source in that relish for the sublime . . . and the beautiful, by which we taste the charms of poetry" (*SPP*, p. 211). Yet as the essay continues, the devotional tastes for the "sublime" and the "beautiful" become not just distinct but opposed. Whereas the enthusiasm of Puritan devotion was consistently coded as sublime, for Barbauld the terms are reversed: the sublime in this essay is the province of abstract philosophy, which, because it opens out to such vast prospects of speculation, exceeds the capacities of the common mind and thus fails to pierce the individual heart: "Philosophy does indeed enlarge our conceptions of the Deity, and gives us the sublimest ideas of his power and extent of dominion; but it raises him too high for our imaginations to take hold of, and in a great measure destroys that affectionate regard which is felt by the common class of pious Christians" (*SPP*, p. 215). This common class requires "some common nature . . . on which to build our intercourse" (*SPP*, p. 216). Philosophy, Barbauld writes, "represents the Deity in too abstracted a manner to engage our affections" (*SPP*, p. 216), and philosophers

dwell too much in generals. Accustomed to reduce every thing to the operation of general laws, they . . . attempt to grasp the whole order of the universe, and in the zeal of a systematic spirit seldom leave room for those particular and personal mercies which are the food of gratitude. They trace the great outline of nature, but neglect the colouring which gives warmth and beauty to the piece.

(*SPP*, pp. 216–17)

Philosophical and rational preaching is sublime, and thus excessive. Where we expect the emotional sublime of Puritan zeal we are given the rational sublime of Socinian reason, and because the rational Christian dedicates his spiritual energies to expounding "general laws" of human, physical, and divine nature, his devotional compositions remain abstract, neither "particular and personal" nor warm and beautiful. Barbauld's position here does participate in the culture of sensibility, but she is participating in that culture by reworking her religious heritage in complex and powerful ways. As a liberal Presbyterian with Unitarian ties, she rejects Calvinism and distances herself from its "gloomy perplexities," but as a devotional writer seeking to critique the very form of rational Dissent that she inhabits, she finds elements of her heritage potentially useful and necessary. The potential becomes realized when the extempore, particular, and experimental methods can be described not as sublime but as "more personal and affecting":

As in poetry it is not vague and general description, but a few striking circumstances clearly related and strongly worked up – as in a landscape it is not such a vast extensive range of country as pains the eye to stretch to its limits, but a beautiful, well-defined prospect, which gives the most pleasure – so neither are those unbounded views in which philosophy delights, so much calculated to touch the heart as home views and nearer objects. The philosopher offers up general praises on the altar of universal nature; the devout man, on the altar of his heart, presents his own sighs, his own thanksgivings, his own earnest desires: the former worship is more sublime, the latter more personal and affecting.

(*SPP*, p. 217)

As William Godwin would later distinguish in "Of History and Romance" (*PPW*, v, pp. 290–301) between the writers of the two genres, privileging the writer of romance, Barbauld here opposes "the philosopher" to "the devout man," bringing devotion home to a local, inhabitable landscape looked upon not as a set of abstract relations that cohere into an ultimately ungraspable magnitude but rather as the picturesque, "well-defined prospect" whose "few striking circumstances clearly related and strongly worked up" produce an aesthetic and devotional experience accommodated to the individual and common eye and heart. As opposed to the philosopher's carefully premeditated, and presumably written, "general praises on the altar of universal nature," the devout man's sighs, thanksgivings, and desires emerge spontaneously as devotion, almost as corporeal emanations without the intervention of reason, and the repetition of "his own" emphasizes the particularity of these individual feelings. "A wise preacher" (*SPP*, p. 221) understands that a good sermon or prayer, like the accompanying devotional taste, proceeds not from the sublime and philosophical reason that "dwell[s] too much in generals" and "attempt[s] to grasp the whole order of the universe," but from the extempore responses of sensibility to the particulars of human nature and divine creation. And always associated with social life, "home views and nearer objects," the domestic language of the beautiful replaces that of the sublime even as the terms of spontaneity and particularity remain constant. Devotional writers and speakers who are not "ignoran[t] of the human heart," therefore, will take "advantage of the impression which particular circumstances, times and seasons, naturally make upon the mind" (*SPP*, pp. 219–20).[71]

A different response to the Puritan sublime emerges in Barbauld's contribution to the Wakefieldian controversy, her *Remarks on Mr. Gilbert Wakefield's Enquiry into the Expediency and Propriety of Public or Social Worship* (1792).[72] Here she follows Hume's model of the communicability or "contagion" of passions in an attempt to defend public worship as "a means of invigorating faith" (p. 41).[73] "None of our feelings," she writes, "are of a more communicable nature than our religious ones. If devotion really exists in the heart of each individual, it is morally impossible it should exist there apart and single. So many separate tapers, burning so near each other, in the very nature of things must catch, and spread into one common flame" (p. 8). If some few individuals can accept truth through reason and, in isolation, stir religious feelings in their own individual hearts, most "minds are not capable of that firmness of decision which embraces truth upon a bare preponderancy of argument . . . These, when they enter a place of worship, amidst all the animating accompaniments of social homage, are seized with a happy contagion" (p. 42). The "contagion" that spreads the fires of "separate tapers . . . into one common flame," of course, evokes the risk of enthusiastic conflagration. Whereas in "Thoughts on the Devotional Taste" the language of spontaneity and particularity allowed Barbauld to recode the sublimity of devotional experience according to the beautiful, here the same set of terms leads her to retain the enthusiastic sublime: "The devout heart . . . bursts into loud and vocal expressions of praise and adoration; and, from a full and overflowing sensibility, seeks to expand itself to the utmost limits of creation" (pp. 18–19). But sensibility does not just facilitate the sublime; its inherently social nature also serves a regulatory function. Just as in "Thoughts" Barbauld reversed the associations of the sublime, mapping it onto abstract philosophy rather than zealous enthusiasm, here she reverses the associations of enthusiasm itself, attributing its origin to the morbid solipsism of isolated individuals rather than to the collective passions of the crowd:

Enthusiasm is indeed most dangerous in a crowd, but it seldom originates there. The mind, heated with intense thinking, adopts illusions to which it is not exposed when its devotion is guided and bounded by addresses which are intended to meet the common sentiments of a numerous assembly. Religion then appears with the most benignant aspect, is then least likely to be mistaken, when the presence of our fellow-creatures points out its connexion with the businesses of life and duties of society. (p. 11)

Contemporary, public worship should reinvigorate devotional feelings, leading to spontaneous and sublime religious experiences dangerously close to enthusiasm yet regulated, "guided and bounded," by the social foundation of sensibility. And it is the preacher's obligation, in turn, to make this social foundation felt by uniting individuals, in their particular natures and characters, into a common community. To do this, in Barbauld's *Remarks*, is to imitate Christ: "His great business in the world was instruction; and this he dispensed, not in a systematic, but a popular manner; nor yet in a vague and declamatory style, but in a pointed and appropriate one . . . Almost all his discourses . . . were delivered as occasion prompted, and therefore it was that they came so home to men's business and bosoms" (pp. 31–32). Once again Barbauld's populism – "Every time Social Worship is celebrated, it includes a virtual declaration of the rights of man" (p. 46) – resists system and champions instead spontaneity and particularity, in this case in order simultaneously to retain the "fervour" and "animation" associated with the sublime while containing the enthusiasm of the crowd within the bounds of sociability, of personal connections and benevolent feelings.

Aware that Dissenting devotional "practices are founded upon a prevalence of religious fervour, an animation and warmth of piety, which, if it no longer exists, it is vain to simulate" (p. 58), Barbauld fears that if the devotional taste among contemporary Dissenting ministers "wants animation, as perhaps it does, the silent pews will be deserted one by one" (p. 59). Her call to animate devotion represented, in part, an attempt to revise some of the most entrenched aspects of rational Dissenters' self-understanding not by simulating their past but by incorporating enthusiastic elements of their heritage into a contemporary affective form of Dissent. And her ideas resonated. Witness the response to "Thoughts" of Harriet Martineau, comparing Barbauld to Hannah More: "Mrs. More awakens and impresses us, and we listen to her warnings with an awe which would make us believe that we are on no equality with her . . . But with Mrs. Barbauld it is different. She meets our ideas, and seems to express what had passed through our own minds . . . We have a fellow-feeling with her in all that she says, and it is thus that we are carried away by her fervour of feeling . . . [S]he paints our passions and emotions [with justice], and touches every chord of feeling in our bosoms."[74] For Martineau, as for Barbauld's more ardent readers both male and female, her appeal is that of the experimental preacher in the guise of the woman writer of sensibility.

The moderated enthusiasm of Barbauld's devotional discourse, however, left her in a difficult position. In the process of accommodating her Dissenting heritage to what she saw as the needs of the contemporary age, Barbauld risks running to the opposite extreme, and in fact her defenses of affective religion seemed to some as a direct betrayal of rational religion in favor of the Established Church, or even as a kind of admiration for the Church of Rome (*SPP*, p. 227). One consequence of Barbauld's attempt to reinvigorate devotion was her apology for the religious experience least acceptable to rational Dissenters: "let us not be superstitiously afraid of superstition," she writes, "It shews great ignorance of the human heart, and the springs by which its passions are moved, to neglect taking advantage of the impressions which particular circumstances, times and seasons, naturally make upon the mind" (*SPP*, pp. 219–20). As it will for the Unitarian Coleridge, Hartleian associationism leads Barbauld to a devotional theory, based on benevolence and the affections, which actually proves to be as much a challenge as a support to rational Dissent, for "The root of all superstition is the principle of the association of ideas, by which, objects naturally indifferent become dear and venerable, through their connection with interesting ones" (*SPP*, p. 220). Knowing the dangerous territory she is entering, she acknowledges that the principle of association "has been much abused: it has given rise to pilgrimages innumerable, worship of relics, and priestly power" (*SPP*, p. 220). She accordingly seeks a middle ground between monkish and tyrannical superstition and the cold reason of "those who call themselves rational Christians": "let us not carry our ideas of purity and simplicity so far as to neglect [superstition] entirely" (*SPP*, p. 220). "A wise preacher," she writes, "will not, from a fastidious refinement, disdain to affect his hearers from the season of the year, the anniversary of a national blessing, a remarkable escape from danger" (*SPP*, p. 221). Such an assertion could not but evoke the four political anniversaries provided for by the late-eighteenth-century *Book of Common Prayer* – Gunpowder Day (5 November), Martyrdom Day (30 January), Restoration Day (29 May), and Accession Day (25 October) – the first and third of which involved national blessings to the Established Church that were also direct escapes from dangers posed by Catholics and Separatists, and the second of which annually reminded the nation of the greatest stigma of Dissent, its association with the killing of a king.

Within Dissent Barbauld met with opposition – Priestley of course balked at her essay, as did Martineau later on: "though it professes to treat of devotional *taste*, and not religious principle, it is still too imaginative."[75] "Thoughts" indeed provoked hostile reactions from various camps, but none was more telling than Priestley's, who responded to her in "a very long and very serious letter," dated 20 December 1775, "on the subject of her late essay, disapproving totally of all the sentiment of it."[76] Long and serious, the letter was semi-public as well; four days later Priestley wrote to William Turner that "Dr. Price, and all my serious and judicious acquaintance in London, think as I do on the subject, and approved of my letter to her."[77] In the letter, Priestley informs Barbauld that his "ideas with respect to devotion, 'sects, and establishments,' are . . . in almost every respect the very reverse of those in your essay" (I, p. 279). He goes out of his way, furthermore, to emphasize what he views as Barbauld's betrayal of Dissent itself, several times suggesting that his remarks speak for the larger Dissenting community: "And really, Mrs. Barbauld, all my more serious and judicious acquaintance, who are among your best friends, are, without exception, of the same opinion, and declared themselves to be so without having had any communication with one another upon the subject" (I, pp. 279–80). Clearly, then, the disagreement was not just about Barbauld's appeal to "the language of the affections" (*SPP*, p. 218), her passages against "cold-hearted philosophy" and its "disputatious spirit" (*SPP*, pp. 212–13), or her inappropriate Rousseauian comparison between the language of devotion and the "strain . . . the lover uses to the object of his attachment" (*SPP*, p. 222); rather, it was about the consequences of all of these positions for the definition and reformation of Dissent itself. When Priestley admits that his "notions on the subjects of your essay were always what are called old-fashioned" and laments, "I used to flatter myself that yours were nearly the same with mine,"[78] he associates himself with a form of Dissent that has kept itself separate from the Church by insisting on its own rational integrity. Barbauld's essay, for Priestley, implies a kind of newfangled Dissent that comes dangerously close to blurring the line between nonconformity and the establishment. There was a good deal of truth to Priestley's accusations, and Barbauld's essay did pose a challenge to rational Dissent in general and Unitarianism in particular. But at the same time it presented as much of a threat to the Established Church by calling for a devotional culture which, if anything, revived and updated an earlier affective and populist brand of nonconformity. In spite of Priestley's assertion that it was his devotional taste which was "old-fashioned," it was in fact Barbauld's which could be understood as bypassing the "new Dissent" of Methodism for a still older civic populism. Rather than turn to the enthusiastic Methodist preacher, Barbauld poses her challenge to both rational Dissent and the Church by combining the old heat of Puritan devotion with the new warmth of sensibility. The novelty of Barbauld's religious thought which seemed so threatening to Priestley and his "serious and judicious acquaintance" lay in its innovative negotiation of deeply rooted denominational, aesthetic, and gendered associations within the eighteenth-century discourse of devotion. By calling for a new, affective religion that would incorporate spontaneity and particularity in a regulated form of enthusiasm, Barbauld accused rational Dissenting reason or "philosophy" of failing to touch the common heart even as she hearkened back to, domesticated, and revised the aesthetic terms of an older Dissenting mode.

HABITUAL DEVOTION AND "AN ADDRESS TO THE DEITY"

As is often the case in arguments, neither Barbauld nor Priestley was able to articulate their common ground as effectively as their differences. As if to call Barbauld back to her true self, Priestley reminded her of a sermon he had preached in the late 1760s, "On Habitual Devotion." In his disapproving letter, he distinguishes between "true philosophy, founded on the most just and exalted conceptions of the Divine Being and his providence that we can attain to," and "spurious and false philosophy,"[79] or argument for argument's sake, which cools devotional sentiments by giving free reign to critical disputation. In her claim that "A prayer strictly philosophical must ever be a cold and dry composition" (*SPP*, p. 217), Priestley suggests, Barbauld has failed to make the distinction. He then writes,

To have the mind habitually impressed with these sentiments, is to set God always before us, and to live as "seeing him who is invisible." It is this that raises the mind above the world, and keeps it fixed, "stayed on God," in all the varieties of prosperity and adversity, and enables us to "rejoice evermore" . . . Such language as this is equally that of the Scriptures, and that of the strictest philosophy, of which you say, (p. 14,) that it "must ever be cold and dry."[80]

Priestley is here not only recalling his sermon "On Habitual Devotion" but also one of the immediate consequences of that sermon, Barbauld's own poem, "An Address to the Deity," first published in *Poems* (1773). In the Preface to his *Two Discourses; I. On Habitual Devotion, II. On the Duty of not living to Ourselves* (1782), Priestley writes that "the former of these discourses . . . was the occasion of that excellent poem of Mrs. Barbauld, intitled *An Address to the Deity*, which was composed immediately after the first delivery of it, before an assembly of ministers at Wakefield in Yorkshire, in the year 1767."[81] For Priestley, this sermon represented the successful synthesis of philosophical and experimental religion. Priestley prefaces his sermons with the apology, "If my theological publications have been more of a *speculative* than of a *practical* nature, it is merely because circumstances have led me to it . . . I hope I shall always consider speculation as subservient to practice" (p. v), and he then concludes his preface by quoting over three stanzas of Barbauld's poem (lines 41–56 and 63–80). These stanzas are intended to affirm that Priestley's theology represents more than cold argumentation. In fact, the circumstances of the poem's composition – "Were I to inform my readers how soon that poem appeared after the delivery of the discourse, it would add much to their idea of the powers of the writer" (p. v) – are meant to suggest the kind of spontaneous effusion of devotional feeling that few would associate with the experiences of Priestley's auditors.

The sermon, in which Priestley seeks to apply "Dr. Hartley's theory of the human affections" (pp. iii–iv), proposes that life should be "as it were, one act of devotion" (p. 4): "a truly and perfectly good man loves, and therefore cherishes the thought of God, his father and his friend; till every production of divine power and skill, every instance of divine bounty, and every event of divine providence, never fails to suggest to his mind the idea of the great Author of all things" (p. 3). An interesting strain of Priestley's thought involves the nature of habits, which, Priestley believed, were formed early in life and to a great extent determined one's entire character. In a sermon published in 1787, "Of the Danger of Bad Habits," Priestley explores the consequences of early associations: "how few are there whose *characters*, whose *dispositions*, or *habits of mind*, undergo any considerable change after they are grown to man's estate. Our *tempers*, and general characters are usually fixed as soon as we have fixed ourselves in a regular employment and mode of life."[82] If, as the materialist Priestley proposed in "On Habitual Devotion," we are to be able to associate God with all of our thoughts, actions, and experiences, then this ability needs to be an integral part of our being, as much a part of the body as of its components, the mind or soul; thus he continues in "Of the Danger of Bad Habits,"

> Any habits that we contract early in life, any particular bias or inclination; any particular cast of thought, or mode of conversation, even any particular gesture of body, as in walking, sitting, &c. we are universally known by among our acquaintance, from the time that we properly *enter life* to the time that we have done with it; as much as we are by the tone of our voice, or our hand writing, which likewise are of the nature of *habits*, or *customs*. (p. 373)

If successfully formed, the habit of devotion will identify the individual as much as any of his or her particular manners or gestures. "On Habitual Devotion" describes the outcome of an early association of life with the thought of God as follows: "Thus he lives, as it were, constantly *seeing him, who is invisible*. He sees God in every thing, and he sees every thing in God. He *dwells in love*, and thereby *dwells in God, and God in him*" (p. 4). From this position, Priestley's sermon builds to a religious experience of the sublime which would provide the immediate inspiration for Barbauld's poem: "by means of a *habitual regard to God*" (p. 7), that is, by means of associating God with quotidian objects and affairs, the individual Christian regulates his or her virtue and also experiences, through a kind of transcendence, the elevation of devotional feelings: "Religion, my brethren, the doctrine of a God, of a providence, and of a future state, opens an immense, a glorious, and most transporting prospect" (p. 10).

In her early children's writing as well as her poetry, Barbauld was deeply influenced by Priestley's Hartleian theories of the habitual. The Preface to her *Hymns in Prose* (1781) announces that "The peculiar design of this publication is, to impress devotional feelings as early as possible on the infant mind," for "a child, to feel the full force of the idea of God, ought never to remember the time when he had no such idea," just as we can never remember a time when our peculiar gestures and mannerisms seemed anything other than simply our own.[83] Her design in *Hymns* is to impress devotional feelings

by connecting religion with a variety of sensible objects; with all that he sees, all he hears, all that affects his young mind with wonder or delight; and thus by deep, strong, and permanent associations, to lay the best foundation for practical devotion in future life. For he who has early been accustomed to see the Creator in the visible appearances of all around him . . . has made large advances towards that habitual piety, without which religion can scarcely regulate the conduct, and will never warm the heart. (pp. vi–vii)

Barbauld's *Hymns in Prose*, then, following Priestley's habitual devotion, represent an attempt to associate God with familiar objects of childhood experience; Hymn VI concludes, "God is in every place; he speaks in every sound we hear; he is seen in all that our eyes behold: nothing, O child of reason, is without God; – let God therefore be in all thy thoughts" (p. 42). The conclusion that Barbauld draws for the "child of reason" is perfectly rational, but the faculty to be strengthened by accepting the conclusion as practice is habitual and affective.

"An Address to the Deity" may be read in this light as the articulation of a poet who has formed such "strong, and permanent associations" between God and nature. The poem, however, unlike either Priestley's sermons or Barbauld's *Hymns in Prose*, suggests that devotional feelings, even when habitual, sometimes fail to cheat so well as they are famed to do. The structure of the poem presents a familiar lyric movement between the moment of inspiration and its necessary termination; habitual devotion thus forms not one constant, steady act of "*seeing him, who is invisible*," as Priestley puts it, but a series of visionary moments that ignite and fade, only to rekindle under the right conditions. The fashioning of the mind and heart in order to enable those conditions becomes the task of the religious poet, and of Barbauld's poem.

"An Address" begins with a movement from the simple naming of God toward the sublime experience of the divinity as the all-encompassing infinite. If the poem were simply a poetic translation of Priestley's sermon, or if Barbauld were not engaging with and revising the relations between specific methods of nonconformist devotion and aesthetic categories, the poem could successfully achieve this state and then conclude with a presage of complete communion after death. Were this the case, the poem would contradict her later devotional theory, and it seems that Priestley at least intended her to see the tensions. But in fact the poem is consistent with her nuanced arbitration between populist Puritanism, rational Dissent, and the Established Church, presenting the failure of the sublime to sustain devotion for the common natures of earthly life. Martineau, indeed, turns directly to this poem from her discussion of "Thoughts" and Barbauld's devotional prose, which "touches every chord of feeling in our bosoms. This is more especially to be said with respect to her poetry. Who has not felt in reading her sublime Address to the Deity, that he meets with his own aspirations, . . . illustrated by loftier imagery than his own imagination could have furnished him with?"[84]

"From gloomy terrors free" (line 71), Barbauld's "Address" is meant to articulate the warmth of religious feeling without the fervid fears of Calvinist doctrine and devotion. God in this poem, as McCarthy and Kraft point out (*PALB*, p. 41), is the benevolent parent, not the angry object of terror who saves the elect by grace and casts the rest into eternal hellfire:

> GOD of my life! and author of my days!
> Permit my feeble voice to lisp thy praise;
> And trembling, take upon a mortal tongue
> That hallow'd name to harps of Seraphs sung. (lines 1–4)

The opening of the poem presents the most basic act of devotion, the naming of the divinity. The "hallow'd name" is the first word of the first line, and by speaking it the poet, habituated to devotion, produces the first link in an associative chain of feelings that leaves the mind and soul empty of all else:

> I feel that name my inmost thoughts controul,
> And breathe an awful stillness thro' my soul;
> As by a charm, the waves of grief subside;
> Impetuous passion stops her headlong tide:
> At thy felt presence all emotions cease,
> And my hush'd spirit finds a sudden peace,
> Till every worldly thought within me dies,
> And earth's gay pageants vanish from my eyes;
> Till all my sense is lost in infinite,
> And one vast object fills my aching sight. (lines 11–20)

At this point in the poem, the devotional act or impulse seems external, like "a charm" that works on the senses and the emotions from without. Thus the emptying process is represented through verbs performed by parts of the speaker's self beyond her agency or will: "waves of grief subside," "impetuous passion stops her headlong tide," "all emotions cease," "every worldly thought within me dies," "earth's gay pageants vanish," and the "sense is lost in infinite." The spirit, "hush'd," thus "finds" rather than makes its peace. The end of the verse paragraph achieves the sublime experience of complete annihilation, an emptiness of all besides the "one vast object" which entirely "fills" the poet's sight. This is an act of vision achieved by allowing the habituated mind to dwell on the infinite and eternal.

It is an act, however, that cannot and does not last:

> But soon, alas! this holy calm is broke;
> My soul submits to wear her wonted yoke;
> With shackled pinions strives to soar in vain,
> And mingles with the dross of earth again. (lines 21–24)

The "wonted yoke" of the poet's soul is not its fallen but rather its common nature; its hours of dross are not consumed by sin but by quotidian distractions from the thought of God. The sublime thus fails to retain the mind, even a mind habituated to devotion, because we require "some common nature . . . on which to build our intercourse." A benevolent God, however, understands this – "But he, our gracious Master, kind, as just, / Knowing our frame, remembers man is dust" (lines 25–26) – and the next turn of the poem returns the poet to a different kind of vision, a less awful one, this time produced by the responsive and reciprocal interaction between the spontaneous expressions of the individual self and the spirit of God:

> His spirit, ever brooding o'er our mind,
> Sees the first wish to better hopes inclin'd;
> Marks the young dawn of every virtuous aim,
> And fans the smoking flax into a flame. (lines 27–30)

Yoked and shackled, its calm broken, the soul nonetheless returns to a state of devotion through this active experience of religious sensibility, as opposed to the passive reception of the religious sublime. God's spirit broods over the mind as it brooded over the waters, simultaneously creating and watching creation unfold. He "sees the first wish to better hopes inclin'd" and "Marks the young dawn of every virtuous aim"; both the wish and the aim are the spark produced by the habitual devotion of the poet. The spark produces smoke, and when God sees and marks this process, he responds by actively fanning the "flax into a flame."[85] The next two couplets then rephrase this process, and the new metaphors suggest the necessarily spontaneous and experimental nature of sustained devotion:

His ears are open to the softest cry,
His grace descends to meet the lifted eye;
He reads the language of a silent tear,
And sighs are incense from a heart sincere. (lines 31–34)

In an almost Blakean moment of lyric innocence, spontaneous effusion produces its reciprocal response in a potentially endless cycle of devotion. The cry, the lifted eye, the tear, and the sighs, all conventional signs of genuine feeling, here find themselves heard, received, read, and accepted as the incense of the sincere heart, and God's response is the mercy and grace characteristic of a benevolent deity who loves what he creates. At this point, the extempore "language of a silent tear" could simply be a generalized expression of human suffering, but following the next section, the poem turns to a sustained devotion that combines spontaneity with the precise terms of particularity and experimentalism we have been considering.

Whereas the experience of the infinite, when "one vast object fills my aching sight," necessarily fades as the soul submits to its "wonted yoke," this second achievement of devotion initiates a sustained form of habituation, pointing the poet's path "to everlasting peace" (line 40). The next two verse paragraphs represent this path not as a simple faith in a final communion with God but rather as the daily course of events and temptations that mark the regular life of the common Christian. The paragraphs (lines 41–48, 49–56) balance one another, describing the poet's ability, following the experience of reciprocal devotion, to encounter the temptations of "winning pleasure" (line 41) and the despair of the "vale of tears" (line 49), respectively. The culmination of the poet's encounter with sorrow is a traditional form of Christian resignation – "Resign'd to die, or resolute to live; / Prepar'd to kiss the sceptre, or the rod" (lines 54–55) – followed by the echo of Priestley's statement that the habitually devoted Christian "sees God in every thing, and . . . every thing in God": the paragraph ends, "While GOD is seen in all, and all in GOD" (line 56).

Having reached this state through the spontaneity of sensibility rather than abstract reflection on the vastness of infinity, the poem returns to the emotion of awe, but with a difference:

I read his awful name, emblazon'd high
With golden letters on th' illumin'd sky;
Nor less the mystic characters I see
Wrought in each flower, inscrib'd on every tree;
In every leaf that trembles to the breeze
I hear the voice of GOD among the trees . . . (lines 57–62)

The "mystic characters" of God's language are "wrought" and "inscribed" on the world of nature, as we might expect, but an inescapable sense of particularity is felt in the emphasis on the individuality of creation: the characters are wrought in "each" flower, inscribed on "every" tree, and the voice of God can be heard in "every" leaf that trembles to the breeze, not just as an undistinguishable member of a choir but also as a single, audible voice. If this is the sublime experience of awe, it is one that is determinedly local and inhabitable, and thus the consequence of the ability to see God in all, and all in God, is the successful and sustained devotion of the individual Christian throughout his or her every experience of common nature:

> With thee in shady solitudes I walk,
> With thee in busy crowded cities talk,
> In every creature own thy forming power,
> In each event thy providence adore. (lines 63–66)

Again, the particularity of the world inheres in Barbauld's repetition of "every" and "each," and the common acts of walking and talking, in either the shady solitudes of the country or the busy crowds of the city, involve not abstract reflection upon God but concrete association of God with daily and personal experience. The extempore, particular, and experimental nature of this process both regulates the poet's virtue – guarding her from temptation and despair alike – and provides her with the comforting faith that, having taught her how to live, God will teach her how to cross from one state into another:

> Then when the last, the closing hour draws nigh,
> And earth recedes before my swimming eye;
> When trembling on the doubtful edge of fate
> I stand and stretch my view to either state;
> Teach me to quit this transitory scene
> With decent triumph and a look serene;
> Teach me to fix my ardent hopes on high,
> And having liv'd to thee, in thee to die. (lines 73–80)

As with the earlier experience of the sublime, every thing "recedes," and the process of learning to die will ultimately leave the poet's senses empty of all but God. But the poet's look now becomes "serene," not "aching." At the end, trembling can give way to serenity and hope because the poet has been habituated by a warm, even ardent devotion sustained and regulated by an intercourse built on common nature, by spontaneous addresses of sensibility from the individual Christian to a Deity who reciprocates.

CHAPTER 3

The "Joineriana": *Barbauld, the Aikin family circle, and the Dissenting public sphere*

In 1775, two years after *Miscellaneous Pieces in Prose, by J. and A. L. Aikin* issued from the press of Joseph Johnson, Anna Barbauld wrote to her brother John, "I think we must some day sew all our fragments together, and make a *Joineriana* of them. Let me see: – I have, half a ballad; the first scene of a play; a plot of another, all but the catastrophe; half a dozen loose similies, and an eccentric flight or two among the fairies" (*Works*, II, p. 9).[1] In her use of the expression "*Joineriana*," Anna implies to John that whereas their half-ballads, first scenes, loose similies, and eccentric flights might remain incomplete on their own, by "sewing" these fragments together the siblings could produce a presentable patchwork. Although this particular project never materialized, she continued to conceive of literary production according to a model of familial collaboration.[2] Twelve years later, as Barbauld and her husband, Rochemont, were settling into their new home in Hampstead, she wrote to her brother, "We are making a catalogue of our books; and I have left a great deal of space under the letters A. and B. for our future publications" (*Works*, II, p. 155). The growth of this catalogue accompanies Barbauld's organization of a new domestic setting in which she, her husband, and their adopted son Charles, the biological child of John and Martha Aikin, will live. The blank space at the beginning of the catalogue, "under the letters A. and B.," signifies a continuity of past and future literary creation defined by the kindred relationship between brother and sister. As with the sewing metaphor of the "*Joineriana*," here Barbauld represents collaborative literary production in private, domestic, and familial terms.[3] If in "An Address to the Deity" she produced a religious lyric out of her own critical devotional thought and powerful Dissenting heritage, her future career would be marked by participation in an extensive and collaborative publishing network that would represent Dissenting culture, its beliefs, practices, interests, and tastes, to the national republic of letters.

The Aikins' collaborative mode asserts an integral connection between the "intimate sphere" of the family, the inherited virtues of religious nonconformity, and the progressive market ethos of middle-class eighteenth-century life, especially in the commercial centers of Northern England. I will return occasionally to the terms generated by Jürgen Habermas' early sociological study, *The Structural Transformation of the Public Sphere* (1962), in order to trace the outlines of what I consider to be a significant variant of classical bourgeois publicity. The Dissenting public sphere was not a "counter-public" in the sense that Geoff Eley, Kevin Gilmartin, and Günther Lottes have used to portray a plebeian public sphere in the late eighteenth and early nineteenth centuries, or in the sense that Joan Landes and Rita Felski have applied to the feminist public sphere of the twentieth century.[4] Nancy Fraser, correspondingly, refers to "a host of competing counter-publics, including nationalist publics, popular peasant publics, elite women's publics, and working-class publics," which "contested the exclusionary norms of the bourgeois public, elaborating alternative styles of political behavior and alternative norms of public speech."[5] Rather than constituting a counter-public, however, the Dissenting public sphere represents a subcategory of the classical public sphere, a fragment that exerted critical pressure from within.[6] At the same time as middle-class Dissenters such as the Aikins and their affiliates were largely excluded by the Corporation and Test Acts from the universities and from ecclesiastical, military, and political avenues of advancement within the English establishment, they nonetheless participated – and saw themselves as participating – in the centers of economic and cultural public life. The legal status of nonconformity gave added impetus to their engagement with public opinion, and their sphere of intervention was thus by necessity an intermediate space between the private realm and the state. By examining the collaborative mode of literary production typical of the Aikin family circle, I will describe a Dissenting public sphere that intervened through religious, political, and cultural debate in the national public sphere by asserting a structural link between the intimate domain of the conjugal family and the civil sphere of middle-class commercial existence. The basis for such an assertion, I hope to demonstrate, lay in the collaborative nature of Dissenting cultural production.

Late-eighteenth-century culture projected sensibility, the essence of humanity inherent in idealized familial relationships, out from the home as a civilizing force that would bind together individuals connected otherwise only by relations of interest and power. Informing this projection was the bourgeois division of the private sphere between the life of the family and the economic functions of civil society and the market.[7] By virtue of this division, in the feminine space of the home, relationships could seem natural, grounded in normative human qualities; in the masculine, competitive world of the market, on the other hand, relationships depended on status and were shaped by property ownership and commodity exchange.[8] For middle-class Dissenting writers such as the Aikins, and especially for Dissenting women writers, a principal end of cultural production was to sustain the progressive force of the market but to inflect its values with the warmer tones of domestic life. Women writers, especially, played a prominent role in this nonconformist project, strategically using their dual status as private family members and professional authors to enter public discourse from a tenuous but potentially privileged station.[9] Considerable negotiation was necessary, but Dissenting women could and did claim to speak with authority about what they perceived to be the proper relations between both spheres of the private realm, and from this position their works entered the "republic of letters," the literary public sphere, with a peculiar force.

For this reason it is again important to qualify the pervasive assumption that the nature of the bourgeois public sphere was uniformly masculinist.[10] Although Habermas and others have emphasized the role of women as readers, and although women were largely excluded from the coffeehouses, taverns, and clubs in which the public sphere thrived, their participation as authors in the literary public sphere has only recently begun to be acknowledged and examined.[11] The political public sphere, on the other hand, was less inclusive: when Barbauld entered the public debate over the repeal of anti-nonconformist legislation in *An Address to the Opposers of the Repeal of the Corporation and Test Acts* (1790), for instance, it was under the ambiguously gendered pseudonym, "A DISSENTER"; her best-known contribution to political discourse, *Sins of Government, Sins of the Nation; or, a Discourse for the Fast, Appointed on April 19, 1793* (1793), was published under the pseudonym, "A Volunteer"; suspicious of the anti-religious tendencies of Jacobinism, Barbauld wrote *The Religion of Nature, A Short Discourse, Delivered before the National Assembly at Paris, . . . With a Short Address to the Jurymen of Great Britain* (1793) under the masculine pseudonym, "Bob Short"; and her *Civic Sermons to the People* (1792) and *Remarks on Mr. Gilbert Wakefield's Enquiry into the Expediency and Propriety of Public or Social Worship* (1792) were both issued anonymously.[12] The pressures on women to resist the publicity of authorship cannot be denied, but neither should the pattern of women's authorship, often in the context of literary families, be overlooked.[13]

Dissenting women such as Barbauld, Joanna Baillie, Maria Edgeworth, Mary Hays, Amelia Opie, Helen Maria Williams, and later Jane and Ann Taylor were well-known names whose works were widely read and reviewed.

Integral to the process by which the Aikins sought to temper the bourgeois sphere of civil society with the nonsectarian, ostensibly human values of the family was their socio-theological assertion of Arminian and Arian Dissent as a middle way between Calvinism and the Church of England. In religious terms, Barbauld's pedagogical project was a vision of the intermediate role to be played by a reinvigorated and reformed Dissenting community between the excessive rigors of Puritan Calvinist nonconformity and the politeness, inclusiveness, and ritual endearments of the Established Church. In Chapter 2 we saw how such a position emerged from a cultural heritage of theological beliefs and denominational characteristics, but the position should be considered in political and economic terms as well. For middle-class Dissenters "rational" heterodox religion and progressive commercialism could be allied. Read in the context of mid- to late-eighteenth-century provincial, heterodox Dissent, Barbauld's proposed "*Joineriana*" suggests that the domestic collaboration signified by the metaphor associated this alliance with sensibility and the plenitude of the intimate sphere – the Aikin family circle and the Warrington community. In Barbauld's writings, reason, science, free enquiry, abstract philosophical speculation, theological disputation, religious liberty, personal self-denial, and a middle-class commercialist ethos could be moderated, made warmer and more beautiful through familial collaboration and poetic techniques of sensibility, which would together affiliate these austere features of nonconformity with the intimate plenitude of the home and the supposedly personal, domestic, and noncompetitive relationships inside its walls. The resulting cultural program thus served to domesticate the progressive and competitive dispositions of Dissent, authorizing Barbauld to disseminate and publicize them, usually through the press of Joseph Johnson, to the nation.

In 1828, forty-two years after the Academy closed, John Aikin's daughter Lucy would recall the Warrington community and her own childhood in a letter to her American correspondent, William Ellery Channing, as follows:

Long before my time . . . my kindred – the Jennings' [*sic*], the Belshams, my excellent grandfather Aikin, and his friend and tutor Doddridge – had begun to break forth out of the chains and darkness of Calvinism, and their manners softened with their system. My youth was spent among the disciples or fellow-labourers of Price and Priestley, the descendants of Dr. John Taylor, the Arian, or in the society of that most amiable of men, Dr. Enfield. Amongst these there was no rigorism . . . in *manners*, the Free Dissenters, as they were called, came much nearer the Church than to their own strict brethren, yet in *doctrine* no sect departed so far from the Establishment.[14]

This account is not merely the voice of nostalgic retrospection; in many ways, individuals brought together by Warrington conceived of themselves as "fellow-labourers" and as kindred of the same religious and intellectual stock. During their years at Warrington, Aikin, Priestley, Taylor, and Enfield, like Price at Hackney, were Arian heterodox Dissenters, and it is in their extensive networks of affiliated critical laborers that I locate the Dissenting public sphere.[15] For the young Barbauld, the process by which the "manners" of these "Free" Dissenters and their immediate ancestors had "softened with their system" constituted more than just a cultural movement away from "the gloomy perplexities of Calvinism." Joined to both the manners and doctrines of Dissent, her literary labors would infuse establishment culture with the distinctive virtues of both the nonsectarian and "human" relationships of the home and the progressive energy of middle-class nonconformist religion and commerce.

THE BUDGET AND THE WORKBAG: "PLEASE TAKE PITY ON TWO"

Between 1792 and 1796 John Aikin and Anna Barbauld wrote and assembled their six-volume collection for children, published by Joseph Johnson, *Evenings at Home; or, The Juvenile Budget Opened. Consisting of A Variety of Miscellaneous Pieces, for the Instruction and Amusement of Young Persons*. With fourteen of the ninety-nine pieces contributed by Barbauld, this educational miscellany presents itself by its frame narrative as the patchwork product of familial literary collaboration, much like Barbauld's proposed "*Joineriana*."

The frame narrative tells the story of the thriving Fairborne family, which consisted of "master and mistress, and a numerous progeny of children of both sexes" (*Evenings*, 1, p. 1). Like the Aikins in Warrington, the Fairbornes in "Beachgrove" received many literary-minded visitors: "as some of them were accustomed to writing, they would frequently produce a fable, a story, or dialogue, adapted to the age and understanding of the young people" (1, p. 2). These literary fragments would then be deposited by Mrs. Fairborne in a box, or "budget," to which only she held the key. During the holidays, when all the children were assembled,

"It was then made one of the evening amusements of the family to *rummage the budget,* as their phrase was" (1, p. 2). One of the younger children would be sent to the box, and one of the older children would then read the piece with which the younger had returned. Over the years,

Other children were admitted to these readings; and as the *Budget of Beachgrove Hall* became somewhat celebrated in the neighbourhood, its proprietors were at length urged to lay it open to the public. They were induced to comply; and have presented its contents in the promiscuous order in which they came to hand, which they think will prove more agreeable than a methodical arrangement.

(1, p. 3)

The patchwork *Juvenile Budget* as published by Johnson, then, is supposed to have originated in these communal compositions on morality, conduct, economics, and history that were jointly sewn together in the Fairborne home and colored by the sympathies of its domestic space. The "promiscuous order" of collective composition will "prove more agreeable" than the "methodical arrangement" of individual authorship, and the narrative thus directly relates the warm and endearing qualities of the family and its circle at Beachgrove to the successful transmission of that community's civil values: children are exhorted not just to be well-behaved, generous, and industrious, but, above all, knowledgeable about European history and the British economy.[16] This frame narrative, then, with its emphasis on collaborative production and communal mediation, emblematizes the literary passage of Dissenting culture from the domestic context of the Aikin family circle to the intermediate community at Warrington and finally, through Johnson's press, to the national reading public.[17]

During the late 1780s and throughout the '90s, in fact, Aikin would use his own family as a sounding board for his writings. Betsy Rodgers records that "Aikin took great care that his style should be clear and accurate . . . To make sure his argument was easily comprehensible, he would have everything he wrote read aloud by one member of the family to the others, and he encouraged comments even from the youngest."[18] Although it is impossible to ascertain precisely which elements of Aikin's arguments or style were indebted to his "household critics," as Rodgers fittingly calls them (p. 122), their presence emerges in the self-presentation of many of his compositions.[19] Aikin repeatedly grounds his writing in the definitions and associations of the specific family, community, and region with which he self-consciously connected his authorship and his work, and the link between the intimate sphere of the conjugal family and the author's public identity is integral to the production of Aikin's texts.

In the fifth volume of *Evenings at Home* (1796), "True Heroism" presents John Howard (1726–90) as a model to the young audience gathered in the bourgeois salon of Beachgrove Hall. Howard's body of work, in fact, was the joint product of Howard, Aikin, and, we may assume, Aikin's household critics; their relationship serves as one of the more concrete examples of the collaborative activity typical of Dissenters at or affiliated with Warrington. The collective process that lay Howard's productions, like the Budget of Beachgrove, "open to the public," provides a case for the collaborative operation of the Dissenting public sphere. Having just worked with Howard on the latter's *State of the Prisons* (1777), printed by Eyres in Warrington, sold by Johnson in London, and highly influenced by Aikin's *Thoughts on Hospitals* (1771), Aikin depicted their professional relationship: "As new facts and observations were continually suggesting themselves to his mind, he put the matter of them upon paper as they occurred, and then requested me to clothe them in such expressions as I thought proper."[20] Educated at the Dissenting academy in Stoke-Newington – described by Lucy Aikin as the "very Elysian field of non-conformity"[21] – Howard provided the research and untiring devotion to the cause while Aikin diligently stitched his notes into a powerful rhetoric of reform that effectively engaged the nation.

This national recognition of Howard's work came in no small part from his affiliation with the expansive cultural force of the Warrington community, and it was in turn maintained and fostered by Barbauld and Aikin, both of whom, like Coleridge in "Reflections on Having Left a Place of Retirement" (1796), paid tribute to Howard in published poems. Barbauld's "Epistle to William Wilberforce" (1791) extended the tradition of relating Howard and the cause of prison reform to Wilberforce and abolitionism: "In Virtue's fasti be inscrib'd your [Wilberforce's] fame, / And utter'd your's with Howard's honour'd name" (lines 108–09).[22] But more suggestively, Aikin's poem to his son Arthur, "An Epistle to Mr. Aikin, Student in New College, Hackney" (1791), describes Howard as intimately associated with the regulated dispositions of Dissent. In this poem, Aikin expects that the academy at Hackney, like nonconformist academies across England, will offer to the nation "forms sublime of *active worth*": the "*Moral Teacher*," the "bold *Assertor of the freeborn mind*," the "*Patriot* firm," and the "*Friend of man*."[23] All these forms, finally, will unite in a single model for Arthur and Dissenting youth, a figure at once benevolent and austere,

> who, scorning soft repose,
> From clime to clime contends with human woes;

Whose mild compassion temp'ring virtuous rage,
Presents a HOWARD to the coming age. (p. 74)

The "mild compassion" of Howard's pity, benevolence, and sensibility
tempers the "virtuous rage" of his libertarian principles, personal self-
denial, and resolute indignation. In Aikin's portrait of their collaboration,
and in his association of Howard's success with the nonconformist academies, the combination of sensibility with virtue and austerity that defines
Howard's career is identified with the Dissenting community by which it
was, to a significant extent, produced. In this league of mild manners and
severe merits lies the definition of Howard's character, and of heterodox
Dissent, that made his career such a heroic ideal for both Aikin and
Barbauld. "True Heroism" thus offers Howard as a model to the young
auditor, "Edmund," much as he had previously been presented in Aikin's
Poems to the actual Edmund's older brother, Arthur:

You have probably heard something of Mr. Howard, the reformer of prisons, to
whom a monument is just erected in St. Paul's church. His whole life almost was
heroism; for he confronted all sorts of dangers with the sole view of relieving the
miseries of his fellow-creatures . . . He at length died of a fever caught in
attending on the sick, on the borders of Crim tartary, honoured and admired
by all Europe . . . Such was *Howard the Good.* (*Evenings,* v, pp. 86–88)

Originating from within the collaborative Dissenting network affiliated
with Warrington and the nonconformist academies, Howard's career
serves as a pattern of domesticated Dissent to be extended from the
Aikins' religious community into St. Paul's itself, the cathedral at the
center of national Anglican culture.

Barbauld's early poetic development also followed a pattern of cooperative literary production and publication grounded in the community of
provincial Dissent: she studied at home, composed and circulated her
poetry in the communal context of Warrington, and published her works,
with explicit stamps of collaboration, through Johnson's press. The motto
on the title page of the Aikins' *Miscellaneous Pieces in Prose* (1773), the
great majority of which were composed by Barbauld, read prominently,
"SI NON UNIUS, QUAESO MISERERE DUORUM" ("If not on one, please take
pity on two").[24] Like Aikin with his "household critics" and Howard in
his professional associations with Aikin, Barbauld fashioned her career
and defined herself as a writer by collaboratively negotiating issues of
manners, politics, and religion that were of central concern to her and her
family's Dissenting community.

Her authorial debut, *Poems* (1773), was marked by a series of collabora-tive relationships associated with the Warrington network. Before she could be persuaded to assume the status of a published author, many of her poems circulated among the students, tutors, and their families at the Academy.[25] The various tastes and interests for which she wrote thus arose from the specific groups represented by the institution. On a more concrete level, Aikin participated in the process by which her poems went from circulated manuscripts to published pieces. According to Lucy Aikin in her *Memoir* of Barbauld, "By his persuasion and assistance her Poems were selected, revised, and arranged for publication" (*Works*, I, p. xii).

The process of production described by the "Juvenile Budget," in fact, may have found its origins in one resonant instance of Warrington's collaborative dynamics. At the Academy students made a game of de-positing anonymous compositions into the workbag of Mary Priestley.[26] From her bag, these writings would make the rounds at Warrington, much as the scraps in *Evenings at Home* made their way from the Fair-bornes' box to the neighborhood of Beachgrove. Like the "*Joineriana*," this emblem associates literary production with the domestic labor of sewing, women's "work," and with the internal space of the conjugal family.[27] And like the budget, to which only Mrs. Fairborne held the key, the workbag into which Anna and others deposited their fragments was monitored by a female figure of benevolence, sweetness, and sensibility – Mary Priestley, whom Barbauld addressed in her poetry as "Amanda" ("deserving of love") and for whose portrait she chose the motto, "Grace was in all her steps" (*PALB*, p. 219). As a personal article identified with domestic labor and belonging to a female figure of sensibility and benevo-lence, then, the work bag receives the various compositions of Warrington and allows for their promiscuous dissemination, thus serving as a trope for Barbauld's association of softened manners and warm attachments with the collaborative literary production of provincial Dissent.

Through this mode of circulation, Anna became the unofficial laureate to the Academy, and subsequently Barbauld's Warrington readership seems to have prepared the national reading public for her *Poems*, a success which went through four editions in its first year. According to William Woodfall in the *Monthly Review* for January 1773,

Before these elegant poems appeared in print, we were not wholly unacquainted with this Lady's extraordinary merit, and fine talents. The pupils of that very useful seminary . . . have, with a genuine and unanimous enthusiasm, celebrated her genius, and diffused her praises far and wide: and some of her compositions have been read & admired by persons of the first taste & judgment in the republic of Letters. ("*Poems. By Miss Aikin*," p. 54)

The emblematic nature of this progression is familiar. In advance of their appearance in print through Johnson's press, Barbauld's poems are "diffused" to a limited but influential reading public ("persons of the first taste & judgment") through private circulation, and thus finally come to national attention in the *Monthly Review* itself marked by association with her distinct community – "that very useful seminary," which Woodfall takes care to footnote, "At Warrington." Like *Evenings at Home*, which emerges from Mrs. Fairborne's "Budget of Beachgrove Hall," Barbauld's poems proceed figuratively from Mary Priestley's workbag at Warrington to a wider network of affiliated readers – the Dissenting public sphere – within the national "republic of Letters," and ultimately present their public voice and subjects in print as colored by the civil, religious, and domestic dispositions of that community.

THE AIKINS' PROSE: "HOME VIEWS AND NEARER OBJECTS"

In Lucy Aikin's *Memoir* of her aunt, published in 1825, her assessment of Barbauld's relation to sensibility is insightful and suggestive; "In some tempers sensibility appears an instinct, while in others it is the gradual result of principle and reflection, of the events and the experience of life. It was certainly so in that of Mrs. Barbauld" (*Works*, I, pp. lxiii–lxiv). Of the change in Barbauld's manners as she aged, Lucy relates, "Her disposition, – of which sensibility was not in earlier life the leading feature, – now mellowed into softness" (*Works*, I, p. liv). Although it is neither possible nor important to ascertain the accuracy of these statements, I would like to underscore their implication that sensibility for the young Anna Barbauld was something that could be learned, applied, and manipulated, not an innate element of femininity but an active result of principle, reflection, and experience. Although the budget and the workbag can be understood as revealing actual Dissenting methods of collaboration, we should remember that they function as much as emblems of representation as of practice. Just as telling as the anecdotes already recounted is an aside by Harriet Martineau: recalling Barbauld as chief among "the really well-educated women of the period," Martineau concedes, "It is true, she was not much of a needlewoman. There is a tradition that the skeleton of a mouse was found in her workbag."[28] When Mary Wollstonecraft in *A Vindication of the Rights of Woman* (1792) chose

Barbauld's "To a Lady, with some painted Flowers" as the focus of her attack on sensibility, therefore, she failed to discern that for Barbauld as a young and highly educated female Dissenter of the early 1770s sensibility could be a strategic device to be applied technically and self-consciously in order to achieve specific cultural ends (*WMW*, v, pp. 122–23).[29] Barbauld invokes sensibility in order to fashion a devotional, didactic, and poetic program that would respond to the particular needs of the present age as she interpreted them in light of what I will describe as her Dissenting and specifically Arminian view of Christian history.

The discrepancy between Wollstonecraft's response to Barbauld's poem, on the one hand, and both Lucy Aikin's portrayal of her aunt's character and the suggestive skeleton of a mouse, on the other, indicates the degree to which contemporary readers need be wary of reducing sensibility to a uniform phenomenon of the late eighteenth century, a mere "*manie* of the day" (*WMW*, v, p. 8), as Wollstonecraft called it in *A Vindication of the Rights of Men* (1790). On the contrary, as G. J. Barker-Benfield has demonstrated, sensibility meant radically different things in the hands of different writers, and its applications varied widely over the course of the period.[30] Thus in *A Vindication of the Rights of Woman*, after quoting Barbauld's offending poem in a footnote Wollstonecraft dismisses its last line ("Your best, your sweetest empire is – to please") with, "So the men tell us; but virtue, says reason, must be acquired by *rough* toils, and careful struggles with worldly *cares*" (*WMW*, v, pp. 122–23). Barbauld, in fact, would have heartily agreed with this as a creed, but she would have countered that as a principle of composition it misses the mark: for Barbauld, whereas reason may demand that virtue be acquired by rough toils and careful struggles, religious devotion and poetic composition demand that these exertions be made endearing to the affections by sympathetic images of beauty, grace, and, most of all, sensibility. Indeed, in "Thoughts on the Devotional Taste, on Sects, and on Establishments," first published in 1775 and appended in the year of Wollstonecraft's *A Vindication of the Rights of Woman* to the new edition of *Miscellaneous Pieces in Prose* (1792), Barbauld anticipates Wollstonecraft's challenge: "In our creeds let us be guarded; let us there way [*sic*, weigh] every syllable; but in compositions addressed to the heart, let us give freer scope to the language of the affections, and the overflowing of a warm and generous disposition" (*SPP*, p. 218).[31]

On the basis of this distinction between "creeds" and "compositions addressed to the heart," we can read *Miscellaneous Pieces in Prose, by J. and A. L. Aikin* as a "*Joineriana*" of modern Dissenting political, religious, economic, and intellectual characteristics associated through topical references, personal addresses, and local subjects with sensibility as embodied in the private and communal aspects of Warrington. From the start, the collection is concerned with identifying opposed communities and establishing balances between their extremes. The first essay, "On the Province of Comedy," treats the comic genre as a curative moral agent that corrects communal vices and other shortcomings by holding them up to ridicule: "Nations, like individuals, have certain leading features which distinguish them from others. Of these there are always some of a ludicrous cast which afford matter of entertainment to their neighbours."[32] The implication is that individuals, social groups, and national cultures have "leading features" among which some are virtuous and others vicious; the reader is for the most part left to distinguish between them on the basis of "nature," but over the course of the volume the delineation of such features becomes increasingly clear. Furthermore, the authors give a historical aspect to their description of communal character: "Although some part of the character of a nation is pretty uniform and constant, yet its manners and customs in many points are extremely variable. These variations are the peculiar modes and fashions of the age; and hence the age, as well as the nation, acquires a distinguishing character" (p. 9). Thus by the end of the first piece the reader has been asked to examine his or her merits and foibles as they participate in those of the larger community and age. The community and the age are implicitly the modern British nation, not subdivided by class, region, or religion but normatively and uniformly understood. The nation's "natural" character, however, is precisely what the volume seeks to establish.

The next piece begins this process with an allegory, "The Hill of Science, A Vision," composed by Anna. Having fallen asleep, the speaker receives a vision of a high mountain rising out of a plain, "the HILL OF SCIENCE. On the top is the temple of Truth, whose head is above the clouds, and whose face is covered with a veil of pure light" (p. 29). Multitudes, chiefly youths, are attempting to climb the mountain, assisted or impeded by a Bunyanesque host of friends and obstacles – Memory, the Muses, the wood of error, the stream of insignificance. Like the "leading features" set forth in "On the Province of Comedy," the characters and sites of the allegory depend for their interpretation on the readers' shared perceptions of normative values. "The Hill of Science," however, fills in these previously unspecified features with an allegory of Dissenting educational practices. The only major approach to the mountain is by "the gate of languages," which is kept by a pensive woman, "MEMORY"

(p. 29). Whereas during the first half of the century Dissenters were often faulted for insufficiently acquiring and teaching the learned languages, by the second half this perception had been largely erased, and indeed the study of modern languages originated among their academies. Priestley's early work, *A Course of Lectures on the Theory of Language and Universal Grammar* (1762), composed for private use at Warrington, followed Jennings' and Doddridge's innovation of incorporating modern languages into the nonconformist curriculum. After passing through "the gate of languages," then, the aspirants ascend or fall on the basis of values the Aikins and their readers would have associated with contemporary Dissenting academies in direct opposition to the universities: "While Genius was thus wasting his strength in eccentric flights, I saw a person of a very different appearance, named APPLICATION" (p. 33). If the public tended to frown on the universities for loose moral standards and propensities to "eccentricity" and indolence, nonconformist academies were widely perceived as pedagogically innovative and academically as well as morally rigorous.[33] Not at Oxford or Cambridge, where the sacramental test excluded Dissenters from attending at all or taking degrees, respectively, but at nonconformist academies such as Warrington, Daventry, Hackney, and Hoxton would students follow the practical and chaste dictates of bourgeois "Application." Finally, then, the vision ends with a union between "Application" and "Virtue," with "Virtue" receiving the last word: "I cheer the cottager at his toil, and inspire the sage at his meditation . . . Science may raise you to eminence, but I alone can guide you to felicity!" (p. 38). What seems at first like a general allegory would have been received by the Aikins' readership as a historically specific nonconformist challenge to the universities, and thus the allegory of science and virtue, eminence and felicity, universalizes the local character of the authors' religious and social community. Indebted to Addison and Steele's program to fashion natural citizens, the Aikins' terms remain normative in their assumption of a national constitution, just as the liberal academies were essentially non-denominational, but the allegory remains ideologically nonconformist, middle-class, and anti-establishmentarian.

Whereas the larger pattern of the volume is to allow tempered Dissenting values to diffuse themselves throughout and thereby leaven national culture, pieces such as "The Hill of Science" and "Against Inconsistency in our Expectations" put forth and endorse the terms of nonconformity with little regard for achieving any sort of balance between denominational and establishment culture. This latter essay, in fact, offers a manifesto of "untempered" middle-class Dissent. Unlike the allegorical

"Hill of Science," however, "Against Inconsistency in our Expectations" describes a universal scenario in the rigorous middle-class free-market vocabulary typical of much nonconformist rhetoric:

We should consider this world as a great mart of commerce, where fortune exposes to our view various commodities, riches, ease, tranquillity, fame, integrity, knowledge. Every thing is marked at a settled price. Our time, our labour, our ingenuity, is so much ready money which we are to lay out to the best advantage. Examine, compare, choose, reject; but stand to your own judgment; and do not, like children, when you have purchased one thing, repine that you do not possess another which you did not purchase. Such is the force of well-regulated industry, that a steady and vigorous exertion of our faculties, directed to one end, will generally insure success. (pp. 62–63; *SPP*, p. 188)

"Our time, our labour, our ingenuity" implies a uniform readership, and personal and national progress together come to rest on this universal individual's freedom to "examine, compare, choose, [and] reject," whether in decisions of private conduct, religion, politics, or economics. The competitive values of the market, however, coincide with the self-conceived levelling libertarianism of rational Dissent: because the world is "a great mart of commerce" in which every thing is valued according to a free market of personal judgment and abilities, it follows that religious tests will not apply and that success will be insured not by inheritance or patronage but by "the force of well-regulated industry" and the "steady and vigorous exertion" of one's faculties.

On a wider scale, then, these two essays offer the extreme middle-class and nonconformist vision of the natural spirit of Britain against which the reader is left to pose the actualities of the present age: landed interests, aristocratic privilege, and hereditary descent; an established Church supported by the Corporation and Test Acts; colonialism sustained by the slave trade; and defense of the status quo on the Continent. In the oppositional rhetoric of Dissent, these pillars of British identity become the vestiges of an *ancien régime* out of step with the true spirit of the modern British nation, which nonconformist writers sought to define as naturally middle-class, anti-establishmentarian or at least latitudinarian, at once mercantilist and abolitionist, and dedicated to the causes of "Liberty" throughout Europe.[34]

Although the moderate Aikins do place great store in this nexus of Whig ideologies, they repeatedly insist that it is but one necessary element or pole of the British dualism between establishment and nonconformist identities. The universalizing move of their prose, and, indeed, of the Dissenting public sphere, does not imply that sectarian manners and beliefs should subsume national character. For Barbauld there exists an abstract national spirit that depends on sectarian activity for its vigor and endurance, just as sectarian identity wholly unmollified by establishment endearments would turn to indifference under the mild conditions of modern religious toleration. The tempered austerity of modern noncon-formity, its local and specific character, should expand from the commu-nity into the national constitution, serving as a salutary check upon cultural dissolution and a dynamic impulse away from cultural stagnation.

The Aikins' prose volume is thus a far cry from middle-class noncon-formist Whig propaganda, and I would suggest that its popularity rested in no small part on its recurring sympathetic identification with trad-itional images of nonsectarian and affective "British" values. The essays, in fact, are consistently critical of attempts to champion any one cultural identity over another without conceding that national vitality subsists in the union or interpenetration of opposed positions. The nonconformist academies present a universalizable model for national education not because they simply *counter* the less austere character of the universities with "application"; rather, because the academies modulate their austerity with the softer tones of nonsectarian culture, their sectarian virtues can be diffused, like medicine made palatable, throughout the national body.

If the first dream vision, "The Hill of Science," allegorizes the need to offset the establishment with nonconformist values, the next, "The Canal and the Brook. An Apologue," reverses the scales. By transferring opposed cultural identities onto the geography of Northern England, the piece submits the Aikins' updated and provincialized version of Denham's seminal image of the Thames in "Cooper's Hill." Whereas for Denham the Thames could stand for his conception of an ideal and royalist England, here two contrary images of flowing water come together in topological dialogue to capture the spirit of the modern nation.[35]

"The Canal and the Brook" narrates a vision in which the contemptuous "Genius" of the Duke of Bridgewater's Canal meets the humbler "Deity of the Stream," and the two exchange their claims to public admiration. The Canal, associated by all of England with the commercialist invention and assiduity of provincial Dissent, rests its claim on utility:

"Wherever I appear I am viewed with astonishment, and exulting commerce hails my waves. Behold my channel thronged with capacious vessels for the convey-ance of merchandise, and splendid barges for the use and pleasure of travellers; my banks crowned with airy bridges and huge warehouses, and echoing with the busy sounds of industry. Pay then the homage due from sloth and obscurity to grandeur and utility." (p. 83)

Figure 2. "View of Barton Bridge," where the Duke of Bridgewater's Canal passed over the River Irwell, from John Aikin, *A Description of the Country from Thirty to Forty Miles round Manchester.* Reproduced by permission of the Library Company of Philadelphia.

The Brook, on the other hand, appeals to "nobler judges" than the "unfeeling sons of wealth and commerce." The philosopher and the poet, "the lovers of nature and the Muses, who are fond of straying on my banks, are better pleased that the line of beauty marks my way, than if, like yours, it were directed in straight, unvaried line. They prize the irregular wildness with which I am decked, as the charms of beauteous simplicity" (p. 84). Their "nobility" dissociates these judges from the middle-class admirers of the Canal, and the opposition between distinct classes of judges consequently implies different sets of values on which their judgments are based. Against middle-class commercialism and its interested aesthetic of utility – "splendid barges," "airy bridges," "huge warehouses" – the dialogue opposes an aristocratic ethos and its disinterested aesthetic of William Gilpin's picturesque – "the line of beauty," "irregular wildness," "the charms of beauteous simplicity." Whereas in "The Hill of Science" and "Against Inconsistency in our Expectations," virtue, nonconformity, and the market-place have the last word, here the Brook's argument carries the day. But this does not discount the utility of the Canal and the force of its commercialist aesthetic; finally, as in the "View of Barton Bridge," the Canal and the Brook together transform the landscape into one useful and beautiful prospect. The essay asks that its readers participate in both the rational aesthetic claims of the Canal and the affective aesthetic claims of the Brook. The Aikins' loco-descriptive prose thus defines national culture according to the "British" dualism of sectarian and establishment identities inscribed by both human invention and nature on the landscape of Lancashire and Yorkshire. The Genius of the Canal bears "certain instruments, used in surveying and levelling" (p. 81), while the Brook "will bestow unvarying fertility on the meadows, during the summers of future ages" (p. 85): the rational demands of the bourgeois sphere of civil commerce and the affective appeal of "nature," implicitly aligned with the humanizing and familial force of sensibility, thus come together in the Aikins' prose to pressure the national landscape into its idealized liberal form.

Another instance of this dialectical movement between establishment and sects is "On Monastic Institutions." One would anticipate from the title a Protestant celebration over the decaying remnants of Popery, and thus at the opening of the piece the speaker reflects how, "like a good protestant, I began to indulge a secret triumph in the ruin of so many structures which I had always considered as the haunts of ignorance and superstition" (pp. 88–89). But this mood rapidly dissipates, and following an ironic reversal the Protestant speaker spends the rest of the piece praising the monastic spirit for its strict austerity, equally unfamiliar among contemporary Catholics as among Protestants of the Established Church of England:

> Though it may not be proper . . . that numbers should seclude themselves from the common duties and ordinary avocations of life . . . yet it is not unuseful that some should push their virtues to even a romantic height; and it is encouraging to reflect in the hour of temptation, that the love of ease, the aversion to pain, every appetite and passion, and even the strongest propensities in our nature, have been controuled; that the empire of the mind over the body has been asserted in its fullest extent; and that there have been men in all ages capable of voluntarily renouncing all the world offers, voluntarily suffering all it dreads, and living independent, and unconnected with it. (p. 112)

Again, self-denial and personal control may not be fit for the generality, but no society will remain healthy without the checks and impulses of sectarian rigor: "*some* should push their virtues to even a romantic height." Barbauld's description of monasticism is, ironically, clearly coded to rehearse as well the public's perception of Puritan nonconformist culture.

Modern Dissenters, however, do not "seclude themselves from the common duties and ordinary avocations of life." Neither "independent" nor "unconnected," they marry, educate, and trade. The essay thus implicitly defines modern Dissent according to its peculiar combination of marginalization and centrality, of immoderately exacting virtues tempered by participation in both domestic and nonsectarian society.

The extreme monastic form of Catholicism, like the extreme Puritan form of Protestantism, therefore has a legitimate place in the progress of gradually refining Christianity. The final basis for Barbauld's analyses in her prose can now be seen to be a Dissenting and, specifically, Arminian view of Christian history; it is the responsibility of each individual Christian to impel history forward according to the proper oppositional relation between establishment and sectarian communities. The clearest articulation of this view came two years after the 1773 volume, in her widely read essay, "Thoughts on the Devotional Taste, on Sects, and on Establishments." Barbauld's Dissenting historical consciousness drives this rhetorically powerful piece. Following her analysis of the devotional taste itself, discussed in Chapter 2, Barbauld describes three stages in the history of sects. The first stage is that of early Christianity:

In this state, all outward helps are superfluous, the living spirit of devotion is among them, the world sinks away to nothing before it, and every object but one is annihilated. The social principle mixes with the flame, and renders it more intense; strong parties are formed, and friends or lovers are not more closely connected than the members of these little communities. (*SPP*, p. 223)

These early Christians are known for their "Severity of manners" (*SPP*, p. 223). But significantly, history in Barbauld's narrative is cyclical, and thus the first stage of arduous Christianity also characterizes English Puritanism after the Civil War: "the austere lives of the primitive Christians counterbalanced the vices of that abandoned period; and thus the Puritans in the reign of Charles the Second seasoned with a wholesome severity the profligacy of public manners" (*SPP*, p. 230). The first period of this modern cycle, from the Restoration through the reign of Queen Anne, gives way to the second, aligned with Hanoverian England especially following the repeals in 1719 of the Occasional Conformity Act (1711) and the Schism Act (1714). Persecution then abates: "Now comes on the period of reasoning and examination . . . Those who before bore testimony to their religion only by patient suffering, now defend it with argument; and all the keenness of polemical disquisition is awakened on either side" (*SPP*, p. 224). Dissenters of this second stage, at the end of which Barbauld would place the present moment, unmistakably resemble the tutors at Warrington and their Arian and Arminian associates:

> Their manners are less austere, without having as yet lost anything of their original purity. Their ministers gain respect as writers, and their pulpit discourses are studied and judicious. The most unfavourable circumstance of this aera is, that those who dissent, are very apt to acquire a critical and disputatious spirit; for, being continually called upon to defend doctrines in which they differ from the generality, their attention is early turned to the argumentative part of religion. (*SPP*, p. 224)

Barbauld's contemporary Presbyterianism, then, is on the cusp of the second and third periods. She values both the politeness and "purity" of nonconformity, but would guard against its excessively "critical and disputatious spirit," the consequence of which in the third period could be cool indifference. This third period, into which the present *might* be descending, must be averted, and such is the task Barbauld assigns both to religious devotion, as we have already seen, and to critical discourse in the Dissenting public sphere: "men grow tired of a controversy which becomes insipid from being exhausted; persecution has not only ceased, it begins to be forgotten; and from the absence of opposition in either kind, springs a fatal and spiritless indifference" (*SPP*, p. 224). Although Barbauld spent a good deal of her early career fighting religious persecution in the form of the Corporation and Test Acts, she is fully aware that in the absence of persecution nonconformist identity might dissolve. Her prose should thus be seen as a sustained attempt to push Christian history forward into an age that would preserve the force of sectarian and establishment "opposition" and preclude "a fatal and spiritless indifference." Opposition without persecution is the proper relation between establishment and sects, a relation which will allow the dynamic impulses of Dissent to continue to act upon the whole: "All the greater exertions of the mind, spirit to reform, fortitude and constancy to suffer, can be expected only from those who, forsaking the common road, are exercised in a peculiar course of moral discipline: but it should be remembered, that these exertions cannot be expected from every character, nor on every occasion" (*SPP*, p. 229). The point is not that all Britons should adhere to sects, but that the values of sects should extend from their small societies – "forsaking the common road" – to exert critical pressure on the national community.

The historical progress of sects thus follows a course maintained or abandoned according to the actions of private individuals come together to form fragments of the national public: "So the purer part of the element, continually drawn off from the mighty mass of waters, forms rivers, which, running in various directions, fertilize large countries; yet, always tending towards the ocean, every accession to their bulk or grandeur but precipitates their course, and hastens their re-union with the common reservoir from which they were separated" (*SPP*, p. 230). One of the "large countries" represents the generality of Britons, for whose dispositions the leniency of the established religion is appropriate, while the refined "rivers" are constituted by members of sects, of sub-publics (not counter-publics), to whose temperaments the discipline of nonconformity is suited. Unregulated by the mild influence of the modern age, these rivers would overflow their banks, involving the country in a flood of Puritan extremism as in 1649, but flowing properly through their appropriate channels, sects "fertilize" the whole. Without sects, Barbauld implies, the waters of Christianity become stagnant and the British nation becomes sterile. By maintaining the proper oppositional relation between the establishment and sects, then, individuals can hasten the present age toward reunion with the Edenic ocean in which all Christian history began.

For Barbauld, sustaining this national vision corresponds to a very practical cultural agenda. If the nation must be energized and stabilized by the oppositional relation between its religious communities, so culture must act on individuals according to the potentially dynamic relations within the human constitution between reason and emotion, philosophy and devotion, creed and prejudice, austerity and pleasure, utility and waste, discipline and desire. As with sects and the establishment within the progression of public providential history, the relationship between these poles of private human nature should not be dissociative; rather, culture should produce rational and affective compositions that join dissociated constitutional elements into dynamic, oppositional – even Blakean – relations. Without contraries, sectarian or interior, is no progression. Like Dissent at the national level, culture at the individual level provides Britons with salutary checks and dynamic impulses necessary for personal vigor and progress.

The "*Joineriana*" can here return as a model to describe the Aikins' mode of cultural production, in which familial and local affiliations endear nonconformist religious and civil definitions, making them both more polite and less exclusive. But still, the subject at hand is religious devotion, specifically the forms of devotion fashioned by Barbauld out of the domestication of her Presbyterian heritage. We have already considered the following passage in terms of its critique of rational Dissent and its revision of the Puritan sublime: "As in poetry it is not vague and general description, but a few striking circumstances clearly related and strongly worked up . . . so neither are those unbounded views in which philosophy delights, so much calculated to touch the heart as home views and nearer objects" (*SPP*, p. 217). The present age, we can now see, demands the same balance from both cultural production and religious devotion. The worship of the "philosopher," who "offers up general praises on the altar of universal nature," is "more sublime"; that of "the devout man," who "on the altar of his heart, presents his own sighs, his own thanksgivings, his own earnest desires," is "more personal and affecting" (*SPP*, p. 217). The philosopher's "unbounded views," the scientist's principles of "universal nature," the rational Dissenter's unbending creeds – "A prayer strictly philosophical must ever be a cold and dry composition" (*SPP*, p. 217) – should be mollified, made palatable to the national taste, "calculated to touch the heart," in literary labors associated with the personal and the affecting, with "home views and nearer objects."

If Barbauld revised and publicized Dissenting dispositions and tastes within a culture of sensibility, she was in this respect part of a larger movement in the late eighteenth century. As we will see in the coming chapters, under the changing political and personal circumstances of the 1780s and '90s, Godwin, Wollstonecraft, Coleridge, and Southey also found themselves engaging with, responding to, and critiquing modes of Dissenting publicity and sociability both as lived experience and abstract representation. The Dissenting public sphere, throughout the entirety of which the Aikin family network extended, to a significant degree shaped the new aesthetic, political, and religious features of early Romantic culture.

CHAPTER 4

Godwinian scenes and popular politics: Godwin, Wollstonecraft, and the legacies of Dissent

By the mid 1790s, the Dissenting public sphere as lived and represented by liberal Dissenters had begun to dissipate. Three years before his permanent departure in 1794 for the banks of the Susquehanna, Joseph Priestley complained that "rational Dissenters . . . are dwindling away almost everywhere,"[1] and by the middle of the decade the representative figures of Dissenting social and intellectual life, such as Priestley, Richard Price, Timothy Hollis, and Robert Robinson, had either died or emigrated.[2] Furthermore, the principal heterodox Dissenting academies throughout England had closed their doors: Hoxton folded in 1785, Warrington in 1786, Daventry in 1789, and the New College in Hackney in 1796.[3] The Dissenting public sphere thus gradually lost its focused and progressive identity, and rational Dissenters would not project such a coherent public front again until the renewed outburst of propaganda against the Corporation and Test Acts in the 1820s.[4] After 1795, a major year of mortality for prominent members of the nonconformist community,[5] liberal Dissent became increasingly retrospective: *The Protestant Dissenter's Magazine*, published monthly from January 1794 to December 1799 "with the Assistance of several Dissenting Ministers of the Three Denominations," can be read as an epitaph to the active phase of late-eighteenth-century Dissenting public life. Consisting mainly of "Biographical Memoirs" and "Ecclesiastical History," the *Magazine* memorialized Dissenting preachers, educators, and intellectuals, accompanying their "Memoirs" with engraved portraits. Compared with the Dissenting pamphlets, poems, essays, and reviews printed by liberal publishers such as Joseph Johnson and George Robinson during the first movement to repeal the Corporation and Test Acts (1787–90), *The Protestant Dissenter's Magazine* already seems more a pantheon of the dead than a testament of living apostles.

The mid to late 1790s, often understood as the so-called "English Terror," the national battle fought and won by Pitt's administration,

Church and King mobs, and anti-Jacobin propagandists against the largely secular radical societies, can thus also be seen as the evening of a coherent and vigorous Dissenting public sphere. In light of this dual interpretation, this chapter examines William Godwin's career during the 1790s as it simultaneously encountered the dissolution of the rational Dissenting community and the rise of new forms of communication, those practiced by the popular political societies which came to dominate moderate to radical political life after 1792. For along with the ascendance of the London Corresponding Society (LCS) and the Society for Constitutional Information (SCI) came new kinds of publicity through which these communities realized their oppositionist identities and expressed their reformist positions, foremost among which were support for a National Convention, annual parliaments, and universal manhood suffrage.[6] Two important developments occurred along with the shift in radical discourse between 1788 and 1792 from support for the Revolution abroad to calls for reform at home. Central to the French Revolution debate, they involved transformations both in the class and religious make-up of the radical societies and in the print medium of radical literature and propaganda.

After 1792 the source of oppositionist discourse shifted from the London Revolution Society to the LCS and SCI. When the Bastille fell in July 1789, the London Revolution Society represented the most vocal community of moderates and radicals in England. Founded in November 1788 to celebrate the one-hundredth anniversary of the English Revolution, it included practically every member of Godwin's circle. Richard Price's 4 November 1789 sermon, *A Discourse on the Love of Our Country*, was delivered to this Society, and it was of course against the published form of Price's *Discourse* (1789) that Burke wrote his *Reflections on the Revolution in France, and on the Proceedings in Certain Societies in London Relative to that Event* (1790). By 1792–93, however, control of the moderate to radical movement had shifted away from the largely middle-class and Dissenting Revolution Society to the corresponding societies, chief among which was the LCS, and the SCI.[7] Founded in 1792 by Thomas Hardy, a shoemaker, the LCS built on the successful models already established by corresponding societies in Derby, Manchester, Sheffield, Norwich, and Edinburgh. These groups, unlike the Revolution Society, were largely working-class: "the great majority of the reformers organised in the societies of 1793 were artisans, wage-earners, small masters and small tradesmen."[8] Furthermore, whereas the Revolution Society represented the tempered dissidence of religious Dissent, the LCS in particular was generally a secular community, at times stridently so: when Francis Place, a tailor who joined the LCS in November 1794 and served as one of its leading members until 1797, described the religious cast of the Society in his *Autobiography*, his original draft recalled that "Nearly all the leading members were either Deists or Atheists."[9] Accordingly, in 1796–97 when Thomas Williams was prosecuted for publishing Paine's *Age of Reason*, Place settled on Stewart Kyd to oversee the defense, explaining his selection: "Mr Kyd was an infidel and a man on whom reliance could be placed."[10] Control of the moderate to radical program thus moved from a community of middle-class Dissenters to the predominantly working-class and secular societies.

Second, the shift in radical discourse between 1789 and 1792 from support for the French Revolution, the main thrust of the London Revolution Society, to calls for reform at home, the objective of the LCS and SCI, had material consequences for the dissemination of radical discourse. Although, as Hannah Barker and Simon Burrows have now shown, over the course of the Romantic period "the newspaper began to supersede the pamphlet as the dominant printed form for political discourse and the dissemination of news,"[11] during the 1790s newspapers were only beginning to rival the pamphlet as the major medium of public opinion. For a variety of reasons, other forms remained the focus of independent radical publishing. Whereas the newspapers reported and commented on public meetings and speeches, chapsheets, handbills, and, most importantly, pamphlets brought them to life by announcing, reproducing, and isolating scenes of public oratory. Both the LCS and SCI had their own printing presses, and the SCI in particular counted a good portion of the print industry among its membership; both were thus ideally positioned to produce large numbers of cheap pamphlets at short notice and to distribute them extensively through their wide networks of corresponding divisions.[12] Furthermore, although the four opposition newspapers, the *Morning Chronicle*, the *Morning Post*, the *Gazeteer*, and the *Star*, remained active throughout the decade, by 1793 the other major London dailies and weeklies were all receiving substantial subsidies from the government; readers, in fact, would have immediately understood Godwin's reference to the London papers, in his 1795 pamphlet against the Gagging Acts, as "treasury prints" (*PPW*, II, p. 136).[13] And newspapers, as Barker and Burrows point out, "by their very nature, were a poor and unlikely medium for truly subversive materials, since they needed to maintain a fixed office and regular impression, and could be suppressed easily or intercepted in the post."[14] Cheap pamphlets thus suited the oratorical medium of radical discourse, the means of the societies, the market for radical literature and propaganda, and the contemporary circumstances of administrative influence and censorship.

In this chapter I will present Godwin's development over the 1790s as an encounter between the legacy of the Dissenting public sphere and the forms of public communication that accompanied populist and largely secular radical culture. In *Godwin's Political Justice* (1986), Mark Philp has persuasively demonstrated that Godwin's revisions of *Enquiry Concerning Political Justice* (1793), published in 1796 and 1798, represent a process of personal and intellectual transformation driven by Godwin's changing social circles and circumstances. The most exciting of Philp's claims is that we need to understand Godwin's utopianism as in a very real sense rooted in the daily life of rational Dissent: "Godwin wrote as if a republic of virtue was possible because he lived in a community which attempted to realise the basic principles of such a republic."[15] It is not my intention here to provide a detailed account of Godwin's changing social circles in the 1790s, a task already admirably undertaken by Philp. Rather, I wish to build on his central argument – that Godwin's faith in the private judgment unfettered by state coercion was "empirically grounded" (p. 173) – by examining the form of moderate to radical communication that replaced what I have called the tempered dissidence of Dissenting discourse after the decline of rational Dissent at the outset of the decade. For it is against this form of communication that Godwin works out his own self-revisions during the 1790s, a process usually attributed to "retreatism" or "apostasy," to the early Romantic withdrawal from the political into the private, interior, and domestic.

Godwin's *Memoirs of the Author of a Vindication of the Rights of Woman* (1798) has generally been seen as the culmination of that progression by which Godwin distanced himself from the ardent rationalism of his early political philosophy. In the *Memoirs*, as Mitzi Myers has noted, Godwin represents himself and Wollstonecraft as polarities of a collaborative opposition: her intuitive boldness and his methodical skepticism correspond in productive dialectical cooperation.[16] Godwin's biographical depiction directs his readers to attribute the modification of his early self-sufficient rationalism to his brief relationship with Wollstonecraft. It is clear, however, that the moderation of Godwin's earlier position was part of a longer and far more complex reflection upon his own religious as well as literary, philosophical, political, and personal history. Critics have recently connected Godwin's more affective theories of human motivation to his growing investment in the novel, or "romance," as he comes to call it in the important essay of 1797, "Of History and Romance." Marilyn Butler and Mark Philp rightly refer to this essay as "a manifesto for the continuation of *Political Justice* by other means, most notably the novel" (*CN*, 1, p. 24).[17] My intention here is to describe another context for our understanding of Godwin's intellectual and artistic development during the 1790s. Throughout the 1780s and into the '90s Dissent had provided a language, style, and tone – a material habitus – with which to express political aspirations in keeping with Godwin's individualist theory of human motivation. In the absence of this religious language of private judgment, however, Godwin is faced in the mid 1790s with a collective political discourse that threatens both private judgment and rational conversation. Whereas Dissenting publicity assumed a universalized reading audience comprising individuals who would engage rationally and freely with public opinion concerning the common good, pamphlet culture, as Godwin rightly understood, implicitly or explicitly associated readers with particular groups and interests, with speech as opposed to writing, with publics as opposed to the public. In this respect, Godwin's career delineates a distinctive early Romantic encounter between two late-eighteenth-century definitions of the public sphere, the contentious political community of the orator and pamphleteer and the professedly tranquil, literary, and domestic one of the novelist, the author of "romance."

Godwin's self-revision in the *Memoirs*, his representation of his marital conversation with Wollstonecraft as a simultaneously cooperative yet individualist dialectic between reason and sensibility, therefore needs to be understood against both the dissolution of the Dissenting community and the contemporaneous emergence of new radical communities, with their correspondent communicative modes of collective persuasion. Such an understanding indicates that Godwin's *Memoirs*, like Wollstonecraft's writings themselves, at times exceeds the common, almost Manichean opposition between reason and sensibility that informs much literary and political discourse during the revolutionary decade. By attending to Godwin's representation of Wollstonecraft's religious character and to the place of religion in her own work, we can see that Wollstonecraft and Godwin both, in fact, arrive at a new conception of sensibility as the basis for, rather than the counterbalance to, reason. This relation produces a modified rational faculty, a kind of intuitively discriminating intelligence or "taste." In addition to embodying, as Godwin claimed in his own autobiographical notes of 1800, the influence of Hume (*CN*, 1, p. 53) – to which we should add that of Rousseau, Smith, and Burke

– such a conception may also be interpreted as Godwin's synthesis of Wollstonecraft's thought with his own efforts to accommodate the individuated, conversational models of Dissenting life to the changing political circumstances of the mid to late 1790s.

THE LEGACY OF DISSENT I: SANDEMANIANISM AND
POLITICAL JUSTICE

Godwin's dogged individualism in the early 1790s was the legacy of his experience of Dissenting cultures. If Presbyterian families such as the Aikins descended or ascended, as the case may be, from Calvinism to Arminianism and Arianism over several generations, Godwin underwent this process of religious liberalization in the space of two decades. Godwin's social and religious experiences of Dissent played a substantial role in determining the grounds on which he would encounter the collective discourses of radical oratory and pamphleteering. Before addressing Godwin's Dissenting sociability, we should therefore review his religious development from Independent orthodoxy to his qualified form of atheism in the 1790s.

Godwin, son and grandson of Calvinist Dissenting ministers, experienced a different trajectory away from orthodoxy than did the Aikin family. The Godwins and the Aikins had roots in the same culture – Godwin's grandfather was a personal friend of Doddridge, and his father, like Barbauld's, was educated by Doddridge at Northampton. But Godwin would become less moderate before turning to heterodoxy. Under the influence of his private tutor in Norwich, Samuel Newton, an Independent minister distinguished by his Wilkite politics and Sandemanian religion, the young Godwin embraced the ultra-Calvinist sect of Particular Baptists known as Sandemanians or Glasites. This sect, originating in Scotland in the late 1720s, took its name from its founder, John Glas (1695–1773), a Presbyterian minister of the Church of Scotland. Glas' son-in-law Robert Sandeman (1718–71) came to be recognized as the leader of the sect, and the name "Sandemanian" became current in England and America. By the end of the century, the major Sandemanian societies were centered in Liverpool, London, Newcastle, Nottingham, and Whitehaven, but they seem to have been few in number, perhaps as few as twenty by the early nineteenth century.[18]

In Godwin's "Of Religion" (1818), he refers to Sandemanian beliefs and practices as "the strictest and severest forms of Christian religion" (*PPW,*

VII, p. 63). If the Calvinists would damn "ninety-nine in a hundred of mankind," Godwin claimed, the Sandemanians had "contrived a scheme for damning ninety-nine in a hundred of the followers of Calvin" (*CN*, I, p. 30). For his early religious severity, in April 1773 Godwin was refused admission to the Homerton Academy in London, on suspicion of Sandemanian tendencies, and instead was placed at the Coward Academy at Hoxton under Andrew Kippis, a Socinian, and Abraham Rees.[19] At Hoxton, under the influence of Kippis, Godwin's Calvinism softened, and by the time he assumed the position of ministerial candidate at Ware, in Hertfordshire, 1778–79, he was moving in the direction of heterodoxy: in his autobiographical notes, titled "The Principal Revolutions of Opinion" and dated 10 March 1800, Godwin writes of this period, "I rejected the doctrine of eternal damnation, and my notions respecting the trinity acquired a taint of heresy" (*CN*, I, p. 53). At Ware he also came under the influence of Joseph Fawcett, a republican minister who in addition to sermons wrote anti-war poetry and "was a declared enemy to the private and domestic affections" (*CN*, I, p. 53).[20] In 1780 and 1781 Godwin held a ministry at Stowmarket in Suffolk, where, according to his notes, after reading d'Holbach's *Système de la Nature* he "became a Deist" (*CN*, I, p. 53). Following a brief stay in London,[21] Godwin moved to Beaconsfield, Buckinghamshire, in late 1782; there he returned to the ministry and, after reading Priestley's *Institutes of Natural and Revealed Religion*, to Protestant Christianity as well: a Deist since 1781, Godwin writes, "I reverted to Christianity under the mitigated form of Socinianism" (*PPW*, VII, p. 64). After leaving Beaconsfield and the ministry in 1783, Godwin remained a heterodox Dissenter throughout the 1780s until 1788 when, as he puts it, he took his "last farewel of the Christian faith" (*CN*, I, p. 53). In his autobiographical notes of 1800 Godwin records that in 1792, under the influence of Thomas Holcroft, he became an "atheist," but these claims about Godwin's unbelief after 1788 bear further examination. Although, according to his own account, since the composition of *Political Justice* in 1792 he had been an "atheist" (*CN*, I, p. 53), in a fragment of 1795 Godwin revealed himself then to have been more of a rational Deist:

I believe in this being, not because I have any proper or direct knowledge of his existence. But I am at a loss to account for the existence and arrangement of the visible universe . . . I perceive my understanding to be so commensurate to his nature, and all his attributes to be so much like what I know – have observed. As instantly to convert mystery into reason and contradictions into certainty.[22]

It is thus important to follow Philp in suggesting that "we have to view claims about Godwin's atheism," including his own, "with caution."[23] Above all, the question of Godwin's atheism should not obscure the role played by religious thought and experience in his political and aesthetic theory.

When Godwin looked back from 1800 on the "principal revolutions" of his opinions since 1793, he singled out his early Calvinism as the basis for his three principal "errors" in *Political Justice*:

> The Enquiry concerning Political Justice I apprehend to be blemished principally by three errors, 1. Stoicism, or an inattention to the principle, that pleasure and pain are the only bases on which morality can rest. 2. Sandemanianism, or an inattention to the principle, that feeling, and not judgment, is the source of human actions. 3. The unqualified condemnation of the private affections.
>
> It will easily be seen how strongly these errors are connected with the Calvinist system. (*CN*, 1, p. 53)

Much attention has justly been paid to Godwin's claims about his own development, but there are several compelling reasons to question his sweeping attribution of these overlapping errors to "the Calvinist system" and to consider some of Godwin's fundamental and enduring tenets in the context of his early religious austerity. Rowland Weston has recently discussed the ways in which Godwin's early "Enlightenment universalism and essentialism [were] heavily tinctured with Calvinist stoicism and immaterialism," but it remains to be explored in detail how Sandemanian doctrines in particular, as Don Locke has proposed, in fact emerged "as leading themes in the atheistical *Political Justice*."[24]

Godwin's reliance on personal censure as the means by which to persuade the private judgment, and thus to regulate morality, demands individual freedom from all institutional control. Since Glas' schism from the Church of Scotland, Sandemanians had rejected all political and secular interference in the kingdom of Christ, which for Dissenters on both sides of the Calvinist/Arminian divide was essentially spiritual. In *A New Universal History of the Religious Rites, Ceremonies, and Customs of the Whole World* (1788), William Hurd lists "The principal heads of that religion laid down by Mr. Glass [*sic*]," the first of which is that "there can be no civil establishments of religion consistent with the plan laid down in the gospel."[25] A national church thus became an imposition on the unmediated relationship between the individual conscience and God. In accord with this justification for the anti-establishmentarian position held in varying degrees by most Dissenters, Godwin's lifelong principle that any form of institutional coercion of the private judgment constituted an impediment to human progress rested on the primacy of the individual conscience. Although Godwin quickly abandoned his Calvinist upbringing, like Kippis he never relinquished his austere and anti-authoritarian emphasis on the private judgment. In a general sense, in England the Jacobin virtue of candor, of civility and open-mindedness respecting opinions with which one disagrees, was always associated with the laws of free enquiry espoused by religious Dissenters in philosophical and theological debate. Absolute candor, according to this model, could provide a form of control by which wrong would naturally defer to right in the absence of any constraint beyond reason alone. In *Political Justice*, Godwin elevates candor to the level of law itself, envisioning a future that is neither democracy nor anarchy proper but rather a kind of government by opinion in which individuals freely censure one another's conduct, leading irresistibly to right action. In place of law, and of rewards and punishments, "in governments of smaller dimensions opinion would be all sufficient; the inspection of every man over the conduct of his neighbours, when unstained with caprice, would constitute a censorship of the most irresistible nature" (*PPW*, II, p. 316). There is a sectarian spirit associated with this irresistible censorship that goes beyond the denominational openness of rational Dissent and its candid brand of free enquiry. Sandemanian churches in fact placed great emphasis on individual censure as the method of regulating behavior within the congregation. "When any one brother gives offence to another, either by word or deed," writes Robert Adam in his account of Sandemanianism in *The Religious World Displayed* (1809), "the person so offending, whatever his rank or station in civil life, is to be immediately told his fault by the brother offended, whatever may be the rank or station of the latter."[26] Having been recently chosen an elder of the Sandemanian congregation in Aldersgate, Samuel Pike relates that should a member of the fellowship misbehave, "he is to be rebuked and censured for it" individually by another member of the congregation; only if the censured congregant persists in his transgression must he then "be brought before the whole Church, and if he will not hear the Church, he must be cut off."[27] Godwin's imagined polity in *Political Justice*, we might say, seeks to transform the nation into a sect and to regulate the conduct of its citizens through the individualist practices of Sandemanian, sectarian censure.

Although Godwin rejects his early stoicism for what can be described as a theory of sympathetic benevolence, another way in which his Sandemanian legacy continues to inform the conclusions of *Political Justice* lies in

the crucial link between the theory of moral duties and Godwin's redefinition of property. If we consider the first error stipulated by Godwin,
stoicism, we find a typical example of the liberal progression among many
Dissenters away from Calvinism and toward the less rigorous religion of
heterodox Presbyterians, General Baptists, and Unitarians. In all editions
of *Political Justice*, however, Godwin's important train of thought from
the rejection of positive rights to the critique of private property remains
rooted in the radical Calvinist tradition. Although he softens his argument
in 1796 in order to moderate his radical challenge to property, Godwin
persistently refuses to accept the existence of positive rights: thus in the
second edition, "Few things have contributed more to undermining the
energy and virtue of the human species, than the supposition that we have
a right, as it has been phrased, to do what we will with our own" (*PPW*,
IV, p. 80). What we think of as our right to behave as we will is "rendered
null by the superior claims of justice" (*PPW*, IV, p. 82); that is, our duties
to satisfy our own needs and the needs of others supersede our perceived
rights to dispose of our own "property." "Strictly speaking," Godwin
writes, "We have in reality nothing that is . . . our own. We have nothing
that has not a destination prescribed to it by the immutable voice of
reason and justice; and respecting which, if we supersede that destination,
we do not entail upon ourselves a certain portion of guilt" (*PPW*, IV,
p. 80). Certainly the incorporation of sympathy and physical sensation
into his account of how benevolence becomes habit could involve a
Humean rejection of "Sandemanianism, or an inattention to the principle,
that feeling, and not judgment, is the source of human actions." But
Godwinian benevolence in combination with the theory of duties over
rights, with its consequent abstract challenge to private property, still
inescapably resembles the most radical component of Sandemanian
practices: members of Sandemanian societies, for whom the accumulation
of wealth was unscriptural and therefore unacceptable, practiced community of property, within the constraints, of course, of daily life in
Liverpool or Newcastle. "They hold it to be unlawful to lay up treasures
on earth," writes Adam in *The Religious World Displayed*, and the radical
Sandemanian Thomas Spence made his opposition to private property,
especially landed property, the centerpiece of his utopian society, "Spensonia."[28] Godwin's very formulation – "We have nothing that has not
a destination prescribed to it by the immutable voice of reason and
justice" – in fact echoes Pike's description of Sandemanian practices in
A Plain and Full Account: "We reckon it unlawful to *lay up Treasures on
Earth*. . . Every one therefore is to look upon all that he has in his

Possession and Power, as open to the Calls of the Poor and church" (pp. 13–14).[29] Throughout the eighteenth century it is impossible to dissociate levelling theories against property rights from the radical Calvinist tradition, and enduring elements of the Godwinian notion of justice as a "voice" or a "call" remain indebted to this tradition.

THE LEGACY OF DISSENT 2: THE GODWINIAN SCENE AND
PAMPHLET CULTURE

The process by which Godwin comes to mitigate his condemnation of the private affections represents an encounter between religious, political, and aesthetic theories and practices of communication. The forms of oratory and print produced by radical speakers and pamphleteers, such as John Thelwall, Daniel Isaac Eaton, Thomas Spence, and many rank-and-file members of the radical societies, posed a problem for Godwin in the mid 1790s. Although political speech and writing, especially as practiced by Thelwall, did in many ways satisfy Godwin's desire in 1794–95 to reconcile rational judgment with the social affections, such radical discourse directed its persuasive methods not toward the individual but the collective mind. Godwin's rejection of the Calvinist system represents one major channel through which sympathy enters his theory of human motivation, but the continuing influence of his Calvinist individualism informs his acceptance of one set of rational and affective media and his rejection of another, more corporate, variety: instead of the individual Christian auditor of a particular sermon or the individual "reader" or "friend" of polite literature, radical speeches and pamphlets addressed "Citizens."

Marilyn Butler and Roy Porter have described the late eighteenth century as, in Butler's phrase, an "age of remarkable sociability."[30] Godwin's sociability during the 1780s proceeded according to the middle-class but oppositionist conventions, manners, and tones of tempered dissidence in the Dissenting public sphere, and his devotion to individualist communication emerged first and foremost from a lived experience of Dissenting sociability in which his Calvinist inheritance merged with and was subsumed by the public nature of moderate, liberal Dissent. For Godwin, this culture existed most saliently at the public dinners given twice a week by Timothy Hollis of Great Ormond Street, at the teas held regularly by Helen Maria Williams, and then within the well-documented social and professional circle radiating outwards from Joseph Johnson's shop in St. Paul's Churchyard.[31] Through John Hollis, a member of Godwin's congregation at Beaconsfield, Godwin entered the Hollis circle, which included John and his uncle Timothy, their adopted relation Brand Hollis, Richard Price, Andrew Kippis, Joseph Priestley, Joseph Towers, Theophilus Lindsey, Thomas Belsham (second cousin of the Aikins and former student of John Aikin), and John Disney.[32] The heyday of these dinners for Godwin was 1788–90, but his frequent associations with the circle continued beyond the death of Timothy Hollis in December 1791 through the following year: a journal entry for 11 June 1792 reads, typically, "June 11 M. Writ 4 pages. Dine at B. Hollis's, with Priestley and Lindsey: the former a republican, lend him [Holcroft's novel] Anna St. Ives. J. Hollis calls."[33] Through the Hollis circle Godwin became acquainted with Williams, and through Williams' tea parties – "the 'arty' side of Dissent"[34] – he met James Barry, Samuel Rogers, Hester Piozzi, John Adams (then the American ambassador), Samuel Romilly, Capel Lofft, Thomas Paine, and Baron Winckelmann.[35] Also through Timothy Hollis' parties Godwin met Thomas Holcroft, who became his almost constant companion after 1788.[36] As I have noted, by 1788 when Godwin's sociability with the Hollis and Williams circles was reaching its peak, he had already taken his "last farewel of the Christian faith." Paul Hamilton writes that "Godwin, true-born Dissenter, follows the secular tendency of part of his culture to write for circles characterised by free thinking no longer obviously connected to a religious ideology."[37] What I am describing as a form of Dissenting sociability, then, needs to be understood in terms of the rhetorical and stylistic legacies of religious communities which continued to inform social manners and values for groups of Dissenters who may no longer have been united by denomination or creed.

Opposed to this Dissenting sociability, the emotive oratory of the largely working-class and secular societies as well as the pamphlet medium came to represent an extreme nearly as threatening to Godwin's convictions as arbitrary government and administrative repression. The consistent fundamental tenet of Godwin's philosophy, first articulated in *Political Justice*, was the endorsement of private judgment refined by conversation with other individuals as the effectual means of discovering truth. Thus in a key passage of *Political Justice*, Godwin writes,

the promoting of the best interests of mankind eminently depends upon the freedom of social communication. Let us imagine to ourselves a number of individuals, who, having first stored their minds with reading and reflection, proceed afterwards in candid and unreserved conversation to compare their ideas, to suggest their doubts, to remove their difficulties, and to cultivate a collected and striking manner of delivering their sentiments. Let us suppose these men, prepared by mutual intercourse, to go forth to the world, to explain with succinctness and simplicity, and in a manner well calculated to arrest attention, the true principles of society. Let us suppose their hearers instigated in their turn to repeat these truths to their companions. We shall then have an idea of knowledge as perpetually gaining ground, unaccompanied with peril in the means of its diffusion. Reason will spread itself, and not a brute and unintelligent sympathy. Discussion . . . may be carried on with advantage in small and friendly societies. (*PPW*, III, p. 121)

This passage captures the essence of what one might call "the Godwinian scene." Influenced by the legacies of more formal eighteenth-century societies, including the Philomathean Society (the monthly debating club of which Godwin was a member), Priestley's Lunar Society of Birmingham, and Benjamin Franklin's "Junto" in Philadelphia, this scene is foremost an idealization of the kind of sociability Godwin experienced in the rational Dissenting circles of the 1780s.[38]

After 1793, indeed, the Godwinian scene risked becoming, or seeming to become, an abstraction; although the LCS and the SCI by no means monopolized radical life – the London Revolution Society and the Whig Association for the Friends of the People both included members of the Dissenting elite – the reality of political communities during the mid 1790s increasingly seemed neither small nor, in Godwin's sense of the term, friendly. Whereas Godwin envisioned the spread of reason through individuated conversation, the mass meetings of the LCS and the intensity of pamphlet production which accompanied and publicized radical oratory came to constitute a very different sphere of communication (see Figure 3 for James Gillray's phobic depiction).[39] As E. P. Thompson's work documents, the radical societies in London, Sheffield, Norwich, Edinburgh, and elsewhere maintained an extensive national correspondence through regional cells, mass meetings, lectures, and, above all, the pamphlet trade.

In opposition to the spectacle of numerous assemblies reproduced for the reading public by radical pamphlets, the Godwinian scene presents the image of several individuals reflecting separately and soberly before coming together in the public sphere to discover truth and determine upon actions through "candid and unreserved" rational conversation. Following Klancher's influential study of Romantic constructions of authorship and audience, Garrett A. Sullivan, Jr. describes the impact of radical communication on definitions of readership in terms of "single" or "multiple" discourses: "What happens in the early 1790s is that, due to changes in the production and consumption of printed texts, the illusion of a single conversation among equals dissolves when confronted with the

Figure 3. James Gillray, "Copenhagen House." Reproduced by permission of the National Portrait Gallery.

emerging reality of multiple conversations."[40] And critically for Godwin, the illusion of a single conversation addressed by individuals to individuals breaks down along with the mass meetings and cheap pamphlets of the LCS: in addition to the reality of multiple conversations, these discursive scenes represent the intense and unpredictable manifestations of oratory directed by an individual to a collective audience.

Political societies, where judgment occurs within the group in response to the emotive rhetoric of a speaker, fostered a form of communication that for Godwin precluded both private judgment as well as individuated conversation. "Associations," Godwin writes in the first edition of *Political Justice*, "must be formed with great caution not to be allied to tumult. The conviviality of a feast may lead to the depredations of a riot. While the sympathy of opinion catches from man to man, especially in numerous meetings, and among persons whose passions have not been used to the curb of judgment, actions may be determined on, which solitary reflection would have rejected" (*PPW*, III, p. 118). As I have suggested, correspondent to Godwin's rationalist distrust of "the conviviality of a feast" was his concern over the print culture through which the "sympathy of opinion" spread, like a contagion, well beyond the already numerous meetings of the societies, the LCS in particular. Behind Godwin's consistent objection to "conviviality" lies the fragmentation of political opposition in the 1790s between middle-class intellectuals such as Godwin and the rational Dissenters on the one hand, and the working-class radical societies on the other. The 1790s brand of political expression typical of LCS meetings and pamphlets evoked fearful and hostile responses not just in published parliamentary debates, "treasury prints," and reactionary propaganda, but among middle-class dissident reformers as well. There was, of course, significant overlap between the radical societies and Godwinian intellectuals – Thelwall, to whom I will return, straddles the two spheres – but in Godwin's writing the distinction between individuated sober and rational conversation and the collective conviviality of radical communication could not have been more stark.

Whereas middle-class radicals such as Godwin and the Dissenters of the London Revolution Society embodied an individualist habitus of tempered dissidence, the more plebeian LCS and its pamphlet literature staged collectivist rituals and celebrations of a more "convivial" nature. The title page of Daniel Isaac Eaton's *Politics for the People*, published in sixteen-page installments and sold for two pence a copy, provides a concentrated instance of the mass audience constructed by the pamphlet form. Along with Thomas Spence and "Citizen" Lee the most active and fearless of the radical publishers, the perpetually prosecuted Eaton here makes his collectivist claims perfectly explicit, precisely the claims Godwin repeatedly rejects. The epigraph on the title page reads,

> The praise of him, who talk'd so big
> For training up one learned Pig,
>   Is far below, friend Daniel, thine!
> The Feast of Words, which you supply
> To your illuminating Stye,
>   Makes Herds of literary Swine.[41]

From *Political Justice* to *The Enquirer* (1797), Godwin propounds the education not of collective herds but of individuals. In the first edition of *Political Justice* he writes,

To conceive an order of society totally different from that which is now before our eyes, and to judge of the advantages that would accrue from its institution, are the prerogatives only of a few favoured minds . . . Time, reading and conversation are necessary to render [these advantages] familiar. They must descend in regular gradation from the most thoughtful to the most unobservant. He, that begins with an appeal to the people, may be suspected to understand little of the true character of mind. (*PPW*, III, p. 118)

Unlike Dissenting dinners and teas where individuated conversation would cultivate "a few favoured minds," Eaton's "feast of Words" "begins with an appeal to the people," granting superior praise to the pamphleteer's ability to make "Herds of literary Swine."

Although Godwin would not brook the imposition of any collective identity on the private judgment, for other radical intellectuals determined to produce "informed" herds, reason and mass sympathy presented no such conflict. John Thelwall, in particular, the great theorist and practitioner of radical communication, successfully integrated rhetorics of rationality and conviviality in his career as political lecturer, radical orator, journalist, and pamphleteer.[42] In theory a Godwinian proponent of "peaceful discussion," Thelwall disseminated the ideas of *Political Justice* both in his lectures and his political journal, *The Tribune*. His lectures from 1794–96, first at New Compton Street, Soho, and then in a larger hall at Beaufort Buildings in the Strand, drew impressive crowds averaging 400–500 and reaching 800 at their peak. Furthermore, these lectures could be purchased in pamphlet form at either Beaufort Buildings or the Newgate-Street publishing house of Daniel Isaac Eaton. At the LCS mass meetings of 1795 and 1796 Thelwall was among the speakers who addressed crowds of over 100,000 from tribunes erected around the fields near Copenhagen House, Islington (see Figure 3).[43] As I have suggested, Thelwall is especially interesting for his ability to straddle middle-class and plebeian societies and to speak the languages of both communities. In pamphlets such as *Peaceful Discussion, and not Tumultuary Violence the Means of Redressing National Grievances* (1795), *The Natural and Constitutional Right of Britons To Annual Parliaments, Universal Suffrage, and the Freedom of Popular Association* (1795), and "Part the Second" of *The Rights of Nature, Against the Usurpations of Establishments* (1796), Thelwall assumes a strong Godwinian stance against tumult and violence and in favor of rational judgment:

> whenever supposed rights (that is to say, particular interests) clash, violence may be prevented, and personal differences be decided by aggregate reason . . .
> It is upon these principles only, that a multitude of individuals can be melted and organized into one harmonious mass. Thus only can they really become a community, or body politic.[44]

But even as he maintains the rational-progressive position of middle-class reformers, Thelwall speaks and writes in the language of a different habitus.

The pamphlet version of Thelwall's speech delivered from the "second tribune" to the mass LCS meeting held on 26 October 1795 begins,

> Remember, Citizens . . . You are listening to . . . a being, who though no longer confined, as of late, in the common charnel-house of Newgate, the common receptacle of the putrid carcases of felons, who died of infectious diseases in the gaol, yet brings to you at this hour, in his veins, and in his constitution, the diseases contracted in that pestiferous den. I hope, however, that though my constitution is injured, my principles are yet sound.[45]

Thelwall's discourse reaches the collective audience, "Citizens," laden with the infectious imagery of "putrid carcases" brought physically by Thelwall from "the common charnel-house of Newgate," where he had been confined from 24 October to 1 December 1794, having previously been imprisoned in the Tower since the middle of May. Thelwall's persuasive method – which to Godwin, in Andrew McCann's suggestive phrase, seemed to participate in a "pathological public sphere"[46] – is to represent his individual body as bearing the collective experience of imprisonment directly from that "pestiferous den" to the audience through his spoken words. Although the radical speaker as a figure is always a powerful and idiosyncratic individual, his body here ceases to be individuated in the sense that it comes to manifest a collective criminalized identity; the sound principles that such a diseased body communicates represent the shared plebeian constitutions and principles of speaker and audience alike. Through its reproduction of the spoken word, the pamphlet medium thus constructs its reading audience of collective citizens as a physiologically and ideologically distinct counter-public. For Godwin, however, the moment the individual mind first becomes part of an individual body and then defers to any collective body, an element of coercion enters the field.[47]

A salient instance of this rhetorical shift from mind to body and from writing to speech facilitated by pamphlet culture can be found in an important genre of political expression during the 1790s, that of the radical toast (see Figure 4). Radical dinners were generally held either at the Globe or the Crown and Anchor, both in the Strand, and the toast, mouthed collectively as if by one indivisible body, is a corporate and corporeal genre through and through.[48] The *Anti-Jacobin*, in fact, devoted extensive attention to toasts in particular, and to the social customs of the radical societies in general. In April 1798, "Mr. Higgins," the magazine's caricature of a radical poet and author of the notorious lampoon of Erasmus Darwin, "Loves of the Triangles," attacks the *Anti-Jacobin*'s bigoted attachment to "*things as they are*," thus aligning himself with the Godwinians.[49] Two months later, in his essay on the drama, Higgins represents radicalism as a curious hodgepodge: "I hold every Government . . . as a *malum in se*, – an evil to be eradicated . . . by force, if force be practicable, if not, – by the artillery of Reason – by Pamphlets, Speeches, Toasts at Club-dinners, and though last, not least, by DIDACTIC POEMS" (II, p. 417). From the perspective of the *Anti-Jacobin*, pamphlets, speeches, toasts, and didactic poems are equally allied within the Jacobin arsenal called "Reason," but this is a very different arsenal, associated with different forms of communication, than that advocated by Godwin.

In *Caleb Williams*, when Caleb hides in London, turning to a career as a hack writer of poetry and periodical essays, it seems for a time that he has escaped Falkland's grasp. While Caleb writes "in the style of Addison's Spectators," Falkland's engine, the criminal Gines, does not use polite literary forms to smear Caleb's reputation.[50] "A Hawker bawling his wares" sells, presumably, pamphlets and handbills: "*Here you have the* MOST WONDERFUL AND SURPRISING HISTORY, AND MIRACULOUS ADVEN-TURES OF CALEB WILLIAMS . . . *All for the price of one halfpenny.*"[51] Falkland's omnipotence over public opinion through Gines, and subsequently through the hawker's wares, reflects Godwin's sense of the irrational persuasive potential of these popular forms. Later, when Laura Denison refuses to listen to Caleb's explanation, it is accordingly Gines' halfpenny

COMMITTEE ROOM, January, 23, 1794.
RESOLVED UNANIMOUSLY,

THAT a hundred thousand Copies of the Address to the people of Great Britain and Ireland, voted at the General Meeting, be printed and distributed by the Society.

Resolved Unanimously. That the following toasts, drank at the Anniversary Dinner of the Society, be printed at the end of the Address,

I. THE RIGHTS OF MAN; and may Britons never want spirit to assert them.

II. *The British Convention,* lately held at Edinburgh; and success to the important object it had in view.

III. *Citizen William Skirvin* charged by the sentence of the Court of Justiciary, with the *honour* of being the cause of calling that Convention.

IV. *The London Corresponding Society,* and other patriotic Societies of Great-Britain and Ireland.

V. *Citizen Maurice Margarot,* the condemned Delegate of this Society; and may his *manly* and *patriotic* conduct be rewarded by the attachment of the people.

Citizen Gerrald then arose, and in a stream of inspiring eloquence, pronounced the just eulogium of this truely valuable Citizen, so emphatically called by *Citizen Aitchinson* (one of the witnesses on his trial) the SECOND SIDNEY. He concluded with wishing we might rather *die* the *last of British Freemen,* than *live* the *first of slaves.*

VI. *Citizen Joseph Gerrald,* the other Delegate of this Society, now under prosecution; and may his concluding sentiment be engraved upon every British heart.

VII. The transactions at *Toulon.* May Briton's remember them as they ought, and profit by *dear bought experience.*

VIII. *Citizen Hamilton Roan,* and the other *true* patriots of *Ireland* ; and may the authors of the *Convention-bill* find that they have committed a *bull.*

IX. *Ditto . . Muir, and Palmer*—May their sentence be speedily reversed. and *Botany-Bay* be peopled with a colony of *real* criminals.

X. Success to the arms of *Freedom* against whomsoever directed; and confusion to *despots* with whomsoever allied.

XI. All that is *good* in *every constitution*; and may we never be superstitious enough to reverence in *any* that which is *good for nothing.*

XII. *Citizen Thomas Paine*—May his virtue rise superior to calumny and suspicion, and his name still be dear to Britons.

XIII. *Lord Loughborough,* the *Earl of Moira, Sir Gilbert Elliot,* and the other apostates from liberty; and may they enjoy the profits of their apostacy *so long as they live.*

XIV. A speedy and honourable *peace* with the *brave republic of France.*

XV. The *starving manufacturers* and *neglected peasantry* of Great Britain and Ireland.

XVI. *Citizen John Frost*; and a speedy restoration of that health which he lost in the dungeons of Newgate.

XVII. The *virtuous and spirited Citizens,* now in confinement for matters of *opinion* : and may we shew them by our conduct, that they are not forgotten.

Figure 4. "Toasts," from *At a General Meeting of the London Corresponding Society, Held at the Globe Tavern Strand: On Monday the 20th Day of January, 1794.* Reproduced by permission of the British Library.

narrative, the "very paper of the WONDERFUL AND SURPRISING HISTORY,"[52] that wins out over Caleb's truth.

BARTERING TONES: *CONSIDERATIONS ON LORD GRENVILLE'S AND MR. PITT'S BILLS*

After establishing himself with *Political Justice, Caleb Williams,* and *Cursory Strictures on the Charge Delivered by Lord Chief Justice Eyre* (1794) as the philosophical spokesman for the radical movement, in *Considerations,* his pamphlet on the proposed Gagging Acts, Godwin broke decisively from his radical allegiances, and along with this break came charges of apostasy. Accusing Godwin of cherishing "*a feebleness of spirit,*" Thelwall classed him by name among other "calumniators," including Burke and John Reeves, founder and chairman of the Association for the Preservation of Liberty and Property against Republicans and Levellers.[53] Godwin, it must be said, was never a member of any of the radical societies, though he did occasionally dine with the London Revolution Society in 1789 and 1790, and it is thus important to note that he could not have been an "apostate," could not have stood apart, from groups he never stood with. Nonetheless, there is a remarkable shift in Godwin's decisions during 1794 and 1795, from the radical philosopher who boldly came forward in *Cursory Strictures* to defend Tooke, Hardy, Thelwall, and others under prosecution for treason, to "A Lover of Order," the pseudonymous polemicist who in the following year chose to issue the schizophrenic pamphlet on the bills of Grenville and Pitt currently before Parliament.[54]

In *Considerations,* Godwin first chastises the radicals for the demagoguery of their oratory but ends by flaying the administration for the legislative restraints it sought to put on public discourse, especially on the freedom of the press. The pamphlet thus doubles back on itself, first opposing the radicalism of the societies and endorsing governmental "vigilance," and then condemning the rabid repressiveness of the government's response, the bills that would become the Two Acts by the end of 1795. This structure allows Godwin to seek a middle way between the two parties controlling "the present irritated and unnatural state of political affairs": "while one party will not endure to hear of any cautionary restraints upon freedom . . . another party . . . conceives that scarcely any restraint can be too vigilant or severe" (*PPW,* II, p. 125). "The great problem of political science," Godwin writes, is to "preserve liberty in all its vigour, while we effectually discountenance licentiousness"

(*PPW*, II, p. 134), and "Liberty without Licentiousness" (*PPW*, II, p. 125) becomes the position from which to express a "moderate and conciliating spirit with respect to the two opposite political systems" (*PPW*, II, p. 161).

Before turning to the rhetorical strategy by which Godwin expresses this spirit, we should mark the extraordinary nature of Godwin's attack on the radical societies. Godwin writes, "The London Corresponding Society is a formidable machine; the system of political lecturing is a hot-bed, perhaps too well adapted to ripen men for purposes, more or less similar to those of the Jacobin Society of Paris. Both branches of the situation are well deserving the attention of the members of the government of Great Britain" (*PPW*, II, p. 134). It is important to remember exactly what this kind of language would have meant in late 1795. Having read through Pitt's and Grenville's bills in early November, and having been personally acquainted with prosecuted radicals from both England and Scotland, Godwin was perfectly aware what "the attention of the . . . government" could lead to. In August and September 1793 Thomas Muir and Thomas Fyshe Palmer, leaders of the Scottish Friends of the People, had been sentenced to fourteen and seven years' transportation to Botany Bay, respectively, and by the following spring Maurice Margarot and Joseph Gerrald, the LCS delegates to the National Convention in Edinburgh, along with the Scottish secretary William Skirving, had been tried, convicted, and sentenced to fourteen years' transportation.[55] Although *Considerations* is ultimately conciliatory, as "A Lover of Order" Godwin nonetheless adds his voice to those loudly calling for governmental interference.

His method is to revive the language of Dissent as a middle way between radical and administrative extremes. Applying the same Dissenting rhetoric of regulated devotion to the opposed parties, Godwin portrays them both as equally unrestrained and, indeed, enthusiastic in their pursuit of opposite ends. When addressing the radical societies, Godwin acknowledges that reform is necessary but cautions that it is "a delicate and an awful task. No sacrilegious hand must be put forth to this sacred work. It must be carried on by slow, almost insensible steps, and by just degrees . . . there must be a grand and magnificent harmony, expanding itself through the whole community" (*PPW*, II, p. 132). Intemperate, disorderly, and precipitous, the radical movement requires a different emotional constitution if it is to approach "the genuine image of reform . . . the lovely and angelic figure that needs only to be shewn, in order to be universally adored. Oh, Reform! Genial and benignant power! how often has thy name been polluted by profane and unhallowed lips!" (*PPW*, II, p. 132). Devotional language here allows Godwin to represent two differ-ent progressions of reformist aspirations, the one gradual and sacred, the other sudden and profane. Furthermore, these two different progressions correspond to opposed methods of persuasion. In the devotional mode, the figure of the orator or writer corresponds to the benevolent character of the rational Dissenting minister whose emotions and ideas retain their individuated quality as they expand throughout the community. It is this communication which represents a "grand and magnificent harmony" as opposed to the discord produced by a different communicative method. When the consecrated ministerial character gives way to the secular nature of the political lecturer, a different tone emerges, a tone dependent not on the individual conscience and reason of the lecturer but on the collective body of the audience, with its "sacrilegious hand" and "profane and unhallowed lips": "The lecturer ought to have a mind calmed, and, if I may be allowed the expression, consecrated by the mild spirit of philosophy . . . It almost universally happens to public speakers, that, though they may begin with the intention of communicating to their auditors the tone of their own minds, they finish with the reality of bartering this tone for the tone of the auditors" (*PPW*, II, p. 132). Godwin, defender of his friend Thelwall and the other English radicals on trial for treason in 1794, thus in 1795 turns around and attacks "the Political Lectures that have been delivered for near two years at Beaufort Buildings, in the Strand," which, as everyone knew, were delivered by Thelwall, asking,

To what end does this intellectual progress in the mind of the lecturer ultimately lead? Quiet disquisition and mere speculative enquiry will not answer his purpose. Strict disquisition . . . does not suit the tone of collected multitudes. Sober inquiry may pass well enough with a man in his closet, or in the domestic tranquillity of his own fire-side: but it will not suffice in theatres and halls of assembly. (*PPW*, II, p. 133)

Opposed to "the conviviality of a feast" and the emotional climate of "theatres and halls of assembly," we here find the chaste sobriety of the "closet," or, more tellingly, "the domestic tranquillity" of the fireside. The "strict disquisition" that emerges from these domestic scenes main-tains progressive and reformist enquiry but curbs the passion, tumult, and artifice with which Godwin always associated "the tone of collected multi-tudes." When the lecturer barters his own tone for that of his auditors, he ceases to communicate the simultaneously sacred, sober, and domesticated habitus of the Dissenting public sphere, instead becoming a mere performative echo of a secular, corporeal, and public collectivity.[56]

If such a tone can be described as a "disease," however, the Two Acts offer no "remedy" (*PPW*, II, p. 157), for, like the very party they oppose, Grenville and Pitt themselves "consult not the coolness of philosophy, but . . . act with the unsteadiness and vehemence of passion" (*PPW*, II, p. 157). When Godwin challenges the Acts, the languages of devotion and the body return. Just as the radical societies should approach the "sacred work" of reform with "No sacrilegious hand," the government should "handle every thing" that relates to liberty "with a tender hand, and a religious fear" (*PPW*, II, p. 157). Complaining of a clause enacting that no one will be prosecuted under Grenville's bill unless by order of the king, his heirs or successors, or by order of the privy council,[57] Godwin concludes, "this bill is a sacred instrument. No ordinary hand may touch it . . . Private men are to know nothing of it, except as they may happen to suffer under its penalties. It is the consecrated engine of tyranny; it is the open and avowed enaction [*sic*] of an arbitrary power" (*PPW*, II, p. 137). Here the Dissenting public sphere provides a model of regulation, just as from the opposite perspective it provided a model of reform. A properly "sacred instrument" would be one that "Private men" could touch and know; here, however, control is not exercised by the communication of public opinion between private individuals but rather by the coercive, even inquisitorial, force of legislative authority. The religious fear with which one should attempt to restrain liberty, as Godwin does in *Considerations*, must be dissociated from all arbitrary and collective power, the chief embodiment of which is the establishment in church and state.

The pamphlet then ends by attempting to conciliate the radical party on the assumption that the bills will pass. Godwin's final injunction involves a high claim for publicity, in a sense replacing the tones of both plebeian multitudes and arbitrary power with the reformist language articulated in Dissenting rhetoric throughout *Considerations*: addressing the "enthusiastic advocates for the extension of liberty," Godwin writes, "Be firm, be active, be temperate. If alarmists are resolved no longer to keep any terms with you, you then, in all just consideration, succeed to the double office, of the advocates of reform, and the moderators of contending and unruly animosities" (*PPW*, II, p. 162). On the one hand this double office incorporates the progressive radicalism of the societies, but on the other it takes over the moderating and restraining role from the establishment. Claiming restraint as the virtue not of coercive legislation, which Godwin's pamphlet explicitly challenges, but of individualist and rational conversation, Godwin's dissident political posture in 1795 attempts to adapt the legacy of the Dissenting public sphere to the new conditions of radical communication and administrative repression.

THE RETURN TO SENSIBILITY: *SKETCHES OF HISTORY*

From the double office of 1795 emerges a highly theorized and determined investment in forms of "polite" literature: the periodical essay, the biographical memoir, and the novel. Before Wollstonecraft's death on 10 September 1797, and before Godwin's reconstruction of their relationship in the *Memoirs*, published five months later, the groundwork for his aesthetic theory at the end of the decade had already been laid in his 1797 volume, *The Enquirer, Reflections on Education, Manners, and Literature, In a Series of Essays*. Of *Political Justice* James T. Boulton writes, "Style is not only a means of conveying ideas, it is at the same time an incarnation of their validity and reasonableness; the qualities of Godwin's style – lucidity, logic, directness, plainness and so on – are themselves witnesses to the philosophical position he maintains on the level of formal argument."[58] In addition to indicating a commitment to a new style, *The Enquirer* can be read as a reincorporation of the devotional language of sensibility which in the previous decade had served Godwin as the basis for his own published sermons, *Sketches of History* (1784).

Godwin's turn to the didactic appeal of "polite" literature does to a significant extent suggest a retreat from the political interventions of *Cursory Strictures* and *Considerations*, but, as Gregory Claeys writes, "In publishing *The Enquirer* Godwin consciously sought an improved mode of influencing the public and, indeed, consequently a new approach to politics."[59] Godwin himself proposes in the Preface to *The Enquirer* that "the cause of political reform, and the cause of intellectual and literary refinement, are inseparably connected" (*PPW*, v, p. 79). Following Claeys, Klancher has described *The Enquirer* as "a methodologically self-conscious attempt to reconstruct a progressive English intelligentsia by literary, educational, and canon-reorganizing means."[60] This progressive intelligentsia, however, is a different English community from that imagined by Godwin in the double office of 1795. Whereas *Considerations* briefly imagined a large and diverse community of "advocates" and "moderators" united by civic-republican models of virtue and the individuated, domesticated conversation of rational Dissent, *The Enquirer* endeavors to fashion through its "polite" style an equally "polite" readership that would serve, much like Coleridge's "clerisy," to define national identity and direct national progress: "A major part of the goal of *The Enquirer* was to state more clearly the need for a cultured elite to lead the nation towards reform, to define the leading characteristics of this group, and to show how they might be educated."[61]

From the opening sentence of its Introduction, *The Enquirer* distinguishes itself methodologically and stylistically from *Political Justice*: "The volume here presented to the reader, is upon a construction totally different from that of a work upon the principles of political science, published by the same author four years ago" (*PPW*, v, p. 77).[62] Unlike *Political Justice*, the deductive method of which was to begin with "one or two simple principles . . . and [follow] them into a variety of inferences," *The Enquirer* will be inductive, proceeding from facts to principles and involving "an incessant recurrence to experiment and actual observation" (*PPW*, v, p. 77). *The Enquirer*, then, as the titles of several essays indicate – "Of an Early Taste for Reading," "Of the Happiness of Youth," "Of Deception and Frankness," "Of Avarice and Profusion," "Of Beggars," "Of Servants" – will begin with quotidian subjects described in a detailed and polite manner rather than with sweeping philosophical or political principles related in the formal, legal, or polemical styles of 1793–95; as Claeys writes, unlike *Political Justice*, *Cursory Strictures*, or *Considerations*, *The Enquirer* will treat "the minutiae of daily life, the realm of the feelings, and the practice of minor virtues."[63]

Throughout the late eighteenth century, this nexus of method and style, of inductive reasoning, quotidian detail, and an emphasis on the social feelings along with minor acts of kindness and benevolence, was inseparable from the school of sensibility. For Godwin and other nonconformists, it was also inseparable from the movement we have witnessed among some heterodox Dissenters to revive affective devotional methods of spontaneity, particularity, and experimentalism. In this context, Godwin's early *Sketches of History. In Six Sermons*, most likely preached during his ministry at Beaconsfield in 1782–83 (*PPW*, vii, p. 3), connects Godwin's own pulpit oratory to the sensibility that we usually associate only with his later career.

For his first sermon, "The Resignation of Aaron," Godwin takes for his text Leviticus 10:3, "And Aaron held his peace." He states his experimental method at the outset – "the mind of man is much more forcibly impressed by instances drawn from real life, than by abstract precepts and dry detail of duty" (*PPW*, vii, p. 7) – and then proceeds to explicate

Aaron's resigned response to God's punishment of his two sons, Nadab and Abihu, for having offered "strange fire before the LORD, which he commandeth them not. And there went out fire from the LORD, and devoured them" (Lev. 10:1). Seeking to express "the genuine language of human nature" (*PPW*, VII, p. 8), Godwin exclaims, "How striking must have been the interview! Aaron, we will suppose, thrown upon his couch, bathed in tears, in all the agony of paternal distress" (*PPW*, VII, pp. 9–10). Godwin next portrays Moses as a "kindred soul" who seeks to comfort and counsel his brother: "The countenance of Moses is marked with the tenderest sympathy . . . He seizes his hand, and tenderly presses it, and seats himself beside him. They look wistfully at each other, and remain for some time in the most uninterrupted silence" (*PPW*, VII, p. 10). In this sermon on resignation, it is of course Aaron's silence, not his speech, which is most expressive. The preacher thus refuses to "interrupt" the "course" of Aaron's silence by translating it into language, and one can imagine Godwin's apparently extempore decision, immediately after returning to the four words of his text, to pause and allow the silence to express itself:

Aaron held his peace. – Expressive silence! Venerable musings! I will not interrupt your course. I will not attempt to translate into language, what language can so imperfectly express. Sure I am, that every susceptible heart, every mind endowed with one spark of sensibility and feeling, will find more dignity . . . and more expression, in this awful stillness of the soul . . . than in the most splendid harangue, and the most polished rhetoric. (*PPW*, VII, p. 11)

The experimental sermon thus presents a novelistic scene of sensibility, in spontaneous yet dignified speech rather than scripted, "polished rhetoric," before turning to the particular application. Godwin next addresses his congregation in the second person, shifting emphasis from the plural to the singular (or at least to a limited group of particular individuals within the collective body) and then back to the plural, and here perhaps we should even imagine the preacher's gestures, marking some of the pronouns, as he indicates various members of the audience:

But if none of you ever suffered an equal calamity, did any of you ever exhibit so . . . pure a resignation? You, will I suppose, have fallen under some dreadful misfortune. Your estate has been impoverished, you have felt all the languors, or all the torments of disease, your good name has been tarnished, your friends have betrayed you, you have been deprived of the partner of your life, or bereaved of your children. And did you never utter a murmur? Have you never, if not in word, yet in thought, arraigned the conduct of the disposer of all things?
(*PPW*, VII, p. 11)

Both the *English Review* and the *European Magazine and London Review* responded by calling Godwin a "man of feeling" (*PPW*, VII, p. 3).[64] The particular and experimental sermon preached by the Calvinist become Socinian Godwin of 1782–83 suggests that the later turn to the techniques of sensibility in *The Enquirer* and subsequent writings was also a return to an earlier devotional mode.

WOLLSTONECRAFT AND ANTI-SECTARIAN NONCONFORMITY

In light of the apparent untenability of individuated political conversation after 1795, Godwin's account of his relationship with Wollstonecraft appears to be less of a retreat than a difficult attempt to conceive a new form of collective discourse. Marriage – or rather the collaborative relationship, unsanctioned by legal or religious institutions, between complementary elements of individual personalities – stands in the *Memoirs* not simply as a retraction of earlier quixotic ideals but as a form of society whose participants converse both as individuals and in a corporate capacity. "Ours was not an idle happiness" (*CN*, I, p. 132), writes Godwin. His narrative of their relationship does not terminate in a conventional novelistic marriage but in a joint authorial identity, a Godwinian variant of Dissenting collaboration. Godwin leaves no doubt that the climax of the *Memoirs* is not the marriage: "We did not marry . . . [C]ertainly nothing can be so ridiculous . . . or so contrary to the genuine march of sentiment, as to require the overflowing of the soul to wait upon a ceremony" (*CN*, I, p. 129). Only after Wollstonecraft becomes pregnant do they marry out of expedience, and thus the emotional climax is not their union but rather Wollstonecraft's death, which emblematizes, for Godwin, the end of "the constancy and uninterruptedness of our literary pursuits" (*CN*, I, p. 133). On "cooperation," Godwin famously wrote in *Political Justice*, "every thing that is usually understood by the term . . . is in some degree an evil" (*PPW*, III, p. 450). Godwin's description of Wollstonecraft's anti-sectarian religious sensibility constitutes an underexplored aspect of the *Memoirs*, yet it plays a key role in his new advocacy for a cooperative relationship and his dialectical reflection upon reason and sensibility, in the tempering of his austere individualism.

In the *Memoirs*, the "rigid, and somewhat amazonian temper" of Wollstonecraft during the early 1790s gives way to that "softness almost more than human" (*CN*, I, p. 122), that "exquisite and delicious sensibility" of the "female Werter" (*CN*, I, p. 117), or later of Marguerite de Damville in *St Leon*.[65] But Godwin does more than reconstruct Wollstonecraft in terms of the very "*manie* of the day" (*WMW*, v, p. 8), sensibility, against which she had written in *A Vindication of the Rights of Men*. If Godwin's frank discussion of Wollstonecraft's unorthodox sexual morality provoked outrage, the aspect of his account that drew the most ire, as Myers points out,[66] was Wollstonecraft's lack of religion on her deathbed. By attending to Godwin's treatment of Wollstonecraft's religion and his organization of her writings, we can understand how he can privilege sensibility as the leading feature of Wollstonecraft's character and place *Letters Written during a Short Residence in Sweden, Norway, and Denmark* (1796) and *Maria, or The Wrongs of Woman* (1798) at the head of her canon yet still call his work *Memoirs of the Author of a Vindication of the Rights of Woman*.

Approaching the scene of her death, Godwin boldly if rashly wrote, "Her religion, as I have shown, was not calculated to be the torment of a sick bed; and, in fact, during her whole illness, not one word of a religious cast fell from her lips" (*CN*, 1, p. 138). The religion that Godwin did show in various passages throughout the *Memoirs* suggests a perceptive understanding of how Wollstonecraft's religious thought, especially its anti-sectarianism and its emphasis on what I will call affective spontaneity, informed her own political and aesthetic theories and practices. What Myers has termed Wollstonecraft's "aesthetic of spontaneity" is primarily a religious, and specifically a nonconformist, aesthetic.[67] Underpinning Wollstonecraft's writings, however, was a form of anti-sectarianism which for her was theoretically inextricable from that same insistence on spontaneity and originality. A comparison of Godwin's representation of Wollstonecraft's religion with her own writings shows that in this respect his conception of a collaborative dialectic between reason and sensibility at the end of the decade owes much to a genuine conversation with Wollstonecraft, as opposed to a mere revision of her thought to suit the needs of his own gendered narrative.

In the *Memoirs*, Godwin carefully positions her early development simultaneously within and against the rational Dissent of Price, her friend and mentor during the mid 1780s at Newington Green: "Mary had been bred in the principles of the church of England, but her esteem for this venerable preacher led her occasionally to attend upon his public instructions. Her religion was, in reality, little allied to any system of forms; and . . . was founded rather in taste, than in the niceties of polemical discussion" (p. 96). Godwin's terms are clear: on the one side there are the "niceties" of rational, doctrinal debate, and on the other side there is the religion of "taste," a warm faith that needs no forms other than those of the heart, which, often in keeping with Hutcheson's "moral sense," would spontaneously feel and worship what is both divine and right. But these simple terms involve Wollstonecraft in a rich discourse in which the fundamental matters of her feminism in particular and radicalism in general were at stake. Barbara Taylor has persuasively shown that the fulcrum of Wollstonecraft's feminism was a form of faith: "Women's rights . . . are an essential prerequisite to women's redemption."[68] I would supplement this argument, that for Wollstonecraft "Only a free soul can seek and know God,"[69] by proposing that the *means* by which a free soul can seek and know God involve an insistence on extemporaneous feeling that places Wollstonecraft's religion, politics, and aesthetics within the larger field of nonconformist devotion.

The great struggle of Wollstonecraft's career was to transform sensibility from the end into the foundation of female subjectivity. Catherine Parke thus refers to "her conception of sensibility as the ground of thinking,"[70] and it is important to remember that for Wollstonecraft sensibility was always something close to Samuel Johnson's definitions, "Quickness of sensation" or "Quickness of perception."[71] In her early works, this spontaneous quickening of ideas and feelings in response to experience serves as a form of discriminating intelligence, often (following Shaftesbury) called "taste" or "relish," and distinct from the judgment. In "The Cave of Fancy" (dated 1787 by Godwin), Sagestus defines sensibility as "the result of acute senses, finely fashioned nerves, which vibrate at the slightest touch, and convey such clear intelligence to the brain, that it does not require to be arranged by the judgment" (*WMW*, I, p. 201). The senses are thus a form of immediate and spontaneous intelligence, and their intuitive vibrations are often associated with religious devotion. Describing her protagonist's youth in *Mary, a Fiction* (1788), Wollstonecraft writes, "Sublime ideas filled her young mind – always connected with devotional sentiments; extemporary effusions of gratitude, and rhapsodies of praise would burst often from her, when she listened to the birds" (*WMW*, I, p. 11). In her two polemics, however, Wollstonecraft needed to call for the judgment to assert itself over excessive, simultaneously effeminate and Burkean emotion, and thus in the *Rights of Woman* she repeats Johnson's definition of sensibility, concluding,

the definition gives me no other idea than of the most exquisitely polished instinct. I discern not a trace of the image of God in either sensation or matter . . .

I come round to my old argument; if woman be allowed to have an immortal soul, she must have, as the employment of life, an understanding to improve. (*WMW*, v, p. 132)

Although such attacks on sensibility are indispensable to her two *Vindications*, they are not wholly incompatible with her early panegyrics, which return in a more sophisticated form in her later works. Throughout her writings, without sensation there is no "understanding to improve," and thus no possibility of redemption. Sensibility, in fact, becomes the basic mechanism implanted by God in the human heart that allows the understanding to develop. In the *Vindications*, women and the various faces of Burkean ideology are all sensation, as if the means were the end. But in both *The Rights of Woman* and her important late essay "On Poetry, and our Relish for the Beauties of Nature" (1797), Wollstone-craft's combination of affective spontaneity and anti-sectarianism leads her to articulate, and subsequently to represent for Godwin, a nuanced synthesis of the rational and intuitive faculties that exceeds the common opposition found throughout much Jacobin and anti-Jacobin discourse.

Wollstonecraft's lapsed Anglican disposition owed much both to the rational Unitarianism of Joseph Johnson's London circle and *Analytical Review* as well as to the more affective Dissenting traditions which, we have seen, appealed to a range of moderate, heterodox nonconformists. But if her devotional taste was akin to that of moderate Dissenters, her anti-sectarianism combined with her feminism to distance her from, and provoke her critiques of, nonconformist communities and practices. Understanding this aspect of her thought, Godwin stresses the personal nature of her faith, insisting that "her religion was almost entirely of her own creation," that "The tenets of her system were the growth of her own moral taste" (*CN*, 1, p. 96). Tilottama Rajan is right to propose that Godwin "de-anglicizes Wollstonecraft by stressing sensibility rather than propriety,"[72] but at the same time his account distances her from organ-ized Dissent by insisting that her personal religion took the place of adherence to the practices of any particular sect: "no person . . . [who] is not the zealous partizan of a sect, can bring himself to conform to the . . . regular routine of sermons and prayers" (*CN*, 1, p. 96).

Behind Godwin's descriptions is the truth that for Wollstonecraft rational Dissent, like the Church, was limited by its lack of affective spontaneity, a lack she finds conspicuous in so-called women of sensibility as well. It is a too seldom observed fact that the *Rights of Woman* ends with a comparison of "the Dissenting and female world" (*WMW*, v, p. 266):

From the tyranny of man . . . the greater number of female follies proceed; and the cunning, which . . . makes at present a part of their character . . . is produced by oppression.

Were not dissenters, for instance, a class of people . . . characterized by cunning? And may I not lay some stress on this fact to prove, that when any power but reason curbs the free spirit of man, dissimulation is practised, and the various shifts of art are naturally called forth? (*WMW*, v, p. 265)

"Cunning," "dissimulation," and the "shifts of art" are precisely the modes of expression that disguise affectation as originality, premeditated display as spontaneity, and self-interest as genuine, "rational" sensibility. Just as a preacher should "habitually feel" the matter of the sermon, as Robert Robinson urged, before delivering it spontaneously yet rationally from the heart, so human beings should express devotional feelings without regard to any of the various manifestations of prejudice or patriotism, for nation, family, or sect. The key to Wollstonecraft's mix of religious nonconformity and political radicalism, I think, is this anti-sectarianism: for Wollstonecraft the identification with a sect, like the identification with a family or a nation, is a form of prejudice, unless the sect, family (read "father"), or nation ("King") has earned the love of its members or subjects, as God should be respected because he has earned the love of his creations, not because he is omnipotent. Thus the comparison between women and Dissenters continues: "I know how many ornaments to human nature have been enrolled amongst sectaries; yet, I assert, that the same narrow prejudice for their sect, which women have for their families, prevailed in the Dissenting part of the community" (*WMW*, v, p. 266). The prejudice of women for family and Dissenters for sect stifles the "rational" course of feeling for what is just.

Written in the last year of Wollstonecraft's life, "On Poetry" takes this delicate synthesis of reason and emotion as its explicit subject: "It may sound paradoxical . . . to assert, that, though genius be only another word for exquisite sensibility, the first observers of nature, the true poets, exercised their understanding much more than their imitators. But they exercised it to discriminate things, whilst their followers were busy to borrow sentiments and arrange words" (*WMW*, vii, p. 9). The "understanding" discriminates "things" – it is a form of perception – and what separates genius from dullness is originality and spontaneity, precisely what Wollstonecraft notoriously finds absent from women of sensibility and so many female novelists, as well as from Dissenting sectaries. Thus true poetry is "the transcript of immediate sensations, in all their native wildness and simplicity . . . At such moments, sensibility quickly furnishes similes, and the sublimated spirits combine images, which rising spontaneously, it is not necessary coldly to ransack the understanding or memory, till the laborious

efforts of judgment exclude present sensations, and damp the fire of enthusiasm" (*WMW*, VII, p. 7). Genuine sensibility is the faculty that spontaneously transforms sensation into expression, and that expression, when
original – not scripted by convention or prejudiced by allegiance to a sect –
is simultaneously art and devotion, a Wollstonecraftian religious aesthetic,
at once nonconformist and anti-sectarian. This aesthetic balances its competing terms of reason and emotion, the understanding and spontaneous
originality: "grand and sublime images strike the imagination – God is seen
in every floating cloud, and comes from the misty mountain to receive
the noblest homage of an intelligent creature – praise . . . These are not the
weak responses of ceremonial devotion; nor, to express them, would the
poet need another poet's aid: his heart burns within him, and he speaks
the language of truth and nature with resistless energy" (*WMW*, VII, p. 8).

   In the *Memoirs*, writes Myers, "Wollstonecraft is treated both as personality and as principle, at once individual woman and symbol of
cultural values, even of an alternate cognitive mode," and the narrative
is "a marital idyll of complementary reciprocity, mutual interdepend-
ence."[73] I wish to stress along with Philp, however, that Godwin's "conversion" to the "new man of feeling" is not a sudden occurrence of
1798–99 rooted in his reflections on the personality and principle of
Wollstonecraft.[74] Godwin's "marital idyll," accordingly, should be seen
as a moment of clarity within a complex process of political and artistic
development, one foundation of which I am placing in the scenes of
conversation Godwin scripted for himself and others sympathetic to the
cause of reform. Godwin and Wollstonecraft together represent a form of
social and intellectual collaboration the polite literary productions of
which would engage numerous individuals emotionally and rationally,
would communicate to large communities the dynamism of reform along
with the ballast of temperate reflection. Although a conjugal conversation,
Godwin's representation of himself and Wollstonecraft in the *Memoirs*
leaves us with more than a simple gendered opposition between reason
and emotion; for both characters, sensibility has to become the individual
ground or basis of rational thought. In the narrative, Wollstonecraft's
spontaneous and affective yet anti-sectarian religion allows her to achieve
this position on her own, and it is conversation with such an individual
that renovates the character of Godwin, a renovation we have already seen
commencing in the writings of the author Godwin, in his returns to the
religious rhetoric of Dissenting conversation and to the sensibility of his
nonconformist sermons.

CHAPTER 5

"Properer for a Sermon": *Coleridgean ministries*

Acquainted in some way with nearly every contemporary figure mentioned in this book, Samuel Taylor Coleridge presents a rewarding case for the study of early Romantic religious Dissent and dissident publicity. From Cambridge in 1794 to his departure for Germany in 1798, Coleridge's Unitarianism informed his fundamental conceptions of community first in the Pantisocracy scheme, the Bristol lectures, and *The Watchman* and then, most enduringly, in the experimental conversation poems which followed. Religious Dissent, however, has too uniformly been applied as a primary context for Coleridge's early development. His Unitarian nonconformity, on the contrary, needs to be understood as in important ways opposed to the public sphere of heterodox Dissenters presented in this study. The public in which Coleridge's radically egalitarian forms of communication would take place developed both within and against the middle-class Dissenting culture opened to Coleridge by his Unitarian beliefs, writings, and oratory.

Throughout the first half of the eighteenth century "old Dissent" comprised the three major denominations of Presbyterians, Independents, and Baptists, but by the end of the century Unitarianism and "new Dissent," Methodism, had augmented the ranks of nonconformity. The Evangelical Revival, furthermore, was beginning to spread from Methodism, especially from Calvinistic Methodism, as well as from Evangelical elements within the Church of England, to energize the older denominations, the orthodox branches in particular. Overlooking tensions between older and newer forms of Dissent, and between heterodox and orthodox communities, literary critics interested in Coleridge's Unitarianism have too often treated Dissenters as a uniform body distinct from the Established Church of England. Coleridge's early career, however, manifests a dissidence alien to the interests and languages of old Dissent as it evolved into the mainstream of Unitarianism. His lectures and conversation poems anticipate the early Romantic figure of Coleridge we associate with his later self-representations in his letters and the *Biographia*; in the 1790s, however, the disinterested persona and public imagined by Coleridge in his political, religious, and poetic writings emerge not from a latent German idealism but from Coleridge's Unitarian rejection of the habitus of rational Dissent, especially with respect to its commercialist nature.

A well-known turning point in Coleridge's early career is January 1798, when the young poet, lecturer, journalist, and preacher received the offer of a £150 annuity from the Wedgwood family. At the time, Coleridge was preparing to accept the position of minister to the Unitarian chapel at Shrewsbury, which came with a salary of £120 and a house worth £30 rent. Shrewsbury was connected to the canal system of the Midlands and North West England by the Ellesmere Canal, which passed from Shropshire northwards into the Mersey River, on which Warrington lies (see Figure 5), and Coleridge's acceptance of the Shrewsbury ministry thus would have placed him physically and symbolically within the network of commercial Dissenters who dominated the economic and intellectual life of the region. To this culture, the Wedgwoods' annuity seemed to offer an alternative. On 16 January 1798, two days after preaching the morning and afternoon sermons at the Unitarian chapel in Shrewsbury, Coleridge wrote from the house of William Hazlitt, Sr., Unitarian minister in nearby Wem, to his friend John Prior Estlin, the Unitarian minister of Lewin's Mead chapel in Bristol, "In a letter full of elevated sentiments Mr Josiah Wedgwood offers me from himself & his brother Thomas Wedgwood 'an annuity of 150£ for life, legally secured to me, *no condition whatever being annexed*'" (*CL*, 1, p. 370). Although based in Bristol, Estlin well understood the nature of Coleridge's situation, for Estlin himself had been a student at the Warrington Academy from 1764–70. Indeed, Estlin's *The Nature and the Causes of Atheism*, published the year before in 1797, begins with a quotation from Coleridge's "The Destiny of Nations," is dedicated to Rochemont Barbauld, and ends with a passage from Anna Barbauld's poem "A Summer Evening's Meditation." Coleridge thus turns to Estlin for assistance, writing, it is "clear to me, that as two distinct & incompatible objects are proposed to me, I ought to chuse between them" (*CL*, 1, p. 371). These "incompatible objects" are the Unitarian ministry as a profession and the more independent and disinterested life of a Unitarian philosopher and poet.

The terms in which Coleridge solicits Estlin's advice capture the definition of "interest" that informs Coleridge's responses to Dissent in the 1790s:

Figure 5. "Canals, Rivers, and Roads," from John Aikin, *A Description of the Country from Thirty to Forty Miles round Manchester*. Reproduced by permission of the Library Company of Philadelphia.

"Shall I refuse 150£ a year for life, as certain, as any fortune can be, for (I will call it) another 150£ a year, the attainment of which is not yet certain, and the duration of which is precarious? –"

You answer – "Yes! – the cause of Christianity & practical Religion demands your exertions. The powers of intellect, which God has given you, are given for this very purpose, that they may be employed in promoting the best interests of mankind." (*CL*, I, p. 371)

For Coleridge's Estlin, religion is a trade to which the practitioner should devote his powers and talents, thereby promoting the "best interests" of the whole. Estlin's advice, Coleridge writes, "should be decisive on my conduct, if I could see any reason why my exertions for Christianity & practical Religion depend . . . on my becoming a stipendiary & regular minister" (*CL*, I, p. 371). Opposed to the interested employment of "a stipendiary & regular" Dissenting minister in Shropshire is the disinterested and innocent, yet still dissident, intellectual life Coleridge envisions as made possible by the annuity.

Although Coleridge claimed in July 1796 that "local and temporary Politics are my aversion" (*CL*, I, p. 222), from 1794 to 1798, the period to which we owe his early poetical productions, Coleridge hardly rejected explicitly political and religious languages and activities in favor of the poetic and hermeneutic writings for which he is most often remembered. Numerous studies have examined Coleridge's political,[1] religious,[2] and philosophical[3] development during the 1790s, and these are the terms I accordingly wish to keep in play.[4] After the Bristol political lectures of February 1795 and the religious lectures of May to June, after the publication of *The Watchman* ceased in May 1796, and especially after the trip to Germany from September 1798 to July 1799, Coleridge's aversion to "local and temporary Politics" seems to accord well with his proclaimed "love of 'the Great', & 'the Whole'" (*CL*, I, p. 354), his devotion to the vast and universal: "My mind feels as if it ached to behold & know something *great – something one* & *indivisible*" (*CL*, I, p. 349). Opposed to the universal is the particular, the "local and temporary," what Coleridge refers to as "*parts* – and all *parts* are necessarily little" (*CL*, I, p. 354). Following the New Historicist critiques of "Romantic ideology" in the 1980s, it has become easy to see this rejection of the particular in favor of the universal as a celebration of the private, internal, and ideal and, conversely, a repression of the public, external, and material.[5] The paradigm of the Romantic poet is thus shaped by the disinterested aesthetic judgment of Kant's third critique, and Coleridge's eventual growth away from his early associationism, Unitarianism, and radicalism comes to represent a retreat from the material interests and political particularities of late-eighteenth-century life. To a significant degree, however, what Coleridge as a Unitarian already rejects in the 1790s is the legacy of old middle-class Dissent, the commercialist culture of Arminian and Arian nonconformity.

COMMERCE AND THE DISSENTING PUBLIC SPHERE

The public sphere most readily open to Coleridge as a Unitarian radical contained strong elements of Dissenting culture, and it is within and against Dissenting forms of publicity that Coleridge first patterns his language of community after leaving Cambridge for Bristol. Coleridge's radical Christianity, which combines his Pantisocratic opposition to property and his anti-Godwinian emphasis on the domestic affections, "joy" or "love," in the formation of a public, necessitates a return to my analysis of the Dissenting public sphere, especially to the role of commerce and property in its reconciliation of interested and disinterested forms of expression. According to Habermas' well-known formulation, "*The fully developed bourgeois public sphere was based on the fictitious identity of the two roles assumed by the privatized individuals who came together to form a public: the role of property owners and the role of human beings pure and simple.*"[6] Terry Eagleton has brought into clear focus the ideological nature of this "fictitious identity." Of the public sphere, Eagleton writes, it is

inconceivable that those without property – without, in the eighteenth-century sense, an "interest" – could participate in this realm. It is not, however, that the public sphere exists for the direct discussion of those interests; on the contrary, such interests become its very concealed problematic, the very enabling structure of its disinterested enquiry. Only those with an interest can be disinterested.[7]

Behind every disinterested enunciation of rational judgment lies the authority to speak about matters of taste and subjectivity. This authority in the eighteenth century materializes not in the court or patron's library but in the coffee-house or salon, and it is engendered not by aristocratic power but by middle-class participation and success in the market economy: "The currency of this realm is neither title nor property but rationality – a rationality in fact articulable only by those with the social interests which property generates."[8]

If bourgeois life in the public sphere sees itself as constituting a disinterested free market of aesthetic judgment, if the bourgeois as natural human being speaks of taste rather than property, commerce, politics, or religion, then the subcategory composed of religious Dissenters presents a somewhat different picture. I have argued that the Dissenting public sphere, because of its peculiar dual position of middle-class economic empowerment and civil marginalization, integrated its commercial, political, and religious interests with the dominant late-eighteenth-century discourse of taste, sensibility, to constitute the language in which it addressed both itself and the national reading public. Whereas the classical public sphere as described by Habermas is now seen by Eagleton and others as the forum and mode in which the emergent middle class ideologically naturalized itself through rational debate in the world of letters, Dissenting critical discourse could and would not so efficiently conceal its interests. Marked by their dissent from the Church of England and their legal proscription but authorized by their commercial success and capital, many Dissenters embraced a form of tempered dissidence that manifested itself in a combination of interested and disinterested rhetorical modes. Dissident almost by definition, marked by separation and opposition, Dissenters naturally spoke, preached, and wrote from the perspective of individuals who, in one sense, could not afford to be disinterested. In another sense, of course, unlike the working-class radicals of the Corresponding Societies in the 1790s, they very well could, and it is this combination of interested and disinterested voices which Coleridge encountered and resisted during the Unitarian phase of his career.

In the pamphlet that provides the epigraph to this book, *An Address to the Opposers of the Repeal of the Corporation and Test Acts* (1790), published anonymously by "A DISSENTER," Anna Barbauld explains the necessary dissidence of Dissent, its "mark of separation," following the third rejection of the movement to repeal Britain's laws barring nonconformists from full participation in civil society: "What we desired, by blending us with the common mass of citizens, would have sunk our relative importance, and consigned our discussions to oblivion. You have refused us; and by so doing, you keep us under the eye of the public, in the interesting point of view of men who suffer under a deprivation of their rights" (*SPP*, p. 272). The partially disenfranchised status of Dissenters "under the eye of the public" places them in an "interesting point of view," but to an important extent that point of view was their own. Aware of their distinctive marks, Dissenters seem almost compelled to promote and celebrate their commercial interests even as they speak the disinterested language of taste. Often the two rhetorical modes are inseparable, as in John Aikin's association of the canal system in North West England with both the "opulence" and "enlarged views" of the commercial class:

The prodigious additions made within a few years to the system of inland navigation, now extended to almost every corner of the kingdom, cannot but impress the mind with magnificent ideas of the opulence, the spirit, and the enlarged views which characterize the commercial interest of this country.

Nothing seems too bold for it to undertake, too difficult for it to atchieve; and should no external changes produce a durable check to the national prosperity, its future progress is beyond the reach of calculation.[9]

When Joseph Johnson's *Analytical Review* came to treat Aikin's *A Description* in November 1795, the reviewer made explicit "The union of taste and science" represented by both the canals themselves and Aikin's encomium on them. For the reviewer, the late eighteenth century "assumes an enlivening aspect, and cheers the spectator with bright images and fair prospects": "In those practical applications of physical science, which contribute to the improvement of agriculture, manufacture, and commerce, and in those exertions of genius and taste, which produce magnificence, elegance and beauty . . . the present age, unquestionably, far surpasses the former."[10] As in Barbauld's "The Canal and the Brook," English progressive history is driven toward its brightest prospects by the engines of science and trade, and science and trade go hand in hand with genius and taste, with magnificence, elegance, and beauty. The languages of interested utility and disinterested taste thus come together in the public self-representations of Dissenters, recalling Barbauld's advice in "Against Inconsistency in our Expectations": "We should consider this world as a great mart of commerce, where fortune exposes to our view various commodities, riches, ease, tranquillity, fame, integrity, knowledge" (*SPP*, p. 188). Here, three years before Adam Smith's *Wealth of Nations* (1776), the principal claim of bourgeois publicity is reversed, and, I would venture, only a liberal Dissenter at this time could have made such an explicit connection between the self-correcting principles of the market and the daily expectations of human life. Rather than merely considering how our interested commercial lives bring us together in a community of equal human beings, we now perceive our interests and our humanity in equally commodified terms: knowledge and integrity, to the same extent as riches, are commodities.

In the second of Barbauld's two pamphlets titled *Civic Sermons to the People* (1792), this double language resonates throughout her paean to social life: "Man, feeble and defenceless in thyself, rejoice that thou art joined to a community! Individuals, rejoice that you are gathered into a public! Its strength becomes your strength, its riches your riches; all its powers of defence to the last man would be drawn out to shield one of your little infants from violence or oppression."[11] The economic interests of the public here blend almost seamlessly into the definitive scene of sensibility, the defenceless infant shielded from a violent oppressor. The collaborative strength of "individuals . . . gathered into a public" is at once calculating and virtuous, in one motion augmenting the nation's wealth and protecting its weaker members. The "problematic" – "Only those with an interest can be disinterested" – to use Eagleton's terms, however, while no longer concealed, is not entirely revealed either: masking competition and inequality as collaboration and progress, the passage explicitly appeals to the middle-class reader's interests and sensibility, his prudence and taste, his dual status as *bourgeois* and *homme*. It is this language that enables John Aikin, in *Address to the Dissenters of England on Their Late Defeat* (1790), to hail his Dissenting readers, "You belong to the most virtuous, the most enlightened, the most independent part of the community, *the middle class.*"[12] To a certain extent this is bourgeois self-congratulation, but in the eighteenth century it is also an assertion of opposition. Although the tempered dissidence of middle-class Dissenting moderates was distinct from the more radical dissidence of the corresponding societies, Isaac Kramnick does well to remind us that the bourgeois radicalism of an emergent middle class in the eighteenth century was very different from the bourgeois conservatism of a triumphant middle class in the twentieth.[13]

Eagleton's Marxist interpretation of eighteenth-century bourgeois publicity does not explore the radicalism of middle-class ideology emphasized by Kramnick and other liberal scholars of Dissent, but Eagleton's overall analysis is nonetheless accurate. The Aikins' alliance of familial collaboration and sensibility on the one hand with provincial commerce and science on the other modulates the harsh keynotes of bourgeois existence – competition and accumulation. Eagleton elucidates the underlying bases of collaboration and rationality in middle-class public life: "Only in this ideal discursive sphere is exchange without domination possible; for to persuade is not to dominate, and to carry one's opinion is more an act of collaboration than of competition . . . What is at stake in the public sphere, according to its own ideological self-image, is not power but reason. Truth, not authority, is its ground, and rationality, not domination, its daily currency."[14] At the forefront of the competitive middle class, Dissenters project this self-image perhaps in its most concise form, and to this extent the Dissenting public sphere may be considered a refinement of the bourgeois public sphere. Their version of Enlightenment publicity, as I hope to have shown, is emphatically collaborative by nature, combining familial literary production with the celebration of middle-class Dissenting religion, politics, and commerce. As truth masks authority and rationality masks domination, for middle-class Dissenters

in particular collaboration masks the competitive nature of the commercial economy in general and the literary market in particular, which, as
Bourdieu's work displays, is itself an important arena of competition for
social and political legitimacy.[15]

The fiction of the solitary genius whose self-reflective poetry explores
and expresses the poetic imagination, the faculty by which the individual
mind synthesizes itself and its objects of thought, can now be seen more
clearly as a rejection not just of collaboration, but of the competition that it
conceals. As Alison Hickey writes, "Collaboration challenges the Coleridgean idea of the work as a reflection of a unitary author."[16] Rather than
return to the matters of Coleridge's ultimately failed collaborations with
Southey, Lamb, and Wordsworth, especially the agon of genius involved in
his relationship with the latter, I want to suggest instead that Coleridgean
"conversation" encodes a kind of "multiple authorship" which is clearly
related to Coleridge's Unitarian thought and oratory but which is distinct
and indeed contrary to bourgeois Dissenting representations of collaborative practices. Coleridge's notions of friendship or "philanthropy" reveal a
conflicted attempt to forge a non-competitive productive community, one
which does not harmonize interest and love but rather effectively transforms self-interest into benevolence within the productive relationship.
Replacing collaboration as practised and represented by Dissenters with
very different forms of sociability, Coleridge's vision of community in the
1790s, from Pantisocracy to the lectures, *The Watchman*, and the conversation poems, is communist-agrarian, domestic, and Unitarian: patterned
after the example of the human Christ, it embodies public discourse
between disinterested and propertyless individuals in close relations of
social affection, in nature, leading to a higher form of communication
with a unified God whose voice speaks through all things. Coleridgean
conversation produces an early Romantic public that seeks alternatives to a
world of getting and spending, of competition, appropriation, and alien-
ation, and its dissident notions of sociability are therefore deeply uncom-
fortable with the kinds of collaboration consistent with the bourgeois
Dissenting response to nonconformity's simultaneous illegitimacy within
the British polity and centrality within the nation's commercial life.

COLERIDGE'S UNITARIANISM, DISSENT, AND DISSIDENCE

The case of Coleridge in the 1790s demands that we treat Dissent in
precise terms if it is to tell us anything new about his early positions and
productions, for several strands of Dissenting religion come together in

the history of Coleridge's early Romanticism. We have already encountered the Arminian and Arian tradition of the Aikin family's Presbyterianism and the ultra-Calvinism of the Particular Baptist Sandemanian sect
with which the young Godwin was affiliated. More extreme in its rationalist creed of Christ's humanity than the Arian Presbyterianism of the
Aikins was the outright Socinianism of the Unitarians, the group with
which Coleridge is commonly identified from his undergraduate experience at Cambridge in early 1794 until his dramatic return to Orthodoxy in
Malta in February 1805. As described in Chapter 2, converts to Unitarianism in the late eighteenth century generally arose from the moderate
Arminian and Arian communities of Presbyterians and General Baptists,
often passing through the Academies, or they converted directly from the
Church of England. The primary cultural distinctions within Unitarianism, then, were between old Dissent and the Church of England, with
Coleridge, of course, emerging from the latter.

Whereas Dissenters like Priestley and Belsham arrived at Socinianism
through nonconformist familial and academic lines, theological debate
and introspection, and active service in the ministry, dissident young
Anglicans such as Coleridge and Southey seem to have been drawn to
Unitarianism for its liberal appeals to free thought and for its anti-
authoritarian associations with political and religious liberty. It was
this seditious edge of Unitarianism that attracted Coleridge, for whom
William Frend's trial at Cambridge in May 1793 for sedition and defam-
ation of the Church served as an introduction to political activism. In the
first issue of *The Watchman*, dated 1 March 1796, Coleridge writes, "the
very act of Dissenting from established opinions must generate habits
precursive to the love of freedom" (*CW*, II, pp. 12–13). For Coleridge,
whose upbringing under his father John Coleridge, vicar of Ottery
St. Mary in Devon, was, as J. Robert Barth puts it, "unexceptionably
Anglican,"[17] Unitarianism could represent the general "habits" of dissidence without bearing the habitus of Dissent. Unlike those who came to
Unitarianism through Dissenting culture, Coleridge can embrace "the
very act of Dissenting" in practically the same terms as those in which
Burke rejects it: responding to Price's sermon, Burke writes, "Let the
noble teachers but dissent, it is no matter from whom or from what. This
great point once secured, it is taken for granted their religion will be
rational and manly."[18] In the absence of the material habitus of old
Dissent, Coleridge's Unitarian Christianity produces a language of dissidence removed from and often opposed to the language of Dissent with
which it is too readily identified. Whereas the middle-class alliance of

Arminian religion with commerce can be traced to the families of old liberal Dissent – as the Warrington alumnus Thomas Barnes put it in 1783, the new academy at Manchester "would contradict the disgraceful idea, that a spirit of merchandize is incompatible with liberal sentiment, and that it only tends to contract and vulgarise the mind"[19] – Coleridge rejects the bourgeois Whig celebration of trade as central to English identity.

If we return to Coleridge's acceptance of the Wedgwood annuity, underlying his reasoning we see an opposition between interested and disinterested, Dissenting and dissident, modes of public engagement. Before the offer of the annuity, Coleridge writes,

Two modes of gaining [a] livelihood were in my power – The press without reference to Religion – & Religion without reference to the Press. – (by the *Press as a Trade* I wish you to understand, reviewing, newspaper-writing, and all those things in which I proposed no fame to myself or permanent good to society – but only to gain that bread which might empower me to do both the one and the other on my vacant days. –) I chose the latter – I preferred, as more *innocent* in the first place, & more *useful* in the second place, the *ministry* as a Trade to the Press as a Trade. – A circumstance arises – & the necessity ceases for my taking up either – that is – as a means of providing myself with the necessaries of Life – Why should I not adopt it? (*CL*, I, p. 372)

Before the Wedgwoods' offer, then, two "trades" were open to Coleridge, the press and the ministry. The former, for Coleridge, produces no "permanent good to society." Had he chosen this path, his "vacant days" alone would have provided the occasion for those activities by which his life would be made productive, and those less interested activities, we can infer, would consist of writing philosophy and poetry. The ministry as a trade, on the other hand, would enable a greater degree of usefulness and a lesser degree of guilt, but the best of all possible situations, that of the disinterested and independent philosopher and poet, demands a complete dissociation of personal life from bourgeois livelihood, from trade, property, and commerce. Whereas the stipendiary minister of Shrewsbury preaches to a congregation of families whose interests and lives are thoroughly grounded in that bourgeois terrain criss-crossed by the canals, the independent scholar writes for an entirely different audience, rooted in different landscapes. This community, far from the Wedgwoods' factories and canals and the Manchester Academy, will see itself reflected in – and in its own imaginings of – the "Sea, hill, and wood" outside Nether Stowey, or the "cloudless, starless lake of blue" by Keswick.[20]

What Barth calls Coleridge's "flirtation with Unitarianism"[21] thus represents a formative stage in his self-construction as a philosopher and poet. This early Romantic figure might be described as a minister with an unconditional annuity instead of a regular stipend, and it would be easy to see in such a pastoral but vocationless calling an early anticipation of what Coleridge will later refer to as the "Clerisy" in *On the Constitution of the Church and State* (1830). But, as Kelvin Everest has argued, Coleridge's ideal community in the 1790s, although it resembles the clerisy in terms of its longing for a small intellectual elite, challenges fundamental aspects of establishment power and culture, whereas the clerisy will invariably support the status quo.[22] The transitions from Coleridge's "small but glorious band . . . of thinking and disinterested Patriots" (*CW*, I, p. 40) in *Conciones ad Populum* (1795) to the conservative clerisy, from Hartleian materialism to Kantian idealism, and from Unitarianism to orthodoxy[23] have been taken to represent various versions of Romantic apostasy, disenchantment, reversal, disillusionment, and retreat. Although readers of Coleridge have benefited from critical assessments of this tell-tale Romantic narrative, aptly named "the Bishop of Llandaff's slide" by E. P. Thompson,[24] my present purpose is to understand Coleridge's Unitarianism in the 1790s on its own terms, and these are the terms of his Socinian, Hartleian, and egalitarian nonconformity.

PERFECT EQUALITY AND THE DOMESTIC AFFECTIONS

When Coleridge arrived in Bristol from Cambridge in August 1795, the Pantisocracy scheme already embraced the two keys to Coleridge's radical socio-political thought: agrarian communism and the private attachments of domestic life. Pantisocracy, in its most basic form, would be a rural community structured by communism and love. Behind these two ideals, however, lies the deeper religious devotion that becomes the pervasive note of Coleridge's early poetry. The ultimate goal of this propertyless community of individuals bound together in nature by the private affections would be to hear and speak the language of God, which for Coleridge is drowned out by the noises of commerce, by cities and their competitive communities. For Coleridge throughout the 1790s, as he baldly puts it in the second lecture on revealed religion (1795), "Property is Power and equal Property equal Power" (*CW*, I, p. 126). In a letter to Thelwall a year later, Coleridge reiterates, "The real source of inconstancy, depravity, & prostitution, is *Property*, which mixes with & poisons every thing good – & is beyond a doubt the Origin of all Evil" (*CL*, I, p. 214). Only in the absence of property will what Coleridge refers to as private attachments unite individuals in disinterested familial communities, and this non-competitive ideal forms the basis of Coleridge's political and religious lectures in Bristol during 1795 and of *The Watchman* in the following year. In the lectures, the Pantisocratic combination of anti-commercialist communism and love within domestic societies merges explicitly with the teachings and example of the human Jesus; the basic structure of the Pantisocracy scheme thus develops into Unitarian Christianity.

Because Pantisocracy has been described in detail many times, I will only provide a brief sketch of its basis in agrarian communism and the domestic affections.[25] From Cambridge in August 1794, Coleridge writes to a prospective participant, Charles Heath, "A small but liberalized party have formed a scheme of emigration on the principles of an abolition of individual property" (*CL*, I, p. 96). In a light-hearted letter to Southey, Coleridge coins the verb "aspheterize" – to make not one's own – for the action that the Pantisocracy scheme will perform upon "the bounties of nature" (*CL*, I, p. 84), and John Morrow accurately calls Pantisocracy a "system of non-property . . . a system which avoided property, not one based on legally regulated equality."[26] As George Burnett makes clear in a retrospective letter written in October 1796, Coleridge and Southey came to see individual property as the cause of moral depravity; "Our grand object then was, the Abolition of Property; at least of individual property. Conceiving the present unequal distribution of property, to be the source of by far the greater part of the moral evil that prevails in the world; by the removal of the *cause*, we thought, and as it appears to me justly thought, that the *effect* must also cease."[27] In order to remove the cause, Coleridge also had to remove the thirty-eighth Article of the Church of England, which states that "The riches and goods of Christians are not common, as touching the right, title, and possession of the same, as certain Anabaptists do falsely boast."[28] The ideal setting for the system of non-property would be a small farming community: Coleridge and Southey decided to settle on the Susquehanna Valley in central Pennsylvania, with Priestley's example in mind, and Coleridge writes that in the course of the winter of 1794 the group intended "to learn the theory and practice of agriculture and carpentry" (*CL*, I, p. 97).

In 1794, Pantisocracy extracts the Godwinian ideal of the select community, "a small but liberalized party," and combines it with the Hartleian benevolence inherent in familial attachments. To Southey in October 1794, Coleridge writes, "In the book of Pantisocracy I hope to have comprised all that is good in Godwin" (*CL*, I, p. 115). All that is not good in Godwin, "the Stoical Morality which disclaims all the duties of

Gratitude and domestic Affection" (*CW*, i, p. 164), will be replaced by a Pantisocratic model of domestic attachments, indebted instead to Hartley's concept of "Sociality." For Hartley, sociality is "the Pleasure which we take in the mere Company and Conversation of others, particularly of our Friends and Acquaintance, and which is attended with mutual Affability, Complaisance, and Candour."[29] Children associate the presence of "Parents, Attendants, or Play fellows" with pleasure, and thus "according to the Doctrine of Association, Children ought to be pleased, in general, with the Sight and Company of all their Acquaintance" (i, p. 472). The "Affections by which we rejoice at the Happiness of others" (i, p. 472), and thereby associate the pleasures of others with our own, lead us to equate self-interest with benevolence, or as Coleridge sometimes calls it, "Philanthropy." Coleridge memorably borrows from this Hartleian process in an early letter to Southey, written in July 1794: "The ardour of private Attachments makes Philanthropy a necessary *habit* of the Soul. I love my *Friend* – such as *he* is, all mankind are or *might* be! The deduction is evident –. Philanthropy (and indeed every other Virtue) is a thing of *Concretion* – Some home-born Feeling is the *center* of the Ball, that, rolling on thro' Life collects and assimilates every congenial Affection" (*CL*, i, p. 86). Philanthropy is a "thing of *Concretion*," and the process of concretion depends on the rolling energy generated by the "home-born Feeling" at the center of the ball. As for Hartley, familial relations in the home provide the origin and engine of benevolence.

Southey, the faithful Godwinian in 1794–95, would remove any reference to the familial unit from the Pantisocratic ideal, but Coleridge insists on maintaining the family as a social principle, so long as individual property does not divert "home-born feelings" from their benevolent course into more selfish channels. In a letter intended on the surface to dissuade Southey from accepting his uncle's advice that he enter the Church, and on a deeper level to counter the selfish principle Coleridge feared was becoming foremost in Southey's character, Coleridge makes an important distinction between retrograde and progressive forms of domesticity: "Domestic Happiness is the greatest of things sublunary – . . . but it is not strange that those things, which in a pure form of Society will constitute our first blessings, should in it's [*sic*] present state, be our most perilous Temptations!" (*CL*, i, p. 158). The family as constituted in contemporary English society too readily lends itself to corruption by the acquisition of property. If for Wollstonecraft love for family could correspond to prejudice for sect or nation, for Coleridge love for family too quickly becomes love of gain, and love for others thus a mere extension of self-interest. Kelvin Everest accordingly writes, "Pantisocracy was not simply an elaborate rationalisation of the ideal of familial community . . . but involved a differentiation between kinds of domesticity."[30] In the Pantisocracy scheme, then, agrarian communism would permit private attachments to function according to the Hartleian associationist process that leads from self-love to benevolence, and only then could the family become a progressive agent of change.

In 1795, as Coleridge prepares and delivers his political and religious lectures, this combination becomes with increasing clarity the defining feature of Coleridge's radical Christianity. The teachings of Jesus describe the communism and love that will structure a revolutionary and benevolent "pure form" of society. If in 1794 the figurative "book of Pantisocracy" would comprise all that is good in Godwin, a year later Coleridge begins to substitute the New Testament for the book of Pantisocracy as the text that contains and surpasses the virtues of *Political Justice*. Throughout this period Coleridge repeatedly mentions his desire to write a response to Godwin; a letter to Thelwall in late 1796 begins, "Enough . . . of Theology. In my book on Godwin I compare the two Systems – his & Jesus's" (*CL*, I, p. 293).[31] The book was never written, but it is nonetheless clear what its argument would have been. Whereas many liberals and radicals such as Southey, Wordsworth, and Thelwall for a time found in *Political Justice* a philosophy "That promised to abstract the hopes of man / Out of his feelings, to be fixed thenceforth / For ever in a purer element" (*The Prelude*, 1805),[32] Coleridge turned to his own brand of Socinian Christianity for the foundation of feeling absent from Godwin's stoic philosophy of rational perfectibility. *Political Justice*, Coleridge writes in the third lecture on revealed religion, is insufficient and dangerous because it "discovers a total ignorance of that obvious Fact in human nature that in virtue and in knowledge we must be infants and be nourished with milk in order that we may be men and eat strong meat" (*CW*, I, p. 164).

The Socinian figure of Jesus not as a God to be worshipped but as a domestic human being, a son and friend, a "Man of Woes . . . whose life was Love!" (lines 8–29) as Coleridge calls him in "Religious Musings," provides the source and pattern of Coleridge's Unitarian faith. In the third religious lecture, this figure consequently emerges as the Hartleian principle of concretion at the center of the ball: "We find in Jesus nothing of that Pride which affects to inculcate benevolence while it does away every home-born Feeling, by which it is produced and nurtured . . . Jesus was a Son, and he cast the Eye of Tenderness and careful regard on his

Mother Mary, even while agonizing on the Cross. Jesus was a Friend, and he wept at the Tomb of Lazarus" (*CW*, 1, pp. 162–63). Coleridge returns to the "home-born Feeling" and explicitly describes his faith in terms of Hartleian associationism. Jesus is the son, parent, and friend, the man of sensibility who pays the passing tribute of a sigh at the tomb of Lazarus. He is the essence of sociality: "Jesus knew our Nature – and that expands like the circles of a Lake – the Love of our Friends, parents and neighbours lead[s] us to the love of our Country to the love of all Mankind" (*CW*, 1, p. 163).[33]

In Coleridge's fifth lecture on revealed religion, delivered in early June 1795 in Bristol, Coleridge presents his Socinian Christianity in more radical terms, bringing together familial affections and "perfect Equality": "That there is one God infinitely wise, powerful and good, and that a future state of Retribution is made certain by the Resurrection of Jesus who is the Messiah – are all the *doctrines* of the Gospel. That Christians must behave towards the majority with loving kindness and submission preserving among themselves a perfect Equality is a Synopsis of its Precepts" (*CW*, 1, p. 195). Coleridge rejects "the pernicious dogma of Redemption" (*CW*, 1, p. 212), general or particular, and dismisses establishmentarian attempts to make the Trinity palatable to rational Christians as "the mysterious cookery of the Orthodox" (*CW*, 1, pp. 207–8). Thus far Coleridge's Unitarianism corresponds to that of Priestley and the majority of Socinian Dissenters, but Coleridge means his audience to take him literally in his determination that, in addition to "loving kindness," Christians must preserve among themselves a "perfect Equality." Although Godwin and Priestley both favor a more equitable distribution of goods through the progressive enlightening of the populace, neither is interested in the abolition of property. Priestley grounds his hopes for greater material equality in equality of rights, but, as Patton and Mann put it, "equality of goods he thought impracticable and unnecessary and of course an idea contrary to the spirit of commerce" (*CW*, 1, p. lxiv). Godwin, who rejects positive rights for moral duties, proposes in *Political Justice* that inequality of property should gradually diminish "not by law, regulation or public institution, but only through the private conviction of individuals" (*PPW*, III, p. 473). Coleridge, on the other hand, whose Christian beliefs diverged from both the commercialist culture of Priestley's Unitarianism and the secular rationalism of Godwin's qualified form of atheism, accepts the words of Acts 2:44–45 in their entirety: "And all that believed were together, and had all things common; And sold their possessions and goods, and parted them to all *men*, as every man had need."

Speaking at the Assembly Coffee-House in Bristol in early June 1796, Coleridge did not mince his words, asserting in his sixth lecture on revealed religion that "Jesus Christ forbids to his disciples all property – and teaches us that accumulation was incompatible with their Salvation!" (*CW*, i, p. 226). In the lecture, he arrives at this position through a lengthy discussion of the evils of commerce:

> Commerce . . . is useless except to continue Imposture and oppression. Its Evils are vast and various . . . The smoakes [*sic*] that rise from our crowded Towns hide from us the face of Heaven. In the country, the Love and Power of the great Invisible are everywhere perspicuous, and by degrees we become partakers of that which we are accustomed to contemplate. The Beautiful and the Good are miniatured on the Heart of the Contemplator as the surrounding Landscape on a Convex Mirror. But in Cities God is everywhere removed from our Sight and Man obtruded upon us – not Man, the work of God, but the debased offspring of Luxury and Want. (*CW*, i, pp. 223–25)

As we will see in Coleridge's Unitarian preaching and in the conversation poems, if the immediate effect of commerce is to debase human beings by fostering the selfish principle, its final effect is to distort perception itself, specifically perception of the divine in nature. In the absence of property, the heart functions as a convex mirror, as a Claude Glass that reduces, concentrates, and clarifies the beautiful and the good.[34] It is not inequality that prevents human beings from perceiving and contemplating the divine but rather the replacement of the divine by our own competitive and appropriating selves. Whereas Godwin and Priestley advocate equalization of property, then, Coleridge's sixth lecture concludes, "Our Saviour by no means authorizes an Equalization of Property," but rather an abolition of property and the common possession of goods: "While I possess anything exclusively mine, the selfish Passions will have full play" (*CW*, i, pp. 227–28).

From the Wedgwoods' realized Etruria to the radically egalitarian and communist "Spensonia" of Thomas Spence and the Spenceans, Enlightenment experimentalism combined with forms of religious belief and sociability to produce deeply principled minorities with distinct models of public life. Unlike either Dissenting visions of utility and taste or the sudden and fantastic images of Messianic millenarianism, Coleridge's utopian minority insists on the gradual and peaceful absorption of "kindred minds" through the very practical and concrete system presented to Coleridge by Unitarian Christianity and familial life made disinterested by the abolition of property and all its perversions. This life structures the "glorious band," a public imagined and preached in Coleridge's first political lecture; although inseparable from his Socinian beliefs, it is a public explicitly conceived in opposition to religious Dissenters.

In his political lecture delivered in late January or early February 1795, Coleridge divides "the professed Friends of Liberty" (*CW*, 1, p. 37) into four classes.[35] The first class is composed of "*dough-baked Patriots*" who unreflectingly "give an indolent Vote in favour of Reform" (*CW*, 1, pp. 37–38). The next refers to the working-class members of the corresponding societies and the audiences at Thelwall's lectures: "Wilder features characterize the second class . . . they listen only to the inflammatory harangues of some mad-headed Enthusiast, and imbibe from them Poison, not Food; Rage, not Liberty" (*CW*, 1, p. 38). The third, considerably less wild, is composed of Dissenting middle-class reformers:

> They pursue the interests of Freedom steadily, but with narrow and self-centering views: they anticipate with exultation the abolition of privileged orders, and of Acts that persecute by exclusion from the right of citizenship . . . Whatever is above them they are most willing to drag down; but every proposed alteration, that would elevate the ranks of our poorer brethren, they regard with suspicious jealousy, as the dreams of the visionary. (*CW*, 1, p. 39)

The "Acts that persecute by exclusion" are the Corporation and Test Acts, and the "narrow and self-centering views" are those of middle-class culture that Coleridge would have known from the Dissenting circles opened to him by his Unitarianism. Like "Gunpowder Priestley," who endorsed capital punishment (and torture in "atrocious cases") as the best means of inspiring "terror" in would-be criminals, and who opposed the poor laws for encouraging idleness and profligacy, these reformers are radical only with respect to the establishment, but the "interests of Freedom" for them often coincide with their own investments, property, and security.[36]

The fourth class, however, contains the potential to absorb the previous three into a new social order: "We turn with pleasure to the contemplation of that small but glorious band, whom we may truly distinguish by the name of thinking and disinterested Patriots. These are the men who have encouraged the sympathetic passions till they have become irresistible habits, and made their duty a necessary part of their self-interest" (*CW*, 1, p. 40). Hartleian in terms of their associationist progress from sympathy to benevolence, Godwinian in their equation of duty and self-interest, these patriots provide a model of equality that will gradually make kindred minds of the wavering reformers, the incendiary working-classes, and the narrow and self-centered Dissenting tradesmen. The political and philosophical process of absorbing these kindred minds, furthermore, resonates with the vocabulary of nature that for Coleridge always opens out to religious experience: "Accustomed to regard all the affairs of man as a process, they never hurry and they never pause. Theirs is not that twilight of political knowledge which gives us just light enough to place one foot before the other; as they advance the scene still opens upon them, and they press right onward with a vast and various landscape of existence around them" (*CW*, I, p. 40). This "vast and various land-scape" provides the setting for the affairs of men regarded not as the competitive dealings of bourgeois Dissenters but as the disinterested actions of human beings pure and simple, as the conversation through which, in Coleridge's preaching and poetry, philanthropy can reform individual auditors and readers, and God's love can express itself as enlightenment, benevolence, and omnipresence.

PERFORMING MINISTRIES: PUBLIC AND SECRET

On the morning of 14 January 1798, two days before Coleridge and Josiah Wedgwood's letter would converge at the house of William Hazlitt, Sr. in Wem, the Unitarian minister's nineteen year-old son walked ten miles from Wem to Shrewsbury. Our most detailed account of Coleridge's preaching comes from William Hazlitt, who made sure to be among the auditors of Coleridge's probationary sermon delivered at the denomina-tionally Presbyterian Unitarian High Street Chapel, where Coleridge was a candidate for the position of ministerial assistant. In Hazlitt's account of his performance, Coleridge presents a strikingly unusual figure in the Unitarian pulpit: "His hair . . . was then black and glossy as the raven's, and fell in smooth masses over his forehead. This long hair is peculiar to enthusiasts, to those whose minds tend heavenward: and is traditionally inseparable (though of a different colour) from the pictures of Christ. It ought to belong, as a character, to all who preach Christ crucified, and Coleridge was at that time one of those!"[37]

Throughout his description, Hazlitt emphasizes Coleridge's physical presence and gestures, and the figure who emerges resembles less a typical Unitarian preacher or rational Dissenter than an enthusiast who addresses the eyes and ears as well as the reason. Thus Hazlitt recalls, "Mr Coleridge rose and gave out his text, 'And he went up into the mountain to pray, HIMSELF, ALONE.' As he gave out this text, his voice 'rose like a steam of rich distilled perfumes,' and when he came to the two last words which he pronounced loud, deep, and distinct, it seemed to me . . . as if the sounds had echoed from the bottom of the human heart" (p. 96). "*As Face answers Face in the Glass, so the Heart of one Man answers to another,*" Isaac Watts proposed in *An Humble Attempt toward the Revival of Practical Religion among Christians,* and emanating from the face and heart of this preacher would have been an unusual set of features and feelings for this congregation to answer.[38] Thus according to Hazlitt, who was not only the son of a Unitarian minister but from 1793–95 had been the student of the Socinian Kippis at the Hackney New College, "A poet and a philosopher getting up into a Unitarian pulpit to preach the Gospel, was a romance in these degenerate days, a sort of revival of the primitive spirit of Christianity, which was not to be resisted."[39] To Unitarians of Shropshire the anti-establishmentarian and libertarian politics of Coleridge's Jacobin sermon would have seemed perfectly familiar – "The sermon was upon peace and war; upon church and state – not their alliance, but their separation – on the spirit of the world and the spirit of Christianity, not as the same, but as opposed to one another" (IX, p. 96). The enthusiasm of the poet-philosopher-preacher, however, would have been novel – "Poetry and Philosophy had met together," for Hazlitt, "under the eye and with the sanction of Religion" (IX, p. 97). Like the "glorious band," and like the conversation poems written during this same period, Coleridge's preaching can be understood as an attempt to reform a public explicitly associated with commercial Dissent.

To Josiah Wade, Coleridge wrote in mid January 1796, "Yesterday I preached twice . . . There were about fourteen hundred present, and my sermons, (great part extempore) were *preciously peppered with Politics*" (*CL*, I, p. 126). His only Unitarian sermon which has survived largely complete was preached soon afterwards, on 31 January 1796, before the High Pavement Chapel in Nottingham, while Coleridge was attempting to raise funds for *The Watchman.* It was delivered partially extempore, and in it Coleridge synthesized many passages from the Bristol lectures on revealed religion, attempting, in effect, to prepare his Unitarian audience to answer the benevolent face and heart of the enthusiastic poet-philosopher-preacher captured in Hazlitt's later description.[40] In a letter written to his brother George in late 1794, Coleridge discusses "the best conceivable mode of meliorating Society," concluding, "Talk not of Politics – *Preach the Gospel!*" (*CL*, I, p. 126). Preaching the gospel of 1 Peter 2:21, "For even hereunto were ye called, because Christ also suffered for us, leaving us an example that ye should follow his steps," Coleridge opened his partially extempore sermon to a congregation of Nottingham's middle-class rational Dissenters as follows: "When Death shall have closed my eye-lids, must I then bid my last farewell to the streams whose murmurs have soothed me, to the fields and woodlands, where I have delighted to wander?" (*CW*, I, p. 349). Having been presented to Nottingham society by the Derby cotton-spinner Jedediah Strutt,[41] Coleridge proceeded to tell the families of Dissenting tradesmen in a commercial town, "when Towns and Cities were built . . . the accumulative system . . . introduced . . . enormous Inequality with its accompanying Vices and miseries" (*CW*, I, p. 350). "In rural scenes," on the other hand, "Love and Power are everywhere conspicuous and by degrees we become partakers of that which we are accustomed to contemplate. The Beautiful and the Good of Creation are miniatured on our Hearts, as the surrounding Landscape on a convex mirror" (*CW*, I, p. 350). In the sermon, members of the Dissenting audience are supposed to forego self-interest and become partakers and reflections of that which they are contemplating, the face of the enthusiastic poet-philosopher-preacher whose own heart, like a convex mirror, has already had the Beautiful and the Good of Creation miniatured on it. The end of this triangular and collaborative process of reflection is political and personal renovation, the replacement of the "accumulative system" and its interior correlate, self-interest, with another system, that of the egalitarian and communist Christ, and its interior correlate, disinterested benevolence.

After his Shrewsbury sermon, Coleridge mentioned that "One shrewd fellow remarked that he would rather hear me *talk* than *preach*" (*CL*, I, p. 375). From the descriptions we have of Coleridge's public speaking, his own writings about religious oratory, and his Nottingham sermon, it is clear that he did not fit the mold of the Unitarian preacher. Like his experimental conversation poems, written at the same time as he was composing weekly sermons, his experimental religious oratory was deeply concerned with the spontaneous renovation, and radicalization, of individual hearts and minds.

The rhetorical mode perfected in the conversation poems has justly received much critical attention, for it has come to represent the evolution of the prospect poetry of Denham, Pope, and Gray and the informal style of Cowper and Akenside into the Romantic lyric. The early Romantic quality of this lyric poetry, then, has been seen as its attempt to bridge the gap between thought and nature, subject and object, in order to produce the third and higher term of the Romantic imagination.[42] This dialectic of interior mind and external world, "the Romantic interfusion of subject and object," is of course the defining feature of M. H. Abrams' greater Romantic lyric.[43] For Abrams, the sonnets of Bowles provide Coleridge

with an important but ultimately insufficient fusion of the mind and
nature. Bowles' sonnets, writes Coleridge, "create a sweet and indissoluble
union between the intellectual and the material world,"[44] but in the
conversation poems, according to Abrams, Coleridge's *"co-adunating
Faculty"* (*CL*, II, p. 866) produces an art that transcends the mere fancy
of Bowles' sonnets. The imaginative dialectic of mind and nature absent
from Bowles leads Coleridge to the higher assertion of "one life within us
and abroad," as famously expressed in "The Eolian Harp" when revised for
Sibylline Leaves (1817).[45] The philosophical correlate of Coleridge's unified
"one life" theory is the post-Kantian rejection of the materialist duality
between elemental mind and nature. For Abrams the first glimpse of
this Romantic imagination comes in the earliest conversation poems: "Even
in 1797, while Coleridge was still a Hartleian associationist ... he had
expressed his recoil from elementarist thinking."[46] Abrams' seminal argument, persuasive as it is, transports German idealism and Coleridge's
definition of fancy and imagination in the *Biographia Literaria* (1817)
back onto the conversation poems of 1796–1802. In addition to looking
forward, however, "Reflections on Having Left a Place of Retirement" and
its companion poem, "The Eolian Harp," represent an astonishing contemporary synthesis of Coleridge's responses, in the 1790s, to the culture of
old Dissent.

The community imagined by Coleridge in these poems depends on a
mode of religious conversation. So many rhetorical traditions – the
Horatian ode, the pastoral lyric, the loco-descriptive poem, the elegiac
meditation – contribute to the conversational genre that its status as
religious performance bears further examination. Whereas the term "conversation" is generally applied retrospectively from the subtitle of "The
Nightingale" in *Lyrical Ballads* (1798), the Horatian motto to "Reflections
on Having Left a Place of Retirement," the second of Coleridge's meditative poems in blank verse, suggests an important association of the
conversational mode with religious oratory. Completed in March or April
1796 and first published in the *Monthly Magazine* in the following
October, the poem was originally titled "Reflections on entering into
active life. A Poem which affects not to be Poetry." In the second edition
of *Poems* (1797) and thereafter, the title is "Reflections on Having Left a
Place of Retirement," and the motto from Horace, "Sermoni propriora,"
is added. William Keach translates this as "more akin to prose" in his
notes to the poem, and given the 1796 subtitle, "A Poem which affects
not to be Poetry," and Horace's original "propiora" ("nearer to"), such
a translation makes sense.[47] The opposite of poetry, however, is not

necessarily prose. Coleridge's corruption, "prop*r*iora," gives the sense of "properer for," and his translation of the uncorrupted form in his disappointed assessment of Bowles' second volume of poems (1802) confirms the inescapable sense of a religious sermon: "They are 'Sermoni propiora' which I once translated – 'Properer for a Sermon'" (*CL*, II, p. 864).[48] A revised fair copy of "Fears in Solitude," signed "S. T. C.," contains the following note: "N.B. The above is perhaps not Poetry, – but rather a sort of middle thing between Poetry and Oratory – sermoni propriora" (*STC*, p. 466). The Latin *sermo*, furthermore, the word that describes Horace's *Satires*, means not simply "prose" but more precisely "conversation." The conversation poems are composed, then, on the middle ground between poetry and oratory, not between poetry and prose. Whereas the later Coleridge will substitute metaphysics as the counterbalance to poetry, in the 1790s this role is played by Coleridge's religious oratory, his Unitarian preaching and lecturing, his ministerial as well as lay sermons.[49] Just as Coleridge's performances in the pulpit and at the lectern, as we have seen, were radically opposed in both style and content to rational Dissenting culture, which they sought to transform, Coleridge's "conversation" as a trope of literary production needs to be firmly distinguished from Dissenting collaboration.

Clearly companion pieces, "The Eolian Harp" and "Reflections" were written several months apart in 1795–96 and were published back-to-back in *Poems* (1797) and all subsequent editions during Coleridge's lifetime.[50] Both begin with synesthetic descriptions of the cottage in Clevedon and its surrounding smells, sights, and sounds. Jasmine, myrtle, and the murmuring sea initiate processes of interior reflection – philosophical in "The Eolian Harp," social and political in "Reflections" – that lead to statements of piety before the poems complete the rondo form, ending again at the cottage. More overtly than "The Eolian Harp," "Reflections" is about the social and political world in which the triangular process of conversation might renovate a selfish perspective associated with Dissent and transform it into a disinterested and dissident vision.

Both poems initiate their distinctive patterns of expansion and contraction[51] by internal full stops that separate the first two sections. Having described the external world of the cottage and its surroundings, the "white-flower'd Jasmin, and the broad-leav'd Myrtle" (line 4), "The Eolian Harp" contracts in the break within line 12 to the definite object, "that simplest Lute": "The stilly murmur of the distant Sea / Tells us of Silence. And that simplest Lute / Plac'd length-ways in the clasping casement, hark!" (lines 11–13). Marked by a line break in *Sibylline Leaves*,

the contraction to the harp allows the speaker's perspective to expand to
the visionary imagery of "twilight Elfins" and "Faery Land" (lines 21–22).
This interaction between the mind and the immediate exterior world then
contracts the perspective into philosophical reflection upon the process
itself, in the second verse paragraph, where the poet considers how the
previous "idle and flitting phantasies" (line 32) traversed his "indolent and
passive brain" (line 33). The philosophical association of his mind with the
lute – the two objects of contraction – then culminates in the famous
second expansion from nature to God:

> And what if all of animated nature
> Be but organic Harps diversly fram'd,
> That tremble into thought, as o'er them sweeps
> Plastic and vast, one intellectual breeze,
> At once the Soul of each, and God of all? (lines 36–40)

"Reflections" follows this pattern as well, but the internal full stop in line
9 between the opening scene of external nature and the first contraction
leads to a different object of immediate perception in place of the harp:

> Low was our pretty Cot: our tallest rose
> Peeped at the chamber-window. We could hear
> At silent noon, and eve, and early morn,
> The sea's faint murmur. In the open air
> Our Myrtles blossomed; and across the porch
> Thick jasmins twined: the little landscape round
> Was green and woody, and refreshed the eye.
> It was a spot which you might aptly call
> The Valley of Seclusion! Once I saw
> (Hallowing his Sabbath-day by quietness)
> A wealthy son of commerce saunter by,
> Bristowa's citizen . . . (lines 1–12)

Whereas the lute leads the poet to reflect upon the processes of perception
and contemplation, and these meditations produce the philosophical
statement of similitude between the wind-swept harp and the "organic"
harp (line 37) of the poet's mind, "Reflections" replaces the lute with
another responsive object, Bristol's "wealthy son of commerce" who is
"Hallowing his Sabbath-day" by walking out of the crowded town and
into the country. Bristol, wealth, commerce, and the sabbath clearly code
this figure as a Dissenting tradesman, for the associations between
Bristol's commercial and Dissenting class were inescapable: when the
Monthly Magazine for June 1799 sought to explain why Bristolians "have

been stigmatized with a want of taste," the writer proposed that they have
been "described as the sordid devotees of Plutos. Another . . . reason may
be alleged for this singularity: no place contains, in proportion to its
inhabitants so many dissenters."[52] Mercantile greed and Dissenting culture combined, for the London review, to turn Bristol's citizens into dull
and self-interested "sons of commerce," and it is the taste of one of these
sons that Coleridge's poem proceeds to renovate. Line 12 continues:

> methought, it calmed
> His thirst of idle gold, and made him muse
> With wiser feelings: for he paused, and looked
> With a pleased sadness, and gazed all around,
> Then eyed our Cottage, and gazed round again,
> And sighed, and said, it was a Blessed Place.
> And we were blessed. (lines 12–18)

If the harp responds to the wind by producing "long sequacious notes"
(line 19), the son of commerce responds to "The Valley of Seclusion"
(line 9) and its "little landscape" (line 6) with both an internal adjustment
of values, "wiser feelings" (line 14), and a benediction (lines 17–18).
Because he will return to his propertied existence as "Bristowa's citizen,"
the adjustment will not last. But, like the Ancient Mariner, he "blesse[s]
them unaware," and for the moment he does so, he is transformed. From
a member of the third class described in *Conciones ad Populum*, the
Dissenting reformers who are characterized by "narrow and self-centering
views," he becomes at least potentially a member of the fourth, the "small
but glorious band." He has left behind the productive life of Bristol and
entered into another of a very different kind. Each life, however, involves
collaboration, commercial in the case of the former and conversational in
the case of the latter. Here we clearly see the triangular process of
reflection proper to Coleridgean conversation, and "properer for a
sermon": God's agency manifests itself in the valley and in the domesticity
of the poet and his beloved, and the combination of the two interact with
the son of commerce, prompting him to bless both the valley and the
couple. This poem's version of the harp's sequacious notes, the sigh and
blessing elicited from Bristol's transformed citizen by the spot of natural
beauty and domestic love before him, then returns to act upon the poet,
expanding his consciousness to a visionary apprehension of the "viewless
sky-lark's note" (line 19), which the poet translates to his "beloved" (line 22):

> "Such, sweet Girl!
> The inobtrusive song of happiness,

Unearthly minstrelsy! then only heard
When the soul seeks to hear; when all is hushed,
And the heart listens!" (lines 22–26)

In place of the "soft floating witchery of sound" made by the "twilight Elfins" (lines 20–21) in "The Eolian Harp," the "Unearthly minstrelsy" here concludes the out-in-out progression from external nature to immediate object to visionary experience.

But what precisely is the visionary experience in "Reflections on Having Left a Place of Retirement"? It is the result of the poet's perceptions of a Dissenting son of commerce as he views the poet's familial community of loving kindness in surroundings of natural beauty. The scene's beauty calms the citizen's "thirst of idle gold," transforming him temporarily from the interested bourgeois of Bristol's bustling and Dissenting commercial society into the disinterested and philosophical "Eolian" human being who muses wisely and sighs. And these sighs, as they merge with the skylark's song, produce in the poet a reciprocal movement between the inner self and the exterior world: the soul actively "seeks to hear" and the heart "listens," but the external "song of happiness" can only be apprehended if the skylark sings and if "all is hushed." Every moment of communal transformation in the opening of the poem, indeed, is enabled by a form of silence: the poet first mentions himself and his beloved as able to hear "At silent noon . . . / The sea's faint murmur" (lines 3–4); the son of commerce is introduced as "Hallowing his Sabbath-day by quietness" (line 10); and the unearthly minstrelsy of the skylark's "inobtrusive song of happiness" (line 23) is only heard "when all is hushed" (line 25). The visionary experience, then, is a simple statement of contentment spoken to the poet's beloved and enabled by both the internal action of the mind and the external song of nature, an "inobtrusive" song only heard because the rural scene is silent.

Unlike "The Eolian Harp," which proceeds from its first expansion (lines 17–25) to philosophical reflection (lines 26–44), "Reflections" inserts another verse paragraph between the "Unearthly minstrelsy" and the poem's major reflective passage (lines 43–62). In the second paragraph, the poet leaves the Valley of Seclusion with its dell and cottage, but before entering active life he climbs "up the stony mount" (line 27) and looks out upon a scene of sublimity. Again, the perception of definite objects, the sheep, clouds, and rocks of "the goodly scene" (lines 29–32), produces an expansion of perspective. Whereas beauty in the first paragraph acts on the son of commerce, causing him momentarily to forego urban interests for the blessings of rural domestic life, sublimity in the second moves the poet to a vision of the divine. Now looking down from the top of the mount on the same "little landscape" (line 6) and its environs, he exclaims,

> It seemed like Omnipresence! God, methought,
> Had built him there a Temple: the whole World
> Seemed imaged in its vast circumference,
> No wish profaned my overwhelmèd heart.
> Blest hour! It was a luxury, – to be! (lines 38–42)

From this distant and high perspective, opposed to the near landscape of the "low dell" (line 27) is the "vast circumference" of a world in which God is omnipresent. As in the beautiful dell where the son of commerce renounces his thirst for gold, in such a sublime world there can be no wish, no interest, to profane the heart.

The poet's community, before he leaves it to enter active life in the third paragraph, thus unfolds in two stages, the beautiful and the sublime. The "green and woody" (line 7) landscape figures forth the domestic love that moves the son of commerce momentarily to relinquish self-interest for benevolence. The "mount sublime" (line 43) then inspires the poet with a vision of God's omnipresence and another renunciation of interest. The small community of the poet and his two companions – the beloved and, for so long as he is transformed, the Dissenting son of commerce – represents a domestic sphere of love and quiet sociability whose members can hear and speak the language of God because the drone of business has ceased for this silent sabbath day. "Reflections," the least read of the conversation poems, provides perhaps the most precise poetic statement of Coleridge's ideal community: rural, egalitarian, domestic, affective, and enabled by disinterested life that apprehends the omnipresence of God, a disinterested life articulated, as in *Conciones*, through a renovation of Dissent.

But as with Christ's disciples in the religious lectures and the glorious band of *Conciones*, this community represents not a retreat from the world but rather a progressive agent of social and political reform. The poem, after all, is about leaving the Valley of Seclusion and entering active, public life. The central reflective paragraph begins, "Ah! quiet Dell! dear Cot, and mount sublime! / I was constrained to quit you" (lines 43–44). "Reflections," it should be recalled, was written upon Coleridge's return from retirement in Clevedon to active life in Bristol. Specifically, the life to which Coleridge returned was that of late November and December 1795, the period which saw the publication of *Conciones* and the conception of *The Watchman*. Both were considered by Coleridge to be vehicles for religious as well as political discourse: just as Coleridge considered *Conciones* to be a "Lay-sermon," *The Watchman*, begun to finance the Pantisocracy scheme, was intended to imitate England's principal Unitarian journal, Benjamin Flower's *The Cambridge Intelligencer*.[53] Akin to these lay-sermon forms, the conversation poem does not exactly renounce "retirement in favour of humanitarian activity," as a common reading would have it,[54] but rather insists that the community imagined in retirement must provide the model that will absorb kindred spirits through useful participation in public life: "retirement was a complement, rather than an alternative, to political intervention in the 1790s."[55]

Coleridge's transition to this active life next evokes a different Dissenting figure who, unlike "Bristowa's citizen," already embodies both humanitarian benevolence and genuine sensibility. The poet reflects:

> Was it right,
> While my unnumbered brethren toiled and bled,
> That I should dream away the entrusted hours
> On rose-leaf beds, pampering the coward heart
> With feelings all too delicate for use?
> Sweet is the tear that from some Howard's eye
> Drops on the cheek of one he lifts from earth. (lines 44–50)

To "dream away" the hours in the Valley of Seclusion or on the mountain-top is certainly not "right," according to the paragraph's ethos of utility, but this is not to say that the community of retirement is simply to be rejected once the poet arrives among his "unnumbered brethren." The prison reformer John Howard here represents a disinterested Dissenter, a figure of sensibility whose feelings are not "too delicate for use," an active man of feeling who sheds a tear as he assists the infirm and oppressed. Unlike the tears of those "Who sigh for wretchedness, yet shun the wretched, / Nursing in some delicious solitude / Their slothful loves and dainty sympathies!" (lines 57–59), Howard's pious drops portray an affective utility. Love is active, not "slothful"; in retirement it moves the son of commerce to sigh and bless, and so too will it act in public. The paragraph ends: "I therefore go, and join head, heart, and hand, / Active and firm, to fight the bloodless fight / Of Science, Freedom, and the Truth in Christ" (lines 60–62). The juxtaposition of the two parallel sets of triple terms is telling: the head and science, the heart and freedom, the hand and truth in Christ. The critique of Godwin implicit in Coleridge's call to join head and heart is clear. The association of the hand with

Christian truth, however, moves beyond opposition to Godwin's rational atheism to a summation of Coleridge's activist and disinterested community. Unlike the French Revolution, this fight will be "bloodless," but not because, like the American Revolution, it will end in the protective stability of capitalism: American emancipation, Coleridge writes, was a "speculation on the probable *Loss and Gain* of . . . Independence," and Congress was "a respectable body of Tradesmen, deeply versed in the ledgers of Commerce, who well understood their own worldly concerns, and adventurously improved them" (*CW*, II, p. 269). Rather, this fight will be fought in public by heads, hearts, and hands both informed and reformed by the benevolent society of retirement, by the disinterested community that joins science, freedom, and the truth in Christ.

Like the humble statement of praise with which "The Eolian Harp" concludes, the last paragraph of "Reflections" pulls back from its overly bold rhetoric to end, back at the cottage, with a simple prayer:

> Yet oft when after honourable toil
> Rests the tired mind, and waking loves to dream,
> My spirit shall revisit thee, dear Cot!
> Thy jasmin and thy window-peeping rose,
> And myrtles fearless of the mild sea-air.
> And I shall sigh fond wishes – sweet abode!
> Ah! – had none greater! And that all had such!
> It might be so – but the time is not yet.
> Speed it, O Father! Let thy kingdom come! (lines 63–71)

Even though "honourable toil" has removed the poet from the peaceful dell, as in Wordsworth's "Tintern Abbey" (1798) the memory of retirement produces both "tranquil restoration" and that blessed mood "of aspect more sublime . . . / While with an eye made quiet by the power / Of harmony, and the deep power of joy, / We see into the life of things" (lines 38–50). On the one hand, the poet's sighs and fond wishes revive the fatigued mind, but the memory of the dell also culminates in the "visionary" statement and millenarian prayer of the last two lines. I qualify "visionary" because, whereas Wordsworth's ability to "see into the life of things" and Coleridge's apprehension of "one life within us and abroad" in "The Eolian Harp" can correspond to the philosophical-idealist visions of Romantic perception to which our more secular tastes are accustomed, "Reflections" presents a social and political vision in Coleridge's idiosyncratic Unitarian terms, the same terms which inform Coleridge's thought as he writes and delivers his lectures, preaches his sermons, and composes the conversation poems, his *sermones*. "It might be so – but the time is not yet," begins the transition to the closing prayer. In the present time the memory of the cottage revives the spirit of the poet for usefulness, but in the contemporary world of competition and interest all do not have such reflections to join head, heart, and hand. However, it might be so, and this is the actual visionary and millennial state for which the poet prays in the last line: "Speed it, O Father! Let thy kingdom come." The kingdom of God, the unitary and loving father to whom prayer is addressed, will exist in the actual truth of the Socinian Christ, the human son of Mary and friend of Lazarus, whose disciples in the late eighteenth century will act in public life, like Howard, not as the interested and selfish bourgeois sons of commerce but as the disinterested and benevolent human sons of God.

Whereas Dissenters sought to allay the competitive nature of commercial life through practices and tropes of collaboration and sensibility, Coleridge replaces collaboration with a different kind of conversation. Alison Hickey has shown that conversation can be read as the outcome of Coleridge's failures to collaborate with Southey: "the obvious impossibility of amalgamation with Southey only draws attention to the incompleteness of both partners and to the distance of their division of labor from the harmonious wholeness that Coleridge envisions for both the poet and the products of his imagination."[56] Here we can mark the distinction between a "*Joineriana*" – a patchwork alliance of the distinctive habitus of liberal Dissent, on the one hand, and the universal sensibility of normative human nature, on the other – and a conversation in the Coleridgean sense. The former seeks to leaven a general and national public with the progressive aspects of a particular community, whereas the latter always transforms the particular into the general and fuses parts into a harmonious whole that will reflect the mind and heart of the poet, be it in the case of the Dissenting reformer with "narrow and self-centering views" revolutionized into a member of that "small" but growing "glorious band," the Nottingham congregation summoned to partake of the preacher's benevolence, or the wealthy son of commerce transmuted into the saunterer who sighs and blesses. As opposed to Dissenting collaboration, Coleridge's conversation poems require "a collaborator to serve as his vehicle" or mirror: "A silent 'collaborator' – a mere auditor, addressee, or co-presence – will do, and actually seems preferable."[57] In each of the conversation poems, the "respondent" – Sara Coleridge in "The Eolian Harp" and "Reflections" (and arguably the son of commerce in the latter);

the absent Charles Lamb in "This Lime-Tree Bower My Prison"; the speechless infant Hartley in "Frost at Midnight"; Stowey itself at the end of "Fears in Solitude"; Sara Hutchinson in the original version of "Dejection: An Ode"; and Wordsworth in "The Nightingale," later versions of "Dejection," and "To William Wordsworth" – facilitates the triangular process by which God's words, miniatured on the poet's heart and expressed as "a sort of middle thing between Poetry and Oratory," can be heard and spoken by others. Jack Stillinger has questioned "whether 'pure' authorship is possible under any circumstances"[58]; conversation emblematizes one form of multiple authorship that resists another, incorporating Coleridge's Unitarian vision of personal and political reform while transforming collaborators in the traditional sense into companionable auditors who reflect and, at times, respond.

If in "Reflections" the poet translates the skylark's song for his beloved, "Frost at Midnight" is an extended translation of "that eternal language, which thy God / Utters, who from eternity doth teach / Himself in all, and all things in himself" (lines 60–62). "Frost at Midnight" maintains the community and language of retirement imagined three years earlier but sheds explicit reference to the public nexus of social and political values which all the conversation poems navigate. Indeed, the poem that articulates the language of God through a conversation with a sleeping infant was composed precisely after Coleridge had weighed his future in the decision, with which I began, to accept the Wedgwoods' annuity. On 14 January 1798, Coleridge preached his probationary sermon at the Unitarian chapel at Shrewsbury; on 16 January he wrote from Shrewsbury to Estlin, requesting his advice; on 17 January he wrote Josiah Wedgwood, again from Shrewsbury, in order to accept the annuity; on 30 January he returned to Bristol and spent a week at Cote House with the Wedgwoods; "Frost at Midnight" was then composed during February 1798.[59] The opening line of the poem, "The frost performs its secret ministry," was thus written immediately following Coleridge's decision not to perform the Unitarian ministry himself in a small commercial town in the Midlands.

The "abstruser musings" (line 6) of "Frost at Midnight" take place in specific surroundings: "Sea, hill, and wood, / This populous village! Sea, and hill, and wood, / With all the numberless goings-on of life, / Inaudible as dreams!" (lines 10–13). The populous village is Nether Stowey in Somerset, but it very well might have been Shrewsbury in Shropshire: it is worth asking how inaudible the numberless goings-on of life would have been in a commercial town on the Ellesmere Canal rather than in

this rural village near Coleridge's native Devon. If the din of cities inter-
feres with our perceptions, the interested lives we lead in cities equally
inhibit our expressions. The reciprocal abilities to hear the language of God
rather than the commotions of urban commerce and to speak that
language undistorted by articulations of self-interest are the principal
consequences of Coleridge's encounter with Dissenting publicity.

In "Frost at Midnight," the alternative initially seems to be a private
community of one:

> The inmates of my cottage, all at rest,
> Have left me to that solitude, which suits
> Abstruser musings: save that at my side
> My cradled infant slumbers peacefully. (lines 4–7)

The infant at first seems to sleep like every other inmate of the cottage,
and the transition "save that" seems slightly peculiar. The infant is asleep,
and besides the inanimate movement of the frost, the poet's is the only
active presence. His solitude leads him to reflect on the extreme silence of
the populous village (lines 10–13), and his sight then falls on his fireplace:
"Only that film, which fluttered on the grate, / Still flutters there, the sole
unquiet thing" (lines 15–16). The motion of the film, the poet thinks,
"Gives it dim sympathies with me who live, / Making it a companionable
form" (lines 18–19). The poet thus seems to have two active or "unquiet"
companions, the frost that performs its ministry and the film that flutters
on the grate, but there is of course a third, more intimate presence,
revealed at the outset of the philosophical paragraph in which the poet
apprehends the "eternal language" of God:

> Dear Babe, that sleepest cradled by my side,
> Whose gentle breathings, heard in this deep calm,
> Fill up the interspersèd vacancies
> And momentary pauses of the thought! (lines 44–47)

The passage elicits the sudden and arresting realization that over the
"extreme silentness" of the entire poem has been and can still be heard
the in-out-in sound of an infant's gentle breathings.

This movement of expansion and contraction, the diastolic and systolic
act of human respiration, the muscular motion that drives life, is the
same involuntary motion that allows communication itself – "articulated
Breath," as Coleridge once called it.[60] On a formal level, this is also the
movement that produces the conversation poems. The ability to hear or
speak the language of God is as involuntary as the spreading frost

"unhelped by any wind," the heated gases shimmering in the grate, or the contractions and expansions of human lungs. For that matter, it is also as involuntary as Hartleian sociality: "Jesus knew our Nature – and that expands like the circles of a Lake" (*CW*, 1, p. 163). The language of God is not just the secret ministry of the frost, the fluttering film, and the breath of the babe; it is the involuntary social principle of concretion, the circular ripples expanding in a lake, the home-born feeling that in the absence of property could permanently transform sons of commerce into human beings pure and simple. Only when no interest profanes the heart, when community is companionship rather than collaboration masking competition, can the systolic and diastolic movements that enable life and structure the conversation poems fuse nature and humanity into one higher language. Unitarian in its reliance on Jesus as a human figure of sensibility and in its fusion of a benevolent God with human virtue and natural beauty, this higher early Romantic language nonetheless represents an alternative to Dissenting models of publicity and production. Composed on the middle ground between poetry and oratory and published as the private meditations of an active mind in retirement, it becomes a public language performed as the sermon not of a stipendiary but rather of a Coleridgean, and secret, ministry.

CHAPTER 6

"A Saracenic mosque, not a Quaker meeting-house": Southey's Thalaba, Islam, and religious nonconformity

While Coleridge's career as a nonconformist preacher was coming to a close, Robert Southey was sketching plans and carrying out research for *Thalaba the Destroyer, a Metrical Romance* (1801). In other words, as Coleridge was weighing the Wedgwood annuity against the Shrewsbury invitation, Southey was worrying that it would "not be easy to find a new way of destroying an enchanter's den." "There will be much to avoid in this poem" (*CPB*, IV, p. 182), he predicted, and although *Thalaba* has had its ardent admirers, including Percy Bysshe Shelley and John Henry Newman, many of Southey's readers have wished that he had simply avoided the poem altogether. The reviewer for the *British Critic* sniped, "A more complete monument of vile and depraved taste no man ever raised"[1]; the early-nineteenth-century reviewers had their reasons, as have critics in the twentieth century who have tended to dismiss the poem, and Southey, for being "unable to break through to the new consciousness that we call 'Romantic,' a consciousness frankly introspective, skeptical, and symbolistic."[2] Southey's apparent inability to "break through" to this "new consciousness" during his heterodox, radical, and Orientalist period provides an important opportunity. Expressing a monotheistic, intuitive, and active faith within the generic form of the quest romance, Southey's "failure" will let us address the ways in which religious heterodoxy, anti-sectarianism, and Enlightenment skepticism inform an anti-authoritarian and experimental poet's fraught engagement with a different religious system, that of Islam.[3]

Responding to a letter in which Southey had announced his plans for "The Destruction of the Dom Danyel," William Taylor wrote in September 1798, "I am glad you are intending to build with the talisman of song a magic palace on the site of the Domdaniel of Cazotte. It remained for you to assert a claim to a certain wildness of fancy – to what shall I call it? – to mythological imagination" (*Taylor*, 1, p. 227). Having emerged from the outward-looking mercantile culture of his native Bristol, Southey's mythological imagination exercised itself upon the European Orientalism of the seventeenth and eighteenth centuries. As Marilyn Butler has observed, Southey was "fascinated by the wider world with which Bristol traded."[4] Before the industrial ascendancy of the North in the early nineteenth century, and of Liverpool in particular, Bristol provided a hub for the westward shift in foreign trade, from the Continent to the New World.[5] This shift turned Bristol, Glasgow, and Liverpool into major cities and transformed England from a London-based economy that looked to the Continent into an imperial and mercantile power that saw the planet as its market.

As in Manchester, Liverpool, Birmingham, and Norwich, Bristol's mercantile character was accompanied by and associated with a strong concentration of Dissenters, but it was the Dissenters of Bristol who engaged the most energy and resources in the early expansion of the missionary movement. If the northern academies were intended to educate young men to be either ministers or tradesmen, the main Baptist academy in Bristol would produce either ministers or missionaries. One of the significant moments leading to the founding of the Baptist Missionary Society in 1792 – the activities of which Southey would later defend in the *Quarterly Review*[6] – was the formation of the Bristol Education Society in 1770 to oversee the Bristol Baptist Academy for the education of ministers and "the encouragement of missionaries to preach the gospel wherever providence opens a door for it."[7] Prior to the Academy, Particular Baptists had been largely indifferent to evangelism, which, for strict Calvinists, seemed like an attempt to intervene in God's salvation of the elect.[8] But the Bristol Baptists were generally less austere in their orthodoxy, and one of the Academy's graduates, John Sutcliff, along with John Ryland and Andrew Fuller, played a key role in the 1791 meeting of the Northamptonshire Baptist ministers which led to the foundation of the Missionary Society.[9] As Bristol's commercial, Dissenting, and missionary elements directed English ships, sailors, and interests overseas, that same combination brought back a wide array of foreign artifacts and "curiosities." The Bristolian public's interest in other religious cultures and mythologies would have been fostered not just by travel narratives and highly publicized voyages of discovery but also by exhibits of artifacts brought or sent back to Bristol by traders and missionaries. By the end of the century, for instance, we find that the Baptist Academy in Bristol, having expanded to accommodate an increasing number of students, had built a "museum, first bequeathed by Dr. Gifford, and since increased by valuable curiosities, particularly of Hindoo mythology, which have been sent by the baptist missionaries in India."[10] From among these Dissenters, missionaries, and merchants, a metropolitan and expansionist culture developed that enabled new kinds of imagination. We have already seen Coleridge's nonsectarian-Unitarian imaginative response to entering the "active life" of Bristol after having left his retirement in Clevedon; Southey's mythological imagination constitutes another response, a less private and more cosmopolitan incorporation of new materials afforded to the mind by the new mercantile cities such as his native Bristol.

Over the course of his long career, Southey sustained an eclectic and bookish fascination with "the manners and mythologies of different nations" (*Taylor*, I, p. 301). Having followed his research through many of the major sources of Orientalist knowledge available in the late eighteenth century, in this chapter I will focus upon the period of Southey's lapsed Anglicanism and political radicalism in order to understand how his "Mahometan" romance participates in an English politico-religious discourse concerning the culture and theology of Islam. Like Coleridge, the heterodox Southey needed to find personal and political alternatives to the public sphere of rational Dissent. As I hope to show, Southey's nonconformist alternative, which he would come to call his "Quakerism," led him to find in Islam material suitable to a Jacobin mythological poem. Reading Southey's Orientalist scholarship and poetry in this light returns us to the undercurrent of early Romantic life that has been the subject of this book: the forces and meanings of theological and sectarian distinctions that shape individual manners and inform public literary and political programs.

"BELONGING TO NO FLOCK, YET NOT WITHOUT A SHEPHERD"

As we have seen, heterodoxy in and of itself could take various forms and manifest itself in various ideologies. Liberal Dissenters such as Barbauld, Price, and Priestley often equated their heterodoxy with models of British nationalism and culture that demanded religious diversity and difference, a harmonic plurality of denominations. For lapsed Anglicans such as Coleridge and Southey in the 1790s, on the other hand, heterodoxy tended to produce visions of a nonsectarian, unified, and progressive British public, be it in the Unitarian mode of Coleridge's conversation poems or in the main strand of syncretic mythography by which Southey and others, like so many Mr. Casaubons, sought to resist sectarian division and enthusiasm by synthesizing historically discordant systems of worship and belief into one originary religion. Like Coleridge, Southey in the 1790s was a kind of dissenter from Dissent; heterodox in religion and radical in his politics, he nonetheless remained unassociated with any denomination and, indeed, opposed to the very idea of sects.[11] The young Southey was an anti-authoritarian radical who was theologically Arminian and Socinian or low Arian but who, to a greater extent than Coleridge, remained unaffiliated with any Dissenting denomination. During the period of his nonconformity he read voraciously on the subject of Islam – "I am qualified in doctrinals to be a Mufti!" he boasted in 1800 (*LC*, II, p. 41) – and wrote the poems that, along with *Lyrical Ballads*, gave rise to a new school of poetry, a school which Francis Jeffrey caricatured as a Dissenting sect.

The famous "*Edinburgh* attempt at Thalabacide" (*NL*, I, p. 306), as Southey called Jeffrey's assault on the "new poets" – by which Jeffrey meant primarily Southey, Coleridge, Lamb, and Wordsworth – begins, "Poetry has this much, at least, in common with religion, that its standards were fixed long ago, by certain inspired writers, whose authority it is no longer lawful to call in question."[12] Although this review has received a good deal of attention, I wish to foreground the often overlooked religious register of Jeffrey's smear campaign and to take seriously the implications of his accusation that the founding poets of British Romanticism constitute a "*sect* of . . . *dissenters*"[13]:

The author who is now before us, belongs to a *sect* of poets, that has established itself in this country within these ten or twelve years, and is looked upon, we believe, as one of its chief champions and apostles. The peculiar doctrines of this sect, it would not, perhaps, be very easy to explain; but, that they are *dissenters* from the established systems in poetry and criticism, is admitted, and proved indeed, by the whole tenor of their compositions. Though they lay claim, we believe, to a creed and a revelation of their own, there can be little doubt, that their doctrines are of *German* origin, and have been derived from some of the great modern reformers in that country. Some of their leading principles, indeed, are probably of an earlier date, and seem to have been borrowed from the great apostle of Geneva. As Mr Southey is the first author, of this persuasion, that has yet been brought before us for judgement, we cannot discharge our inquisitorial office conscientiously, without premising a few words upon the nature and tendency of the tenets he has helped to promulgate.

The disciples of this school boast much of its originality, and seem to value themselves very highly, for having broken loose from the bondage of ancient authority, and re-asserted the independence of genius.[14]

In spite of Southey's level-headed retort – "The damned lying Scotch son of a bitch"[15] – Jeffrey was in fact mixing truth with falsehood in his insinuations that poetical experimentation and disdain for established authorities coincided with religious heterodoxy.

The "disciples of this school" – which would not become the "Lake School" until another attack by Jeffrey in the *Edinburgh*, this time on Wordsworth's *Poems, in Two Volumes* (1807) – form a "sect," with "chief . . . apostles," "peculiar doctrines," and "a creed and a revelation of their own." The sectarians are "*dissenters* from the established systems in poetry and criticism," and although Jeffrey protests, as do most writers against Dissent, that their creed is too complex and, by implication, too obscure to merit the trouble of either the writer or the reader, he does eventually explain it in detail. Jeffrey's subjects are "poetry and criticism," and *Thalaba* in particular, yet the "*German* origin" of ostensibly original Dissenting doctrines intimates political and religious as well as poetical imitation: Luther comes to mind along with "(*horresco referens*) . . . Kotzebue and Schiller."[16] and "the great apostle of Geneva" refers to Rousseau in a phrase that could equally denominate Calvin, "l'apôtre de Genève," as Voltaire in fact called him.[17] Marilyn Butler accounts for Jeffrey's primary reference by proposing that Thalaba "leaves his pastoral origins for a corrupt advanced society, which he overthrows, restoring the primal simplicity by force."[18] The juxtaposition of Luther, Calvin, and Rousseau, furthermore, effectively characterizes the new creed as both the doctrine of a zealous reforming sect as well as another version of Jacobin infidelity. The distortion as well as the success of the strategy lies in a kind of sleight of hand that comically disguises the real tensions between actual denominations or sects of Dissenters and heterodox, experimentalist poets such as Southey, "the first author, of this persuasion" brought before Jeffrey's ecclesiastical court.

Because of Southey's eventual fierce defense of the Established Church against both Catholicism and nonconformity, most biographies of Southey focus on the *remnants* of his heterodoxy during the period of his Toryism.[19] But in order to examine the relationship between Southey's heterodoxy and Orientalism in the 1790s, we need once again to rethink the powerful narrative of apostasy, which can obliterate other stories that may not conform to its characteristic teleology. At Oxford in 1794, Southey's doubts about taking orders did not necessarily bear within them any seeds of future conservatism: "What is to become of me at ordination, heaven only knows! . . . the Test Act will be a stumbling-block to honesty."[20] As a young boy, Southey was a day student at a school "then esteemed the best in Bristol, kept by Mr. Foot, a dissenting minister of that community who are called General Baptists . . . Like most of his denomination, he had passed into a sort of low Arianism, if indeed he were not a Socinian" (*LC*, I, p. 45).[21] Southey's Bristol roots brought him into contact with numerous Dissenting families, and when it came time for him to arrange for the education of his younger brother Henry in 1798, he placed him under George Burnett, minister to the Unitarian Congregation at Yarmouth. At Yarmouth, Southey began his friendship with William Taylor of Norwich, who, along with Thomas Martineau and Frank Sayers, had been educated by the Barbaulds at Palgrave. Explaining the origins of his association with Southey, the editor of Taylor's *Memoir* writes that Taylor's "near connexion with some of the leading dissenters in that town naturally brought about an introduction between two persons, already known to each other by reputation, and both pursuing the same career with similar tastes, congenial ardour and accordant views" (*Taylor*, I, p. 212). In spite of these connections, and although Southey was nonconformist in his religious beliefs, he never considered himself a Dissenter.

According to Thomas Poole in his well-known description of the Pantisocracy scheme, Southey "is more violent in his principles than even Coleridge himself. In Religion, shocking to say . . ., I fear he wavers between Deism and Atheism."[22] Bernhardt-Kabisch follows this line, calling Southey's Christianity "the 'reasonable' and 'not mysterious' one of Deism."[23] I will return below to Bernhardt-Kabisch's emphasis on the rationalistic impulse in Southey, but here it is necessary to demonstrate that Southey's early religion could not really be described as either rational Deism or, still less, atheism. Although he would have been playing up his heterodoxy in his utopian enthusiasm over Pantisocracy in front of Poole, as he no doubt reverted to this radical posture during his later interview with Shelley in 1811,[24] it is true that his rhetoric in the mid 1790s could lead one to conclude that his Socinianism bordered on outright Deism: "Were I a legislator," he wrote in the summer of 1793, "I would build a temple to the One Eternal Universal God. My national creed should be God is one, Christ is the Saviour of Mankind. For the Metaphysical disquisitions of subtle disputants . . . I would reject them all" (*NL*, I, p. 31). He consistently remains "an enemy to an establishment" (*NL*, I, p. 31), but in his insistence upon the divinity of Christ's mission and his rejection of "Metaphysical disquisitions" the foundations of Southey's later low Arianism and "Quakerism" are visible. As late as 1800, Southey could still refer to himself as a Socinian, though we should not overlook the context of the remark.

Writing of a Trinity Sunday festival he witnessed in Lisbon, Southey first describes an illuminated "mountebank-stage" with "barrels of pitch blazing all along it" and then reflects, "It was somewhat terrible – they were bonfires of superstition – and I could not help thinking how much finer a sight the spectators would have thought it, if there had been a Jew or a Socinian like me in every barrel."[25] This is less an outright assertion of Socinian beliefs than a satirical lumping together of Jews and Socinians as heretics in the bigoted eyes of the Papist crowd. Throughout the period, indeed, Christ remained for Southey "the Saviour of Mankind," and by 1803 his friendship with Taylor had become marked by his resistance to Taylor's Socinianism and Taylor's light-hearted jibes at Southey's low Arianism. "Your theology does nothing but mischief," Southey wrote to Taylor in 1803, "it serves only to thin the miserable ranks of Unitarianism . . . The Monthly Magazine is read by all the Dissenters . . . and here are you eternally mining, mining, under the shallow faith of their half-learned, half-witted, half-paid, half-starved pastors" (*Taylor*, 1, pp. 459–60). Southey, then, not Taylor, is the true "believer" (*Taylor*, 1, p. 460), a claim which Taylor took up in his response a week later when he recommended an essay he had written attributing the authorship of the apocryphal book *The Wisdom of Solomon* to Jesus: "I am very glad you are a believer. I think you will desert your low Arian for pure Socinian ground, when you have read my paper about the 'Wisdom'" (*Taylor*, 1, pp. 463–64).

As we will see below, the period during which Southey composed *Thalaba* witnessed a transformation of his religious thought from nominal Socinianism, based more upon a firm anti-establishmentarianism than a rejection of the divinity of Christ, into a far more moderate position. In a later letter, of April 1808, Southey writes, "My creed is what I cannot so explicitly lay down – That there was in Christ a far greater portion of the Divine Mind than has ever been imparted to any other of the Sons of men I believe" (*NL*, 1, p. 473). Southey goes on, however, to lay down his creed quite clearly: "Of the Trinity I cannot discover a trace in the words of Christ, nor even in the whole New Testament . . . My heresy inclines rather to Arius than to Socinus" (*NL*, 1, p. 474). Like other low Arians, Southey was generally Arminian in his beliefs regarding original sin and general redemption: "Original sin as it is commonly understood is not consistent with the Justice of the Creator, nor indeed with the language of Christ . . . I prefer Pelagius to St. Augustine" (*NL*, 1, pp. 473–74). Referred to by Bogue and Bennett in their *History of Dissenters* as "the gordian knot in theology" (IV, p. 225), the controversy between Arminian-ism and Calvinism with its roots in the debate between Pelagius and

Augustine concerned the nature of redemption: for the Arminian, as for Southey, Christ's death and sufferings atoned for all men in general, whereas for the orthodox Calvinist, Christ's death and sufferings atoned for the elect in particular. Although there were high Arians (such as Samuel Clarke) within the Church of England, and throughout the eighteenth century many clergymen were generally Arminian – in the famous formula attributed to Pitt the Elder, the Church had a Calvinistic creed, a Popish liturgy, and an Arminian clergy[26] – Southey's Arminianism and low Arianism place him theologically more in line with liberal Dissent than with either Deism or atheism, on the one hand, or the Established Church, on the other.

In spite of Southey's theological accordance with liberal Dissent, his religious dispositions during his oppositionist period would soon lead him to an important and lasting affinity not for the rational Dissenters but rather for the Quakers, whom he came to know well first through the family of his brother-in-law and fellow Pantisocrat Robert Lovell and then through his friendship with the abolitionist Thomas Clarkson.[27] After meeting Clarkson in 1803, Southey came to see the Quakers as presenting a warm and inspired religion without devolving into Methodist enthusiasm. Comparing John Wesley unfavorably with George Fox, Southey writes in that same year, "A worse danger than the spread of methodism can scarcely be apprehended for England; a greater blessing for mankind cannot be desired or devised, than that the system of George Fox should become the practical system of the Christian world."[28] By 1807 Southey could go so far as to refer to the Quakers as "a body of Christians from whom, in all important points, I feel little or no difference in my own state of mind" (*Selections,* I, p. 426). To James Grahame Southey writes soon afterwards, "As to my own faith I am what would have been called a Seeker in former times: belonging to no flock, yet not without a shepherd. I incline to Quakerism, and if the present Quakers abstained from insisting on articles of faith, and left those points which are not explained in the Gospels, untouched, with the same reverence as their fathers do – I should perhaps call myself a Quaker" (*NL,* I, p. 467). The attraction of Quakerism lay not in theology, then, but in the absence of dogma characteristic of the Quakers' vaunted refusal to enter into religious debate,[29] a refusal which Southey sees the "present Quakers" as having partially abandoned. Just as he had rejected religious disputation in 1793, the now Arian Southey "with the true Quakers . . . would rather be reverently silent than dogmatise . . . upon a subject that is out of our reach" (*NL,* I, p. 474).

Southey's reverent silence evokes the most characteristic feature of Quaker devotion, its substitution of intuitive and spontaneous faith – Robert Barclay's "inner light" – for religious polemic. Samuel Fothergill's extempore sermon, "Thanks be to God for his unspeakable Gift," delivered in 1768 at Stockport, expresses the kind of Quaker distrust of religious discourse that appealed to Southey. "This unspeakable gift, the religion of Jesus, works secretly, powerfully, and effectually; sometimes it draws to expressions, oftentimes otherwise: the occasion of praise ceased not when there was silence in heaven for half an hour," Fothergill preached according to the published version: "I have feared the multitude of conversation has betrayed the minds of the people . . . there is a possibility of talking away religion, by a multiplicity of conversation, passing beyond our own light. I would rather know what the Holy Ghost meant by that silence in heaven for half an hour, than make religion too cheap by conversation: – Keep it in the heart: too much discourse carries off the essence of religion."[30] As an alternative to the "multiplicity of conversation" – or, in a more sympathetic phrase, the "free enquiry" – that characterized rational Dissenting public life, Quakerism presents spontaneous intuition as the faculty through which God communicates with individual human beings, and, in response, through which human beings worship and express their faith in God.

Insofar as Southey's interest in Quakerism involves his desire for a moderate worship that would avoid superstition and idolatry yet maintain religious fervor, his conception of a tempered form of Dissent coincides with that of the Dissenting public sphere. "The Papists are, beyond all doubt Idolaters," Southey writes, "but in flying from idolatry, what a fearful chasm have we left between man and God! What a void have we made in the Universe!" (*NL*, 1, p. 474). Here Southey echoes Barbauld's typical moderate Dissenting assertion that "A prayer strictly philosophical must ever be a cold and dry composition" (*SPP*, p. 217), that Socinianism is "Christianity in the frigid zone."[31] Coleridge too identifies Socinian Dissent with excessive frigidity, jotting in his notebook in 1799, "Socinianism Moonlight – Methodism &c A Stove! O for some Sun that shall unite Light & Warmth,"[32] and Southey would later claim that Socinianism "neither interests the imagination, nor awakens the feelings, nor excites the passions, nor satisfies the wants of the human heart."[33] But if Southey and Coleridge agreed with liberal Dissenters in their ideal of enlightened yet affective religious devotion, they both understood their religious heterodoxy as opposed to the corrupting power of the establishment, in the manner of the Quakers, rather than as identified with the purifying leaven of any sect, in the manner of the liberal Dissenters. Coleridge could easily have spoken for Southey as well when he wrote, "I approve altogether & embrace entirely the *Religion* of the Quakers, but exceedingly dislike the *sect*" (*CL*, II, p. 893). Certainly Dissenters such as Barbauld and Price would agree with Southey's premise, that religion should not be so cold and dry as to produce a void in the universe, but not with his conclusion: in the same letter in which Southey expresses his inclination to Quakerism, he also writes, "All sects appear to me to think unworthily both of man and his maker" (*NL*, I, p. 467).

Southey's eventual Quakerism, like Coleridge's Unitarianism, emerges from an enduring resistance to sectarianism in and of itself, and this resistance, I believe, makes manifest the crucial tension between heterodox belief and Dissenting culture, between religious affinities impelled by political and social opposition to the establishment and affiliations thoroughly implicated in individual, communal, political, economic, doctrinal, and devotional conceptions of a Dissenting public sphere. Southey does not come to prefer "true" Quakerism primarily or solely as an alternative to the establishment, as we might expect from a young radical, but also as an alternative to other particular sects, to the very *idea* of sects: "Many Xtian sects, or societies, seem to me to have been founded upon a strong perception of *part* of the Xtian system; none to have a clear steady comprehension of the whole, perfectly pure and simple as that system is" (*NL*, I, p. 472). For Southey during both his radical and conservative periods, the partial nature of Dissenting sects fails to comprehend the whole of Christianity, a system which is "perfectly pure and simple." If pure and simple, though, as both Unitarians and Deists tended to assert, the system should be articulable through rational articles of faith, yet that is not what Southey means by purity. Characterized by its excessive dogmatism, by "Metaphysical disquisitions of subtle disputants," Dissent for Southey multiplies religious doctrines through reason whereas his idealized form of Quakerism intuitively, simply, and silently reveres the system itself in its unity and entirety. If the imagination, according to Coleridge's famous definition in the *Biographia*, "at all events . . . struggles to idealize and to unify,"[34] Southey's religious thought too is based in part on an anti-rationalist and imaginative premise. The void made in the universe by rational faith, by Dissent, is synonymous with the proliferation of religious doctrines, just as for Fothergill "too much discourse carries off the essence of religion." "Had the senses and the imagination their wholesome food set before them," Southey writes, "they would not prey upon such garbage as that of the bedeadening and bedarkening sectaries" (*NL*, 1, p. 474). Habitually averse to belonging to any flock, Southey cannot conceive of rational debate, the sustenance of the Dissenting public sphere, as either invigorating or enlightening. Although Southey's shepherd, the Socinian or low Arian Christ, is a thoroughly radical and anti-authoritarian Pantisocrat – "To me nothing can be clearer than Christ Jesus has expressly forbidden his disciples either riches or authority; that his words . . . lead to nothing short of a total revolution in the whole constitution of human governments, and the establishment of a new order of things, in which no man is to exercise authority over another" (*NL*, 1, p. 472) – the new social and political order over which this shepherd will preside is an imaginative Utopian vision based on the resolution, not proliferation, of religious difference and discourse. In surprising ways, Southey's alternative to rational Dissent, which after 1803 he would come to think of as his "Quakerism," led him to find in eighteenth-century accounts of Islam the proper religion for the hero of his Jacobin romance.

ISLAM AND DISSENT

The East did not always serve as Europe's Other in which the subject saw itself reflected by virtue of difference from its object.[35] Especially after the 1690s a strain of Orientalism emerged that reflected dissident elements of European subjectivity in a fundamentally homologous East. As much as Orientalism was a Foucauldian discourse of European control over the Orient, in Britain it was also part of a Gramscian struggle to unify and define a nation in which, following the political and religious upheavals of the seventeenth century, the internal processes of hegemony were still very much dynamic and uncertain. Many Orientalist texts throughout the seventeenth and eighteenth centuries drew analogies between East and West in order to critique and indeed subordinate dissident groups within the West itself. Gramscian hegemony functions differently than the Foucauldian episteme in that it is a process in which a multitude of forces seek to realise unity in the form of the State by subordinating other forces and winning "the active or passive assent" of "auxiliaries or allies."[36] Orientalism in seventeenth- and eighteenth-century Britain was part of such a process in which the hegemony of the ruling classes faced internal conflict with other groups, groups defined primarily as religious sects. Furthermore, eighteenth-century religious pluralism could easily be over-simplified as the culmination of a history of dissension reaching directly back to the once hegemonic Puritan Commonwealth. At times, the sects that emerged after the Act of Uniformity came to represent a real threat to British stability, but the perception of them as a cause for national anxiety was fairly persistent over the course of the following century. To establishmentarian writers, in other words, Islam could look all too familiar, not as absolute Other but as just another Dissenting sect. The side of Orientalism we can understand in terms of hegemony depicts the East in order to combat the Dissenting challenge of Socinianism, into which establishmentarian writers tend to lump Deism and atheism, in order both to subordinate those actual nonconformist sects and to win the active or passive assent to Anglican hegemony of the vast majority of nonsectarian Britons. The consequence of this perspective is a far less unified discursive field, involving Orientalisms that either represent a coherent Europe as superior to its Other or suggest a fragmented and unstable Europe in which alien cultures could be homologous to dissident religious and political groups vying for supremacy within the state and civil society. It is from these latter kinds of accounts, of which I will give a brief catalogue, that Islam emerged as an alternative to rational Dissent suited to the revolutionary hero of Southey's fatalistic romance.

In defense of the Trinitarianism of the Established Church, eighteenth-century establishmentarian religious thinkers faced three rigidly monotheistic alternatives: Unitarianism, Judaism, and Islam. The theological basis of the first, Socinianism, was a sixteenth-century Polish heresy that had become an accepted if despised component of Protestant heterodoxy following the Trinitarian debates of the 1690s.[37] Its roots were firmly planted in Church history, in the controversy between Arius and Athanasius, which was decided in favor of the latter at the Council of Nicaea in A.D. 325. Modern Judaism and Islam, on the other hand, for the most part represented distinct forms of religious alterity, not part of but opposed to the Christian world. Unlike Judaism, however, Islam posed the longest and greatest political and theological threat both as the religion of the Ottoman and Mughal Empires and as a doctrinally coherent monotheistic *response* to what many Protestants themselves viewed as the polytheistic corruptions of Christianity. John Toland, in fact, went so far as to refer to "Mahometan Christianity" in the subtitle of his *Nazarenus: Or, Jewish, Gentile, and Mahometan Christianity* (1718), explaining, "tho the very title of Mahometan Christianity may be apt to startle you . . . yet . . . there is a sense, wherin [*sic*] the Mahometans may not improperly be reckon'd and call'd a sort or sect of Christians, as Christianity was at first esteem'd a branch of Judaism."[38] To a late-eighteenth-century English reader, the nature of Islam could run the gamut from the most pernicious imposture perpetrated on the ignorant and superstitious to the manifestation of divine providence, a symbol of God's will that Protestant reformers complete the purification of the true monotheistic faith preached by Jesus Christ but corrupted by the idolatry of Catholicism and even of its reformed progeny, the Church of England in particular.

It is no coincidence that the 1690s saw so many Orientalist publications, for the decade of the Trinitarian debates brought together both discourses, as exemplified by the full title of Humphrey Prideaux's enormously influential *The True Nature of Imposture Fully Displayed in the Life of Mahomet. With A Discourse annexed, for the Vindicating of Christianity from this Charge; Offered to the Consideration of the Deists of the present Age* (1697). Prideaux, Arch Deacon of Suffolk and later Dean of Norwich, wrote primarily to draw analogies between the imposture of Islam and the impositions of Deists and Socinians "of the present Age" upon the present nation. In the same year, d'Herbelot's *Bibliothèque Orientale* described Islam as "une heresie qui a pris le nom de Religion que nous apellons Mahometane." Not a religion but essentially a Christian heresy given the name of a religion, Islam corresponds to Arianism or Socinianism: "Les Interpretes de l'Alcoran & autres Docteurs de la Loy Musulmane ou Mahometane ont appliqué à ce faux Prophete tous les éloges que les Ariens, Paulitiens, ou, Paulianistes & autres Heretiques ont attribués à Jesus-Christ en luy ôtant sa Divinité."[39] Another in a series of works to associate Islam with Socinianism and other Christian heresies was an oft-cited edition titled *Four Treatises Concerning the Doctrine, Discipline and Worship of the Mahometans* (1712), which included Adrian Reland's "A Defence of the Mahometans from several Charges falsly laid against them by Christians" along with an anonymous pamphlet called "Reflections on Mahometanism and Socinianism," frequently misattributed to Reland but in fact a translation of "Reflexions historique et critique sur le mahometisme, & sur le socinianisme" (1707) by Mathurin Veyssière de la Croze (1661–1739).[40] By the time the reader of the edition gets to "Reflections on Mahometanism and Socinianism," he or she has been prepared by Reland to believe that although Islam is a false imposture, it is essentially no different from other heresies, for "Sense and Reason are equally distributed among Men: And . . . that Religion, which hath largely spread it self over *Asia, Africa,* and even *Europe,* commends it self to Men by a great Appearance of Truth, which is ready to allure them; nor is it so foolish as many Christians esteem it."[41] According to "Reflections upon Mahometanism and Socinianism," the "two Sects" are both "proud to be call'd *Unitarians*; a name that signifies the same thing with both Parties. Therefore I cannot see with what reason the *Socinians* should make such a bustle as they do, when they are accus'd of entertaining the same Opinions of the Deity with the *Mahometans*" (p. 182). The tone of the pamphlet assumes that the reader is already familiar with the charge: "I know the Charge of *Mahometanism* enrages the *Socinians* extremely, but I could not hinder my self from laying it home to them" (p. 195). After the 1690s, then, Islam could be represented not as absolutely different from the West but rather as yet another heretical sect, a homologous variation of the antitrinitarian Dissent which would pose a major theological challenge to the religious establishment throughout the eighteenth century: the pamphlet shows "that the false Prophet *Mahomet* reviv'd all these Impieties, and that his *Sect* is so like these *Heresies*, and consequently so like *Socinianism*, that it is impossible to distinguish them" (p. 156). In a clear attempt to win the assent of a social group which, two years after the Sacheverell riots, constituted a more than doctrinal threat to Anglican hegemony, the pamphlet hopes that "This Resemblance of Doctrines . . . ought to frighten the *Socinians*, and bring them back to the *true Religion*" (p. 156). It is not only the Socinians, however, who could be brought *back* to the true religion, for the Mahometans too become another sect that has separated from the Christian fold over the unity of God: the Socinians thus "agree with the *Mahometans* in the essential Article of their Separation" (p. 184). The pamphlet, and the volume, ends with "A Letter from Mr. Leibniz to the Author of the Reflections upon the Origin of Mahometanism," in which Leibniz asserts, "I am not at all astonish'd at the great Progress of *Mahometanism*. 'Tis a kind of Deism" (p. 245).

Predictably, after the 1690s the next wave of Orientalism directed against heterodox Dissent came in the late eighteenth century, especially after the 1770s, with Priestley's repeated defences of Socinianism in sermons and pamphlets and with the foundation of the Essex Street congregation. Two orthodox Dissenters, staunch Trinitarians and Calvinists both, took up the attempt to associate Socinianism with Mahometanism, the one a Particular Baptist minister, John Macgowan (who published under the pseudonym "ANTISOCINUS"), and the other an Independent minister, George Townsend. The full title of one of Macgowan's pamphlets sums up his argument: *Socinianism Brought to the Test: or Jesus Christ Proved to be Either the Adorable God, or a Notorious Impostor. In a Series of Letters to the Reverend Doctor Priestley. In which it Appears, That if Jesus Christ is not a Divine Person, the Mohammedan is in all Respects, preferable to the Christian Religion, and the Koran is a better Book than the*

Bible (1773). The late 1780s then saw another outburst of anti-Socinian writings during the movement to repeal the Corporation and Test Acts, and William Frend's two *Address[es] to the Inhabitants of Cambridge, exhorting them to turn from the false worship of Three Persons to the worship of the one true God* (1788) provoked Townsend to respond in *The Replication; or, A Familiar Address to Mr. William Frend* (1789), the final third of which was dedicated to demonstrating "The affinity and tendency of Socinianism to Mahometanism: with the name of noted Socinians who have left the one for the other."[42] As we have seen, defenders of orthodoxy viewed the trajectory from truth to error as a descent through a series of Christian heterodox beliefs to Deism or even atheism; here, however, we find a surprising resting point as the apostate nears the bottom of this slippery slope:

> the most celebrated champion of Socinianism, in this day, Joseph Priestley, L.L.D. could give you a *little* history . . . of this *retrograde motion*, in apostazing [*sic*] from Truth and embracing error. How a Calvinistic Trinitarian goes to Arianism; and so on to Socinianism. He might add in the way to Mahometanism, and then to Deism, and one step more, and then, with David Hume, of famous memory; *doubt all things*, and dwindle into practical Atheism.[43]

Looking back on the rise of Unitarianism from the vantage point of 1809, Robert Adam cites Warburton's claim that Unitarianism represents "a sort of infidelity in disguise," Wilberforce's that it is a "sort of *half-way house* from nominal orthodoxy to absolute infidelity," and Barbauld's that it is "*Christianity in the Frigid Zone.*" Adam himself asserts, "the Unitarians hold so few opinions which are peculiarly Christian, that many . . . class them with Jews, Mohammedans, and Deists, with whom they hold common principles."[44]

As these examples show, Unitarianism could seem to be a form of infidelity warranting a defensive response in and of itself, but by the end of the century the Socinian threat to the Anglican establishment had also been subsumed by the broader oppositionist category of Jacobin, and Orientalist attacks followed suit. Although there were serious internal divisions between liberal Dissenters and members of the Corresponding Societies, Orientalist writers in support of the establishment in church and state found a single target in the so-called Jacobin opposition. From the paranoid perspective of 1796, Mahomet could just as easily be equated with sensual and effeminate Eastern tyranny as with religious and political enthusiasm. Nathan Alcock's *The Rise of Mahomet, Accounted for on Natural and Civil Principles* (1796), for instance, seeks to discount the divine inspiration of Islam by placing Mahomet in a line of fanatical reformers and revolutionaries. "Enthusiasm," writes Alcock,

may cause a man to deceive himself, and take his own fancies or conceptions for divine suggestions. This probably was the case with Mahomet . . . Many other enthusiasts have thus deceived themselves. Oliver Cromwell was a very great enthusiast, and, I doubt not, really believed many of his divine illuminations and consultations with the Lord, although they might often be hypocritical, and made use of as a cloak to cover his worldly views.[45]

Similarly, in 1799 Henry Kett, one of the King's preachers at Whitehall, published *History the Interpreter of Prophecy*, an extreme statement of proto-fascist order in politico-theological terms. Kett's work "DISPLAYS THE HARMONY OF PROPHECY – THE ONE GREAT SCHEME THAT PERVADES ALL ITS PARTS – AND THE CONCURRENCE OF ALL HUMAN EVENTS TO ACCOMPLISH ITS STUPENDOUS PLAN."[46] All history, for Kett, can be accommodated to God's will as revealed in prophecy, and God's will decrees the supremacy of the Protestant Church of England. According to the title of the "Introductory Chapter" to Volume Two, Kett's premise is that "the PAPAL, the MAHOMETAN, and the INFIDEL POWERS, are different branches or forms of THE SAME ANTICHRISTIAN POWER – and that ALL are expressly foretold in Scripture, as permitted to arise in different ages of the world, for the purposes of punishment and trial to the Church of Christ." Islam, Catholicism, and other forms of infidelity from Paganism to Hinduism are all essentially the same; they are branches of Antichrist, and are therefore essentially different from the true church of God. However, the Orientalism of the work does not schematically represent this alterity in terms of East and West. "I am much deceived," writes Kett, "if the Reader will not see ample confirmation of the system, respecting the three great forms of Antichrist . . . in the following sketch of the nature and effects of the Mahometan scourge of the *East* – more especially if he will compare the description of this power, with that which has tyrannized over the *West*, for the same purposes of trial and punishment."[47] The infidel system "which has tyrannized over the *West*" is Jacobinism, and God has decreed the French Revolution and the English Jacobins for "the same purposes" as He has unleashed "the Mahometan scourge of the *East*." After Volume Two, which treats Mahometanism, Volume Three accordingly tracks the "rise and progress of *Jacobinism*, which seems to include every species of Infidelity, and may be defined to mean Hostility to Religion, to Virtue, to Monarchy, to Laws, to Social Order, Rank and Property."[48] Kett, like other anti-Jacobins, here relies heavily on the conspiracy theories of the Abbé Barruel's *Memoirs, Illustrating the History of Jacobinism* (1797–98) and John Robison's *Proofs of a Conspiracy Against All the Governments of Europe* (1797). God's unified plan to try and punish the Christian church equates Eastern Islam with Western Jacobinism, and Orientalism thus becomes a hegemonic discourse to justify the violent eradication of religious and political dissident groups even as it assumes the historical legitimacy of violent conflicts with Arabs and Saracens, who, Kett writes, have been "*like locusts upon the earth* for their numbers and the rapidity of their progress; and *like scorpions of the earth* for their venom."[49]

In the 1790s Orientalism could therefore serve to oppose European Jacobinism by equating it with Eastern threats to Western stability, and consequently East and West could be confused as well in arguments against Dissenters. In the debate over the repeal of the Corporation and Test Acts in the House of Commons on 2 March 1790, one MP opposed the repeal by arguing that it would permit not only the English Dissenters to hold offices of trust and power "but Dissenters of every denomination: the Jew, the Mahometan, the disciples of Brama, Confucius, and of every head of a sectary" (Fox is reported to have deflated this scare tactic by crying out "*Hear! hear!*").[50] In this context, Dissenters are associated with Mahometans not because of their shared Unitarian theology but simply because both appear hostile, like Jacobins according to the Manichean view of *The Anti-Jacobin*, to Anglican uniformity and established order.[51]

Like Unitarianism, then, Islam could be understood by the end of the eighteenth century as both rigorously monotheistic and politically dissident. But in other important ways, Islam would have seemed extremely different from rational Dissent, particularly in its active enthusiasm and its perceived resistance to religious disputation, both of which were thought to stem from an absolute belief in fatalism. Above all, authorities from various perspectives return to the Orientalist depiction of Islam as characterized chiefly by submission to God's will. Describing "the name of Islâm," George Sale's "Preliminary Discourse" to the Koran explains that the "word signifies resignation, or submission to the service and commands of GOD."[52] The "orthodox doctrine" of predestination is "that whatever hath, or shall come to pass in this world, whether it be good, or whether it be bad, proceedeth entirely from the divine will, and is irrevocably fixed and recorded from all eternity in the preserved table."[53] Repeatedly, Islamic submission corresponds to an active strain of enthusiastic courage and austerity, on the one hand, and a refusal to take part in rational debate about questions of faith, on the other. "The belief of predestination," Richard Pococke writes, "is very st[r]ongly rooted in them . . . which often inspires them with very great courage,"[54] just as for Alcock "This principle of fixed fate, or predestination, was exactly adapted to the character of the eastern nations, and particularly to Arabia . . . as it has a tendency to inspire a people of their genius and temperament with an enthusiastic courage and resolution, and render them fearless of danger and regardless of death."[55] If submission to fate kindles active courage, it also induces silent reverence in the form of a reticence to engage in controversy, and thus according to Reland, the Mahometans "neither love to dispute about their Religion, nor to commend it to others."[56] "Sense and Reason are equally distributed among Men," and it is therefore not the case that Mahometans are incapable of rational discourse, "But they will not dispute about their Religion."[57] From the less sympathetic perspective of Prideaux, the very existence of Mahometanism can be attributed to God's anger with Christendom for weakening religion through excessive controversy: the Eastern Churches

having drawn the abstrusest Niceties into Controversy . . . and divided and subdivided about them into endless Schisms and Contentions, did thereby so destroy that Peace, Love, and Charity from among them . . . that they lost the whole Substance of their Religion . . . and in a manner drove Christianity quite out of the World by those very Controversies in which they disputed with each other about it. So that at length having wearied the patience and long-suffering of God . . . he raised up the Saracens to be the Instruments of his Wrath to punish them for it.[58]

Unlike rational Dissent, then, Islam can be viewed sympathetically as a religion that shuns rational debate and instead embraces submission to God's ineffable will, or less sympathetically as a scourge to remind Christians of their own history of schisms, contentions, and disunity.

The anti-sectarian, heterodox, and Jacobin Southey, the experimental poet to whom "Quakerism" would appeal, found two things in Islam: first, because of the types of Orientalism I have been discussing, Southey found a dissident religion, theologically homologous to his own antitrinitarian nonconformity, that challenged Christian orthodoxy and established power; but second, because of the reputed austere and submissive fatalism of Islam, Southey also found a religion that, unlike Dissenting sects themselves, he perceived to be intuitive and active rather than rational and skeptical. Although Islam, as opposed to "true Quakerism," would suggest the exotic heroism appropriate to an "Arabian poem of the wildest nature" (*Taylor*, 1, p. 223), for Southey the two in fact have a good deal in common – both are abstractions that could seem dissident yet intuitive and unified, reverent without the risk of "talking away religion." While writing *Thalaba* in 1799 Southey even had to remind himself, "I must build a Saracenic mosque, not a Quaker meeting-house" (*NL*, I, p. 272). Strange as it may sound, in Southey's mind his wild Arabian romance risked becoming a Quaker poem.

THALABA

Southey accordingly presents a very different take on Islam than Gibbon, for whom Islam was the rational religion, "less inconsistent with reason, than the creed of mystery and superstition, which, in the seventh century, disgraced the simplicity of the gospel."[59] The romance narrative of *Thalaba* advances a totalizing vision of history and morality for which Islam rather than rational Dissent or Deism provides the appropriate frame in which to express Southey's heterodox and Jacobin opposition to established authorities. For the poem certainly was intended to be Jacobin in its allegorical representation of evil. In his plans for the poem Southey wrote, "Wealth, Power, and Priestcraft form the Trinity of Evil," asking "Cannot the Dom Danael [*sic*] be made to allegorize those systems that make the misery of mankind?" and "Can the evils of established systems be well allegorized? Can Thamama [the original name for Thalaba] see them in the realms where the Magicians govern?" (*CPB*, IV, pp. 182–83). The sorcerers do subsequently allegorize "the evils of established systems," but not in the way that Burkean mystification represents for a Wollstonecraft, Paine, or Godwin the duplicity of aristocratic and Anglican power. For Southey, on the other hand, established systems do not mystify but rather systematize power: in *Thalaba*, evil is skeptical and rational whereas good resists analysis and instead intuitively recognizes itself in the will of God and acts accordingly.[60] Metaphysics, William Haller reminds us, "had become anathema to Southey, and the evil sorcerers in his poem are metaphysicians of the school of Locke, but Thalaba staunchly defends revelation and innate truth."[61]

Inspired by *The Faerie Queene*, Southey's childhood favorite from which he took the epigraph to the first Book of *Thalaba* in editions after 1801, Southey presents a romance hero who conquers duplicitous evil in order to champion a God of unity. It is often claimed that the poem is betrayed by its combination of absolute fatalism with the Spenserian allegory of inner purification.[62] As part of his larger design "of exhibiting the various mythologies of the world in a set of poems founded upon the characteristics of each," *Thalaba* was to exhibit Islam in the form of a romance, and, as Southey writes to Taylor in 1804, "Fatalism is the corner-stone of Mahometry, the hero of the Islamic romance was to act therefore under the impulse of Destiny" (*Taylor*, I, p. 502). Repeatedly throughout the poem the reader is reminded, "thou canst not change / What in the Book of Destiny is written" (II.85–86). From Azrael's prophecy at the end of Book I, let alone from the title itself, we know that Thalaba is the destined destroyer, the "chosen Arab" (VI.28), and although Southey throws numerous and fantastic hindrances in his way, we seldom fear for either his faith or virtue, for "Ye can shake the foundations of earth, / But not the Word of God: / But not one letter can ye change / Of what his Will hath written!" (II.219–22). Thalaba's vengeance is "long delayed" (III.375), but, because the poem is so "severely unilinear," to borrow a phrase from Bernhardt-Kabisch,[63] each delay merely reinforces the poem's guiding principle that "Blindly the wicked work / The righteous will of Heaven" (V.457–58).

"Where singleness is virtue," Herbert F. Tucker writes of *Thalaba*, "the villainous are, as might be expected, the poem's double agents."[64] The fundamental conflict between the physical unity of good and the metaphysical duplicity of evil forms the generic basis of the romance. One of the reasons Bernhardt-Kabisch dismisses Southey as falling short of "the new consciousness that we call 'Romantic'" is that *Thalaba* is hardly an "internalized quest romance."[65] The Arabian protagonist, predictably, is among the most corporeal heroes of the Romantic period (see Figure 6), and thus instead of internalizing faith in his quest to conquer the evil of this rationalist priesthood, Southey's hero comes to embody the will of God.[66] Although Thalaba must give up material talismans in order to conquer through spiritual faith, the poem refuses to accept this faith as purely internal or ideal. In Southey's Islamic frame, faith, like fate, resides less in the spirit than in skin and muscle; a note to Book V reads, "The Mahummedans [*sic*] believe that the decreed events of every man's life are impressed in divine characters on his forehead."[67] Unlike the bodies of other physicalized figures of Orientalist romance, such as Beckford's Vathek or Moore's veiled prophet Mokanna, Thalaba's is associated with neither luxury nor appetite but rather with immediacy, agency, and simplicity. Although there is much to be dismissed in Islam, in the Koran itself, Southey writes, "there is nothing to shock belief," and although it may be "dull and full of repetitions, . . . there is an interesting simplicity in the tenets it inculcates" (*Selections*, I, p. 77). The religion, however, "has been miserably perverted" (*Selections*, I, p. 78): in Southey's poem the

Figure 6. "The Garden of Aloadin," from William Hawkes Smith, *Essays in Design . . .*
Illustrative of the Poem of Thalaba the Destroyer. Reproduced by permission of the
British Library.

unperverted form of the religion embodied by Thalaba presents an austere
and enthusiastic subordination of reason and doubt to the will. The severe
unilinearity of the poem, the courageous enthusiasm of a hero who acts
under the impulse of destiny, and the unfailing rectitude of intuitive
judgment combine to equate the will of the hero with that of God, and
it is this "ecstasy of agency"[68] which results from Southey's strange
syncretism of Saracenic mosque and Quaker meeting-house. In the two
symmetrically arranged philosophical temptations of Thalaba, by the
sorcerers Lobaba, in Book IV (three books from the beginning), and
Mohareb, in Book IX (three books from the end), Southey's hero is
revealed to be a monotheistic revolutionary, opposed to the "evils of
established systems," who remains loyal to an imaginative ideology of
unity, intuition, and action over the skeptical proliferation of discourses,
doubts, and contingencies.

The first test comes from Lobaba, who, like Archimago, assumes the
form of an "antient man" (IV.63) and places himself in the hero's way. As
they proceed, Lobaba involves Thalaba in a discussion of the nature of

truth, for Thalaba has asked Lobaba to confirm the story he has heard of
the fall of the Angels Haruth and Maruth, a story Southey took from
various sources including d'Herbelot and Sale's "Preliminary Discourse"
to the Koran. The position of evil rests on duplicity and contingency, for
Lobaba will not allow one version of truth to predominate. According
to Lobaba, "all things feel / The power of Time and Change! thistles and
grass / Usurp the desolate palace, and the weeds / Of Falshood root in
the aged pile of Truth" (IV.107–10). Set among the ruins of Babylon, the
conversation questions the ordering principles of history. For Thalaba, the
fall of Haruth and Maruth is explained by the determinate truth of their
sin, for sent by Allah to be judges on earth, they gazed on the beautiful
Zohara "With fleshly eyes" (IV.128). Therefore, their residence among the
ruins of Babylon must be explained by a narrative of expiation – "I have
heard the Angels expiate their guilt" (IV.102) – and punishment – "penal
ages might at length restore them / Clean from offence" (IV.140–41).
Similarly, the "power of Time and Change" which brings about the rise
and fall of empires must also be ordered by providence and manifest the
will of Allah. Whereas for Lobaba the ruin represents the "weeds / of
Falshood," according to Thalaba's position the ruin represents divine
truth just as much as the palace it replaced, for both participate in a
unified narrative of historical transformation. After Thalaba relates his
version of the story, however, Lobaba responds, "Son what thou sayest is
true, and it is false" (IV.167). Opposed to Thalaba's intuitive and monotheistic faith in truth is Lobaba's rational and duplicitous skepticism,
which takes the form of heresy: "All things have a double power, / Alike
for good and evil. the same fire / That on the comfortable hearth at eve /
Warmed the good man, flames o'er the house at night" (IV.239–42).
Lobaba does not replace Thalaba's narrative of local (Haruth and Maruth)
and historical (Babylon) change with an alternative story, for, like that of
all the sorcerers, Lobaba's evil represents a world of power in which right
and wrong are not absolute but are contingent on reason, cunning,
and strength. "Nothing in itself is good or evil, / But only in its use"
(IV.251–52), Lobaba insists. It is almost as if Lobaba encourages a romance
plot in which the hero *could* fail, but subsequent events assure us that
Haruth and Maruth do suffer for their sin and that Babylon did fall
because Allah willed it. As throughout the poem, faith in determinate
truth asserts its power by expressing itself on the body of Thalaba. After
Lobaba convinces Thalaba to remove the magic ring that protects him
from the sorcerer's blade, a wasp settles on Thalaba's finger and stings
him, making it impossible to remove the stone: "The baffled Sorcerer

knew the hand of Heaven, / And inwardly blasphemed" (IV.333–34). God's intervention upon the physical body of Thalaba, not Thalaba's internalization of God's will, foils Lobaba, and here it is only the sorcerer's blasphemy that is "inward." Lobaba persists in his attempt, however, and leads Thalaba into a sandstorm, where he tries to persuade Thalaba to invoke the powers of his ring rather than rely on God: "If Allah and the Prophet will not save / Call on the Powers that will!" (IV.522–23). Allah and the Prophet will save, however, and when Lobaba mounts a magic car and attempts to abandon Thalaba to the storm, "Driven by the breath of God / A column of the Desert met his way" (IV.568–69). Southey's generic assumptions link absolute fatalism with a stoic vision of individual and historical transformation according to which right and wrong are determinate and stories are singular in their truth, in which good is a unity defended by an intuitive and physical faith.

In the second philosophical temptation, which occurs in Book IX, Thalaba is held captive on Mohareb's island, and the Sultan takes the opportunity to challenge Thalaba's monotheism, his allegiance to the one true God. Mohareb "build[s] skilfully the sophist speech": "Hear me! in Nature are two hostile Gods, / Makers and Masters of existing things, / Equal in power" (IX.150–52). A kind of Zoroastrian polytheism, Mohareb's sophistry insists on equal and independent forces, Allah and Eblis, that govern human existence: "Be sure, had Allah crushed his Enemy, / But that the power was wanting. From the first, / Eternal as themselves their warfare is, / To the end it must endure" (IX.166–69). In this struggle, which will only end with the end of time, human beings must choose sides, and the only basis on which they can make that choice is power: "Evil and Good . . . / What are they Thalaba but words? in the strife / Of Angels, as of men, the weak are guilty; / Power must decide" (IX.169–72). After death human souls do not reside in heaven or hell, but rather "each joins the host / Of his great Leader," either Allah or Eblis, "aiding in the war / Whose fate involves his own" (IX.176–78). According to Mohareb's eschatology, at the end of time one of these two coeternal and independent forces will vanquish the other: "Woe to the vanquished then! / . . . Thou Thalaba hast chosen ill thy part, / If choice it may be called, where will was not, / Nor searching doubt, nor judgement wise to weigh" (IX.179–85). Although Mohareb predicts the victory of Eblis, the history he describes is purely contingent – indeed, Volneyan – for it depends not on fate but on power and will. Thalaba, according to Mohareb's dogma, has "chosen ill" his part because the weak intuitive faith of Islam is opposed to the rational skepticism of "searching doubt" and "judgement" that wins power for the sect of Eblis. In Mohareb's scheme of things, Allah must necessarily be the weaker party because he requires the resignation of the will, and Mohareb, an utter ideologue, would be perfectly correct if the world of Southey's romance were in fact a chaotic struggle for power between various competing parties rather than an ordered theocracy. In Southey's romance narrative, however, there remains one truth, and according to the Islamic frame, that one truth is a spontaneous, physical, and fatalistic submission of the human will to that of God. The poem ends with the destruction of Mohareb and all the sorcerer brood by the strong right arm of Thalaba, a repetition of Thalaba's first encounter with Mohareb, a victory of faith described as follows: "Mohareb reels before him! he right on / With knee, with breast, with arm, / Presses the staggering foe!" (v.483–85). Having defeated the foe "With knee, with breast, with arm," "Thalaba's breath came fast, / And panting he breathed out / A broken prayer of thankfulness" (v.493–95). Thalaba here affirms his faith not in words of rational prayer but in "broken" and inarticulate panting breaths, in reverence by and of the body.

In spite of Thalaba's unifying intuition as he proceeds single-mindedly toward the predestined destruction of his Archimagos, Duessas, and Acraslas, the wizards of the Domdaniel, the poem's notes, which outweigh the text of the poem, force the reader into digressions from the narrative telos – digressions into Orientalist scholarship, travel literature, popular ballads, vulgar superstition, and, as Marilyn Butler calls it, Southey's "sardonic comparativist commentary."[69] Whereas Victorian editions pruned or omitted the notes in an effort to present Southey as a lesser Lake Schooler, leading to the earnest song of stoic triumph presented by Maurice Fitzgerald in the 1909 Oxford edition of Southey's poetry,[70] they are now seen as a central part of the work. Ingeniously read by Herbert Tucker as "Inoculating *Thalaba* against itself," as demarcating "a European, English, and urbane perspective that, precisely because it is vigilantly orientalist, runs no risk of going oriental,"[71] and by Clare Simmons as establishing Southey's "authority not merely over the text but also over the monumentalized 'Orient' they expose to the reader,"[72] the notes provide powerfully skeptical and parodic elements which form a negative and critical counterpart to the triumphalist romance. In them we find a rationalistic impulse apparently at odds with the poem's intuitive and fatalistic heroism. This impulse serves, however, not to obscure Thalaba's Mahometan "inner light" but rather to check its potential excesses by presenting a negative critique of irrationalism, of the superstition, priestcraft, and fanaticism that accompany various forms of religious enthusiasm. As Bernhardt-Kabisch rightly proposes, Southey "feared . . . the threat which the irrational appeal of religion and other 'epidemics of the mind' posed to the rational judgment in the form of fanaticism and divisiveness."[73] Along with fear, of course, came fascination with the sources of infection: these epidemics could as easily issue from Islam as from Catholicism, Hinduism, Methodism, Calvinism, or popular superstition and folklore, precisely the subjects in which Southey immersed himself. In the tradition of biblical criticism, especially that introduced by Pierre Bayle, in whose *Dictionnaire Historique et Critique* "the real action takes place" not in the entries themselves but in the "remarks,"[74] Southey's skeptical commentary divests history and religion of the enthusiastic excesses associated both with popular beliefs and established orthodoxies or dogmas even as it revels in its source materials. Especially in its parodic moments, the commentary's syncretism, on the one hand, and narrative self-reflexivity, on the other, are demystifying: providing the negative counterpart to the unified heroism of the romance, syncretism effectively bridges the gap between the mythological and the actual while the notes' self-reflexivity contains ("inoculates" the poem against) the possibility of its own hero's fanaticism.

Southey's syncretic notes tend to combine myth with social and/or natural history in order to suggest that remote mythological and historical realms are not absolutely separate or alien from present realities. When subject to the Enlightenment gaze of the syncretic mythographer, these realms in fact prove not to be mystical or even symbolic at all. To this extent, Southey's commentary produces a novelistic supplement to the poem's romance, and, in keeping with Bakhtin's terms, this generic hybridity brings the romance narrative into "living contact with unfinished, still-evolving contemporary reality."[75] Considering the eventual destruction of the Domdaniel in his common-place book, for instance, Southey writes,

A good mock-philosophic note might be made upon the changes produced in the earth by the falling in of the Dom-Daniel. The origin of the Maelstrom proved to have been this. Increase of cold also in those regions, the rush of the waters having put out a great portion of the central fire; hence no vineyards in England as formerly. Consequences from the immense quantity of steam thus generated. – Geyser. (*CPB*, IV, pp. 212–13)[76]

Southey's relentless mythopoesis drives him to imagine the fantastical conclusion of the poem, in which Thalaba dies Samson-like when the walls of the underwater seminary crash down around him, as the historical origin of contemporary natural phenomena. While the romance allows the reader to understand the allegorical and transcendent meanings of Thalaba's final victory over the various forms of evil represented by the seminary, the hybridization of the genre also produces a kind of mock-philosophy in which the allegory accounts for contemporary experiences of the natural world. "The falling in of the Dom-Daniel" comes into contact with the still-evolving realities of meteorological and geological change.

Southey decided not to include this note, but when it comes time for Zeinab, Thalaba's mother, to express her resignation in losing her husband and children, she recites, "He gave, he takes away, / The Lord our God is good!" (1.41–42), and the note explains,

I have placed a scripture phrase in the mouth of a Mohammedan; but it is a saying of Job, and there can be no impropriety in making a modern Arab speak like an ancient one . . . It had been easy to have made Zeinab speak from the Koran, if the tame language of the Koran could be remembered by the few who have toiled through its dull tautology. I thought it better to express a feeling of religion in that language with which our religious ideas are connected. (p. 193)

As Southey knew, Job, after all, was an Edomite sheikh of the classical Arabian empire, and the syncretism of the passage unites the resignation of a modern Arab with contemporary Christian stoicism in the common Judeo-Arabic origin. On the one hand, Southey's condescension to the Koran, which he could only read in translation, dismisses the language of Islam as inferior to its more sublime classical and European scriptural counterparts. But, like all syncretism, Southey's is double-edged, and thus on the other hand the modern Arab and Christian share the same feelings, for those feelings share the same paternity in the expressions of the ancient Arab and Old Testament archetype. Connecting the past to the present and synthesizing religious languages even while denigrating the Koran, the note finds the common stoicism of Christianity and Islam not in scripture as mythology but rather in the originary, historical, and demystified Job, an ancient Arab.

Syncretism provided Southey with a range of often contradictory opportunities, which suggest that in reading *Thalaba* we should follow Nigel Leask in his attempt "to focus upon anxieties and instabilities rather than positivities and totalities in the Romantic discourse of the Orient."[77] Thus the superstitious Mohammedans can correspond to Catholics in their shared use of the rosary, in a note to Book V, and at the same time they can portray Southey's idealized version of pastoral simplicity and radical equality. Describing Moath's virtuous domesticity, Southey offers a note from Volney: "We must not . . . when we speak of the Bedouins, affix to the words Prince and Lord, the ideas they usually convey; we should come nearer the truth by comparing them to substantial farmers . . . whose simplicity they resemble in their dress as well as in their domestic life and manners " (p. 216). And earlier, when Moath invites the disguised Abdaldar to rest and eat, Southey provides a note from Pococke's *A Description of the East*: "an Arab Prince will often dine in the street before his door and call to all that pass even beggars, in the usual expression, *Bisimillah*, that is, in the name of God . . . for the Arabs who are great levellers, put every body on a footing with them" (p. 208). If many Orientalist accounts could suppress internal dissidence by associating religious and political oppositionist groups with Islam, Southey's syncretism could just as readily appropriate Islam in order either to critique Catholic superstition or to bolster the Rousseauean ideals of his own Pantisocratic utopianism.

Another way in which Southey's commentary serves as a negative critique of religious excess involves the parodic reflection of the notes upon the generic qualities of the romance itself. When taken as a whole, including its eclectic patchwork of sources and commentary, *Thalaba* simultaneously narrates the high heroic tale of destiny and ironically contemplates the artifice of generic narration. Southey's primary debt, as we have seen, is to Spenser, but in other respects Southey also takes his cues from Cervantes' self-conscious revelation of the underside of romance, the open-ended and contingent nature of narrative. In this manner, the notes contain and check the single-mindedness of both the narrative and Thalaba himself, whose actions and faith border on a kind of virtuous fanaticism, thus revealing Southey's profound sense of the hazards of enthusiasm raised by his own hero. Thalaba, according to Southey, is a "male Joan of Arc" (*Taylor*, II, p. 82), and in a memorable letter of 1804 he wrote that he feared meeting Joan in heaven and "upon nearer acquaintance" finding her to be "a crazy papist" (*Selections*, I, p. 268). In 1801 Southey had recommended to a friend, "Observe the growth of methodism, perhaps more nearly connected with popery than is generally imagined" (*Selections*, I, p. 146), and Thalaba's Islamic heroism thus risks shading into other forms of enthusiastic zealotry.

Several times the commentary insists that we laugh at the poem's manipulation of fantastical circumstances, introducing a kind of imaginative and parodic free-play by asserting the constructed nature of the narrative. In Book VIII, Thalaba meets the sorcerer Mohareb for the second time, "Whom erst his arm had thrust / Down the bitumen pit" (VIII.449–50). Earlier, in Book V, Mohareb failed to deceive Thalaba into betraying his faith in Allah and the Prophet. Angered by his failure, Mohareb called Thalaba a "camel-kneed prayer-monger" (V.431), and in the ensuing fight Thalaba cast Mohareb into an abyss. In Book VIII, however, Thalaba is taken captive and brought to an island where he finds Mohareb not only restored to life but now ruling as Sultan. Lest the attentive reader of romance should wonder how this could be so, the footnote reads, "How came Mohareb to be Sultan of this Island? Every one who has read Don Quixote knows that there are always Islands to be had by Adventurers. He killed the former Sultan and reigned in his stead. what [*sic*] could not a Domdanielite perform? The narration would have interrupted the flow of the main story" (p. 270). It would be easy to dismiss such a note by attributing it to authorial laziness: if he had really tried, *without* interrupting the flow of the main story Southey could have resurrected Mohareb from the abyss by yet another magic talisman and narrated the subsequent events by which he came to be Sultan. Such a dismissal, however, would miss the effect of the note, which is to signify that the audience of *Thalaba* is one that "has read Don Quixote" and knows that the generic contract between author and reader of this particular romance involves the awareness that "there are always Islands to be had by Adventurers" and that enchanted helmets can turn out to be imaginatively transformed barbers' basins. Further-more, if "the *narration* would have interrupted the flow of the main story," then the *note* certainly does so as well. But whereas the interruption of the main story by the narration would have simply detracted from the romance, the actual interruption of the story by the note introduces an instability in the genre itself. The fatalistic plot of a romance in which supposedly nothing whatsoever can "check the chariot-wheels of Destiny" (XI.2), when so checked, proves to be a plot constructed by a parodic consciousness aware of the conventionality and artifice of the form.

A final check upon the poem's excesses comes in the form of one note's parodic, self-reflexive, and syncretic pretense of conflating literature and myth with theology. If, unlike the sorcerers, the Quakerish Mahometan Thalaba resists "talking away religion, by a multiplicity of conversation," the commentary shares no such concern. As Aeneas must discover the entrance to the underworld from the Cumaean Sibyl, Thalaba must learn the way to the underwater seminary of the Domdaniel from the Simorg.[78]

"Reverently the youth approached / That old and only Bird" (xi.137–38), and the description is accompanied by a note, which begins, "In the Bahar-Danush the Simorg is mentioned as a genus – not an individual. this [*sic*] is heresy, – the unity of the Simorg being expressed in all the books of canonical Romance" (p. 297). Parodying the language of theological debate, Southey's note first conflates the "books of canonical romance" with the scriptures of revealed religion. Southey here takes the supposedly orthodox line of asserting that the Simorg is a unitary individual against the heterodox belief that it is a genus, a "heresy" taken from the *Bahar-Danush; or, Garden of Knowledge. An Oriental Romance* (1799) by Jonathan Scott, who had served in the East India Company as Persian Secretary to Warren Hastings. The poet of *Thalaba* becomes a kind of dual consciousness as both the Orientalist recaster of the Virgilian convention and the syncretic mythographer who must yet again interrupt the plot by introducing his own mock commentary. There is an extreme sense of skeptical containment – and of belatedness – in the repetition of the epic visit to the oracular figure detoured by mock scholarship in which the now ludicrously dogmatic poet pretends earnestly to defend his representation of the Persian Phoenix in the language of Christological debate.

Southey's notes have led to the common criticism that *Thalaba* is merely a patchwork of Orientalist sources. Jeffrey was among the first to attack Southey's manic borrowings and pastings: "the book is entirely composed of scraps, borrowed from the oriental tale-books, and travels into the Mahometan countries, seasoned up for the English reader with some fragments of our own ballads, and shreds of our older sermons."[79] Peacock, in *The Four Ages of Poetry*, agrees that "Mr. Southey wades through ponderous volumes of travels and old chronicles . . . and when he has a commonplace book full of monstrosities, strings them into an epic."[80] And Herman Merivale, in the *Edinburgh Review* for January 1839, repeats the charge: "He plunges into the learning of remote and half-romantic ages – . . . the stories of Eastern fable collected by Sale, D'Herbelot, and other Orientalists . . . and little labour is required to construct a story by way of thread to string together these choice extracts of his commonplace book."[81] The position is summed up by Maurice Fitzgerald in the 1909 Oxford edition: "He can construct rather than create."[82] But a different interpretation of Southey's pastiche-work could bracket off the opposition between creative and scholarly impulses and see their interaction as an early Romantic alternative to the ideology of transcendence. Unlike the great Romantic fragment poems such as

"Kubla Khan" and *Hyperion*, Southey's scraps of Eastern learning and digressions into popular superstition do not necessarily gesture toward a knowledge of a whole to be reconstituted in the private mind of the reader. *Thalaba*, instead, is a "monument of vile and depraved taste," a dissident composite of Saracenic mosque and Quaker meeting-house. In Southey's Orientalist romance we find an anti-sectarian yet nonconformist, heterodox, and revolutionary revision of the old conflict between the Redcrosse Knight, who defends Una, the true and unitary religion, and the forces of Archimago and Duessa, of superstition, duplicity, and error. At the same time, the hybrid poem checks its own enthusiasm, supplying skeptical and Cervantean counter-tones to the triumph of unity in its eclectic wanderings through the thorny woods of sardonic commentary, syncretic mythography, and generic parody.

Conclusion

"It is as impossible to establish an unity of religious opinion, as it is for man to regulate the great movements of the ocean," wrote Benjamin Bousfield in 1791.[1] Early Romanticism arose during an era in which literary innovations and political identities were shaped by diverse currents of belief and practice, by waves of religious opinion. Impelled by heterogeneous doctrines, tastes, interests, and ideologies, individuals formed themselves into sectarian, denominational, non-denominational, and established societies, assuming a series of correspondent personal, social, and aesthetic perspectives. The variety and popularity of religious writing during the early Romantic period suggest that to many, including the range of figures that this book has considered, efforts to comprehend the natures of and relationships between individuals, communities, and God played complex and crucial roles in the development of publicly oriented literary and political programs.

The meaning of religious organization itself provided a conflicted field of debate and representation through which early Romantic writers understood themselves and their work. If during the late eighteenth century many nonconformist writers associated themselves with liberal Dissenting denominations whereas others, especially lapsed Anglicans, embraced either non-denominational or anti-sectarian varieties of nonconformity, early-nineteenth-century literary culture saw a steady diminution of the former, denominational mode. As liberal Dissent gave way to Methodism, Evangelicalism, and the missionary movement, and as the progress of the French Revolution and the Revolutionary War drove England into a period of political and religious retrenchment, the public viability of denominational or sectarian identities dwindled in the minds of many heterodox nonconformist writers, and so did the possibilities of literary affiliations explicitly rooted in the values and interests of these clearly defined religious organizations. (Think how different Hazlitt would have been had he been born the son of a Dissenting minister in

Shropshire in 1758 rather than 1778.) In the absence of these affiliations there emerged a different spirit of the age, one that would find its religious articulation in the Oxford Movement of the 1830s rather than in the ultimately successful attempt to repeal the Corporation and Test Acts in 1828.

Thus by 1816, in her bluntly titled "Poetry and Reality," the Dissenting poet and children's writer Jane Taylor – raised in Independent congregations but sympathetic to Methodism, to which she converted – could oppose the spirit of "Poetry" to the "Reality" of religious Dissent. Taylor describes the figure of the poet as

> a high-flown, mental thing,
> As fine and fragile as *libella's* wing,
> All soul and intellect, the ethereal mind
> Scarcely within its earthly house confin'd.[2]

Immaterial and removed from the social realities of his immediate surroundings, the poet nonetheless considers himself to be devout and his poetry to be a form of worship. It is the Sabbath, and his

> inmost soul responsive swells
> To every change of those religious bells; . . .
> His mind exalted, melted, sooth'd, and free
> From earthly tumult, all tranquility; –
> If this is not devotion what can be? (pp. 79–80, lines 27–33)

The poet, however, muses "not with others" (p. 85, line 135), and his devotion to the abstract and distant God of nature – "There he can sit, and thence his soul may rise, / Caught up in contemplation, to the skies, / And worship nature's God on reason's plan" (p. 80, lines 42–44) – takes place in the private confines of his own mind and heart, not in the public space of the meeting-house: "But, gentle poet, wherefore not repair / To yonder temple? God is worshipp'd there" (p. 80, lines 36–37). Opposed to this "Poetry" of natural religion and interior transcendence is the "Reality" of an itinerant nonconformist preacher, a Methodist:

> A poor Itinerant – start not at the sound!
> To yonder licens'd barn his course is bound;
> To christen'd heathens, upon Christian ground,
> To preach – or if you will, to rant and roar
> That Gospel news they never heard before. (p. 89, lines 201–05)

Next to Taylor's caricature of the ethereal Romantic poet, the ranting Methodist preacher presents a perspective incompatible with the "spilt religion" of "natural supernaturalism" found in trees, hills, and woods, or in pagan, classical antiquity, "For that which turns poor non-conformists sick, / Touches poetic feeling to the quick" (p. 86, lines 153–54). Between Romantic poetry and Methodist reality there is now no middle ground, no moderate public Dissenting life suited to preserve and foster English literary culture and expression. Whereas the poet is insensible to the gospel, the itinerant preacher is insensible to nature: his pace is rapid, and "he checks it not, / To gaze or muse on that sequester'd spot" (p. 88, lines 191–92). Taylor ends by bidding the poet,

> Pluck a wild daisy, moralise on that,
> And drop a tear for an expiring gnat,
> Watch the light clouds o'er distant hills that pass,
> Or write a sonnet to a blade of grass. (p. 92, lines 258–61)

In 1816, then, Taylor could satirically claim that the gospel, preached by enthusiastic Evangelical ministers to individual Christians come together for public worship, as opposed to a sonnet written by a solitary poet to a single blade of grass, "was ne'er design'd, / To please the morbid, proud, romantic mind" (p. 87, lines 166–67). This "romantic mind" clearly inhabits a different world from that of Milton, Bunyan, or Defoe, or, for that matter, of the late eighteenth century, and thus in 1813 Southey could dismissively assert in the *Quarterly Review*, "The spirit of dissent is as little favourable to literature as to manners; the Muses as well as the Graces are heathenish."[3]

But, as I hope to have shown, if the rising soul of the non-denominational, private poet needed to distance itself from public, clearly defined Dissenting affiliations, this Romantic subjectivity was itself in part the legacy of a late-eighteenth-century field of conflict in which Dissenting communities already seemed to be losing, or at least struggling to sustain, their individual and focused characteristics. The most salient example of this late-eighteenth-century failure to discriminate between distinct communities is Burke's scornful attack in *Reflections* on Richard Price. Having accused Price of encouraging the proliferation of Dissent for its own sake – "Let the noble teachers but dissent . . . This great point once secured, it is taken for granted their religion will be rational and manly" – Burke continues, "I doubt whether religion would reap all the benefits which the calculating divine computes from this 'great company of preachers.' It would certainly be a valuable addition of nondescripts to the ample collection of known classes, genera and species, which at present beautify the *hortus siccus* of dissent."[4] Burke's famous reduction of Dissent to a *hortus siccus* at the end of the eighteenth century, echoed by Hazlitt at the beginning of the nineteenth, represents an early moment in a long tradition which has affected both those hostile and sympathetic to religious dissidence. For many since Burke, Dissent has been divided into various classes, genera, and species, but essentially these have too often conformed to one unified image of Enlightenment rationality and Whiggish opposition to the establishment in church and state. The "great point" of their dissent from the Church of England homogenizes the collective identities of Dissenters and flattens the very real cultural and social differences that accompanied their theological and organizational distinctions. Whether the garden is viewed as withered or flourishing, it too often remains one uniform tract according to both hostile and sympathetic systems of classification.

Descriptions of late-eighteenth-century Dissent, both from within the Romantic period and from later vantage points, have tended to follow Burke's lead, but the accounts of two early-nineteenth-century Dissenters, Walter Wilson and Josiah Conder, suggest that a more complex process was taking place, and accordingly that a more nuanced account is required. In *The History and Antiquities of Dissenting Churches and Meeting Houses* (1808), Wilson writes,

A spirit of inquiry as to the distinguishing features of nonconformity, has, with the exception of the Baptists, wholly fled from the different sects. The Presbyterians have either deserted to the world, or sunk under the influence of a lukewarm ministry; and the Independents have gone over in a body to the Methodists. Indifference and enthusiasm have thinned the ranks of the old stock, and those who remain behind are lost in the croud [*sic*] of modern religionists.[5]

In the first decade of the new century, Wilson felt himself to be alone in his "inquiry as to the distinguishing features of nonconformity," for the "old stock" of Presbyterians and Independents seemed to have lost both those distinguishing features themselves along with the desire to represent them to a wider, nonsectarian public. Partially due to the rise of Evangelicalism and the enduring popular appeal of Calvinism, the Particular Baptists maintained their unity, but for the most part old Dissent gave way to Methodism on the one hand and the undistinguished "croud of modern religionists" on the other.[6] It is this crowd that many Dissenters themselves saw as a symptom of an indifferent age when public, sectarian virtues and values had given way to petty self-interest and, as Coleridge put it in 1798, a confined and confining "sectarian mannerism, which generally narrows the Intellect itself, and always narrows the sphere of it's [*sic*] operation" (*CL*, i, p. 366). But Dissenters did not lose the sense that a different set of sectarian manners had existed. Thus in 1811 Josiah Conder, one of Jane Taylor's fellow "Associate Minstrels," laments that "the republic of taste and letters" is in "a declining state," for "It is divided, not into parties, but factions; numerous little sects, not indeed the independents of old, – hostile to each other, without the magnanimity of ambition, or the firmness of principle; and only according in a vague impatience of old establishments and superior power."[7] To Conder, a member of the Aikin circle and an active collaborator in Dissenting publishing networks, the "republic of taste and letters" has lost its focused energy and principled integrity precisely because its writers are now divided into "factions," not "parties," and into "numerous little sects," not the vigorous sects of "the independents of old." Mapping the religious onto the literary world, Conder echoes Burke in seeing contemporary Dissenters and writers alike as distinguished only by their shared "vague impatience of old establishments and superior power." But unlike Burke, Conder and Wilson consider the loss of Dissenting sectarian identity to be a loss to British character and culture. At the heart of this loss, according to this retrospective Dissenting vision, was the libertarian tradition that publicly foregrounded connections between "magnanimity of ambition" and "firmness of principle," between the interests and dispositions of patriotic yet dissident Protestants whose Dissenting party integrity and activity sustained British liberty and letters. There is a notable contrast between Conder's and Wilson's nostalgic retrospection and Barbauld's confident claim – by "A DISSENTER" – to the national reading public in 1790, "If our writers are solid, elegant, or nervous, you will read our books and imbibe our sentiments" (*SPP*, p. 272).

Although the erasure of Dissenting particularity and sectarian or denominational models of public life may have been a necessary stage in the subsequent development of dominant forms of Romanticism, we have seen that in fundamental ways the Dissenting tradition shaped the literary and political cultures of the late eighteenth century. If nineteenth- and twentieth-century movements either found this tradition to be limiting or needed to suppress the vitality of its history, it is then all the more important to return it to an account of early Romanticism that seeks to address the period on its own, contemporary terms. The conflicting narratives of early Romantic culture that have emerged in this study's contextualization of Godwin, Wollstonecraft, Coleridge, and Southey in relation to the Dissenting public sphere, a sphere represented and sustained to a great extent by members of the Aikin network, suggest that current attempts to understand Romantic publicity and sociability, as well as their genesis in the literary and political communities of the late eighteenth century, require detailed attention to the beliefs, practices, interests, affiliations, tastes, and tones of religious nonconformity.

Notes

INTRODUCTION

1 William Hazlitt, "On the Tendency of Sects," in *The Selected Writings of William Hazlitt*, ed. Duncan Wu, 9 vols. (London: William Pickering, 1998), II, p. 51.

2 Ibid., II, p. 50. I use the term "nonconformist" to describe a range of religious beliefs and dispositions that prevented English Protestants from conforming to the Articles and rites of the Church of England. By "Dissent" I mean the three principal denominations of "old Dissent" – the Presbyterians, Independents (or Congregationalists), and Baptists – as well as the Unitarians (see Fig. 1), whose evolution out of old Dissent I discuss in Chapter 2. Methodists were often thought of as "new Dissenters," and the Quakers, whom I discuss in Chapter 6, were usually considered to be a nonconformist sect distinct from the Dissenting communities.

3 It will be important to distinguish between sectarianism and denominationalism. With a few exceptions, most of the Dissenting groups addressed constitute denominations, not sects, in the late eighteenth century. Please see below for a discussion of these terms.

4 Isabel Rivers, *Reason, Grace, and Sentiment: A Study of the Language of Religion and Ethics in England, 1660–1780*, vol. I, *Whichcote to Wesley* (Cambridge University Press, 1991) and vol. II, *Shaftesbury to Hume* (Cambridge University Press, 2000); Edward H. Davidson and William J. Scheick, *Paine, Scripture, and Authority: The Age of Reason as Religious and Political Idea* (Bethlehem: Lehigh University Press, 1994); and the important collection, *Enlightenment and Religion*, ed. Knud Haakonssen (Cambridge University Press, 1996). Other major sources include James E. Bradley, *Religion, Revolution, and English Radicalism: Nonconformity in Eighteenth-Century Politics and Society* (Cambridge University Press, 1990); Richard Brown, *Church and State in Modern Britain* (London: Routledge, 1991); Robert Hole, *Pulpits, Politics and Public Order in England 1760–1832* (Cambridge University Press, 1989); and Deryck W. Lovegrove, *Established Church, Sectarian People: Itinerancy and the Transformation of English Dissent, 1780–1830* (Cambridge University Press, 1988). All students of Dissent are indebted to Michael R. Watts' indispensable companion volumes, *The Dissenters: From the Reformation to*

the French Revolution, vol. 1 (Oxford: Clarendon Press, 1978) and *The Dissenters: The Expansion of Evangelical Nonconformity*, vol. 11 (Oxford: Clarendon Press, 1995).

5 M. H. Abrams, *Natural Supernaturalism: Tradition and Revolution in Roman-
tic Literature* (New York: Norton, 1971); T. E. Hulme, *Speculations: Essays on
Humanism and the Philosophy of Art*, ed. Herbert Read (1924; London:
Routledge, 1949), p. 118.

6 Robert M. Ryan, *The Romantic Reformation: Religious Politics in English
Literature, 1789–1824* (Cambridge University Press, 1997).

7 Ryan dedicates a chapter to each of these writers, with the exception of
Coleridge (ibid., p. 10).

8 Ibid.

9 Martin Priestman, *Romantic Atheism: Poetry and Freethought, 1780–1830*
(Cambridge University Press, 1999).

10 Mark Canuel, *Religion, Toleration, and British Writing, 1790–1830* (Cambridge
University Press, 2002).

11 Ibid., p. 38.

12 In this and the following five notes, I offer working definitions of several basic
theological terms. Arminianism, named after the Dutch theologian Jacobus
Arminius (1560–1609), opposed or qualified each of the five points of Calvinist doctrine (see n. 15, below). The following account comes from a popular
pamphlet of the 1790s, *A Sketch of the Several Denominations into which the
Christian World is Divided; accompanied with a Persuasive to Religious Moderation*, 2nd edn. (London, 1795), by the General Baptist minister John Evans
(1767–1827): "1st. That God has not fixed the future state of mankind by an
absolute unconditional decree; but determined from all eternity, to bestow
salvation on those whom he foresaw would persevere to the end in their faith
in Jesus Christ, and to inflict punishment on those who should continue in
their unbelief, and resist to the end his divine assistance. 2ndly. That Jesus
Christ, by his death and sufferings, made an atonement for the sins of all
mankind in general, and of every individual in particular; that however none
but those who believe in him can be partakers of this divine benefit. 3dly.
That mankind are not totally depraved, and that depravity does not come
upon them by virtue of Adam's being their public head, but that mortality
and natural evil only are the direct consequences of his sin to posterity. 4thly.
That there is no such thing as irresistible grace in the conversion of sinners; –
and, 5thly. That those who are united to Christ by faith, may fall from their
faith, and forfeit finally their state of grace" (p. 36).

13 The core of Arianism was the belief in Christ's pre-existence as a divine but
subordinate and created being. High and low Arians differed on the degree of
dignity assigned to Christ: Arians "owned Christ to be God in a subordinate
sense, and considered his death to be a propitiation for sin . . . [They]
acknowledge that the Son was the *word*, though they deny its being eternal;
contending, that it had only been created prior to all other beings. Christ, say
they, had nothing of man in him except the flesh, with which the λόγος, or

word, spoken of by the Apostle John, was united, which supplied the rest. In modern times the term Arian is indiscriminately applied to those who consider Jesus simply subordinate to the Father. Some of them believe Christ to have been the creator of the world; but they ALL maintain that he existed previous to his incarnation, though in his pre-existent state they assign him different degrees of dignity. Hence the appellations High and Low Arian" (Evans, *A Sketch*, p. 26).

14 William Hurd's "An Account of the Presbyterians," in *A New Universal History of the Religious Rites, Ceremonies, and Customs of the Whole World* (London, 1788), begins, "The Presbyterians may be divided into the four following classes; First, Calvinists; secondly, Arminians; thirdly, Arians; and, lastly, Socinians" (p. 578). See Chapter 2 for a discussion of divisions among Presbyterians, particularly as those divisions contributed to the rise of Unitarianism.

15 The five points of eighteenth-century Calvinism are here synthesized from the Westminster Confession (1647) by Charles Lloyd (1766–1829), *Particulars of The Life of a Dissenting Minister* (London, 1813): "1. That God elected a certain number in Christ to everlasting glory, before the foundation of the world, according to his immutable purpose, and of his free grace and love, without the least regard to faith, to good works, or to any conditions to be performed by the creature; and that the rest of mankind he was pleased to ordain to dishonour and wrath for the glory of his vindictive justice (*Predestination*). 2. That Jesus Christ, by his sufferings and death, made an atonement for the sins of the elect, and for the sins of the elect alone (*Particular Redemption*). 3. That mankind are totally depraved in consequence of the fall; and, by virtue of Adam's being their federal head, the guilt of his sin was imputed, and a corrupt nature was conveyed to all his posterity, from which proceed all actual transgressions; and that by sin we are made subject to death, and to all miseries, temporal, spiritual, and eternal (*Original Sin*). 4. That all whom God has predestined to life, he is pleased in his appointed time effectually to call by his word and Spirit out of that state of sin and death, in which they are by nature, to grace and salvation by Jesus Christ (*Irresistible Grace*). 5. That those whom God has effectually called and sanctified by his Spirit shall never finally fall from a state of grace (*Perseverance of the Saints*)" (p. x).

16 Sandemanians were a sect of ultra-Calvinists, to be discussed in Chapter 4, characterized chiefly by a plurality of church elders in each congregation, literal translation of the New Testament, and the attempt to replicate primitive Christianity, including practices such as foot-washing and weekly feasts.

17 Theologically, Unitarians were Arminian, and either Arian or Socinian. Socinianism, of which Priestley became the philosophical champion during the early 1780s, stressed the complete humanity of Christ; Socinians believed in his divine mission but not in his divine nature or pre-existence, holding Christ to have been a man chosen by God to be His revelation. Socinians, as described by Evans, held that "Christ had no existence until born of the Virgin Mary, and that, being a man like ourselves, though endowed with a

large portion of the divine wisdom, the only objects of his mission were to teach the efficacy of repentance without an atonement, as a medium of the divine favour – to exhibit an example for our imitation; to seal his doctrine with his blood; and, in his resurrection from the dead, to indicate the certainty of our resurrection at the last day" (*A Sketch*, p. 29). Like many Unitarians, Priestley began as an Arian and a Presbyterian, but he was converted to Socinianism in the late 1760s by reading Nathaniel Lardner's *A Letter . . . Concerning . . . the Logos* (London, 1759).

18 Robert Southey, *Letters from England: By Don Manuel Alvarez Espriella*, 3 vols. (London, 1807), II, pp. 27–28.

19 Constantin François Volney, *Les Ruines, ou Méditations sur les Révolutions des Empires* (Paris, 1791).

20 In *A New Translation of Volney's Ruins* (Paris, 1802), begun by Thomas Jefferson and finished by Joel Barlow, the passage reads: "the subaltern sects, subdivided from the principal divisions, the Nestorians, the Eutycheans, the Jacobites, the Iconoclasts, the Anabaptists, the Presbyterians, the Wicliffites, the Osiandrians, the Manicheans, the Pietists, the Adamites, the Contemplatives, the Quakers, the Weepers, and a hundred others; all of distinct parties, persecuting when strong, tolerant when weak, hating each other in the name of a God of peace" (p. 186).

21 Max Weber, *The Theory of Social and Economic Organization*, ed. Talcott Parsons, trans. A. M. Henderson and Talcott Parsons (New York: Free Press, 1947), pp. 156–57; *The Sociology of Religion* (Boston: Beacon Press, 1922), p. 100; H. Richard Niebuhr, *The Social Sources of Denominationalism* (New York: Holt, 1929), p. 19; Peter L. Berger, "The Sociological Study of Sectarianism," *Social Research* 21 (Winter 1954): 467–85.

22 Bryan Wilson, *Patterns of Sectarianism: Organisation and Ideology in Social and Religious Movements* (London: Heineman, 1967), p. 23.

23 Ibid., p. 25.

24 Theophilus Lindsey, *A Sermon Preached At the Opening of the Chapel in Essex-House, Essex-Street, in the Strand, on Sunday, April 17, 1774* (London, 1774), pp. 5, 13.

25 Ibid., p. 14.

26 Robert Robinson, *An Essay on the Composition of a Sermon. Translated from the original French of The Revd. John Claude*, 2 vols. (London, 1778–79), II, p. lvi.

27 Richard Price, *A Discourse on the Love of Our Country, Delivered on Nov. 4, 1789, at the Meeting-House in the Old Jewry, to the Society for Commemorating the Revolution in Great Britain* (London, 1789), p. 18. Burke responded to this passage in *Reflections on the Revolution in France, and on the Proceedings in Certain Societies in London Relative to that Event* (London, 1790), p. 15.

28 "Letters on Preaching. Doctrinal, Practical, Experimental, Allegorical. Printed in the Evangelical Magazine for 1808; with Some Enlargements," in *The Preacher's Manual* (London, 1812), p. 105.

29 See Russell E. Richey, "The Origins of British Radicalism: The Changing Rationale for Dissent," *Eighteenth-Century Studies* 7 (1973–74): 179–92. James

E. Bradley has persuasively shown that eighteenth-century Dissenters did not act politically as a unified body: "Whigs and Nonconformists: 'Slumbering Radicalism' in English Politics, 1739–89," *Eighteenth-Century Studies* 9.1 (1975): 1–27.

30 See Wilfrid Prest, "Law, Lawyers and Rational Dissent," in *Enlightenment and Religion*, pp. 169–92.

31 Sometimes called the Clarendon Code, the four acts of anti-nonconformist legislation comprised the Corporation Act, the Act of Uniformity, the Conventicle Act, and the Five Mile Act.

The Corporation Act (1661): every magistrate and every civic and municipal officer must take the Sacrament according to the rites of the Church of England within a year of his election, and must take the oaths of allegiance and supremacy.

The Act of Uniformity (1662): deprived of their livings clergy who would not subscribe to the Thirty-Nine Articles and declare their assent to the Book of Common Prayer, and denied them the rights to preach or to earn livings as schoolmasters or private tutors, unless they had a license from a Bishop.

The Conventicle Act (1664): forbade more than five people over the age of sixteen to gather together for worship except in a church. The first offence bore a sentence of three months imprisonment or a penalty of £5; the second offence bore six months or £10; and the third would result in banishment for seven years or a penalty of £100, and in case of return or escape from banishment, the offender would suffer death without benefit of clergy.

The Five Mile Act (1665), also called the Oxford Act: no nonconformist ex-minister or teacher should come within five miles of any town where he had formerly taught, on penalty of £40, without taking the following oath: "I—do swear that it is not lawful upon any pretence whatsoever to take arms against the King, or against those commissioned by him; and that I will not at any time endeavour any alteration of government either in church or state."

According to the Test Act (1672), the Commons' response to Charles II's pro-Catholic Declaration of Indulgence earlier the same year, it became compulsory for anyone who held any civil or military office in the state to take the Sacrament according to the rites of the Church of England within three months after his appointment. Although aimed primarily at Catholics, it equally penalized Dissenters.

The Toleration Act (1689) exempted Dissenters, except Papists and those who denied the Trinity, from all penal laws relating to religion, provided they would take the oaths of allegiance and supremacy, subscribe to the declaration against Popery, and repair to some congregation registered in the Bishop's court or at the sessions. Dissenting teachers had to subscribe to the Thirty-Nine Articles, except those relating to church government and infant baptism.

The Corporation and Test Acts were ultimately repealed in 1828, following the Unitarian Toleration Act of 1813 (sometimes called the Unitarian Relief Act), which extended the Toleration Act (1689) to Unitarians.

32 Bradley, "Whigs and Nonconformists," p. 15.
33 Parliament passed the Occasional Conformity Act in 1711, preventing any person in office from entering a nonconformist meeting-house. The Schism Act of 1714 would have prohibited Dissenters from educating their own children by forbidding tutors from attending any conventicle or Dissenting place of worship. Had the Schism Act not been repealed under George I, it would have led to the extermination of nonconformist academies.
34 In order to matriculate at Oxford it was necessary to subscribe to the Thirty-Nine Articles and take the Oath of Supremacy, and therefore Dissenters could not attend, but they could attend Cambridge, though there they were disqualified from taking degrees.
35 Charles James Fox, *A Letter from the Right Honourable Charles James Fox to the Worthy and Independent Electors of the City and Liberty of Westminster* (London, 1793), pp. 13–14; qtd. in Nicholas Roe, *Wordsworth and Coleridge: The Radical Years* (Oxford: Clarendon Press, 1988), p. 100.
36 Haddon Smith, *The Church-Man's Answer to the Protestant-Dissenter's Catechism* (London, 1795), p. ix.
37 Joseph Priestley, *A Free Address to Protestant Dissenters, As Such, By a Dissenter,* 3rd edn. (1769; London, 1788), pp. 25–26.
38 For a nearly identical formulation, see *The Protestant Dissenter's Magazine* (March 1795): 101.
39 Samuel Palmer, *The Protestant-Dissenter's Catechism,* 9th edn. (1773; London, 1792), p. 35. In his speech to the House of Commons on 2 March 1790, during the debate over the repeal of the Corporation and Test Acts, Burke cited "two printed catechisms for the use of young Non-conformists," Palmer's along with Robert Robinson's *Political Catechism* (London, 1782), as among his reasons for opposing the repeal. *The Debate in the House of Commons on the Repeal of the Corporation and Test Acts, March 2d, 1790,* 2nd edn. (London, 1790), p. 44. See also Haddon Smith's *The Church-Man's Answer to the Protestant Dissenter's Catechism* (1795), to which Palmer responded in *The Protestant-Dissenter's Magazine* (October 1795): 428–31.
40 See anthologies edited by David Perkins, *English Romantic Writers,* 2nd edn. (Harcourt Brace, 1995); Anne K. Mellor and Richard E. Matlak, *British Literature 1780–1830* (Harcourt Brace, 1996); Susan Wolfson and Peter Manning, *The Romantics and Their Contemporaries* (Longman, 1999), and M. H. Abrams and Stephen Greenblatt, *The Norton Anthology of English Literature,* 7th edn., vol. II (Norton, 2000); in Duncan Wu's *Romanticism: An Anthology,* 2nd edn. (Blackwell, 2000), Barbauld is the fourth poet.
41 In addition to his collaborations with his sister, John Aikin wrote essays on song-writing and the applications of natural history to poetry; edited the *Monthly Magazine* after 1796; oversaw the production of the ten-volume *General Biography;* edited and introduced editions of Goldsmith, Green, Armstrong, Somerville, Milton, and Pope; and authored medical treatises, an influential work on hospitals, a volume of poetry, a popular geographical description of the Manchester area, and a number of religious pamphlets.

42 William McCarthy, "'We Hoped the *Woman* Was Going to Appear': Repression, Desire, and Gender in Anna Letitia Barbauld's Early Poems," in *Romantic Women Writers: Voices and Countervoices*, ed. Paula R. Feldman and Theresa M. Kelley (Hanover: University Press of New England, 1995), pp. 113–37. For the most part, "rational" and "liberal" were synonymous terms, though it is helpful at times to see "rational Dissent" as a subcategory of "liberal Dissent." Both phrases designate the heterodox communities and distinguish them from the orthodox, but not all liberal Dissenters in the late eighteenth century fit comfortably under the former appellation, which tended to be embraced by Unitarians.

43 See Watts, *The Dissenters*, II, p. 29, "Table III. Nonconformists as a percentage of the total population: 1715–1718 and 1851."

44 Jon Klancher, *The Making of English Reading Audiences, 1790–1832* (Madison: University of Wisconsin Press, 1987), p. 24.

45 Kevin Gilmartin, "Popular Radicalism and the Public Sphere," *Studies in Romanticism* 33.4 (1994): 553.

46 Klancher, *The Making*, p. 24.

47 Pierre Bourdieu, *Distinction: A Social Critique of the Judgment of Taste*, trans. Richard Nice (Cambridge: Harvard University Press, 1984), pp. 101–02, 123. Bourdieu's concept of "habitus" will appear several times throughout this book, and I take the following definition of the term from Moishe Postone, Edward LiPuma, and Craig Calhoun, "Introduction: Bourdieu and Social Theory," in *Bourdieu: Critical Perspectives*, ed. Calhoun et al. (University of Chicago Press, 1993): "The habitus is . . . a system of dispositions that is both objective and subjective. So conceived, the habitus is the dynamic intersection of structure and action, society and the individual" (p. 4). By the term, then, Bourdieu describes the manners, gestures, tones, prejudices, and general dispositions that, as Jon Klancher succinctly puts it, "a particular group acquires by internalizing objective conditions that it has, more or less unwittingly, produced as historical agents in the first place" (*The Making*, p. 13).

48 Francis Jeffrey, "*Thalaba, the Destroyer*: A Metrical Romance. By Robert Southey," *The Edinburgh Review* 1 (October 1802): 63.

1 "TRUE PRINCIPLES OF RELIGION AND LIBERTY": LIBERAL DISSENT AND THE WARRINGTON ACADEMY

1 For an overview of Dissenting national networks, see Stuart Andrews, *Unitarian Radicalism: Political Rhetoric, 1770–1814* (Houndmills: Palgrave, 2003), pp. 107–35.

2 G. M. Trevelyan, *Illustrated English Social History. Volume Three. The Eighteenth Century* (London: Longmans, 1951), p. 3.

3 Isaac Kramnick, "Religion and Radicalism: English Political Theory in the Age of Revolution," *Political Theory* 5.4 (1977): 506. Kramnick takes his figures from Everett Hagen, *On the Theory of Social Change* (Homewood: Dorsey Press, 1962), pp. 294–309, who analyzes the ninety-two entrepreneurs

and inventors described in T. S. Ashton's *The Industrial Revolution 1760–1830* (Oxford University Press, 1948).

4 See W. D. Rubinstein, *Men of Property* (New Brunswick: Rutgers University Press, 1981), pp. 145–75.

5 "Gentlemen, the Church of England, and the Crown commanded an intellectual and social hegemony." J. C. D. Clark, *English Society 1688–1832: Ideology, Social Structure and Political Practice during the Ancien Regime* (Cambridge University Press, 1985), p. 7; see also *Revolution and Rebellion: State and Society in England in the Seventeenth and Eighteenth Centuries* (Cambridge University Press, 1986).

6 Thomas Sherlock, *Bishop Sherlock's Arguments against a repeal of the Corporation and Test Acts* (London, 1787), p. iv.

7 Benjamin Hoadly, *Bishop Hoadly's Refutation of Bishop Sherlock's Arguments against a repeal of the Corporation and Test Acts* (London, 1787), p. iv.

8 John Aikin, *The Spirit of the Constitution and that of the Church of England, Compared* (London, 1790), p. 10. See the Catholic Joseph Berington's *The Rights of Dissenters from the Established Church, in relation, principally, to English Catholics* (London, 1789): "an idea is often thrown out, that the legislatures of different kingdoms have now adopted such modes of religion, as are most conformable to the genius of their respective governments . . . On this airy hypothesis it is asserted, that the religion of Rome is fitted to despotic states; presbyterianism to republics; and the episcopal form of this country to its mixed government, confessedly, it is added, the best that ever existed" (p. 51).

9 According to Evans' *A Sketch of the Several Denominations*, whereas the Presbyterians "are less attached to Calvinism, and consequently admit a greater latitude of religious sentiment," the Independents "deny not only the subordination of the clergy, but also all *dependency* on other assemblies. Every congregation (they say) has in itself what is necessary for its own government, and is not subject to other churches or to their deputies" (pp. 80–81).

10 On Johnson, see Gerald P. Tyson, *Joseph Johnson: A Liberal Publisher* (Iowa City: University of Iowa Press, 1979), and most recently Helen Brathwaite, *Romanticism, Publishing and Dissent: Joseph Johnson and the Cause of Liberty* (Houndmills: Palgrave, 2003).

11 John Thelwall, *Political Lectures, Volume the First* (London, 1795), p. 57.

12 David Bogue and James Bennett, *History of Dissenters, from the Revolution in 1688, to the Year 1808*, 4 vols. (London, 1808–12), I, p. 179. David Bogue (1750–1825), minister of an Independent chapel at Gosport, in 1789 became tutor at that town's academy for the education of young men destined for the Independent ministry; he was one of the founders of the London Missionary Society in 1795, and in addition to the *History of Dissenters* published sermons and theological tracts. James Bennett (1774–1862) was a student at Gosport under Bogue, and in 1797 was ordained Independent minister at Romsey; he was the author of many theological works as well as Bogue's memoirs.

13 Ibid., I, p. xxxi.

14 See Linda Colley, *Britons: Forging the Nation 1707–1837* (London: Pimlico, 1992), p. III.

15 John Locke, *An Essay Concerning Human Understanding*, ed. Peter H. Nidditch (Oxford: Clarendon Press, 1975), p. 237.

16 Richard Price, *Observations on the Nature of Civil Liberty, the Principles of Government, and the Justice and Policy of the War with America* (London, 1776), p. 6.

17 Quoted in Clark, *English Society*, p. 193.

18 John Wesley, *Some Observations on Liberty: Occasioned by a Late Tract* (London, 1776), pp. 3–4.

19 Dissenters were acutely aware of their need to assert their patriotism and to distance themselves from the execution of Charles I; the text of this sermon (1 Peter 2:16) also appears as the citation on the title page of the first issue of *The Protestant Dissenter's Magazine* (January 1794).

20 Alexander Gerard, *Liberty The Cloke of Maliciousness, Both in the American Rebellion, and in the Manners of the Times. A Sermon Preached at Old Aberdeen, February 26, 1778, Being the Fast-Day appointed by Proclamation, on account of the Rebellion in America* (Aberdeen, 1778), pp. 16–17.

21 *Ibid.*, p. 23.

22 Price, *Observations*, pp. 12–13.

23 Wesley, *Some Observations*, p. 20.

24 Priestley's first living (1755–58) was as assistant and successor to John Meadows, Presbyterian minister at Needham Market in Suffolk. According to Priestley's biographer Anne Holt, in *A Life of Joseph Priestley* (Oxford University Press, 1931), "His predecessor had received £40 a year, partly from the congregation and partly from the Presbyterian and Independent Funds. But the young Priestley felt that it would scarcely become him, whose views were heretical, to accept any grant from the orthodox Independent Fund. His congregation acquiesced and undertook to make good the deficiency" (p. 15). Priestley's Arianism, nonetheless, became a point of contention, and disagreements both theological and personal between Priestley and his congregation led to his departure in September 1758 for Nantwich, Cheshire, where he took charge of a smaller congregation.

25 Priestley, *An Essay on the First Principles of Government, and on the Nature of Political, Civil, and Religious Liberty, Including Remarks on Dr. Brown's Code of Education, and on Dr. Balguy's Sermon on Church Authority*, 2nd edn. (1768; London, 1771), p. 210.

26 Clark, *English Society*, p. 44.

27 I call Barbauld by her married name, occasionally referring to her, before her marriage, as Anna; when referring to Barbauld and her brother, John Aikin, or to the family, I use "the Aikins."

28 Although the official dates of the Warrington Academy are usually accurately given as 1757–86, the Academy ceased to function in 1783. The last entries in the register of students are for 1782. On 23 September 1784 the Trustees resolved "That the Institution be resumed at Warrington," but they were

unsuccessful; on 29 June 1786 the Academy was dissolved and it was determined that the library and remaining endowments be transferred to the "intended Academy in Manchester," which opened in September 1786. Betsy Rodgers, *Georgian Chronicle: Mrs Barbauld and Her Family* (London: Methuen, 1958), pp. 83–85. Manchester New College would eventually be incorporated into Oxford University as Manchester College, where the Warrington Academy library is to be found today.

29 The standard works on the Academy are Herbert McLachlan, *English Education under the Test Acts: Being the History of the Nonconformist Academies 1662–1820* (Manchester University Press, 1931) and *Warrington Academy: Its History and Influence* (Manchester: The Chetham Society, 1943); P. O'Brien, *Warrington Academy, 1757–86: Its Predecessors and Successors* (Wigan: Owl Books, 1989); and Irene Parker, *Dissenting Academies in England: Their Rise and Progress and their Place among the Educational Systems of the Country* (Cambridge University Press, 1914). For a list of the tutors at the Academy, see Parker, *Dissenting Academies*, p. 108.

30 D. L. Wykes, "The Contribution of the Dissenting Academy to the Emergence of Rational Dissent," in *Enlightenment and Religion*, p. 133.

31 Gregory Claeys, "Virtuous Commerce and Free Theology: Political Economy and the Dissenting Academies 1750–1800," *History of Political Thought* 20 (Spring 1999): 141.

32 *The Debate on a Motion for the Abolition of the Slave-Trade, in the House of Commons, on Monday the second of April, 1792* (London, 1792), p. 64.

33 Gilbert Wakefield, *Memoirs of the Life of Gilbert Wakefield*, 2 vols., A New Edition (London, 1804), I, p. 214.

34 See Rodgers, *Georgian Chronicle*, pp. 49–50.

35 *Profiles of Warrington Worthies, Collected and Arranged by James Kendrick, M. D.* (Warrington, 1853), p. 5. On Eyres, see H. R. Plomer et al., *Dictionaries of the Printers and Booksellers Who Were at Work in England, Scotland and Ireland 1726–1775* (Ilkley: The Bibliographical Society, 1968), p. 87, and Michael Perkin, "William Eyres and the Warrington Press," in *Aspects of Printing From 1600*, ed. Robin Myers and Michael Harris (Oxford Polytechnic Press, 1987), pp. 69–89.

36 Roscoe, later the abolitionist MP for Liverpool, was the author of *Mount Pleasant* (1777) and *The Wrongs of Africa* (1787–88). In keeping with the familial literary dynamics of the nonconformist network I will discuss, Roscoe and his daughters later published *Poems for Youth, by a Family Circle* (London, 1820).

37 The other original tutors were Dr. John Taylor of Norwich (author of the great Hebrew concordance), tutor in Divinity, and John Holt of Kirkdale, tutor in Mathematics.

38 Quoted in McLachlan, *English Education*, p. 141.

39 Ibid. Baxterian theology, after Richard Baxter (1615–91), was considered a "Middle Way" between Calvinism and Arminianism. In the eighteenth century Baxterianism chiefly allowed Calvinists to introduce repentance as a condition of grace, thus moderating the orthodox insistence upon free grace

without any regard to faith. As Michael Watts writes, "the Baxterian of one generation was likely to foster the Arians or Socinians of the next" (*The Dissenters*, 1, p. 465).

40 Andrew Kippis, "A Life of the Author," in Philip Doddridge, *The Family Expositor*, 7th edn. (London, 1792), p. lx.

41 According to Daniel Defoe, in *The Present State of the Parties in Great Britain* (London, 1712), Charles Morton "Read all his Lectures, gave all his Systems, whether of *Phylosophy* [*sic*], or *Divinity*, in *English*; had all his Declaimings and Dissertations in the *English* tongue" (p. 319). Defoe was a student at Morton's Academy, at Newington Green, in the late 1670s.

42 A. Victor Murray, "Doddridge and Education," in *Philip Doddridge 1702–51: His Contribution to English Religion*, ed. Geoffrey F. Nuttall (London: Independent Press, 1951), p. 114.

43 Isabel Rivers, *The Defence of Truth through the Knowledge of Error: Philip Doddridge's Academy Lectures* (London: Dr. Williams's Trust, 2003), p. 4.

44 Rodgers, *Georgian Chronicle*, p. 46.

45 Quoted in ibid., p. 39.

46 John Aikin, *A Description of the Country from Thirty to Forty Miles round Manchester* (London, 1795), p. 304. By the end of the period in question bills of mortality were being kept; during the latter half of the century Warrington's population was on the rise.

47 Anna Letitia Le Breton, *Memoir of Mrs. Barbauld, Including Letters and Notices of Her Family and Friends* (London: George Bell and Sons, 1874), p. 31. The town, at least, seems to have shared the title with Edinburgh, and the nationalist implications of Warrington's status as a provincial Athens resonate throughout Anna Aikin's description of the Academy in her poem "The Invitation: To Miss B*****," *Poems* (London, 1773), lines 81–182 of which were reprinted by William Enfield in *The Speaker* (1774) under the title "Warrington Academy."

48 According to John Aikin, "half of the heavy sail-cloth used in the navy has been computed to be manufactured" in Warrington, and other significant manufactures were pins, locks, hinges, glassware, and refined sugar. The town also had an active iron foundry and was noted for its malt and ale. The Mersey was well stored with salmon and smelt, and the surrounding country-side raised potatoes, up to "thirty or forty thousand bushels" of which were exported annually from Bankquay. *A Description*, pp. 300–08.

49 McLachlan, *Warrington Academy*, pp. 1–3. On the canals, see T. S. Ashton, *An Eighteenth-Century Industrialist* (Manchester University Press, 1939), and John Aikin's "Account of River and Canal Navigation" in *A Description*, pp. 105–39. Barbauld describes the canal in "The Invitation: To Miss B*****," and for an imaginative encounter with the "Genius" of the Duke of Bridgewater's canal, see "The Canal and the Brook," a dream vision in John and Anna Aikin's *Miscellaneous Pieces in Prose* (London, 1773) which I discuss in Chapter 3. For a discussion of canal-building in late-eighteenth-century England and Ireland in relation to the sentimental novel, see Markman Ellis,

The Politics of Sensibility: Race, Gender and Commerce in the Sentimental Novel (Cambridge University Press, 1996), pp. 129–60.

50 Colley, *Britons*, p. 167.

51 Wykes, "The Contribution," p. 107.

52 Parker, *Dissenting Academies*, p. 105.

53 Quoted in Rodgers, *Georgian Chronicle*, pp. 33–34.

54 Parker, *Dissenting Academies*, p. 107.

55 Rodgers, *Georgian Chronicle*, pp. 33–34.

56 Ibid.

57 See Claeys, "Virtuous Commerce," on the role played by "small, non-sectarian commercial academies" in preparing for the "introduction of commerce into the curriculum at Dissenting academies during the eighteenth century" (p. 145).

58 Thomas Barnes, "A Plan for the Improvement and Extension of Liberal Education in Manchester . . . Read April 9, 1783," in *Memoirs of the Literary and Philosophical Society of Manchester*, vol. II (Warrington, 1785), p. 21.

59 Ibid., II, p. 42.

60 The course on PRACTICAL MATHEMATICS, which would have included "the principal branches of NATURAL and EXPERIMENTAL PHILOSOPHY – GEOGRAPHY – and the use of the GLOBE," was not delivered (ibid., II, p. 45).

61 Ralph Harrison, *A Sermon Preached at the Dissenting Chapel in Cross-Street, Manchester* (Warrington, 1786), p. 26.

62 Ibid., p. 24.

63 For a discussion of the curriculum itself, as well as a timetable of students' daily activities beginning at 7:00 A.M. and ending at 9:00 P.M., see McLachlan, *English Education*, pp. 209–27. See also Claeys, "Virtuous Commerce," pp. 155–56.

64 Parker, *Dissenting Academies*, p. 118.

65 Joseph Priestley, *An Essay on a Course of Liberal Education for Civil and Active Life. With Plans of Lectures on I. The Study of History and general Policy. II. The History of England. III. The Constitution and Laws of England. To which are added, Remarks on a Code of Education, Proposed by Dr. Brown, in a Late Treatise, Intitled, Thoughts on Civil Liberty, &c.* (London, 1765), p. 21.

66 Priestley's arguments against Brown were no doubt central to his larger project of defending liberty from civil and religious establishments, for he expanded on this response in his more widely circulated and influential *An Essay on the First Principles of Government, and on the Nature of Political, Civil, and Religious Liberty* (1768).

67 John Brown, *Thoughts on Civil Liberty, on Licentiousness and Faction* (Dublin, 1765), p. 44.

68 Ibid., pp. 62–63.

69 Joseph Priestley, *The Rudiments of English Grammar, Adapted to the Use of Schools*, A New Edition (1761; London, 1769), pp. xix–xx.

70 Ibid., p. xx.

71 "Virtuous Commerce," p. 156. Claeys goes on to suggest, rightly, that "Priestley's attitude towards commercial society was not entirely unambiguous"

(p. 158). In particular, like other Dissenters he was concerned that successful trade would debase the middle classes by increasing their appetite for luxuries, an appetite to be restrained less by discipline than by the necessary progress of manners, politeness, and refinement (pp. 158–59).

2 ANNA BARBAULD AND DEVOTIONAL TASTES: EXTEMPORE, PARTICULAR, EXPERIMENTAL

1 For Barbauld's reported criticism of *The Rime*, see *CW*, xiv, part 1, *Table Talk*, ed. Carl Woodring (Princeton University Press, 1990), p. 272.
2 William McCarthy is currently writing a biography, but an authoritative edition of Barbauld's complete works remains wanting.
3 Anna Letitia Le Breton, *Memoir of Mrs. Barbauld, Including Letters and Notices of Her Family and Friends* (London: George Bell and Sons, 1874), p. 84.
4 Ibid., pp. 86–87.
5 See William McCarthy, "Why Anna Letitia Barbauld Refused to Head a Women's College: New Facts, New Story," *Nineteenth-Century Contexts* 23.3 (2001): 349–79. Discussions of this incident usually rely on Lucy Aikin's selective reprinting of the letter in which Barbauld rejects the proposal (*Works*, I, pp. xvi–xxiv). McCarthy reprints and discusses in its extant entirety Barbauld's letter to Rochemont Barbauld in which she justifies her refusal, and McCarthy's analysis of her motives – "her case against schools for girls is more rhetorical than theoretical: she is throwing cold water on a scheme *she* wants to evade, not on the principle that women should be educated" (p. 357) – leads him to conclude, justly, that "it should no longer be permissible to cite this letter as adequate evidence of Barbauld's supposed antifeminism" (p. 363).
6 McCarthy, "'We Hoped the *Woman* Was Going to Appear': Repression, Desire, and Gender in Anna Letitia Barbauld's Early Poems," in *Romantic Women Writers: Voices and Countervoices*, ed. Paula R. Feldman and Theresa M. Kelley (Hanover: University Press of New England, 1995), pp. 125–30. Barbara Taylor has recently discussed Barbauld's anti-feminism in relation to female Jacobinism, in *Mary Wollstonecraft and the Feminist Imagination* (Cambridge University Press, 2003), pp. 182–87.
7 Le Breton, *Memoir*, p. 87.
8 Anne Janowitz sees a transition from the amiability of Warrington conversation and friendship to the ardour of Barbauld's poetry and pamphlets produced in Hampstead and London: "In her urban poetry of the late 1780s and early '90s, Barbauld concretized and dialectically criticized the abstractions of Warrington values and manners." Janowitz, "Amiable and radical sociability: Anna Barbauld's 'free familiar conversation,'" in *Romantic Sociability: Social Networks and Literary Culture in Britain, 1770–1840*, ed. Gillian Russell and Clara Tuite (Cambridge University Press, 2002), p. 63. Lucy Newlyn and others have focussed on the "ambiguity" and "androgyny"

of her negotiations: Barbauld's "aesthetic of sensibility," Newlyn proposes, "mediated between masculinity and femininity . . . Positioning herself ambiguously in relation to gender-oppositions, Barbauld demands from her own readers a response that is similarly androgynous and empathetic." Newlyn, *Reading, Writing, and Romanticism: The Anxiety of Reception* (Oxford University Press, 2000), pp. 156–57. (Pamela Plimpton, to whom I am indebted for conversation about Barbauld, used the term "androgyny" in discussing her authorial persona, in "The Canonizing of Anna Letitia Barbauld: Agency in the Act of Editing – History, Theory, and Practice," Special Session, MLA convention, Chicago, 28 December 1995.) And writing of Barbauld's conflicts with Priestley, Jon Mee suggests that "Understanding their relationship only in terms of feminine-gendered sensibility versus masculine-gendered reason obscures both the nuances and vicissitudes of their exchanges." Mee, *Romanticism, Enthusiasm, and Regulation: Poetics and the Policing of Culture in the Romantic Period* (Oxford University Press, 2003), p. 174. See as well Deirdre Coleman, "Firebrands, letters and flowers: Mrs Barbauld and the Priestleys," in *Romantic Sociability*, pp. 82–103.

9 Coleman, "Firebrands," pp. 83–84.

10 Coleman's apt phrase, ibid., p. 83.

11 Murray, "Doddridge and Education," p. 120.

12 On the evolution of Unitarianism and "rational Dissent," see Watts, *The Dissenters*, I, pp. 445–90; H. L. Short, "Presbyterians Under a New Name," in *The English Presbyterians: From Elizabethan Puritanism to Modern Unitarianism* (London: George Allen, 1968), pp. 219–86; and R. K. Webb, "The Unitarian Background," in *Truth, Liberty, Religion: Essays Celebrating Two Hundred Years of Manchester College*, ed. Barbara Smith (Oxford: Manchester College, 1986), pp. 1–30.

13 Priestley's early pamphlets against the Trinity include *An Appeal to the Serious and Candid Professors of Christianity* (London, 1771), *A Familiar Illustration of Certain Passages of Scripture* (London, 1772), and *A General View of the Arguments for the Unity of God, and Against the Divinity and pre-existence of Christ, from Reason, from the Scriptures, and from History* (London, 1783). Bogue and Bennett write that Priestley's *Institutes of Natural and Revealed Religion*, 3 vols. (London, 1772–74), "may be considered as a socinian body of divinity" (*History of Dissenters*, IV, p. 249).

14 Andrews, *Unitarian Radicalism*, p. 3. On the Essex Street congregation, see pp. 44–53.

15 Wakefield's situation was, as Barbauld described it, "peculiar and insulated": "Separating through the purest motives from one church, he has not found another with which he is inclined to associate . . . he worships alone because he stands alone." *Remarks on Mr. Gilbert Wakefield's Enquiry into the Expediency and Propriety of Public or Social Worship* (London, 1792), p. 57.

16 When Lindsey himself left the Church in 1773, he nonetheless intended the new congregation he would found in London to be Anglican as well as Unitarian.

17 Russell E. Richey, "Did the English Presbyterians Become Unitarian?," *Church History* 42 (1973): 58.

18 Andrew Fuller, *The Calvinistic and Socinian Systems Examined and Compared, as to their Moral Tendency* (Market-Harborough, 1793), p. 42. Although an Arian, and in spite of the Socinianism of the Unitarian Society for Promoting Christian Knowledge, Price was a founding member of the Society in 1791. See R. K. Webb, "Price among the Unitarians," *Enlightenment and Dissent* 19 (2000): 147–70.

19 William Woodfall, "*Poems. By Miss Aikin*," *Monthly Review* 48 (January 1773): 57.

20 Red Lion Hill is now Rosslyn Hill, and the chapel is now Unitarian.

21 Le Breton, *Memoir*, p. 66.

22 Wykes, "The Contribution," p. 135.

23 "Appendix No. I. Manchester Academy," in Ralph Harrison, *A Sermon*, p. 1.

24 "Appendix No. II. Manchester Academy," in Ralph Harrison, *A Sermon*, p. 10.

25 John Aikin, *Letters from a Father to His Son, on Various Topics, Relative to Literature and the Conduct of Life* (London, 1794), pp. 100–01.

26 On Watts' funeral, see Gordon Rupp, *Religion in England 1688–1791* (Oxford: Clarendon Press, 1986), p. 161, and on Toulmin's, see *DNB*.

27 For an excellent overview of devotional writing and publishing, see Isabel Rivers, "Dissenting and Methodist Books of Practical Divinity," in *Books and their Readers in Eighteenth-Century England*, ed. Isabel Rivers (New York: St. Martin's Press, 1982), pp. 127–64.

28 Barbauld, "Thoughts on the Devotional Taste, on Sects, and on Establishments," in *SPP*, p. 211.

29 George Gregory, "Thoughts on the Composition and Delivery of a Sermon," in *Sermons* (London, 1787), pp. iii–iv.

30 Rupp, *Religion in England*, pp. 156–57. The quotation is from Johnson's "The Life of Isaac Watts, D. D.," in *Lives of the English Poets*, ed. G. B. Hill, 3 vols. (Oxford: Clarendon Press, 1905), III, p. 306.

31 Watts, *The Dissenters*, I, p. 312.

32 Barbara Taylor, "For the Love of God: Religion and the Erotic Imagination in Wollstonecraft's Feminism," in *Mary Wollstonecraft and 200 Years of Feminisms*, ed. Eileen Janes Yeo (London: Rivers Oram Press, 1997), p. 18.

33 Barbara Taylor, "The Religious Foundations of Mary Wollstonecraft's Feminism," in *The Cambridge Companion to Mary Wollstonecraft*, ed. Claudia L. Johnson (Cambridge University Press, 2002), p. 104. See also Taylor's *Mary Wollstonecraft and the Feminist Imagination*, pp. 95–142.

34 "Discipulus" [Harriet Martineau], "Female Writers on Practical Divinity," *Monthly Repository* 17 (October 1822): 593.

35 Jean Jacques Rousseau, *Julie ou La Nouvelle Héloïse*, ed. Michel Launay (Paris: GF-Flammarion, 1967), p. 575. "As the enthusiasm of devotion borrows the language of love, the enthusiasm of love also borrows the language of devotion."

36 My uses of the term "regulation" and its cognates are indebted to Mee, *Romanticism, Enthusiasm, and Regulation*, pp. 37–49. Mee describes regulation as the means by which eighteenth-century religious and philosophical discourses sought to recuperate enthusiasm and reclaim it from association with disorder and fanaticism: "regulation offered a way of confirming the fundamental importance of sociability without abandoning society to the crowd" (p. 41). At the same time, "the discourse of regulation produced a supplement, an anxiety that regulated enthusiasm could always transmute back into its vulgar alter ego . . . the unruliness of the crowd" (pp. 48–49).

37 Geoffrey F. Nuttall, *Studies in English Dissent* (Weston Rhyn: Quinta Press, 2002), pp. 84, 92. Nuttall's essay, "Puritan and Quaker Mysticism," here reprinted, was first published in *Theology* 78 (October 1975): 518–31.

38 Gregory, "Thoughts," p. xi.

39 Bogue and Bennett, *History of Dissenters*, II, pp. 166–67.

40 James Glazebrook, *What is called Extempore Preaching Recommended* (Warrington, 1794), pp. iii, 4. Another churchman who advocated the practice was John Byrom, who included among his *Miscellaneous Poems* "Advice to the Rev[s] . . . H— and H— . . . on Preaching Extempore," in which the poet suggests that the stores of a rational, "thoughtful mind" can be revealed "without the help of pen and ink": "Speak from *within*, not from without," Byrom's advice concludes, "And Heart to Heart will turn about." *Miscellaneous Poems* (Manchester, 1773), pp. 125–26.

41 Glazebrook, *What is called Extempore Preaching*, p. 2.

42 Gregory, "Thoughts," p. lxxxi.

43 Gilbert Burnet, *The History of the Reformation of the Church of England* (London, 1679), I, p. 316.

44 Ibid., pp. 317–18.

45 *A Discovery of 29, Sects here in London, all of which, except the first, are most Divelish and Damnable* ([London], 1641), p. 3. The first sect is "*The Protestant* . . . like to a diamond, which, though it bee cast to the Dung-hill, loseth not a jot of its splendor" (p. 1).

46 For assistance during the early stages of my research on Unitarian sermons, I am grateful to R. K. Webb for his private correspondence.

47 Joseph Priestley, *A Course of Lectures on Oratory and Criticism* (London, 1777), pp. 112–14.

48 Quoted in David Wykes, "'A good discourse, well explained in 35 minutes': Unitarians and Preaching in the Early Nineteenth Century," *Transactions of the Unitarian Historical Society* 16.3 (1997): 181.

49 Defoe, *The Present State of the Parties in Great Britain*, pp. 287–89. I thank John Richetti for suggesting that I consider Defoe's discussion of Dissenting preaching.

50 Defoe, *The Present State*, p. 305. As a model of one who preached with both "becoming Gravity" and "an affectionate Zeal" (p. 289), Defoe could have had in mind Samuel Annesley (1620?–96), minister to the congregation in Cripplegate attended by Defoe's family, and, in fact, first cousin of Barbauld's

maternal great grandmother, Lady Anne Annesley (d. after 1687). Samuel Annesley's daughter Susanna (1669–1742) would marry Samuel Wesley (1662–1735), and among their numerous children would be John and Charles Wesley, who were thus Barbauld's (distant) cousins.

51 Hugh Blair, *Lectures on Rhetoric and Belles Lettres*, 3 vols. (1783; London, 1790), II, pp. 326–27.

52 Ibid., II, p. 327.

53 The other sect that practiced extempore preaching was of course the Quakers, whose devotional spontaneity will be discussed in Chapter 6.

54 Robert Robinson, *An Essay on the Composition of a Sermon. Translated from the original French of The Revd. John Claude*, 2 vols. (Cambridge, 1778–79), and Charles Simeon, *Claude's Essay on the Composition of a Sermon: with Alterations and Improvements*, 2nd edn. (1796; Cambridge, 1801). In addition to the texts on sermon composition and delivery discussed below, other important sources included works by Richard Baxter, James Beattie, William Cowper, Fénelon, John Howe, John Newton, and John Witherspoon.

55 "There are in general five parts of a sermon . . . but, as connection and division are parts which ought to be extremely short, we can properly reckon only three parts; exordium, discussion, and application" (Robinson, *An Essay*, I, pp. 1–2). In the connection the preacher discusses the text in relation to surrounding scriptural passages, and in the division the preacher sets forth the order in which he will explicate the terms of the text.

56 See Graham Werden Hughes, *With Freedom Fired: The Story of Robert Robinson, Cambridge Nonconformist* (London: Carey Kingsgate Press, 1955), and Nuttall, "Robert Robinson (1721–1790) and the Cambridge Baptists," first published in 1971 and reprinted in Nuttall, *Studies in English Dissent*, pp. 183–204. For a brief account of Robinson's life which corrects several errors originating in George Dyer's *Memoirs of the Life and Writings of R. Robinson* (London, 1796), especially the claim that Robinson converted to Unitarianism shortly before his death in 1790, see Len Addicott, "Introduction," in *Church Book: St Andrew's Street Baptist Church, Cambridge 1720–1832* (London: Baptist Historical Society, 1991), pp. viii–xviii. I am grateful to Gina Luria Walker for correspondence concerning Robinson's life and work.

57 Isaac Watts, "Preface," in John Jennings, *Two Discourses: The First, Of Preaching Christ; the Second, Of Particular and Experimental Preaching . . . With a Preface by the Reverend Dr. Isaac Watts*, 3rd edn. (1723; London, 1736), p. x.

58 Isaac Watts, *An Humble Attempt toward the Revival of Practical Religion among Christians, And particularly the Protestant Dissenters* (London, 1731), pp. 54–55. *An Humble Attempt* provoked John White's *A Letter to a Gentleman Dissenting from the Church of England* (London, 1743), which in turn provoked Micaiah Towgood's *A Dissent from the Church of England, Fully justified* (London, 1746), the text to which generations of Dissenting polemicists referred their readers for "the grounds upon which dissent from the established church is founded" (Evans, *A Sketch*, p. 74).

59 Philip Doddridge, *Lectures on Preaching, and the Several Branches of the Ministerial Office* (London, 1821), p. 44.

60 Bogue and Bennett, *History of Dissenters*, II, p. 163. Similarly, John Wilkins (1614–72), who would marry Cromwell's sister before becoming Bishop of Chester after the Restoration, had recommended in his influential *Ecclesiastes* that preaching should proceed "from the heart, and an experimentall acquaintance with those truths which we deliver . . . 'Tis a hard matter to affect others, with what wee are not first affected our selves." *Ecclesiastes, or, A Discourse concerning the Gift of Preaching as it fal[l]s under the rules of Art* (London, 1646), p. 73.

61 *Scotch Presbyterian Eloquence Display'd: Or, the Folly of their Teaching Discover'd, from their Books, Sermons, Prayers, &c.* (1692; London, 1789), p. 99.

62 Jennings, *Two Discourses*, pp. 65–66.

63 Quoted in Nuttall, *Studies in English Dissent*, p. 91.

64 Bogue and Bennett, *History of Dissenters*, II, pp. 166–67.

65 Hereafter I will for the most part use the term "particularity" as shorthand for the two related methods of "particular and experimental" preaching.

66 *The Fashionable Preacher: or, Modern Pulpit Eloquence Displayed* (London, 1792), pp. 8–14, first published as *The Fashionable Preacher: An Essay* (Glasgow, 1773).

67 For the development of these opposed perspectives in England, see Nicholas Tyacke, *Anti-Calvinists: The Rise of English Arminianism c. 1590–1640* (Oxford: Clarendon Press, 1987).

68 A. L. Barbauld, *Remarks on Mr. Gilbert Wakefield's Enquiry into the Expediency and Propriety of Public or Social Worship* (London, 1792), pp. 67–68.

69 Ibid., p. 76. The challenges facing the dissemination of Barbauld's position were many. Thus John Wesley's *The Question, What is an Arminian? Answered* (Bristol, 1770), published anonymously "By a Lover of Free Grace," begins: "To say, 'This man is an Arminian,' has the same effect on many Hearers, as to say, 'This is a mad dog' . . .: they run away from him . . . [a]nd will hardly stop, unless it be to throw a stone at the dreadful, and mischievous animal" (p. 2). A decade later the pious young poetess, Susannah Harrison, could confidently transform a number of disparate theological terms into one web of error. *Songs in the Night; By a Young Woman under deep Afflictions* (London, 1780) ends with "Meditations in Blank Verse," the tenth of which calls on a Calvinist and Trinitarian Deity to preserve the poet's soul

> From all th'abounding Errors of this Age, –
> From all the conscious pains that DEISTS know; –
> Thou shalt preserve me from th'ARMINIAN's Shame,
> From all the Horrors ANTINOMIANS feel. –
> From all the Terrors that Thou hast prepar'd
> For ARIAN Monsters, and SOCINIAN Fools. (p. 144)

70 Barbauld, *Remarks*, p. 69.

71 Barbauld's resistance to abstraction and "the zeal of a systematic spirit" may seem reminiscent of Burke's, but its origins and ends are rather different: for

Barbauld, particularity in contemporary religious devotion could produce a
tempered form of that "wholesome severity" with which "the Puritans in the
reign of Charles the Second seasoned . . . the profligacy of public manners"
(*SPP*, p. 230).

72 In *Remarks* (1792), Barbauld is answering Gilbert Wakefield's *An Enquiry into
the Expediency and Propriety of Public or Social Worship* (London, 1791), in
which he argued against communal worship on scriptural grounds and because
Christianity had matured beyond its Hebraic infancy, when "Material impressions and manual services were . . . necessary to occupy the attention and engage
the senses" (p. 4). Mary Hays responded in *Cursory Remarks on an Enquiry into
the Expediency and Propriety of Public or Social Worship* (London, 1792). On the
ensuing controversy, see Gina Luria Walker, "Mary Hays (1759–1843): An
Enlightened Quest," in *Women, Gender and Enlightenment*, ed. Sarah Knott
and Barbara Taylor (London: Palgrave, 2005), pp. 493–518.

73 As described by Hume in *Treatise of Human Nature* (1739–40), "The passions
are so contagious, that they pass with the greatest facility from one person to
another, and produce correspondent movements in all human breasts."
Quoted in John Mullan, *Sentiment and Sociability: The Language of Feeling
in the Eighteenth Century* (Oxford: Clarendon Press, 1988), pp. 23–24.

74 Martineau, "Female Writers on Practical Divinity," *Monthly Repository* 17
(December 1822): 749.

75 Ibid.

76 Priestley, *Life and Correspondence*, in *The Theological and Miscellaneous Works
of Joseph Priestley*, ed. J. T. Rutt, 25 vols. (London, 1818–31), I, p. 288. For an
excellent discussion of Barbauld's relationship with the Priestleys, see Coleman, "Firebrands," pp. 82–103.

77 Priestley, *Life*, I, p. 288.

78 Ibid., I, p. 279.

79 Ibid., I, pp. 281–82.

80 Ibid., I, p. 282.

81 Priestley, *Two Discourses; I. On Habitual Devotion, II. On the Duty of not
living to Ourselves* (Birmingham, 1782), p. v. It seems likely that the correct
date of Priestley's sermon and Barbauld's poem is 1769, not 1767. See David
Chandler, "Barbauld's 'Address to the Deity': Two Notes," *Notes and Queries*
245.2 (2000): 208–10.

82 Priestley, *Discourses on Various Subjects, Including several on Particular Occasions* (Birmingham, 1787), p. 373.

83 Barbauld, *Hymns in Prose for Children* (London, 1781), pp. v–vi.

84 Martineau, "Female Writers on Practical Divinity," *Monthly Repository* 17
(December 1822): 749.

85 Lucy Newlyn notes that "Poems addressed to those unable to reciprocate are
unusual in [Barbauld's] oeuvre" (*Reading, Writing, and Romanticism*, p. 141).
I would include the addressee of "An Address to the Deity" as among those
who can, by their nature, respond and reciprocate.

3 THE *"JOINERIANA"*: BARBAULD, THE AIKIN FAMILY CIRCLE, AND THE DISSENTING PUBLIC SPHERE

1 The term was current due to Samuel Paterson's *The Joineriana: or The Book of Scraps*, 2 vols. (London, 1772), where the metaphor pertained to carpentry: "JOINERIANA, or the book of SCRAPS?" Paterson asks, "Ay, or CARPENTERIANA, or the Book of CHIPS, if you had rather" (1, p. 2).

2 The landmark study addressing familial collaboration and Dissent during the Romantic period is Leonore Davidoff and Catherine Hall, *Family Fortunes: Men and Women of the English Middle Class, 1780–1850* (University of Chicago Press, 1987).

3 On the relationships between needlework and literary production, see Carol Shiner Wilson, "Lost Needles, Tangled Threads: Stitchery, Domesticity, and the Artistic Enterprise in Barbauld, Edgeworth, Taylor, and Lamb," in *Re-Visioning Romanticism: British Women Writers 1776–1837*, ed. Carol Shiner Wilson and Joel Haefner (Philadelphia: University of Pennsylvania Press, 1994), pp. 167–90.

4 Geoff Eley, "Nations, Publics, and Political Cultures: Placing Habermas in the Nineteenth Century," in *Habermas and the Public Sphere*, ed. Craig Calhoun (Cambridge: MIT Press, 1992), pp. 289–339; Kevin Gilmartin, "Popular Radicalism and the Public Sphere," *Studies in Romanticism* 33.4 (1994): 549–57, and *Print Politics: The Press and Radical Opposition in Early Nineteenth-Century England* (Cambridge University Press, 1996); Günther Lottes, *Politische Aufklärung und plebejisches Publikum: Zur Theorie und Praxis des englischen Radikalismus im späten 18. Jahrhundert* (Munich: Old-enbourg, 1979); Joan B. Landes, *Women and the Public Sphere in the Age of the French Revolution* (Ithaca: Cornell University Press, 1988); Rita Felski, *Beyond Feminist Aesthetics* (Cambridge: Harvard University Press, 1989). On the concept of alternative or counter-public spheres, see Oskar Negt and Alexander Kluge's 1972 revisionist critique of Habermas, *Public Sphere and Experience: Toward an Analysis of the Bourgeois and Proletarian Public Sphere*, trans. Peter Labanyi et al. (Minneapolis: University of Minnesota Press, 1993).

5 Nancy Fraser, "Rethinking the Public Sphere: A Contribution to the Critique of Actually Existing Democracy," in *The Phantom Public Sphere*, ed. Bruce Robbins (Minneapolis: University of Minnesota Press, 1993), pp. 7–8.

6 See Orrin N. C. Wang, "Romancing the Counter-Public Sphere: A Response to Romanticism and its Publics," *Studies in Romanticism* 33.4 (1994): 579–88, especially its critique of the tendency to equate women's writing with the production of a counter-public sphere.

7 Jürgen Habermas, *The Structural Transformation of the Public Sphere: An Inquiry into a Category of Bourgeois Society*, trans. Thomas Burger (1962; Cambridge: MIT Press, 1989), pp. 27–31.

8 Ibid., pp. 55–56.

9 On the "ironically fortuitous position" of the Dissenting woman writer, see Marlon Ross, "Configurations of Feminine Reform: The Woman Writer

and the Tradition of Dissent," in Wilson and Haefner, eds., *Re-Visioning Romanticism*, pp. 92–93.

10 Markman Ellis has focused attention on women who did participate in coffee-house culture, primarily as servers and prostitutes, in "Coffee-women, 'The Spectator' and the public sphere in the early eighteenth century," in *Women, Writing and the Public Sphere 1700–1830*, ed. Elizabeth Eger et al. (Cambridge University Press, 2001), pp. 27–52.

11 Anglican women, such as the Bluestockings Frances Boscawen, Elizabeth Carter, Hester Chapone, Mary Delaney, Hannah More, Elizabeth Montagu, and Elizabeth Vesey, tended to emerge from salons and *soirées*. Although Barbauld corresponded with More and Montagu, she and Maria Edgeworth always conceived of themselves as separate from the Bluestocking circle.

12 On the exclusion of women writers from the political public sphere, see Elizabeth Heckendorn Cook, *Epistolary Bodies: Gender and Genre in the Eighteenth-Century Republic of Letters* (Stanford University Press, 1996), p. 11.

13 For precisely the kind of familial production I am discussing, see the Conder and Taylor family circle's volume, *The Associate Minstrels* (London, 1810). Published by Josiah Conder's father Thomas, the book included poems by Josiah and Thomas Conder, Ann and Jane Taylor, and their close friend Eliza Thomas, soon to be the wife of Josiah Conder. This circle was affiliated with the Aikins: Josiah Conder was a contributor to John Aikin's *The Athenaeum* (1807–09) and was editor of *The Eclectic Review* from 1814–36.

14 Anna Letitia Le Breton, ed., *Correspondence of William Ellery Channing, D. D., and Lucy Aikin, from 1826 to 1842* (Boston, 1874), pp. 28–29.

15 In accordance with the classical model of bourgeois publicity, periodicals played a fundamental role in the Dissenting public sphere. From 1790–1810, the Aikin network dominated the periodical industry in England. This industry helped forge Dissenters into a public that "held up a mirror to itself," to use Habermas' phrase, in Priestley's *Theological Repository* (1769–71, 1784–88), Joseph Johnson's *The Analytical Review* (1788–99), *The Christian Miscellany* (1792), *The Evangelical Magazine* (first series, 1793–1822; continued until 1904), *The Monthly Magazine* (1796–1843; edited by John Aikin until 1806), *The Protestant Dissenter's Magazine* (1794–99), *The Theological Magazine* (1801–14?), *The Annual Review* (1802–08; edited by John Aikin's son Arthur Aikin), John Aikin's *The Athenaeum* (1807–09), *The Eclectic Review* (1805–36; edited by Josiah Conder from 1814), and Robert Aspland's *The Monthly Repository* (1806–26). See Marilyn Butler, "Culture's Medium: The Role of the Review," in *The Cambridge Companion to British Romanticism*, ed. Stuart Curran (Cambridge University Press, 1993), pp. 120–47; Klancher, *The Making of English Reading Audiences, 1790–1832*; and for an overview of religious periodicals from 1700–1825, Francis E. Mineka, *The Dissidence of Dissent: The Monthly Repository, 1806–1838* (Chapel Hill: University of North Carolina Press, 1944), pp. 27–101. For an interesting contemporary account by an insider, see Josiah Conder's *Reviewers Reviewed; Including An Enquiry into the Moral and Intellectual Effects of Habits of Criticism, and Their Influence on the*

General Interests of Literature. To which Is Subjoined A Brief History of the Periodical Reviews Published in England and Scotland (London, 1811).

16 The majority of the pieces are clearly aimed at children of the middle classes. In "On Manufactures," young Henry strikes up a casual conversation with his father:

> *Hen.* My dear father, you observed the other day that we had a great many *manufactures* in England. Pray what is a Manufacture?
>
> *Fa.* A Manufacture is something made by the hand of man. It is derived from two Latin words, *manus*, the hand, and *facere*, to make.
>
> (*Evenings*, II, p. 97)

The piece ends with a discussion of Josiah Wedgwood, Sr. (1730–95), whose son John attended the Warrington Academy. The bourgeois homes in which the Wedgwoods' wares found their market would have been the same homes in which the Aikins' children's literature found its readership.

17 This idea that Dissent, and Dissenting domesticity in particular, provided an intermediate space between private and public allowing for literary transmission to both a Dissenting and national audience, first proposed in my "The 'Joineriana': Anna Barbauld's Prose, the Aikin Family Circle, and the Collaborative Production of the Dissenting Public Sphere," *Eighteenth-Century Studies* 32.4 (1999): 516–17, finds support in Lucy Newlyn's *Reading, Writing, and Romanticism* (Oxford University Press, 2000), in which Barbauld's writings perform a "sophisticated negotiation of the intermediate terrain between public and private" (p. 137) and create "an ethic of interconnectedness which . . . spreads out from the immediate network of family and friends into the nation at large" (p. 144).

18 Rodgers, *Georgian Chronicle*, p. 122.

19 There was a steady supply of young readers and commentators: John and Martha Aikin's first two children, Arthur and George, were born in 1773 and 1774, respectively, and were followed by Edmund and Lucy, for whom *Evenings at Home* would be written, in 1780 and 1781. Their third son, Charles, born in 1775, was raised by the otherwise childless Anna and Rochemont Barbauld, who persuaded the Aikins to let them adopt Charles soon before his second birthday.

20 Cited in Rodgers, *Georgian Chronicle*, p. 56. Lucy Aikin's *Memoir of John Aikin, M. D.* (1823; Philadelphia, 1824) reproduces a letter written in February 1777 by John Aikin to his sister: "[Howard] has been here [at Warrington] superintending the printing, for three or four weeks, and will stay as much longer. I have the pleasure of seeing him every day, being his corrector and revisor and so forth" (pp. 30–31). Another typical example of collaboration at Warrington involves John Aikin and the naturalist and topographer Thomas Pennant.

21 Le Breton, *Memoir*, p. 81.

22 Howard's name was often coupled with those of abolitionists Wilberforce and Thomas Clarkson: "The miserable prisoners in the dungeons of Europe had a

Howard to feel for their distresses . . . The groans and lamentations of the children of Africa . . . awakened the pity of a Clarkson and a Wilberforce" (Bogue and Benett, *History of Dissenters*, IV, p. 185).

23 Aikin, *Poems* (London, 1791), pp. 73–74.

24 *Miscellaneous Pieces in Prose, by J. and A. L. Aikin*, 3rd edn. (1773; London, 1792).

25 See *PALB*, p. xxix; cf. Rodgers, *Georgian Chronicle*, p. 57.

26 The anecdote appears in Henry Bright, *A Historical Sketch of Warrington Academy* (Liverpool, 1859), p. 14; Holt, *A Life of Joseph Priestley*, p. 28; and Herbert McLachlan, "Mary Priestley: A Woman of Character," in *Motion Toward Perfection: The Achievement of Joseph Priestley*, ed. A. Truman Schwartz and John G. McEvoy (Boston: Skinner House Books, 1989), p. 255. Mary Priestley's younger brother, William Wilkinson, was enrolled in the Academy in 1761. William Turner, *The Warrington Academy* (Warrington: Library and Museum Committee, 1957), p. 56. A first edition of Barbauld's *Poems*, inscribed "To Mrs. Priestley from the Author," is in the Library Company of Philadelphia.

27 During the seventeenth and eighteenth centuries, a workbag could be referred to simply as a "housewife" (Wilson, "Lost Needles," p. 190 n. 17). Pamela, for instance, deceives Mrs. Jewkes' spy by purposely dropping her *"hussey."* Samuel Richardson, *Pamela; or, Virtue Rewarded* (1740; London: Penguin, 1980), p. 161.

28 Martineau, "What Women are Educated For," *Once a Week* (10 August 1861): 175–79; in *Harriet Martineau on Women*, ed. Gayle Graham Yates (New Brunswick: Rutgers University Press, 1985), pp. 102–04.

29 See Isobel Armstrong, "The Gush of the Feminine: How Can We Read Women's Poetry of the Romantic Period?," in *Romantic Women Writers*, pp. 13–32.

30 G. J. Barker-Benfield, *The Culture of Sensibility: Sex and Society in Eighteenth-Century Britain* (University of Chicago Press, 1992).

31 Wollstonecraft herself had previously quoted approvingly from Barbauld's essay in *The Female Reader* (1789), including this very passage in the preface (*WMW*, IV, pp. 57–58) along with another excerpt at the head of Book VI (IV, p. 323).

32 *Miscellaneous Pieces in Prose*, pp. 6–7.

33 Wykes, "The Contribution," in *Enlightenment and Religion*: "Recent studies (of Oxford in particular) have qualified earlier assessments of the eighteenth-century university as educationally moribund" (p. 132). The public's perception of the nonconformist academies as morally rigorous should be qualified as well: when the Warrington Academy initially closed in 1783, a breakdown in discipline was cited as a cause along with a want of adequate support. For some excellent anecdotes, see Bright, *A Historical Sketch*, pp. 22–23, and Holt, *A Life of Joseph Priestley*, pp. 40–41.

34 Barbauld's politics were formed in relation to a set of Whig positions during the late 1760s and early '70s, including support for Corsican independence, "Wilkes and Liberty," and concern over domestic commerce and the national

debt. See *PALB*, pp. 232–33. On Wilkes and the "cult of England," see Colley, *Britons*, pp. 106–12. Like the followers of Wilkes in London, Dissenters in Northern England vigorously supported the cause of "Liberty" against French militarism in Corsica during 1768–69 and against the partition of Poland by Austria, Prussia, and Russia in 1772. 1772 also saw the Feather's Tavern Petitions seeking removal for the established clergy of the necessity of subscription under the Corporation and Test Acts, a motivating cause for the early publishing endeavors of Joseph Johnson.

35 On relations between the regional political networks involved in the canal scheme and both regional and national identity, see John Money, *Experience and Identity: Birmingham and the West Midlands 1760–1800* (Manchester University Press, 1977), pp. 24–30.

4 GODWINIAN SCENES AND POPULAR POLITICS: GODWIN, WOLLSTONECRAFT, AND THE LEGACIES OF DISSENT

1 Quoted in Watts, *The Dissenters*, I, p. 487.
2 Robinson died in 1790, Price and Hollis in 1791. Priestley went into permanent exile on 7 April 1794, settling in Northumberland, Pennsylvania.
3 Mark Philp, *Godwin's Political Justice* (London: Duckworth, 1986), p. 162.
4 From January to December 1828, the year in which the Acts were finally repealed, *The Test-Act Reporter* was issued monthly.
5 1795 saw the deaths of Samuel Stennett, Andrew Kippis, Rice Harris, Benjamin Beddome, Samuel Clark, Thomas Toller, Roger Flexman, Henry Beaufoy, and Josiah Wedgwood, Sr. James Fordyce, Thomas Christie, and Stephen Addington followed in 1796.
6 On the radical societies, see Thompson, *The Making*, pp. 17–185, and Albert Goodwin, *The Friends of Liberty: The English Democratic Movement in the Age of the French Revolution* (Cambridge: Harvard University Press, 1979). See also Carl B. Cone, *The English Jacobins: Reformers in Late 18th Century England* (New York: Charles Scribner's Sons, 1968), pp. 187–209; Iain McCalman, *Radical Underworld: Prophets, Revolutionaries and Pornographers in London, 1795–1840* (Cambridge University Press, 1988), pp. 8–14, 114–15; and David Worrall, *Radical Culture: Discourse, Resistance and Surveillance, 1790–1820* (Detroit: Wayne State University Press, 1992), pp. 19–38.
7 Although the SCI was founded in 1780, it was reinvigorated in 1792 with the formation of the LCS, the participation of Thomas Holcroft, who joined in November 1792, and the Scottish Reform Convention of late 1793.
8 Thompson, *The Making*, p. 122.
9 Place, *The Autobiography of Francis Place (1771–1854)*, ed. Mary Thale (Cambridge University Press, 1972), p. 197n. Place joined the LCS at the request of his landlord, a cabinet maker (p. 129).
10 Ibid., p. 162. Although it is generally wise to treat Place's *Autobiography* with reserve as "in part a personal *apologia*, in which the 'sober thinking

men' (i.e. Francis Place) are elevated, and the less temperate denigrated" (Thompson, *The Making*, p. 134n), there are instances such as this when Place seems reliable: his discussion of infidelity in the LCS does not further his often revisionary project.

11 Hannah Barker and Simon Burrows, "Introduction," in *Press, Politics and the Public Sphere in Europe and North America, 1760–1820*, ed. Barker and Burrows (Cambridge University Press, 2002), p. 4.

12 Lucyle Werkmeister, *A Newspaper History of England 1792–1793* (Lincoln: University of Nebraska Press, 1967), pp. 21–22, and Richard D. Altick, *The English Common Reader: A Social History of the Mass Reading Public 1800–1900* (University of Chicago Press, 1957), pp. 69–72.

13 Barker and Burrows, *Press, Politics and the Public Sphere*, provide the apt phrase "contingent autonomy" (p. 14) to describe the typical relationship of newspapers to state power.

14 Ibid., p. 8.

15 Philp, *Godwin's Political Justice*, p. 216. Philp's thesis is anticipated by M. Fitzpatrick, "William Godwin and the Rational Dissenters," *Price-Priestley Newsletter* 3 (1979): 17: "If . . . the attainment of his ideal rested upon the twin pillars of honest enquiry and candid discussion, then it can be maintained that his utopia was in so many ways the society of his London friends and acquaintances multiplied."

16 Myers, "Godwin's Memoirs of Wollstonecraft: The Shaping of Self and Subject," *Studies in Romanticism* 20.3 (1981): 299–316.

17 "Of History and Romance" was first published as an appendix to *Caleb Williams*, ed. Maurice Hindle (London: Penguin, 1988). See Evan Radcliffe, "Godwin from 'Metaphysician' to Novelist: *Political Justice*, *Caleb Williams*, and the Tension between Philosophical Argument and Narrative," *Modern Philology* 97.4 (2000): 528–53.

18 See Bogue and Bennett, *History of Dissenters*, IV, pp. 327–28. On another Sandemanian, the ultra-radical Thomas Spence, see Thompson, *The Making*, p. 36, and below.

19 During the 1780s, Kippis assisted both Godwin and their mutual friend Helen Maria Williams. In 1784, on the recommendation of Kippis, Godwin became the editor of the British and Foreign History section in the *New Annual Register*, for which he worked from 1784–91. Kippis helped Williams publish her first poem, *Edwin and Eltruda*, in 1781, and he seems to have been a strong advocate for her during the early 1780s, her first years in London. See the *Monthly Review* 57 (July 1782): 26–30.

20 Along with George Dyson, Thomas Holcroft, and Coleridge, Fawcett was one of the four friends Godwin referred to as his "oral instructors." Fawcett's poetry remained popular among liberal Dissenting circles after his death; see *Poems, by Joseph Fawcett. To which are Added Civilised War, Before Published under the Title of The Art of War* (London, 1798).

21 Godwin's year in London led to his first burst of publications, in 1783–84: *An Account of the Seminary That will be opened On Monday the Fourth Day of*

August, At Epsom in Surrey (1783), *A Life of Chatham* (1783), *A Defence of the Rockingham Party* (1783), *Damon and Delia: A Tale* (1784), *Italian Letters; or, The History of the Count de St. Julian* (1784), *Imogen: A Pastoral Romance* (1784), *The Herald of Literature* (1784) and *Instructions to a Statesman* (1784).

22 Quoted in Philp, *Godwin's Political Justice*, p. 161.

23 Ibid.

24 Rowland Weston, "Politics, Passion and the 'Puritan Temper': Godwin's Critique of Enlightenment Modernity," *Studies in Romanticism* 41. 3 (2002): 446. Don Locke, *A Fantasy of Reason: The Life and Thought of William Godwin* (London: Routledge, 1980), p. 17.

25 William Hurd, *A New Universal History of the Religious Rites, Ceremonies, and Customs of the Whole World* (London, [1788]), p. 571.

26 Robert Adam, *The Religious World Displayed; or, A View of the Four Grand Systems of Religion, Judaism, Paganism, Christianity, and Mohammedism; and of the Various Existing Denominations, Sects and Parties, in the Christian World*, 3 vols. (Edinburgh, 1809), III, p. 183.

27 Samuel Pike, *A Plain and Full Account of the Christian Practices Observed by the Church in St. Martin's-le-grand, London* (London, 1766), p. 21.

28 Adam, *The Religious World Displayed*, III, p. 190. Spence envisioned, essentially, a welfare state in which all land would be possessed in common by all citizens – men, women, and children – of individual parishes. These would constitute "parochial corporations" which would control all land within the parish boundary. See H. T. Dickinson, ed., *The Political Works of Thomas Spence* (Newcastle upon Tyne: Avero Publications, 1982); T. R. Knox, "Thomas Spence: The Trumpet of Liberty," *Past & Present* 76 (August 1977): 75–98; and Marcus Wood, *Radical Satire and Print Culture, 1790–1822* (Oxford: Clarendon Press, 1994), pp. 57–95. Spence has received detailed attention from Michael Scrivener in *Seditious Allegories: John Thelwall & Jacobin Writing* (University Park: Pennsylvania State University Press, 2001), ch. 4.

29 John Bell's *The Wanderings of the Human Intellect; or, A New Dictionary of the Various Sects into which the Christian Religion, in Ancient and in Modern Times, has been Divided* (Newcastle, 1814) similarly describes Sandemanian "community of goods" as follows: "each one is to consider whatever he possesses, as liable to the calls of the poor, and of their society" (p. 342).

30 Marilyn Butler, *Romantics, Rebels, and Reactionaries: English Literature and its Background 1760–1830* (Oxford University Press, 1981), p. 25; Roy Porter, "The Enlightenment in England," in *The Enlightenment in National Context*, ed. Roy Porter and Mikulas Teich (Cambridge University Press, 1981), pp. 15–16; see also Philp, *Godwin's Political Justice*, pp. 127–29, 164–66.

31 See Tyson, *Joseph Johnson*, and Brathwaite, *Romanticism, Publishing and Dissent*. The "intellectual tea parties" of Williams' Dissenting circle "represented the height of radical fashion." Locke, *A Fantasy of Reason*, p. 30.

32 Fitzpatrick, "William Godwin," p. 14. Though the heir of Timothy's republican cousin Thomas Hollis, Brand was not related to the Hollises by blood.

Timothy Hollis was affiliated with Theophilus Lindsey's Essex Street Chapel (Watts, *The Dissenters*, I, p. 488), of which Brand Hollis was a founding member, contributing £100 towards the purchase of Essex House. Both John and Brand Hollis were original members of the Unitarian Society for Promoting Christian Knowledge and the Practice of Virtue, by Distributing Books, formed in 1791. Thomas Belsham, who succeeded Priestley as pastor at Hackney, wrote the biography of Lindsey, and served as minister of the Essex Street congregation after 1804, was a second cousin of the Aikins: his mother was the sister of Anna Laetitia Jennings, the maternal grandmother of Anna and John Aikin, and Belsham commenced his education at John Aikin's school at Kibworth. Barbauld's "The Invitation. To Miss B*****" was addressed to her closest friend Elizabeth Belsham, Thomas' sister, who was "no infrequent visitant at Warrington" (*PALB*, p. 225). Disney, a member of Lindsey's Essex Street congregation who succeeded Lindsey as minister in 1793 and in turn was succeeded by Belsham, was a powerful writer in the Unitarian cause. When the London Revolution Society was formed in November 1788, this community was at its center: Price, Priestley, Kippis, Rees, Lindsey, Belsham, and Brand Hollis were all influential members. The SCI also included members of this Dissenting circle, such as Price, Brand Hollis, Thomas Rogers, John Jebb, and Capel Lofft (Fitzpatrick, "William Godwin," pp. 14–15).

33 Quoted in Fitzpatrick, "William Godwin," p. 11.
34 Philp, *Godwin's Political Justice*, p. 163.
35 Fitzpatrick, "William Godwin," p. 8.
36 From 1788–95, Godwin and Holcroft dined together in each other's lodgings almost every other day. Their friends were affiliated with the extensive publishing circles of George Robinson and Joseph Johnson, both of whom threw regular literary parties. Godwin first met Mary Wollstonecraft at Johnson's in November 1791. Peter H. Marshall, *William Godwin* (New Haven: Yale University Press, 1984), pp. 86–89.
37 Paul Hamilton, "Coleridge and Godwin in the 1790s," in *The Coleridge Connection: Essays for Thomas McFarland*, ed. Richard Gravil and Molly Lefebure (New York: St. Martin's Press, 1990), p. 42.
38 The Philomathean Society, the membership of which was limited to twenty-one, was the only society Godwin seems to have joined in the 1790s. See Locke, *A Fantasy of Reason*, p. 80, and Marshall, *William Godwin*, p. 87. On the Lunar Society, see Jenny Uglow, *The Lunar Men: Five Friends Whose Curiosity Changed the World* (New York: Farrar, Straus, and Giroux, 2002); R. E. Schofield, *The Lunar Society of Birmingham: A Social History of Provincial Science and Industry in Eighteenth-Century England* (Oxford: Clarendon Press, 1963); Butler, *Romantics, Rebels, and Reactionaries*, p. 26; and Ian Wylie, "Coleridge and the Lunaticks," in Gravil and Lefebure, eds., *The Coleridge Connection*, pp. 25–40. On Franklin's Junto, from which the first circulating library in America resulted, see Franklin, *Benjamin Franklin*.

Autobiography and Other Writings, ed. Ormond Seavey (Oxford University Press, 1993), pp. 61–81.

39 "Copenhagen House" depicts the mass meeting held by the LCS on 26 October 1795 but integrates scenes from the meeting of 12 November held in response to Pitt and Grenville's proposed Two Acts. The bills of the Two Acts were first read in Parliament on 6 and 12 November 1795: Lord Grenville's "Act for the Safety and Preservation of his Majesty's Person and Government against Treasonable and Seditious Practices and Attempts" (36 Geo. III. c. 7), and William Pitt's "An Act for the more Effectually Preventing Seditious Meetings and Assemblies" (36 Geo. III. c. 8). The bills were printed in the *Morning Chronicle,* Monday 9 November 1795, and passed into law on 18 December. Regarding the 26 October meeting, in Copenhagen Fields, Islington, "The claim that 100,000 to 150,000 attended cannot be dismissed" (Thompson, *The Making,* p. 144). On 12 November between 200,000 and 300,000 were claimed to have attended. Gillray shows Thelwall in the foreground at the right, Gale Jones on the tribune at the left, William Hodgson in the distant center, and Priestley behind and to the left of the gaming wheel (Hill, *The Satirical Etchings,* pp. 108–09). The gaunt Jacobin behind Thelwall holds a handbill of "Resolutions of the London Corresponding Society," and the torn breeches, grotesque figures, and "Real Democratic Gin" of the audience represent the incendiary, carnivalesque elements of the working classes feared by Gillray and conspicuously absent from Francis Place's account of these scenes (pp. 144–45).

40 Garrett A. Sullivan, Jr., "'A Story to Be Hastily Gobbled Up': *Caleb Williams* and Print Culture," *Studies in Romanticism* 32.3 (1993): 329–30. Cf. Klancher, *The Making of English Reading Audiences,* pp. 14, 60.

41 *Politics for the People: or, A Salmagundy for Swine,* vol. II (London, 1795).

42 For a discussion of Thelwall's centrality to a vital Jacobin culture that "did not collapse of its own inadequacies and contradictions" but rather "was coerced into silence and disguise" (p. 290), see Scrivener's *Seditious Allegories.* See also Judith Thompson, "'A Voice in the Representation': John Thelwall and the Enfranchisement of Literature," in *Romanticism, History and the Possibilities of Genre: Re-forming Literature, 1789–1837,* ed. Tilottama Rajan and Julia M. Wright (Cambridge University Press, 1998), pp. 122–48.

43 It is difficult to say with precision how many hearers Thelwall's voice may have reached at any given meeting. Benjamin Franklin recounts in his *Autobiography* that the voice of a good speaker at the Court House on Market Street and Second Street in Philadelphia could still be heard at Market Street and Front Street, a distance (by my estimate) of approximately 460 feet (140 meters); Franklin then calculates that in that space "he might well be heard by more than Thirty-Thousand" (*Autobiography,* p. 111).

44 John Thelwall, *The Rights of Nature, Against the Usurpations of Establishments . . . Part the Second* (London, 1796), p. 45. After the Gagging Acts of December 1795, Thelwall chose to lecture on contemporary politics

obliquely through other subjects; see *Sober Reflections on the Seditious and Inflammatory Letter of the Right Hon. Edmund Burke, to a Noble Lord* (London, 1796), pp. 110–11.

45 *The Speech of John Thelwall, at the General Meeting of the Friends of Parliamentary Reform, Called by the London Corresponding Society, and Held in the Neighbourhood of Copenhagen-House; On Monday, October 26, 1795*, 3rd edn. (London, 1795), p. 21. Thelwall's speech was also published as *Peaceful Discussion, and not Tumultuary Violence the Means of Redressing National Grievances* (London, 1795).

46 Andrew McCann, *Cultural Politics in the 1790s: Literature, Radicalism and the Public Sphere* (Houndmills: Macmillan, 1999), p. 82.

47 For Bakhtin, plebeian rituals include carnivalesque representations of the grotesque body, which is not "individualized": "Manifestations of this life refer not to the isolated biological individual . . . but to the collective ancestral body of all people." Mikhail Bakhtin, *Rabelais and His World*, trans. Helene Iswolsky (Bloomington: Indiana University Press, 1984), p. 19. See also Terry Eagleton, *Walter Benjamin: Towards a Revolutionary Criticism* (London: Verso, 1981), pp. 148–49, and Peter Stallybrass and Allon White, *The Politics and Poetics of Transgression* (Ithaca: Cornell University Press, 1986), pp. 1–26, 80–124.

48 See James Epstein, "Radical Dining, Toasting and Symbolic Expression in Early Nineteenth-Century Lancashire: Rituals of Solidarity," *Albion* 20.2 (1988): 271–91.

49 *The Anti-Jacobin, or Weekly Examiner*, 2 vols. (London, 1799), II, pp. 163–64. See also Gillray's "The Loyal Toast" (London, 1798), a depiction of the Duke of Norfolk's widely reported toast to "Our Sovereign, the Majesty of the People"; repr. in John Brewer, *The Common People and Politics, 1750–1790s* (Cambridge: Chadwyck-Healey, 1986), p. 93.

50 Godwin, *Caleb Williams*, ed. Gary Handwerk and A. A. Markley (Peterborough: Broadview, 2000), p. 357.

51 Ibid., p. 368.

52 Ibid., p. 406.

53 Thelwall, *Sober Reflections*, p. 105.

54 Whereas *Cursory Strictures*, which first appeared in the *Morning Chronicle* on 21 October 1794, was published by Daniel Isaac Eaton, for the publication of *Considerations* Godwin turned to Joseph Johnson. On the Treason Trials, see Alan Wharam, *The Treason Trials, 1794* (Leicester University Press, 1992), and David Erdman, "Treason Trials in the Early Romantic Period," *The Wordsworth Circle* 19.2 (1988): 76–82.

55 Godwin himself visited Muir, Palmer, and Gerrald, among others, during their imprisonment in Newgate and the Tower. Skirving and Gerrald would both die within a year of their arrival in New South Wales. At the National Convention, which met from late October through early December 1793, French forms of procedure and address ("Citizen") had been used, and minutes were dated, "First Year of the British Convention" (Thompson, *The Making*, p. 127).

56 McCann has offered an insightful reading of these passages, to a different end, in *Cultural Politics in the 1790s,* pp. 65–66.
57 The clause ultimately did not appear in the Act, but it was included in the 9 November *Morning Chronicle* printing of the Act read by Godwin (*PPW,* ii, p. 137).
58 James T. Boulton, *The Language of Politics in the Age of Wilkes and Burke* (London: Routledge, 1963), p. 209.
59 Gregory Claeys, "From True Virtue to Benevolent Politeness: Godwin and Godwinism Revisited," in *Empire and Revolutions: Papers Presented at the Folger Institute Seminar,* ed. Gordon J. Schochet (Washington, D. C.: Folger Institute, 1993), p. 197. Cited with permission from the author.
60 Jon P. Klancher, "Godwin and the Republican Romance: Genre, Politics, and Contingency in Cultural History," *Modern Language Quarterly* 56.2 (1995): 153–54. See Klancher's revised version, "Godwin and the Genre Reformers: on Necessity and Contingency in Romantic Narrative Theory," in Rajan and Wright, eds., in *Romanticism, History, and the Possibilities of Genre,* pp. 21–38. Pamela Clemit has discussed *The Enquirer* as a "turning-point in Godwin's career," in which Godwin first "elevates books above conversation as a means of improvement"; after *The Enquirer,* "Godwin's interest in the formation of individual personality becomes central, and he moves into the realms of biography and fiction." Clemit, "Godwin's Educational Theory: *The Enquirer,*" *Enlightenment and Dissent* 12 (1993): 3, 9–10.
61 Claeys, "From True Virtue," p. 200.
62 Early in the first chapter of *St. Leon,* Godwin similarly alerts his reader, "I do not sit down now to write a treatise of natural philosophy." Godwin, *St. Leon,* ed. Pamela Clemit (Oxford University Press, 1994), p. 2.
63 Claeys, "From True Virtue," p. 206.
64 Henry Mackenzie's *The Man of Feeling* had appeared in 1771, and Godwin would later title his 1805 novel *Fleetwood: Or, the New Man of Feeling.*
65 On Marguerite de Damville in *St. Leon,* in the context of Godwin's memorialization of Wollstonecraft in the *Memoirs* "as the Revolutionary feminist in domestic as well as public life," see Gary Kelly, *Revolutionary Feminism: The Mind and Career of Mary Wollstonecraft* (New York: St. Martin's Press, 1992), p. 224.
66 Myers, "Godwin's Memoirs," p. 314.
67 Myers, "Sensibility and the 'Walk of Reason': Mary Wollstonecraft's Literary Reviews as Cultural Critique," in *Sensibility in Transformation: Creative Resistance to Sentiment from the Augustans to the Romantics,* ed. Syndy McMillen Conger (Rutherford: Fairleigh Dickinson University Press, 1990), p. 123.
68 Taylor, "For the Love of God," p. 24.
69 Ibid.
70 Catherine Parke, "What Kind of Heroine is Mary Wollstonecraft?," in Conger, ed., *Sensibility in Transformation,* p. 105.
71 *Samuel Johnson's Dictionary: Selections from the 1755 Work that Defined the English Language,* ed. Jack Lynch (Delray Beach: Levenger Press, 2002), p. 461.

72 Tilottama Rajan, "Framing the Corpus: Godwin's 'Editing' of Wollstonecraft in 1798," *Studies in Romanticism* 39.4 (2000): 514.
73 Myers, "Godwin's Memoirs," pp. 300, 316.
74 Philp, *Godwin's Political Justice*, p. 217.

5 *"PROPERER FOR A SERMON"*:
COLERIDGEAN MINISTRIES

1 Nicholas Roe, "Coleridge and John Thelwall: the Road to Nether Stowey," in Gravil and Lefebure, eds., *The Coleridge Connection*, pp. 60–80; Roe, *The Politics of Nature: Wordsworth and Some Contemporaries* (New York: St. Martin's Press, 1992), and *Wordsworth and Coleridge: The Radical Years*; Carl Ray Woodring, *Politics in English Romantic Poetry* (Cambridge: Harvard University Press, 1970), and *Politics in the Poetry of Coleridge* (Madison: University of Wisconsin Press, 1961). See also John Beer, "The 'revolutionary youth' of Wordsworth and Coleridge: Another View," *Critical Quarterly* 19.2 (1977): 79–87; John Colmer, *Coleridge: Critic of Society* (Oxford: Clarendon Press, 1959), and "Coleridge and Politics," in *S. T. Coleridge*, ed. R. L. Brett (London: G. Bell, 1971), pp. 244–70; John Cornwell, *Coleridge, Poet and Revolutionary, 1772–1804; A Critical Biography* (London: A. Lane, 1973); Kelvin Everest, *Coleridge's Secret Ministry: The Context of the Conversation Poems 1795–98* (Sussex: Harvester Press, 1979); Paul Hamilton, *Coleridge's Poetics* (Oxford: Basil Blackwell, 1983); Nigel Leask, *The Politics of Imagination in Coleridge's Critical Thought* (London: Macmillan, 1988); John Morrow, *Coleridge's Political Thought: Property, Morality and the Limits of Traditional Discourse* (London: Macmillan, 1990); E. P. Thompson, "Disenchantment or Default? A Lay Sermon," in *Power & Consciousness*, ed. Conor Cruise O'Brien and William Dean Vanech (University of London Press, 1969), pp. 149–81.
2 H. W. Piper, "Coleridge and the Unitarian Consensus," in Gravil and Lefebure, eds., *The Coleridge Connection*, pp. 273–90; Basil Willey, "Coleridge and Religion," in Brett, ed., *S. T. Coleridge*, pp. 221–43, and Willey, *Samuel Taylor Coleridge* (New York: Norton, 1972). See also J. Robert Barth, S. J., "Coleridge and the Church of England," in Brett, ed., *The Coleridge Connection*, pp. 291–307; David Jasper, *Coleridge as Poet and Religious Thinker: Inspiration and Revelation* (London: Macmillan, 1985); Peter J. Kitson, "The Whore of Babylon and the Woman in White: Coleridge's Radical Unitarian Language," in *Coleridge's Visionary Languages*, ed. Tim Fulford and Morton D. Paley (Rochester: Brewer, 1993), pp. 1–14; Thomas McFarland, *Coleridge and the Pantheist Tradition* (Oxford: Clarendon Press, 1969); Jonathan Mulrooney, "'Sounding on His Way': Coleridgean Religious Dissent and Hazlitt's Conversational Style," in *The Fountain Light: Studies in Romanticism and Religion In Honor of John L. Mahoney*, ed. J. Robert Barth, S. J. (New York: Fordham University Press, 2002), pp. 176–92; Stephen Prickett, *Romanticism and Religion: The Tradition of Coleridge and Wordsworth in the Victorian Church* (Cambridge University Press, 1976); Ronald

C. Wendling, *Coleridge's Progress to Christianity: Experience and Authority in Religious Faith* (Lewisburg: Bucknell University Press, 1995).

3 M. H. Abrams, "Structure and Style in the Greater Romantic Lyric," in *From Sensibility to Romanticism: Essays Presented to Frederick A. Pottle*, ed. F. W. Hilles and H. Bloom (Oxford University Press, 1965), pp. 527–60; J. A. Appleyard, *Coleridge's Philosophy of Literature: The Development of a Concept of Poetry, 1791–1819* (Cambridge: Harvard University Press, 1965); Jerome Christensen, *Coleridge's Blessed Machine of Language* (Ithaca: Cornell University Press, 1981), and "Philosophy/Literature: The Associationist Precedent for Coleridge's Late Poems," in *Philosophical Approaches to Literature: New Essays on Nineteenth- and Twentieth-Century Texts*, ed. William E. Cain (Lewisburg: Bucknell University Press, 1984), pp. 27–50; Leonard W. Deen, "Coleridge and the Sources of Pantisocracy: Godwin, the Bible, and Hartley," *Boston Studies in English* 5 (1961): 232–45; A. C. Goodson, "Coleridge on Language: A Poetic Paradigm," *Philological Quarterly* 62.1 (1983): 45–68; James C. McKusick, *Coleridge's Philosophy of Language* (New Haven: Yale University Press, 1986).

4 I take the following as models of criticism that have integrated these categories of Coleridge's early development: Hamilton, "Coleridge and Godwin in the 1790s," in Gravil and Lefebure, eds., *The Coleridge Connection*, pp. 41–59; Terence Allan Hoagwood, *Politics, Philosophy, and the Production of Romantic Texts* (DeKalb: Northern Illinois University Press, 1996); Klancher, *The Making*; Lewis Patton and Peter Mann, "Editor's Introduction," in *CW*, I, pp. xxiii–lxxx.

5 Jerome McGann, *The Romantic Ideology* (University of Chicago Press, 1983); Marjorie Levinson, "The New Historicism: Back to the Future," in *Rethinking Historicism: Critical Readings in Romantic History*, ed. Marjorie Levinson (London: Blackwell, 1989), pp. 18–63; Alan Liu, *Wordsworth: The Sense of History* (Stanford University Press, 1989).

6 Habermas, *Structural Transformation*, p. 56.

7 Terry Eagleton, *The Function of Criticism, From the Spectator to Post-Structuralism* (London: Verso, 1984), p. 16.

8 Ibid., p. 26.

9 John Aikin, *A Description of the Country from Thirty to Forty Miles round Manchester* (1795), p. 136.

10 *Analytical Review* 22 (November 1795): 449.

11 Anna Letitia Barbauld, *Civic Sermons to the People. Number II* (London, 1792), pp. 19–20.

12 John Aikin, *Address to the Dissenters of England on Their Late Defeat* (London, 1790), p. 18; quoted in Kramnick, "Religion and Radicalism," p. 517.

13 Kramnick, "Religion and Radicalism," p. 530.

14 Eagleton, *Function of Criticism*, p. 17.

15 Pierre Bourdieu, *The Field of Cultural Production*, ed. Randal Johnson (New York: Columbia University Press, 1993), pp. 40–43.

16 Alison Hickey, "Coleridge, Southey 'and Co.': Collaboration and Authority," *Studies in Romanticism* 37.3 (1998): 306.

17 Barth, "Coleridge and the Church," p. 291.
18 Burke, *Reflections*, p. 15.
19 Barnes, "A Plan," p. 29.
20 "Frost at Midnight" (line 10) and "Dejection: An Ode" (line 36). All quotations of Coleridge's poetry are from *STC*, and I give line numbers parenthetically.
21 Barth, "Coleridge and the Church," p. 291.
22 Everest, *Coleridge's Secret Ministry*, p. 90.
23 Ibid., p. 86.
24 Thompson, "Disenchantment or Default?," p. 179. See Hoagwood's reassessment in *Politics, Philosophy, and the Production of Romantic Texts*.
25 For the individuals involved in the projected emigration, see Everest, *Coleridge's Secret Ministry*, p. 75; see also Roe, *The Politics of Nature*, pp. 52–55, 156–57, and "Pantisocracy and the Myth of the Poet," in *Romanticism and Millenarianism*, ed. Tim Fulford (Houndmills: Palgrave, 2002), pp. 87–102; and Nigel Leask, "Pantisocracy and the Politics of the 'Preface' to *Lyrical Ballads*," in *Reflections of Revolution: Images of Romanticism*, ed. Alison Yarrington and Kelvin Everest (London: Routledge, 1993), pp. 39–58.
26 Morrow, *Coleridge's Political Thought*, pp. 25–27. In September 1794 Southey wrote to his brother that he and Coleridge had been preaching "Pantisocracy and Aspheterism every where. There Tom are two new words, the first signifying the equal government of all – and the other – the generalization of individual property, words well understood now in the city of Bristol" (*NL*, 1, p. 75).
27 Quoted in Roe, *The Politics of Nature*, p. 157.
28 *Articles, Agreed upon by the Archbishops and Bishops of both Provinces, and the Whole Clergy, in the Convocation Holden at London in the Year 1562, for Avoiding of Diversities of Opinions, and for the Establishing of Consent, Touching True Religion* (London, 1813), p. 22.
29 David Hartley, *Observations on Man*, 2 vols. (London, 1749), 1, p. 472.
30 Everest, *Coleridge's Secret Ministry*, p. 69.
31 Similarly, Coleridge writes to Benjamin Flower on 11 December 1796: "My answer to Godwin will be a six shilling Octavo; and is designed to shew not only the absurdities and wickedness of *his* System, but to detect what appear to me the defects of all the systems of morality before & since Christ, & to shew that wherein they have been right, they have exactly coincided with the Gospel" (*CL*, 1, p. 267). Everest, Hamilton (1990), Patton and Mann, Morrow, and Roe (1988 and 1990) provide in-depth treatments of the role played by Godwin in Coleridge's thought, and see Nicola Trott, "The Coleridge Circle and the 'Answer to Godwin,'" *Review of English Studies* 41.162 (1990): 212–29.
32 Book x, lines 806–09. William Wordsworth, *The Prelude 1799, 1805, 1850*, ed. Jonathan Wordsworth, M. H. Abrams, and Stephen Gill (New York: Norton, 1979), p. 402.
33 Coleridge takes the image of circles expanding in a lake, as well as the progression of benevolence, from Pope's *Essay on Man*, Epistle IV, lines

363–68. *The Poems of Alexander Pope*, ed. John Butt (New Haven: Yale University Press, 1963), p. 546.

34 Compare Coleridge's letter to George Dyer of 19 March 1795 (*CL*, 1, p. 154).

35 First published as *A Moral and Political Lecture*, the essay was revised over the summer for the "Introductory Address" to *Conciones ad Populum*, which appeared in early December.

36 For Priestley's sentiments on capital punishment, see *Lectures on History and General Policy* (Birmingham, 1788), pp. 348–58; and on the poor laws, see *An Appeal to the Public, on the Subject of the Riots in Birmingham* (Birmingham, 1791), p. 86, and *Letters to the Right Honourable Edmund Burke* (Birmingham, 1791), p. 119.

37 Hazlitt, "My First Acquaintance with the Poets," in *The Selected Writings of William Hazlitt*, IX, pp. 97–98. Hazlitt's essay first appeared in full in *The Liberal* 2 (April 1823): 23–46.

38 Watts, *An Humble Attempt*, p. 57.

39 Hazlitt, "My First Acquaintance with the Poets," in *The Selected Writings of William Hazlitt*, IX, p. 96.

40 *CW*, I, pp. 346–56. The sermon comes to us in a transcription made by Ernest Hartley Coleridge, VCL (Victoria College Library, University of Toronto) MS BT 5 ff 169–78. E. H. Coleridge, interestingly, went out of his way to reproduce the physical configuration of Coleridge's original manuscript, marking where the pages began and ended and even, in copying a fragment of another sermon, at one point writing exclusively down the left margin of one page and right margin of the next where the bottom right corner of the original double-sided manuscript page must have been torn off. See Patton and Mann's description, *CW*, I, p. 336. When Coleridge turns to the application (the part of the sermon traditionally calling for the most pathos), the transcription presents the last two consequences followed by ellipses and then leaves the remainder of the page blank, with the conclusion of the sermon only starting again at the top of the next. Presumably, as Patton and Mann propose, Coleridge here "intended to extemporise" (*CW*, I, p. 346); in doing so he also presumably did not even want to see how the conclusion would begin.

41 Andrews, *Unitarian Radicalism*, p. 116.

42 On the conversation poems as a discrete body, see George Maclean Harper, "Coleridge's Conversation Poems," *Quarterly Review* 244 (1925): 284–98; Richard Harter Fogle, "Coleridge's Conversation Poems," *Tulane Studies in English* 5 (1955): 103–10; Albert Gérard, "The Systolic Rhythm: The Structure of Coleridge's Conversation Poems," *Essays in Criticism* 10.3 (1960): 307–19; A. R. Jones, "The Conversational and other Poems," in Brett, ed., *S. T. Coleridge*, pp. 91–122; Max F. Schulz, "The Conversation Voice," in *The Poetic Voices of Coleridge: A Study of His Desire for Spontaneity and Passion for Order* (Detroit: Wayne State University Press, 1963) pp. 73–99; and George Watson, "The Conversation Poems," in *Coleridge the Poet* (New York: Barnes & Noble, 1966), pp. 61–84.

43 Abrams, "Structure and Style," p. 550.
44 *Poems, by S. T. Coleridge*, 2nd edn. (Bristol, 1797), p. 72.
45 The passage first appears in the *Errata*, following the "Preface."
46 Abrams, "Structure and Style," p. 545.
47 From Horace's *Satires* i.iv.42. *STC*, p. 466.
48 See Richard T. Martin, "Coleridge's Use of 'sermoni propriora,'" *The Words-worth Circle* 3 (1972): 71–75.
49 Coleridge later refers to *Conciones* as "the first of my 'Lay-sermons'" (*CW*, I, p. 25n).
50 "The Eolian Harp" was first published in *Poems* (1796) under the title "Effusion xxxv." I will continue to call the poem "The Eolian Harp," but for historical accuracy I will quote from the 1796 version (*STC*, pp. 85–86).
51 Gérard, "The Systolic Rhythm," p. 311.
52 Quoted in Peter T. Marcy, "Eighteenth Century Views of Bristol and Bristolians," in *Bristol in the Eighteenth Century*, ed. Patrick McGrath (Newton Abbott: David & Charles, 1972), p. 38.
53 Flower published some of Coleridge's poems in *The Cambridge Intelligencer* and printed Coleridge and Southey's *The Fall of Robespierre* (Cambridge, 1794). Coleridge praises Flower's journal in the last number of *The Watchman* (*CW*, II, p. 374).
54 John Spencer Hill, *A Coleridge Companion* (London: Macmillan, 1983), p. 30.
55 Leask, *Politics of Imagination*, p. 13.
56 Hickey, "Coleridge, Southey," p. 318.
57 Ibid., p. 321.
58 Jack Stillinger, *Multiple Authorship and the Myth of Solitary Genius* (Oxford University Press, 1991), p. 183.
59 Valerie Purton, *A Coleridge Chronology* (London: Macmillan, 1993), pp. 31–32.
60 *The Notebooks of Samuel Taylor Coleridge*, ed. Kathleen Coburn and A. J. Harding, 5 vols. (London: Routledge, 1957–2002), III.4022.

6 "A SARACENIC MOSQUE, NOT A QUAKER MEETING-HOUSE": SOUTHEY'S *THALABA*, ISLAM, AND RELIGIOUS NONCONFORMITY

1 *British Critic* 18 (September 1801): 309; quoted in *Robert Southey: The Critical Heritage*, ed. Lionel Madden (London: Routledge, 1972), p. 63.
2 Ernest Bernhardt-Kabisch, *Robert Southey* (Boston: Twayne Publishers, 1977), p. i.
3 Because "sect" is the word used by Southey, Coleridge, Jeffrey, and the various Orientalist writers I will discuss, in this chapter I will for the most part use the word and its variants to refer to groups that elsewhere I have specified as denominations.
4 Butler, "Literature as a Heritage," p. 9.

5 At the turn of the eighteenth century, trade with North America and the Caribbean accounted for 11 percent of the value of English exports and 20 percent of imports; by 1798, trade with the New World accounted for 57 percent of exports and 32 percent of imports. Kenneth Morgan, *Bristol and the Atlantic Trade in the Eighteenth Century* (Cambridge University Press, 1993), p. 2. For a further description of Bristol's expansionist economy, see Walter Minchinton, "The Port of Bristol in the Eighteenth Century," in McGrath, ed., *Bristol in the Eighteenth Century*, pp. 127–60; see also C. M. MacInnes, "Bristol and the Slave Trade," in McGrath, ed., *Bristol in the Eighteenth Century*, pp. 161–84.

6 "Account of the Baptist Missionary Society," *Quarterly Review* 1 (February 1809): 193–226.

7 Caleb Evans, *The Kingdom of God* (Bristol, 1775), p. 24; quoted in Brian Stanley, *The History of the Baptist Missionary Society 1792–1992* (Edinburgh: T&T Clark, 1992), p. 3.

8 Stanley, *The History*, p. 3.

9 Ibid., p. 10.

10 Bogue and Bennett, *History of Dissenters*, IV, p. 291.

11 For Canuel, on the other hand, *The Watchman*, *The Friend*, and Coleridge's later defenses of the Established Church all regard "religious sectarianism as a strength rather than a weakness of British civil institutions" (*Religion, Toleration, and British Writing*, p. 88). He later qualifies this position significantly, however, emphasizing the "extent to which even Coleridge's earlier writing can be . . . deeply immersed in the rhetoric of religious uniformity" (p. 101) and arguing that Coleridge conceptualizes "establishment . . . as a way of providing contending beliefs with a public context that in turn awards those beliefs with increased distinction, articulation, and protection" (p. 108). I would agree that Coleridge more consistently regards diversity of beliefs, rather than diversity of sects, as a national strength.

12 Jeffrey, "*Thalaba*," p. 36.

13 One critic who has considered the implications of Jeffrey's religious rhetoric is Robert Ryan in *The Romantic Reformation*: "Jeffrey's comparison of the Romantics with religious nonconformists was not so whimsical a conceit as it may appear to us . . . In 1802, Dissent provided the most familiar example . . . of rebellion against intellectual coercion, setting a pattern which any other movement for cultural innovation might be seen as imitating" (p. 32).

14 Jeffrey, "*Thalaba*," p. 36.

15 Quoted in Mark Storey, "'A Hold upon Posterity': The Strange Case of Robert Southey," Inaugural lecture delivered on 20 February 1992 at the University of Birmingham (School of English, 1993), p. 4. To his friend Wynn, Southey wrote in December 1802, "*Vidi* the Review of Edinburgh. The first part is designed evidently as an answer to Wordsworth's Preface to the second edition of the Lyrical Ballads; and, however relevant to me, *quoad* Robert Southey, is certainly utterly irrelevant to Thalaba" (*LC*, II, p. 196).

16 Jeffrey, "*Thalaba*," p. 64.

17 Voltaire, *Essai sur les mœurs et l'esprit des nations*, 2 vols. (Paris: Garnier Frères, 1963), II, p. 242.
18 Butler, "Literature as a Heritage," p. 14.
19 See the appendix dedicated to "Southey's Religious Beliefs after 1811" in Geoffrey Carnall, *Robert Southey and His Age: The Development of a Conservative Mind* (Oxford: Clarendon Press, 1960), pp. 215–20.
20 Quoted in Jack Simmons, *Southey* (New Haven: Yale University Press, 1948), p. 36.
21 Southey had been a student there for a little over a year when Foot died and was replaced by the Socinian John Prior Estlin, at which point Southey's father withdrew him from the school: "Had I Continued," Southey wrote of Estlin, "he would have grounded me well" (*LC*, I, p. 46).
22 Quoted in Simmons, *Southey*, p. 44.
23 Bernhardt-Kabisch, *Robert Southey*, p. 58.
24 According to Shelley after his disappointing visit in 1811, "Southey calls himself a Christian, but he does not believe that the Evangelists were inspired . . . He rejects the Trinity, and thinks that Jesus Christ stood precisely in the same relation to God as himself." Quoted in Carnall, *Robert Southey*, p. 217.
25 Robert Southey, *Journals of a Residence in Portugal 1800–1801 and a Visit to France 1838*, ed. Adolfo Cabral (Oxford: Clarendon Press, 1960), pp. 94–95.
26 *The Debate in the House*, p. 41.
27 On Southey's Quakerism, see Carnall, *Robert Southey*, pp. 74–80.
28 Quoted in Carnall, *Robert Southey*, p. 74, from Southey's review of William Myles' *A Chronological History of the People Called Methodists* (1803) in the *Annual Review* (1803): 207.
29 Carnall, *Robert Southey*, p. 75.
30 Samuel Fothergill, *Discourses Delivered Extempore at Several Meeting Houses of the People Called Quakers* (Philadelphia, 1800), pp. 165–66.
31 As reported by Fuller, *The Calvinistic & Socinian Systems*, p. 4.
32 *The Notebooks of Samuel Taylor Coleridge*, 1.467. Similarly, in 1806 Coleridge complained of the "fine *respectable* attendants of Unitarian Chapels, and the moonshine Head-Work of the Sermons" (II.2892), and he came to see the Unitarian God as "a mere power in darkness . . . no sun, no Light with vivifying Warmth, but a cold and dull moonshine, or rather starlight, which shews itself but shews nothing else" (*CL*, II, p. 1196).
33 "On the Evangelical Sects," *Quarterly Review* 4 (November 1810): 486.
34 *Biographia Literaria*, ed. James Engell and W. Jackson Bate, 2 vols. (Princeton University Press, 1983), I, p. 304.
35 According to Edward Said, Orientalism "assumed an unchanging Orient, absolutely different (the reasons change from epoch to epoch) from the West." *Orientalism* (New York: Vintage Books, 1978), p. 96.
36 Antonio Gramsci, *Selections from the Prison Notebooks of Antonio Gramsci*, ed. and trans. Quintin Hoare and Geoffrey Nowell Smith (New York: International Publishers, 1971), pp. 51–53. See Dennis Porter, "*Orientalism* and its Problems," in *Colonial Discourse and Post-Colonial Theory: A Reader*, ed.

Patrick Williams and Laura Chrisman (New York: Harvester Wheatsheaf, 1993), p. 152.

37 Laelius Socinus (1525–62) and his nephew Faustus Socinus (1539–1604) were Italians, but Faustus settled in Poland in 1579, and it was there that the doctrine took hold, especially among the international student body of Rakow and with the formation of the Polish Brethren. The Trinitarian debates gained steam following the publication of William Sherlock's controversial *A Vindication of the Doctrine of the Holy and Ever Blessed Trinity* (London, 1690) and were then re-energized by the founding text of English Deism, John Toland's *Christianity not Mysterious: or, A Treatise Shewing, That there is nothing in the Gospel Contrary to Reason, Nor Above it: And that no Christian Doctrine can be properly call'd a Mystery* (London, 1696).

38 John Toland, *Nazarenus: Or, Jewish, Gentile, and Mahometan Christianity* (London, 1718), pp. 4–5.

39 Barthélemy d'Herbelot, *Bibliothèque Orientale, ou Dictionaire Universel contenant généralement Tout ce qui regarde la connoissance des Peuples de l'Orient* (Paris, 1697), p. 598. "A heresy that has taken the name of the religion that we call Mahometan." "The Interpreters of the Koran and other doctors of Muslim or Mahometan law have applied to this false prophet all the praises that the Arians, Paulitians, or, Paulianists and other heretics have attributed to Jesus Christ in denying him his divinity." Paul of Samosate was taken to be a predecessor of Socinus.

40 [Mathurin Veyssière de la Croze,] "Reflections on MAHOMETANISM and SOCINIANISM . . . To which is prefix'd, The Life and Actions of MAHOMET, extracted chiefly from Mahometan Authors," in *Four Treatises Concerning the Doctrine, Discipline and Worship of the Mahometans* (London, 1712), a translation of "Reflexions historique et critique sur le mahometisme, & sur le socinianisme," in vol. 1 of *Dissertations historique sur divers sujets*, 2 vols. (Rotterdam, 1707–08). Reland's "A Defence of the Mahometans" is a reprint of his *Of the Mahometan Religion* (1705).

41 Reland, "A Defence," p. 41.

42 George Townsend, *The Replication; or, A Familiar Address to Mr. William Frend* (Canterbury, 1789), p. 29.

43 Ibid., p. 33.

44 Adam, *Religious World Displayed*, II, p. 172.

45 Nathan Alcock, *The Rise of Mahomet, Accounted for on Natural and Civil Principles* (London, 1796), pp. 30–31.

46 Henry Kett, *History the Interpreter of Prophecy, or, A View of Scriptural Prophecies and their Accomplishment in the Past and Present Occurrences of the World; with Conjectures respecting their Future Completion*, 3 vols. (Oxford, 1799), I, p. viii.

47 Ibid., II, pp. 309–10.

48 Ibid., III, pp. 2–3.

49 Ibid., II, p. 264. Charles Butler's *Horae Biblicae; Part the Second: Being a Connected Series of Miscellaneous Notes on the Koran, the Zend-Avesta, the*

Vedas, the Kings, and the Edda (London, 1802) similarly claims that "between the rapid march of Islamism, and the rapid march of French Democracy, the resemblance is . . . striking. In each may be found the same zeal to propagate the tenets of their sect, the same thirst of plunder, the same ardour of destruction, the same enthusiasm, and the same patient and adventurous courage" (p. 83).

50 *The Debate in the House*, p. 38.

51 Because of the broad analogy between internal dissident communities and Islam, the organization of descriptions of the religious world throughout the century made it clear that readers needed to familiarize themselves with both nonconformist and Mahometan sects in order to understand and defend the truth of the Anglican church. Bernard Picart's *The Ceremonies and Religious Customs of the Various Nations of the Known World*, 6 vols. (London, 1733–39), Southey's early favorite and the inspiration for his mythological poems, divides Volume VI into two parts: "Part I. Containing the Doctrine and Discipline of the Church of England, of the Presbyterians, Independents, Anabaptists, Quakers, &c." (1737) and "Part II. Containing the Various Sects of Mahometans, with an Appendix of the Lives of Mohammed, Omar, and Ali" (1739). (Although usually referred to as Picart's work – Southey calls it "the great work of Picart" [*LC*, III, p. 351] – Bernard Picart was in fact the engraver; for the most part the work is a translation of *Ceremonies et coutumes religieuses de tous les peuples du monde*, 8 vols. [Amsterdam, 1723–43], written and collected by Jean Frédéric Bernard and Antoine Augustin Bruzen de la Martinière, among others.) John Lawrence Mosheim's *An Ecclesiastical History, Antient and Modern, from the Birth of Christ, to the Beginning of the Present Century* (1765) and Hurd's *A New Universal History* also take the reader through similar accounts. A later example of this organizational analogy is Adam's *The Religious World Displayed* in which Volume I gives a general account of Mahometanism followed by a detailed description of the principal Sonnite and Schiite sects, in addition to which "a numerous and powerful party of Deists or Infidels, known by the name of *Wahabees*, have arisen . . . and . . . are daily gaining ground, so as to threaten the very downfall of Mohammedism" (I, p. 266). If for Leibniz Islam itself was a "kind of Deism," for Adam the major religions repeat the same pattern of strict orthodoxy undermined by infidel sects. Volumes II and III, accordingly, then provide an account of Christianity along with the "Various Existing Denominations, Sects and Parties, in the Christian World," concluding with "A View of Deism and Atheism," which threaten Christianity just as the Mahometan "Deists" threaten Islam.

52 George Sale, "A Preliminary Discourse," in vol. I of *The Koran, commonly called The Alcoran of Mohammed*, trans. George Sale, A New Edition (1734; Bath, 1795), p. 92.

53 Ibid., p. 137.

54 Richard Pococke, *A Description of the East, and Some other Countries. Volume the First. Observations on Egypt* (London, 1743), p. 180.

55 Alcock, *The Rise of Mahomet*, p. 29.

56 Reland, "*A Defence*," p. 12.

57 Ibid., p. 57.

58 Humphrey Prideaux, *The True Nature of Imposture Fully Displayed in the Life of Mahomet* (London, 1697), pp. vii–viii. Henri de Boulainvilliers' *The Life of Mahomet* (London, 1731) repeated Prideaux's argument: "The prospect of the infinite disputes . . . of the Christian World . . . which GOD so remarkably punished by the arms of the Mussulmen, may teach us at this day prudence, and charity, caution, and mutual forbearance" (p. vi).

59 Edward Gibbon, *The History of the Decline and Fall of the Roman Empire*, ed. David Womersley, 3 vols. (London: Penguin, 1994), III, p. 316.

60 I would therefore qualify Nigel Leask's claim that *Thalaba* presents "Islam as a rational Unitarian religion." *British Romantic Writers and the East: Anxieties of Empire* (Cambridge University Press, 1992), p. 26. Islam serves Southey's ends, rather, because he holds it to be a Unitarian religion that is intuitive.

61 William Haller, *The Early Life of Robert Southey 1774–1803* (New York: Columbia University Press, 1917), p. 248.

62 Bernhardt-Kabisch, *Robert Southey*, p. 95; Curran, *Poetic Form*, p. 134.

63 Bernhardt-Kabisch, *Robert Southey*, p. 92.

64 Herbert F. Tucker, "Southey the Epic-Headed," *Romanticism on the Net* 32–33 (November 2003–February 2004): par. 17. 19 March 2005. <http://www.erudit.org/revue/ron/2003/v/n32-33/009263ar.html>.

65 See Harold Bloom's influential essay, "The Internalization of Quest-Romance," in *Romanticism and Consciousness: Essays in Criticism*, ed. Harold Bloom (New York: Norton, 1970), pp. 3–23.

66 As Tim Fulford's discussion of the witch Khawla suggests, and in keeping with the Spenserean frame, the pagan female body in *Thalaba* represents a different kind of physicality altogether from that of the Islamic male body. The physicalized faith of *Thalaba* is thus also a masculine one. Fulford, "Pagodas and Pregnant Throes: Orientalism, Millenarianism and Robert Southey," in Fulford, ed., *Romanticism and Millenarianism*, pp. 129–31.

67 *Thalaba the Destroyer*, ed. Tim Fulford, vol. III of *Robert Southey: Poetical Works 1793–1810*, gen. ed. Lynda Pratt, 5 vols. (London: Pickering & Chatto, 2004), p. 247. All quotations of *Thalaba* are from this edition; I provide book and line numbers parenthetically for passages of verse, and page numbers for passages from the notes.

68 Tucker, "Southey," par. 16.

69 Butler, "Literature as a Heritage," p. 13.

70 *Poems of Robert Southey*, ed. Maurice Fitzgerald (Oxford University Press, 1909).

71 Tucker, "Southey," par. 23.

72 Clare Simmons, "'Useful and Wasteful Both': Southey's *Thalaba the Destroyer* and the Function of Annotation in the Romantic Oriental Poem," *Genre* 27 (Spring–Summer 1994): 84.

73 Bernhardt-Kabisch, *Robert Southey*, p. 58.

74 Thomas M. Lennon, *Reading Bayle* (University of Toronto Press, 1999), p. 7.
75 Mikhail Bakhtin, "Epic and Novel," in *The Dialogic Imagination: Four Essays by M. M. Bakhtin*, ed. Michael Holquist, trans. Caryl Emerson and Michael Holquist (Austin: University of Texas Press, 1981), p. 7.
76 Southey repeated the idea for this note in a letter to Coleridge of January 1800 (*LC*, II, p. 39).
77 Leask, *British Romantic Writers*, p. 2. For diametrically opposed accounts, see Eric Meyer, "'I know thee not, I loathe thy race': Romantic Orientalism in the Eye of the Other," *ELH* 58.3 (1991): 657–99, in which "The texts of Romantic Orientalism must . . . be read as part of the cultural apparatus whereby the Orient is contained and represented by ideological frameworks that serve both to incite confrontation and to seal off contestation within the larger structures of imperial history" (p. 661), and Mohammed Sharafuddin, *Islam and Romantic Orientalism: Literary Encounters with the Orient* (London: I. B. Tauris, 1994), in which the demystifying and "realistic" (p. xviii) Orientalism of Southey, Landor, Moore, Byron, Shelley, and Leigh Hunt was "critical of Europe – on the one hand for its despotic tendencies, on the other for its cultural imperialism or short-sightedness" (p. xxii).
78 In the *Mantiq al-teyr*, the late-thirteenth-century Persian allegorical poem by Farid ud-Din Attar, the birds, or Sufis, seek the mythical Simorgh in order to make it their king. When they complete their quest and find the Simorgh, they see themselves reflected in its countenance and realize that they and it are one. *The Conference of the Birds*, trans. Afkham Darabandi and Dick Davis (Harmondsworth: Penguin, 1984).
79 Jeffrey, "*Thalaba*," p. 77.
80 Quoted in Storey, "'A Hold upon Posterity,'" p. 4.
81 Herman Merivale, *Edinburgh Review* 68 (January 1839): 354–76; quoted in Madden, ed., *Robert Southey: The Critical Heritage*, p. 400.
82 Fitzgerald, *Poems of Robert Southey*, p. v.

CONCLUSION

1 Benjamin Bousfield, *Observations on the Right Hon. Edmund Burke's Pamphlet, on the Subject of the French Revolution*, 2nd edn. (1791; London, 1792), pp. 99–100.
2 Jane Taylor, *Essays in Rhyme*, 2nd edn. (London, 1816), p. 78, lines 11–18. Hereafter I provide both page numbers and line numbers parenthetically.
3 Robert Southey, "*History of Dissenters*," *Quarterly Review* 10 (October 1813): 132.
4 Burke, *Reflections*, p. 15.
5 Walter Wilson, *The History and Antiquities of Dissenting Churches and Meeting Houses, in London, Westminster, and Southwark; Including their Ministers, from the Rise of Nonconformity to the Present Time*, 4 vols. (London, 1808–14), I, pp. xi–xii.

6 As we have seen, between 1715–18 and 1851 Presbyterians and Unitarians shrank from 3.30 percent to 0.50 percent of the population; the Independent and Baptist denominations did grow, from 1.10 to 3.88 percent and from 1.09 to 2.95 percent respectively, but the greatest gains were among the Arminian Methodists, who by 1851 accounted for 8.80 percent of the English population, more than the Independents, Baptists, Quakers, Presbyterians, and Unitarians combined. Watts, *The Dissenters*, II, p. 29, "Table III. Nonconformists as a percentage of the total population: 1715–1718 and 1851."

7 Conder, *Reviewers Reviewed*, p. 27. On Conder and *The Associate Minstrels* (1810), see Chapter 3, n. 13.

Bibliography

PRIMARY SOURCES

Adam, Robert, *The Religious World Displayed; or, A View of the Four Grand Systems of Religion, Judaism, Paganism, Christianity, and Mohammedism; and of the Various Existing Denominations, Sects and Parties, in the Christian World*, 3 vols. (Edinburgh, 1809).

Aikin, John, *Address to the Dissenters of England on Their Late Defeat* (London, 1790).

A Description of the Country from Thirty to Forty Miles round Manchester (London, 1795).

Letters from a Father to His Son, on Various Topics, Relative to Literature and the Conduct of Life (London, 1794).

Poems (London, 1791).

The Spirit of the Constitution and that of the Church of England, Compared (London, 1790).

Aikin, Lucy, *Memoir of John Aikin, M.D.* (1823; Philadelphia, 1824).

Alcock, Nathan, *The Rise of Mahomet, Accounted for on Natural and Civil Principles* (London, 1796).

Articles, Agreed upon by the Archbishops and Bishops of both Provinces, and the Whole Clergy, in the Convocation Holden at London in the Year 1562, for Avoiding of Diversities of Opinions, and for the Establishing of Consent, Touching True Religion (London, 1813).

Attar, Farid ud-Din, *The Conference of the Birds*, trans. Afkham Darabandi and Dick Davis (Harmondsworth: Penguin, 1984).

Barbauld, Anna Letitia, *An Address to the Opposers of the Repeal of the Corporation and Test Acts*, 4th edn. (London, 1790).

Anna Letitia Barbauld: Selected Poetry and Prose, ed. William McCarthy and Elizabeth Kraft (Peterborough: Broadview, 2002).

Civic Sermons to the People. Number II (London, 1792).

Hymns in Prose for Children (London, 1781).

Poems (London, 1773).

The Poems of Anna Letitia Barbauld, ed. William McCarthy and Elizabeth Kraft (Athens: University of Georgia Press, 1994).

Remarks on Mr. Gilbert Wakefield's Enquiry into the Expediency and Propriety of Public or Social Worship (London, 1792).

The Works of Anna Laetitia Barbauld. With a Memoir by Lucy Aikin, ed. Lucy Aikin, 2 vols. (London, 1825).

Barbauld, Anna Letitia, and John Aikin, *Evenings at Home*, 6 vols. (London, 1792–96).

Miscellaneous Pieces in Prose, by J. and A. L. Aikin, 3rd edn. (1773; London, 1792).

Barnes, Thomas, "A Plan for the Improvement and Extension of Liberal Education in Manchester . . . Read April 9, 1783," in *Memoirs of the Literary and Philosophical Society of Manchester*, vol. II (Warrington, 1785).

Barruel, Augustin, *Memoirs, Illustrating the History of Jacobinism* (London, 1797–98).

Bell, John, *The Wanderings of the Human Intellect; or, A New Dictionary of the Various Sects into which the Christian Religion, in Ancient and in Modern Times, has been Divided* (Newcastle, 1814).

Berington, Joseph, *The Rights of Dissenters from the Established Church, in relation, principally, to English Catholics* (London, 1789).

Blair, Hugh, *Lectures on Rhetoric and Belles Lettres*, 3 vols. (1783; London, 1790).

Bogue, David, and James Bennett, *History of Dissenters, from the Revolution in 1688, to the Year 1808*, 4 vols. (London, 1808–12).

Boulainvilliers, Henri de, *La Vie de Mahomed* (London, 1730).

The Life of Mahomet (London, 1731).

Bousfield, Benjamin, *Observations on the Right Hon. Edmund Burke's Pamphlet, on the Subject of the French Revolution*, 2nd edn. (1791; London, 1792).

Brown, John, *Thoughts on Civil Liberty, on Licentiousness and Faction* (Dublin, 1765).

Burke, Edmund, *Reflections on the Revolution in France, and on the Proceedings in Certain Societies in London Relative to that Event. In a Letter Intended to have been Sent to a Gentleman in Paris* (London, 1790).

Burnet, Gilbert, *The History of the Reformation of the Church of England*, 3 vols. (London, 1679).

Butler, Charles, *Horae Biblicae; Part the Second: Being a Connected Series of Miscellaneous Notes on the Koran, the Zend-Avesta, the Vedas, the Kings, and the Edda* (London, 1802).

Clarke, Samuel, *The Scripture-Doctrine of the Trinity* (London, 1712).

Coleridge, Samuel Taylor, *Biographia Literaria*, ed. James Engell and W. Jackson Bate, 2 vols. (Princeton University Press, 1983).

The Collected Letters of Samuel Taylor Coleridge, ed. Earl Leslie Griggs, 6 vols. (Oxford: Clarendon Press, 1956–71).

The Collected Works of Samuel Taylor Coleridge, gen. ed. Kathleen Coburn, 16 vols. (Princeton University Press, 1971–).

The Notebooks of Samuel Taylor Coleridge, ed. Kathleen Coburn and A. J. Harding, 5 vols. (London: Routledge, 1957–2002).

Poems, by S. T. Coleridge, 2nd edn. (Bristol, 1797).

Poems on various Subjects, By S. T. Coleridge (London, 1796).

Samuel Taylor Coleridge: The Complete Poems, ed. William Keach (London: Penguin, 1997).

Conder, Josiah, *Reviewers Reviewed; Including An Enquiry into the Moral and Intellectual Effects of Habits of Criticism, and Their Influence on the General Interests of Literature. To which Is Subjoined A Brief History of the Periodical Reviews Published in England and Scotland* (London, 1811).

[Conder, Josiah, Ann Taylor, Jane Taylor, and Eliza Thomas,] *The Associate Minstrels* (London, 1810); facsimile repr., *The Associate Minstrels and The Star in the East*, ed. Donald Reiman (New York: Garland, 1977).

[Croze, Mathurin Veyssière de la,] "Reflections on MAHOMETANISM and SOCINIANISM . . . To which is prefix'd, The Life and Actions of MAHOMET, extracted chiefly from Mahometan Authors," in *Four Treatises Concerning the Doctrine, Discipline and Worship of the Mahometans* (London, 1712). A translation of Croze, "Réflexions historique et critique sur le mahometisme, & sur le socinianisme" in vol. 1 of *Dissertations historique sur divers sujets*, 2 vols. (Rotterdam, 1707–08).

The Debate in the House of Commons on the Repeal of the Corporation and Test Acts, March 2d, 1790, 2nd edn. (London, 1790).

The Debate on a Motion for the Abolition of the Slave-Trade, in the House of Commons, on Monday the second of April, 1792, Reported in Detail (London, 1792).

Defoe, Daniel, *The Present State of the Parties in Great Britain* (London, 1712).

A Discovery of 29, Sects here in London, all of which, except the first, are most Divelish and Damnable ([London], 1641).

Disney, John, *An Arranged Catalogue of the Several Publications which have Appeared, Relating to the Enlargement of the Toleration of Protestant Dissenting-Ministers; and the Repeal of the Corporation and Test Acts* (London, 1790).

Doddridge, Philip, *The Correspondence and Diary of Philip Doddridge, D.D.*, ed. John Doddridge Humphreys, 2 vols. (London, 1829).

Lectures on Preaching, and the Several Branches of the Ministerial Office (London, 1821).

Estlin, John Prior, *The Nature and the Causes of Atheism, Pointed Out in a Discourse, Delivered at the Chapel in Lewin's-Mead, Bristol* (Bristol, 1797).

Evans, Caleb, *The Kingdom of God* (Bristol, 1775).

Evans, John, *A Sketch of the Several Denominations into which the Christian World is Divided; accompanied with a Persuasive to Religious Moderation*, 2nd edn. (London, 1795).

Fawcett, Joseph, *Poems, . . . To which are Added Civilised War, Before Published under the Title of The Art of War, With Considerable Alterations; and The Art of Poetry, According to the Latest Improvements, with Additions* (London, 1798).

Fothergill, Samuel, *Discourses Delivered Extempore at Several Meeting Houses of the People Called Quakers* (Philadelphia, 1800).

Four Treatises Concerning the Doctrine, Discipline and Worship of the Mahometans (London, 1712).

Fox, Charles James, *A Letter from the Right Honourable Charles James Fox to the Worthy and Independent Electors of the City and Liberty of Westminster* (London, 1793).

Franklin, Benjamin, *Benjamin Franklin, Autobiography and Other Writings*, ed. Ormond Seavey (Oxford University Press, 1993).

Fuller, Andrew, *The Calvinistic and Socinian Systems Examined and Compared, as to their Moral Tendency* (Market-Harborough, 1793).

Gerard, Alexander, *Liberty The Cloke of Maliciousness, Both in the American Rebellion, and in the Manners of the Times. A Sermon Preached at Old Aberdeen, February 26, 1778, Being the Fast-Day appointed by Proclamation, on account of the Rebellion in America* (Aberdeen, 1778).

Gibbon, Edward, *The History of the Decline and Fall of the Roman Empire*, ed. David Womersley, 3 vols. (London: Penguin, 1994).

Gillray, James, "Copenhagen House" (London, 1795) and "The Loyal Toast" (London, 1798); repr., *The Satirical Etchings of James Gillray*, ed. Draper Hill (New York: Dover, 1976).

Glazebrook, James, *What is called Extempore Preaching Recommended* (Warrington, 1794).

Godwin, William, *Caleb Williams*, ed. Gary Handwerk and A. A. Markley (Peterborough: Broadview, 2000).

Caleb Williams, ed. Maurice Hindle (London: Penguin, 1988).

The Collected Novels and Memoirs of William Godwin, gen. ed. Mark Philp, 8 vols. (London: William Pickering, 1992)

Political and Philosophical Writings of William Godwin, gen. ed. Mark Philp, 7 vols. (London: William Pickering, 1993).

St Leon, ed. Pamela Clemit (Oxford University Press, 1994).

Gregory, George, *Sermons, . . . To which are prefixed,* "Thoughts on the Composition and Delivery of a Sermon" (London, 1787).

Harrison, Ralph, *A Sermon Preached at the Dissenting Chapel in Cross-Street, Manchester . . . on occasion of the Establishment of an Academy in that Town* (Warrington, 1786).

Harrison, Susannah, *Songs in the Night; By a Young Woman under deep Afflictions* (London, 1780).

Hartley, David, *Observations on Man*, 2 vols. (London, 1749).

Hazlitt, William, *The Selected Writings of William Hazlitt*, ed. Duncan Wu, 9 vols. (London: William Pickering, 1998).

Herbelot, Barthélemy d', *Bibliothèque Orientale, ou Dictionaire Universel contenant généralement Tout ce qui regarde la connoissance des Peuples de l'Orient* (Paris, 1697).

Hoadly, Benjamin, *Bishop Hoadly's Refutation of Bishop Sherlock's Arguments against a repeal of the Corporation and Test Acts: Wherein the Justice and Reasonableness of such a Repeal are Clearly Evinced* (1718; London, 1787).

Hurd, William, *A New Universal History of the Religious Rites, Ceremonies, and Customs of the Whole World* (London, 1788).

Jeffrey, Francis, "*Thalaba, the Destroyer*: A Metrical Romance. By Robert Southey," *The Edinburgh Review* 1 (October 1802): 63–83.

Jennings, John, *Two Discourses: The First, Of Preaching Christ; the Second, Of Particular and Experimental Preaching . . . With a Preface by the Reverend Dr. Isaac Watts*, 3rd edn. (1723; London, 1736).

Johnson, Samuel, *Lives of the English Poets*, ed. G. B. Hill, 3 vols. (Oxford: Clarendon Press, 1905).

Samuel Johnson's Dictionary: Selections from the 1755 Work that Defined the English Language, ed. Jack Lynch (Delray Beach: Levenger Press, 2002).

Kendrick, James, *Profiles of Warrington Worthies, Collected and Arranged by James Kendrick, M.D.* (Warrington, 1853).

Kett, Henry, *History the Interpreter of Prophecy, or, A View of Scriptural Prophecies and their Accomplishment in the Past and Present Occurrences of the World; with Conjectures respecting their Future Completion*, 3 vols. (Oxford, 1799).

Kippis, Andrew, "A Life of the Author," in Philip Doddridge, *The Family Expositor*, 7th edn. (London, 1792).

Lardner, Nathaniel, *A Letter Writ in the Year 1730 Concerning the Question Whether the Logos Supplied the Place of a Human Soul in the Person of Jesus Christ* (London, 1759).

Le Breton, Anna Letitia, *Correspondence of William Ellery Channing, D.D., and Lucy Aikin, from 1826 to 1842* (Boston, 1874).

Memoir of Mrs. Barbauld, Including Letters and Notices of Her Family and Friends (London: George Bell and Sons, 1874).

Lindsey, Theophilus, *A Sermon Preached At the Opening of the Chapel in Essex-House, Essex-Street, in the Strand, on Sunday, April 17, 1774* (London, 1774).

Lloyd, Charles, *Particulars of The Life of a Dissenting Minister* (London, 1813).

Locke, John, *An Essay Concerning Human Understanding*, ed. Peter H. Nidditch (Oxford: Clarendon Press, 1975).

Martineau, Harriet ["Discipulus"], "Female Writers on Practical Divinity," *Monthly Repository* 17 (October 1822): 593–96 and 17 (December 1822): 746–50.

"What Women are Educated For," *Once a Week* (10 August 1861): 175–79.

Memoirs of the Literary and Philosophical Society of Manchester, vol. II (Warrington, 1785).

Palmer, Samuel, *The Protestant-Dissenter's Catechism. Containing, I. A Brief History of the Nonconformists: II. The Reasons of the Dissent from the National Church. Designed to instruct and establish Young Persons among the Dissenters in the Principles of Nonconformity*, 9th edn. (1773; London, 1792).

Paterson, Samuel, *The Joineriana: or The Book of Scraps*, 2 vols. (London, 1772).

Picart, Bernard, engraver, *The Ceremonies and Religious Customs of the Various Nations of the Known World*, 6 vols. (London, 1733–39). Translation of Jean Frédéric Bernard, Antoine Augustin Bruzen de la Martinière, et al., *Ceremonies et coutumes religieuses de tous les peuples du monde*, 8 vols. (Amsterdam, 1723–43).

Pike, Samuel, *A Plain and Full Account of the Christian Practices Observed by the Church in St. Martin's-le-grand, London* (London, 1766).

Place, Francis, *The Autobiography of Francis Place (1771–1854)*, ed. Mary Thale (Cambridge University Press, 1972).

Pococke, Richard, *A Description of the East, and Some other Countries. Volume the First. Observations on Egypt* (London, 1743).

Politics for the People: or, A Salmagundy for Swine, vol. II (London, 1795).

Pope, Alexander, *The Poems of Alexander Pope*, ed. John Butt (New Haven: Yale University Press, 1963).

The Preacher's Manual (London, 1812).

Price, Richard, *A Discourse on the Love of Our Country, Delivered on Nov. 4, 1789, at the Meeting-House in the Old Jewry, to the Society for Commemorating the Revolution in Great Britain* (London, 1789).

    Observations on the Nature of Civil Liberty, the Principles of Government, and the Justice and Policy of the War with America (London, 1776).

Prideaux, Humphrey, *The True Nature of Imposture Fully Displayed in the Life of Mahomet. With A Discourse annexed, for the Vindicating of Christianity from this Charge; Offered to the Consideration of the Deists of the present Age* (London, 1697).

Priestley, Joseph, *An Appeal to the Public, on the Subject of the Riots in Birmingham* (Birmingham, 1791).

    An Appeal to the Serious and Candid Professors of Christianity (London, 1771).

    A Course of Lectures on Oratory and Criticism (London, 1777).

    A Course of Lectures on the Theory of Language and Universal Grammar (Warrington, 1762).

    Discourses on Various Subjects, Including several on Particular Occasions (Birmingham, 1787).

    An Essay on a Course of Liberal Education for Civil and Active Life. With Plans of Lectures on I. The Study of History and general Policy. II. The History of England. III. The Constitution and Laws of England. To which are added, Remarks on a Code of Education, Proposed by Dr. Brown, in a Late Treatise, Intitled, Thoughts on Civil Liberty, &c. (London, 1765).

    An Essay on the First Principles of Government, and on the Nature of Political, Civil, and Religious Liberty, Including Remarks on Dr. Brown's Code of Education, and on Dr. Balguy's Sermon on Church Authority, 2nd edn. (1768; London, 1771).

    A Familiar Illustration of Certain Passages of Scripture (London, 1772).

    A Free Address to Protestant Dissenters, As Such, By a Dissenter, 3rd edn. (1769; London, 1788).

    A General View of the Arguments for the Unity of God, and Against the Divinity and Pre-existence of Christ, from Reason, from the Scriptures, and from History (London, 1783).

    Institutes of Natural and Revealed Religion, 3 vols. (London, 1772–74).

    Lectures on History and General Policy (Birmingham, 1788).

    Letters to the Right Honourable Edmund Burke (Birmingham, 1791).

    Life and Correspondence, vol. I of *The Theological and Miscellaneous Works of Joseph Priestley*, ed. J. T. Rutt, 25 vols. (London, 1818–31).

The Rudiments of English Grammar, Adapted to the Use of Schools, with Observations on Style, A New Edition (1761; London, 1769).

Two Discourses; I. On Habitual Devotion, II. On the Duty of not living to Ourselves (Birmingham, 1782).

The Protestant Dissenter's Magazine (1794–95).

Reland, Adrian, "A Defence of the Mahometans from several Charges falsly laid against them by Christians," in *Four Treatises.*

Richardson, Samuel, *Pamela; or, Virtue Rewarded* (1740; London: Penguin, 1980).

Robinson, Robert, *An Essay on the Composition of a Sermon. Translated from the original French of The Revd. John Claude*, 2 vols. (London, 1778–79).

Political Catechism (London, 1782).

Robison, John, *Proofs of a Conspiracy Against All the Governments of Europe* (Edinburgh, 1797).

Roscoe, William, *Mount Pleasant* (London, 1777).

Poems for Youth, by a Family Circle (London, 1820).

The Wrongs of Africa, a Poem (London, 1787–88).

Sale, George, "A Preliminary Discourse," in vol. 1 of *The Koran, commonly called The Alcoran of Mohammed*, trans. George Sale, A New Edition (1734; Bath, 1795).

Scotch Presbyterian Eloquence Display'd: Or, the Folly of their Teaching Discover'd, from their Books, Sermons, Prayers, &c. (1692; London, 1789).

Sherlock, Thomas, *Bishop Sherlock's Arguments against a repeal of the Corporation and Test Acts: Wherein Most of the Pleas Advanced in a Paper now Circulating, styled The Case of Protestant Dissenters, &c. are Discussed. With a Dedication to the Right Honourable Wm. Pitt* (1718; London, 1787).

Sherlock, William, *A Vindication of the Doctrine of the Holy and Ever Blessed Trinity* (London, 1690).

Simeon, Charles, *Claude's Essay on the Composition of a Sermon: with Alterations and Improvements*, 2nd edn. (1796; Cambridge, 1801).

Smith, Haddon, *The Church-Man's Answer to the Protestant-Dissenter's Catechism* (London, 1795).

Southey, Robert, "Account of the Baptist Missionary Society," *Quarterly Review* 1 (February 1809): 193–226.

"History of Dissenters," *Quarterly Review* 10 (October 1813): 90–139.

Journals of a Residence in Portugal 1800–1801 and a Visit to France 1838, ed. Adolfo Cabral (Clarendon Press, 1960).

Letters from England: By Don Manuel Alvarez Espriella, 3 vols. (London, 1807).

The Life and Correspondence of Robert Southey, ed. Charles Cuthbert Southey, 6 vols. (London, 1849–50).

New Letters of Robert Southey, ed. Kenneth Curry, 2 vols. (New York: Columbia University Press, 1965).

"On the Evangelical Sects," *Quarterly Review* 4 (November 1810): 480–514.

Poems of Robert Southey, ed. Maurice Fitzgerald (Oxford University Press, 1909).

Selections from the Letters of Robert Southey, ed. John Wood Warter, 4 vols. (London, 1856).

Southey's Common-Place Book, ed. John Wood Warter, 4 vols. (London, 1849–51).

Thalaba the Destroyer, ed. Tim Fulford, vol. III of *Robert Southey: Poetical Works 1793–1810*, gen. ed. Lynda Pratt, 5 vols. (London: Pickering & Chatto, 2004).

Spence, Thomas, *The Political Works of Thomas Spence*, ed. H. T. Dickinson (Newcastle upon Tyne: Avero Publications, 1982).

Taylor, Jane, *Essays in Rhyme*, 2nd edn. (London, 1816).

Taylor, William, *A Memoir of the Life and Writings of the Late William Taylor of Norwich . . . Containing his Correspondence of Many Years with the late Robert Southey, Esq.*, ed. J. W. Robberds, 2 vols. (London, 1843).

The Test-Act Reporter (London, 1828).

Thelwall, John, *Peaceful Discussion, and not Tumultuary Violence the Means of Redressing National Grievances* (London, 1795).

Political Lectures, Volume the First (London, 1795).

The Rights of Nature, Against the Usurpations of Establishments . . . Part the Second (London, 1796).

Sober Reflections on the Seditious and Inflammatory Letter of the Right Hon. Edmund Burke, to a Noble Lord (London, 1796).

The Speech of John Thelwall, at the General Meeting of the Friends of Parliamentary Reform, Called by the London Corresponding Society, and Held in the Neighbourhood of Copenhagen-House; On Monday, October 26, 1795, 3rd edn. (London, 1795).

Toland, John, *Christianity not Mysterious: or, A Treatise Shewing, That there is nothing in the Gospel Contrary to Reason, Nor Above it: And that no Christian Doctrine can be properly call'd a Mystery* (London, 1696).

Nazarenus: Or, Jewish, Gentile, and Mahometan Christianity (London, 1718).

Towgood, Micaiah, *A Dissent from the Church of England, Fully justified* (London, 1746).

Townsend, George, *The Replication; or, A Familiar Address to Mr. William Frend* (Canterbury, 1789).

Volney, Constantin François, *A New Translation of Volney's Ruins*, trans. Thomas Jefferson and Joel Barlow (Paris, 1802).

Les Ruines, ou Méditations sur les Révolutions des Empires (Paris, 1791).

Voltaire, *Essai sur les mœurs et l'esprit des nations*, 2 vols. (Paris: Garnier Frères, 1963).

Wakefield, Gilbert, *An Enquiry into the Expediency and Propriety of Public or Social Worship* (London, 1791).

Memoirs of the Life of Gilbert Wakefield, 2 vols., A New Edition (London, 1804).

Watts, Isaac, *An Humble Attempt toward the Revival of Practical Religion among Christians, And particularly the Protestant Dissenters* (London, 1731).

"Preface," in Jennings, *Two Discourses*.

Wesley, John, *The Question, What is an Arminian? Answered* (Bristol, 1770).

Some Observations on Liberty: Occasioned by a Late Tract (London, 1776).

White, John, *A Letter to a Gentleman Dissenting from the Church of England* (London, 1743).

Wilkins, John, *Ecclesiastes, or, A Discourse concerning the Gift of Preaching as it fal[l]s under the rules of Art* (London, 1646).

Wilson, Walter, *The History and Antiquities of Dissenting Churches and Meeting Houses, in London, Westminster, and Southwark; Including their Ministers, from the Rise of Nonconformity to the Present Time,* 4 vols. (London, 1808–14).

Wollstonecraft, Mary, *The Works of Mary Wollstonecraft*, gen. ed. Janet Todd and Marilyn Butler, 7 vols. (London: William Pickering, 1989).

Wordsworth, William, *Lyrical Ballads*, ed. R. L. Brett and A. R. Jones, 2nd edn. (London: Routledge, 1991).

The Prelude 1799, 1805, 1850, ed. Jonathan Wordsworth, M. H. Abrams, and Stephen Gill (New York: Norton, 1979).

SECONDARY SOURCES

Abrams, M. H., "Coleridge's 'A Light in Sound': Science, Metascience, and Poetic Imagination," *Proceedings of the American Philosophical Society* 116 (1972): 458–76.

"English Romanticism, The Spirit of the Age," in *Romanticism Reconsidered: Selected Papers from the English Institute*, ed. Northrop Frye (New York: Columbia University Press, 1963), pp. 26–72.

Natural Supernaturalism: Tradition and Revolution in Romantic Literature (New York: Norton, 1971).

"Structure and Style in the Greater Romantic Lyric," in *From Sensibility to Romanticism: Essays Presented to Frederick A. Pottle*, ed. Frederick W. Hilles and Harold Bloom (Oxford University Press, 1965), pp. 527–60.

Adburgham, Alison, *Women in Print: Writing Women and Women's Magazines From the Restoration to the Accession of Victoria* (London: George Allen and Unwin, 1972).

Addicott, Len, "Introduction," in *Church Book: St Andrew's Street Baptist Church, Cambridge 1720–1832* (London: Baptist Historical Society, 1991), pp. viii–xviii.

Ahmad, Aijaz, "*Orientalism* and After," in Williams and Chrisman, eds., *Colonial Discourse and Post-Colonial Theory: A Reader*, pp. 162–71.

Altick, Richard D., *The English Common Reader: A Social History of the Mass Reading Public 1800–1900* (University of Chicago Press, 1957).

Andrews, Stuart, *Unitarian Radicalism: Political Rhetoric, 1770–1814* (Houndmills: Palgrave, 2003).

Appleyard, J. A., *Coleridge's Philosophy of Literature: The Development of a Concept of Poetry, 1791–1819* (Cambridge: Harvard University Press, 1965).

Armstrong, Isobel, "The Gush of the Feminine: How Can We Read Women's Poetry of the Romantic Period?," in Feldman and Kelley, eds., *Romantic Women Writers: Voices and Countervoices*, pp. 13–32.

Ashton, T. S., *An Eighteenth-Century Industrialist* (Manchester University Press, 1939).

The Industrial Revolution 1760–1830 (Oxford University Press, 1948).

Aspinall, Arthur, *Politics and the Press c. 1780–1850* (1949; Brighton: Harvester Press, 1973).

Bakhtin, Mikhail, "Discourse in the Novel," in *The Dialogic Imagination: Four Essays by M. M. Bakhtin*, ed. Michael Holquist, trans. Caryl Emerson and Michael Holquist (Austin: University of Texas Press, 1981), pp. 259–422.

"Epic and Novel," in Bakhtin, *The Dialogic Imagination*, pp. 3–40.

Rabelais and His World, trans. Helene Iswolsky (Bloomington: Indiana University Press, 1984).

Barker, Hannah, and Simon Burrows, "Introduction," in *Press, Politics and the Public Sphere in Europe and North America, 1760–1820*, ed. Barker and Burrows (Cambridge University Press, 2002), pp. 1–22.

Barker-Benfield, G. J., *The Culture of Sensibility: Sex and Society in Eighteenth-Century Britain* (University of Chicago Press, 1992).

Barlow, Richard Burgess, *Citizenship and Conscience: A Study in the Theory and Practice of Religious Toleration in England during the Eighteenth Century* (Philadelphia: University of Pennsylvania Press, 1957).

Barnet, George L., " 'That Cursed Barbauld Crew' or Charles Lamb and Children's Literature," *The Charles Lamb Bulletin* 25 (January 1979): 1–18.

Barrell, John, *Poetry, Language and Politics* (Manchester University Press, 1988).

Barth, J. Robert, S. J., "Coleridge and the Church of England," in Gravil and Lefebure, eds., *The Coleridge Connection*, pp. 291–307.

Bate, Walter Jackson, *Coleridge* (Cambridge: Harvard University Press, 1968).

Beer, John, "The 'revolutionary youth' of Wordsworth and Coleridge: Another View," *Critical Quarterly* 19.2 (1977): 79–87.

Beljame, Alexandre, *Men of Letters and the English Public in the Eighteenth Century*, ed. Bonamy Dobrée, trans. E. O. Lorimer (1897; London: Kegan Paul, 1948).

Berger, Peter L., "The Sociological Study of Sectarianism," *Social Research* 21 (Winter 1954): 467–85.

Bernhardt-Kabisch, Ernest, *Robert Southey* (Boston: Twayne Publishers, 1977).

Bindman, David, *The Shadow of the Guillotine: Britain and the French Revolution* (London: British Museum Publications, 1989).

Bloom, Harold, "The Internalization of Quest-Romance," in *Romanticism and Consciousness: Essays in Criticism*, ed. Harold Bloom (New York: Norton, 1970), pp. 3–23.

Boulton, James T., *The Language of Politics in the Age of Wilkes and Burke* (London: Routledge, 1963).

Bourdieu, Pierre, *Distinction: A Social Critique of the Judgment of Taste*, trans. Richard Nice (Cambridge: Harvard University Press, 1984).

The Field of Cultural Production, ed. Randal Johnson (New York: Columbia University Press, 1993).

Bradley, James E., *Religion, Revolution, and English Radicalism: Nonconformity in Eighteenth-Century Politics and Society* (Cambridge University Press, 1990).

"Whigs and Nonconformists: 'Slumbering Radicalism' in English Politics, 1739–89," *Eighteenth-Century Studies* 9.1 (1975): 1–27.

Brathwaite, Helen, *Romanticism, Publishing and Dissent: Joseph Johnson and the Cause of Liberty* (Houndmills: Palgrave, 2003).

Brett, R. L., ed., *S. T. Coleridge* (London: G. Bell & Sons, 1971).

Brewer, John, *The Common People and Politics, 1750–1790s* (Cambridge: Chadwyck-Healey, 1986).

Party Ideology and Popular Politics at the Accession of George III (Cambridge University Press, 1976).

Briggs, Asa, *The Age of Improvement 1783–1867* (London: Longmans, 1979).

Bright, Henry, *A Historical Sketch of Warrington Academy* (Liverpool, 1859).

Brown, Marshall, *Preromanticism* (Stanford University Press, 1991).

Brown, Richard, *Church and State in Modern Britain* (London: Routledge, 1991).

Brown, W. C., "Robert Southey and the English Interest in the Near East," *ELH* 5 (1938): 218–24.

Burdon, Christopher, *The Apocalypse in England: Revelation Unravelling, 1700–1834* (Houndmills: Macmillan, 1997).

Butler, Marilyn, "Culture's Medium: The Role of the Review," in *The Cambridge Companion to British Romanticism*, ed. Stuart Curran (Cambridge University Press, 1993), pp. 120–47.

"Godwin, Burke, and *Caleb Williams*," *Essays in Criticism* 32 (1982): 237–57.

"Literature as a Heritage or Reading Other Ways," Inaugural Lecture, 10 November 1987 (Cambridge University Press, 1987).

"Myth and Mythmaking in the Shelley Circle," in *Shelley Revalued: Essays from the Gregynog Conference*, ed. Kelvin Everest (Totowas: Barnes and Noble, 1983), pp. 1–19.

Romantics, Rebels, and Reactionaries: English Literature and its Background 1760–1830 (Oxford University Press, 1981).

Butler, Marilyn, ed., *Burke, Paine, Godwin, and the Revolution Controversy* (Cambridge University Press, 1984).

Butterfield, Herbert, *The Whig Interpretation of History* (London: G. Bell and Sons, 1950).

Canuel, Mark, *Religion, Toleration, and British Writing, 1790–1830* (Cambridge University Press, 2002).

Carnall, Geoffrey, *Robert Southey and His Age: The Development of a Conservative Mind* (Oxford: Clarendon Press, 1960).

Castle, Terry, "Unruly and Unresigned," *Times Literary Supplement*, 10–16 November 1989, pp. 1227–28.

Chandler, David, "Barbauld's 'Address to the Deity': Two Notes," *Notes and Queries* 245.2 (2000): 208–10.

Chandler, James K., *Wordsworth's Second Nature: A Study of the Poetry and Politics* (University of Chicago Press, 1984).

Christensen, Jerome, *Coleridge's Blessed Machine of Language* (Ithaca: Cornell University Press, 1981).

Claeys, Gregory, "From True Virtue to Benevolent Politeness: Godwin and Godwinism Revisited," in *Empire and Revolutions: Papers Presented at the*

Folger Institute Seminar, ed. Gordon J. Schochet (Washington, D.C.: Folger Institute, 1993), pp. 187–226.

"Virtuous Commerce and Free Theology: Political Economy and the Dissenting Academies 1750–1800," *History of Political Thought* 20 (Spring 1999): 141–72.

Claeys, Gregory, ed., *The Politics of English Jacobinism: Writings of John Thelwall* (University Park: Pennsylvania State University Press, 1995).

Clark, J. C. D., *English Society 1688–1832: Ideology, Social Structure and Political Practice during the Ancien Regime* (Cambridge University Press, 1985).

The Language of Liberty, 1660–1832: Political Discourse and Social Dynamics in the Anglo-American World (Cambridge University Press, 1994).

Revolution and Rebellion: State and Society in England in the Seventeenth and Eighteenth Centuries (Cambridge University Press, 1986).

Clemit, Pamela, "Godwin's Educational Theory: *The Enquirer*," *Enlightenment and Dissent* 12 (1993): 3–11.

Coleman, Deirdre, "Firebrands, Letters and Flowers: Mrs Barbauld and the Priestleys," in Russell and Tuite, eds., *Romantic Sociability: Social Networks and Literary Culture in Britain, 1770–1840*, pp. 82–103.

"The Unitarian Rationalist and the 'Winged Spider': Anna Letitia Barbauld and Samuel Taylor Coleridge," in *Imperfect Apprehensions: Essays in English Literature in Honour of G. A. Wilkes*, ed. Geoffrey Little (Sydney: Challis, 1996), pp. 148–63.

Colley, Linda, *Britons: Forging the Nation 1707–1837* (London: Pimlico, 1992).

Collins, A. S., *Authorship in the Days of Johnson: Being a Study of the Relation between Author, Patron, Publisher and Public, 1726–1780* (London: Robert Holden, 1927).

Colmer, John, *Coleridge: Critic of Society* (Oxford: Clarendon Press, 1959).

"Coleridge and Politics," in Brett, ed., *S. T. Coleridge*, pp. 244–70.

Cone, Carl B., *The English Jacobins: Reformers in Late 18th Century England* (New York: Charles Scribner's Sons, 1968).

Conger, Syndy McMillen, ed., *Sensibility in Transformation: Creative Resistance to Sentiment from the Augustans to the Romantics* (Rutherford: Fairleigh Dickinson University Press, 1990).

Cook, Elizabeth Heckendorn, *Epistolary Bodies: Gender and Genre in the Eighteenth-Century Republic of Letters* (Stanford University Press, 1996).

Cookson, J. E., *The Friends of Peace: Anti-War Liberalism in England, 1793–1815* (Cambridge University Press, 1982).

Cornwell, John, *Coleridge, Poet and Revolutionary, 1772–1804; A Critical Biography* (London: A. Lane, 1973).

Curran, Stuart, *Poetic Form and British Romanticism* (Oxford University Press, 1986).

Daffron, Eric, "'Magnetical Sympathy': Strategies of Power and Resistance in Godwin's *Caleb Williams*," *Criticism* 37.2 (1995): 213–32.

Davidoff, Leonore, and Catherine Hall, *Family Fortunes: Men and Women of the English Middle Class, 1780–1850* (University of Chicago Press, 1987).

Davidson, Edward H., and William J. Scheick, *Paine, Scripture, and Authority:*
The Age of Reason as Religious and Political Idea (Bethlehem: Lehigh
University Press, 1994).

Davis, Thomas W., ed., *Committees for Repeal of the Test and Corporation Acts,*
Minutes, 1788–90 and 1827–28 (London Record Society, 1978).

Deen, Leonard W., "Coleridge and the Sources of Pantisocracy: Godwin, the
Bible, and Hartley," *Boston Studies in English* 5 (1961): 232–45.

Dickinson, H. T., *Liberty and Property: Political Ideology in Eighteenth-Century*
Britain (New York: Holmes and Meier, 1977).

Ditchfield, G. M., "Anti-trinitarianism and Toleration in Late Eighteenth-
Century British Politics: The Unitarian Petition of 1792," *Journal of Ecclesi-*
astical History 42.1 (1991): 39–67.

"The Parliamentary Struggles over the Repeal of the Test and Corporation
Acts, 1787–90," *English Historical Review* 89.352 (1974): 551–77.

Donnelly, F. K., "Levellerism in Eighteenth and Early Nineteenth Century
Britain," *Albion* 20.2 (1988): 261–69.

Downie, J. A., and Thomas N. Corns, eds., *Telling People What to Think: Early*
Eighteenth-Century Periodicals from The Review *to* The Rambler (London:
Frank Cass, 1993).

Duff, David, *Romance and Revolution: Shelley and the Politics of a Genre*
(Cambridge University Press, 1994).

Eagleton, Terry, *The Function of Criticism, From the Spectator to Post-Structuralism*
(London: Verso, 1984).

The Ideology of the Aesthetic (Oxford: Basil Blackwell, 1990).

Walter Benjamin: Towards a Revolutionary Criticism (London: Verso, 1981).

Eley, Geoff, "Nations, Publics, and Political Cultures: Placing Habermas in
the Nineteenth Century," in *Habermas and the Public Sphere*, ed. Craig
Calhoun (Cambridge: MIT Press, 1992), pp. 289–339.

Ellis, Markman, "Coffee-women, 'The Spectator' and the Public Sphere in the
Early Eighteenth Century," in *Women, Writing and the Public Sphere 1700–*
1830, ed. Elizabeth Eger et al. (Cambridge University Press, 2001), pp. 27–52.

The Politics of Sensibility: Race, Gender and Commerce in the Sentimental Novel
(Cambridge University Press, 1996).

Ellison, Julie, "The Politics of Fancy in the Age of Sensibility," in Wilson and
Haefner, eds., *Re-Visioning Romanticism*, pp. 228–55.

Engell, James, "Imagining into Nature: 'This Lime-Tree Bower My Prison,'" in
Critical Essays on Samuel Taylor Coleridge, ed. Leonard Orr (New York:
G. K. Hall, 1994), pp. 81–96.

Epstein, James, "Radical Dining, Toasting and Symbolic Expression in Early
Nineteenth-Century Lancashire: Rituals of Solidarity," *Albion* 20.2 (1988):
271–91.

Erdman, David, "Treason Trials in the Early Romantic Period," *The Wordsworth*
Circle 19.2 (1988): 76–82.

Everest, Kelvin, *Coleridge's Secret Ministry: The Context of the Conversation Poems*
1795–98 (Sussex: Harvester Press, 1979).

Fairchild, H. Neale, *Religious Trends in English Poetry*, 3 vols. (New York: Columbia University Press, 1939–49).

Feldman, Paula R., and Theresa M. Kelley, eds., *Romantic Women Writers: Voices and Countervoices* (Hanover: University Press of New England, 1995).

Felski, Rita, *Beyond Feminist Aesthetics* (Cambridge: Harvard University Press, 1989).

Ferguson, Francis, *Solitude and the Sublime: Romanticism and the Aesthetics of Individuation* (New York: Routledge, 1992).

Ferguson, Moira, and Janet Todd, *Mary Wollstonecraft* (Boston: Twayne Publishers, 1984).

Fitzpatrick, M., "William Godwin and the Rational Dissenters," *Price-Priestley Newsletter* 3 (1979): 4–28.

Fogle, Richard Harter, "Coleridge's Conversation Poems," *Tulane Studies in English* 5 (1955): 103–10.

Forbes, D., "Sceptical Whiggism, Commerce and Liberty," in *Essays on Adam Smith*, ed. A. Skinner and T. Wilson (Oxford: Clarendon Press, 1975), pp. 179–201.

Foucault, Michel, *The Archaeology of Knowledge and the Discourse on Language*, trans. A. M. Sheridan Smith (New York: Pantheon Books, 1972).

Fraser, Nancy, "Rethinking the Public Sphere: A Contribution to the Critique of Actually Existing Democracy," in *The Phantom Public Sphere*, ed. Bruce Robbins (Minneapolis: University of Minnesota Press, 1993), pp. 1–32.

 Unruly Practices: Power, Discourse, and Gender in Contemporary Social Theory (Minneapolis: University of Minnesota Press, 1989).

Fruchtman, Jack, Jr., "Joseph Priestley on Rhetoric and the Power of Political Discourse," *Eighteenth-Century Life* 7.3 (1982): 37–47.

Fulford, Tim, "Pagodas and Pregnant Throes: Orientalism, Millenarianism and Robert Southey," in Fulford, ed., *Romanticism and Millenarianism*, pp. 121–37.

Fulford, Tim, ed., *Romanticism and Millenarianism* (Houndmills: Palgrave, 2002).

Gérard, Albert S., *English Romantic Poetry: Ethos, Structure, and Symbol in Coleridge, Wordsworth, Shelley, and Keats* (Berkeley: University of California Press, 1968).

 "The Systolic Rhythm: The Structure of Coleridge's Conversation Poems," *Essays in Criticism* 10.3 (1960): 307–19.

Gill, Frederick C., *The Romantic Movement and Methodism: A Study of English Romanticism and the Evangelical Revival* (London: The Epworth Press, 1937).

Gilmartin, Kevin, "Popular Radicalism and the Public Sphere," *Studies in Romanticism* 33.4 (1994): 549–57.

 Print Politics: The Press and Radical Opposition in Early Nineteenth-Century England (Cambridge University Press, 1996).

Gleadle, Kathryn, *The Early Feminists: Radical Unitarians and the Emergence of the Women's Rights Movement, 1831–51* (New York: St. Martin's Press, 1995).

Goldsmith, M. M., "The Principles of True Liberty: Political Ideology in Eighteenth-Century Britain," *Political Studies* 27 (1979): 141–46.

Goodson, A. C., "Coleridge on Language: A Poetic Paradigm," *Philological Quarterly* 62.1 (1983): 45–68.

Goodwin, Albert, *The Friends of Liberty: The English Democratic Movement in the Age of the French Revolution* (Cambridge: Harvard University Press, 1979).

Graham, Kenneth W., *The Politics of Narrative: Ideology and Social Change in William Godwin's* Caleb Williams (New York: AMS Press, 1990).

Graham, Walter, *English Literary Periodicals* (New York: Thomas Nelson & Sons, 1930).

Gramsci, Antonio, *Selections from the Prison Notebooks of Antonio Gramsci*, ed. and trans. Quintin Hoare and Geoffrey Nowell Smith (New York: International Publishers, 1971).

Gravil, Richard, and Molly Lefebure, eds., *The Coleridge Connection: Essays for Thomas McFarland* (New York: St. Martin's Press, 1990).

Guillory, John, *Cultural Capital: The Problem of Literary Canon Formation* (University of Chicago Press, 1993).

"Gray's 'Elegy,' Anna Laetitia Barbauld, and the Vernacular Canon," in *Early Modern Conceptions of Property*, ed. John Brewer and Susan Staves (London: Routledge, 1995), pp. 389–410.

Gunn, J. A. W., *Beyond Liberty and Property: The Process of Self-Recognition in Eighteenth-Century Thought* (Kingston: McGill-Queen's University Press, 1983).

Haakonssen, Knud, ed., *Enlightenment and Religion* (Cambridge University Press, 1996).

Habermas, Jürgen, "Further Reflections on the Public Sphere," in *Habermas and the Public Sphere*, ed. Craig Calhoun (Cambridge: MIT Press, 1992), pp. 421–61.

Moral Consciousness and Communicative Action, trans. Christian Lenhardt and Shierry Weber Nicholson (Cambridge: MIT Press, 1990).

The Structural Transformation of the Public Sphere: An Inquiry into a Category of Bourgeois Society, trans. Thomas Burger (1962; Cambridge: MIT Press, 1989).

Hagen, Everett, *On the Theory of Social Change* (Homewood: Dorsey Press, 1962).

Halévy, Elie, *The Birth of Methodism in England*, trans. and ed. Bernard Semmel (University of Chicago Press, 1971).

The Liberal Awakening 1815–1830, trans. E. I. Watkin (1923; London: Ernest Benn, 1949).

Haller, William, *The Early Life of Robert Southey 1774–1803* (New York: Columbia University Press, 1917).

Hamilton, Paul, "Coleridge and Godwin in the 1790s," in Gravil and Lefebure, eds., *The Coleridge Connection*, pp. 41–59.

Coleridge's Poetics (Oxford: Basil Blackwell, 1983).

Handwerk, Gary, "Of Caleb's Guilt and Godwin's Truth: Ideology and Ethics in *Caleb Williams*," *English Literary History* 60.4 (1993): 939–60.

Harper, George Maclean, "Coleridge's Conversation Poems," *Quarterly Review* 244 (1925): 284–98.

Hayden, John O., *The Romantic Reviewers 1802–1824* (London: Routledge, 1969).

Helfield, Randa, "Constructive Treason and Godwin's Treasonous Constructions," *Mosaic* 28.2 (1995): 43–62.

Hewitt, Regina, *The Possibilities of Society: Wordsworth, Coleridge, and the Sociological Viewpoint of English Romanticism* (Albany: State University of New York Press, 1997).

Hickey, Alison, "Coleridge, Southey 'and Co.': Collaboration and Authority," *Studies in Romanticism* 37.3 (1998): 305–49.

"Double Bonds: Charles Lamb's Romantic Collaborations," *ELH* 63.3 (1996): 735–71.

Hill, Bridget, *Women, Work, and Sexual Politics in Eighteenth-Century England* (Oxford: Basil Blackwell, 1989).

Hill, Christopher, *Reformation to Industrial Revolution: A Social and Economic History of Britain, 1530–1780* (London: Weidenfeld & Nicolson, 1967).

Hill, John Spencer, *A Coleridge Companion* (London: Macmillan, 1983).

Hoagwood, Terence Alan, *Politics, Philosophy, and the Production of Romantic Texts* (DeKalb: Northern Illinois University Press, 1996).

Hobsbawm, Eric, *Industry and Empire: An Economic History of Britain since 1750* (London: Weidenfeld & Nicolson, 1968),

Hoffpauir, Richard, "The Thematic Structure of Southey's Epic Poetry," *The Wordsworth Circle* 6.4 (1975): 240–48.

Hole, Robert, *Pulpits, Politics and Public Order in England 1760–1832* (Cambridge University Press, 1989).

Holmes, Richard, *Coleridge: Early Visions* (London: Hodder & Stoughton, 1989).

Holt, Anne, *A Life of Joseph Priestley* (Oxford University Press, 1931).

Holub, Robert C., *Jürgen Habermas: Critic in the Public Sphere* (London: Routledge, 1991).

Hughes, Graham Werden, *With Freedom Fired: The Story of Robert Robinson, Cambridge Nonconformist* (London: Carey Kingsgate Press, 1955).

Hulme, T. E., *Speculations: Essays on Humanism and the Philosophy of Art*, ed. Herbert Read (1924; London: Routledge, 1949).

Ingram, David, *Habermas and the Dialectic of Reason* (New Haven: Yale University Press, 1987).

Innes, Joanna, "Jonathan Clark, Social History and England's 'Ancien Regime,'" *Past and Present* 115 (May 1987): 165–200.

Janowitz, Anne, "Amiable and Radical Sociability: Anna Barbauld's 'free familiar conversation,'" in Russell and Tuite, eds., *Romantic Sociability*, pp. 62–81.

Jasper, David, *Coleridge as Poet and Religious Thinker: Inspiration and Revelation* (London: Macmillan, 1985).

The Sacred and Secular Canon in Romanticism: Preserving the Sacred Truths (Houndmills: Macmillan, 1999).

Jaszi, Peter, "On the Author Effect: Contemporary Copyright and Collective Creativity," in Woodmansee and Jaszi, eds., *The Construction of Authorship: Textual Appropriation in Law and Literature*, pp. 29–56.

Jewson, C. B., *The Jacobin City: A Portrait of Norwich in its Reaction to the French Revolution 1788–1802* (London: Blackie, 1975).

Jones, A. R., "The Conversational and other Poems," in Brett, ed., *S. T. Coleridge*, pp. 91–122.

Jones, Gareth Stedman, *Languages of Class: Studies in English Working Class History 1832–1982* (Cambridge University Press, 1983).

Keach, William, "A Regency Prophecy and the End of Anna Barbauld's Career," *Studies in Romanticism* 33.4 (1994): 569–77.

Keane, Angela, "The Market, the Public and the Female Author: Anna Laetitia Barbauld's Gift Economy," *Romanticism* 8.2 (2002): 161–78.

Kelly, Gary, *The English Jacobin Novel, 1780–1805* (Oxford: Clarendon Press, 1976).

Revolutionary Feminism: The Mind and Career of Mary Wollstonecraft (New York: St. Martin's Press, 1992).

Women, Writing, and Revolution, 1790–1827 (Oxford: Clarendon Press, 1993).

Kernan, Alvin, *Printing Technology, Letters, and Samuel Johnson* (Princeton University Press, 1987).

Kitson, Peter J., "'To Milton's Trump': Coleridge's Unitarian Sublime and the Miltonic Apocalypse," in Fulford, ed., *Romanticism and Millenarianism*, pp. 37–52.

"The Whore of Babylon and the Woman in White: Coleridge's Radical Unitarian Language," in *Coleridge's Visionary Languages*, ed. Tim Fulford and Morton D. Paley (Rochester: Brewer, 1993), pp. 1–14.

Klancher, Jon P., "Godwin and the Genre Reformers: on Necessity and Contingency in Romantic Narrative Theory," in Rajan and Wright, eds., *Romanticism, History, and the Possibilities of Genre*, pp. 21–38.

"Godwin and the Republican Romance: Genre, Politics, and Contingency in Cultural History," *Modern Language Quarterly* 56.2 (1995): 145–65.

The Making of English Reading Audiences, 1790–1832 (Madison: University of Wisconsin Press, 1987).

Knox, T. R., "Thomas Spence: The Trumpet of Liberty," *Past & Present* 76 (August 1977): 75–98.

Kraft, Elizabeth, "Anna Letitia Barbauld's 'Washing-Day' and the Montgolfier Balloon," *Literature and History* 4.2 (1995): 25–41.

Kramnick, Isaac, "Religion and Radicalism: English Political Theory in the Age of Revolution," *Political Theory* 5.4 (1977): 505–34.

Landes, Joan B., *Women and the Public Sphere in the Age of the French Revolution* (Ithaca: Cornell University Press, 1988).

Leask, Nigel, *British Romantic Writers and the East: Anxieties of Empire* (Cambridge University Press, 1992).

"Pantisocracy and the Politics of the 'Preface' to *Lyrical Ballads*," in *Reflections of Revolution: Images of Romanticism*, ed. Alison Yarrington and Kelvin Everest (London: Routledge, 1993), pp. 39–58.

The Politics of Imagination in Coleridge's Critical Thought (London: Macmillan, 1988).

Leaver, Kristen, "Pursuing Conversations: *Caleb Williams* and the Romantic Construction of the Reader," *Studies in Romanticism* 33.4 (1994): 589–610.

Lennon, Thomas M., *Reading Bayle* (University of Toronto Press, 1999).

Levinson, Marjorie, "The New Historicism: Back to the Future," in *Rethinking Historicism: Critical Readings in Romantic History*, ed. Marjorie Levinson (London: Blackwell, 1989), pp. 18–63.

Lincoln, Anthony, *Some Political and Social Ideas of English Dissent 1763–1800* (Cambridge University Press, 1938).

Liu, Alan, *Wordsworth: The Sense of History* (Stanford University Press, 1989).

Locke, Don, *A Fantasy of Reason: The Life and Thought of William Godwin* (London: Routledge, 1980).

Lottes, Günther, *Politische Aufklärung und plebejisches Publikum: Zur Theorie und Praxis des englischen Radikalismus im späten 18. Jahrhundert* (Munich: Oldenbourg, 1979).

Lovegrove, Deryck W., *Established Church, Sectarian People: Itinerancy and the Transformation of English Dissent, 1780–1830* (Cambridge University Press, 1988).

McCalman, Iain, *Radical Underworld: Prophets, Revolutionaries and Pornographers in London, 1795–1840* (Cambridge University Press, 1988).

McCann, Andrew, *Cultural Politics in the 1790s: Literature, Radicalism and the Public Sphere* (Houndmills: Macmillan, 1999).

McCarthy, Thomas, *The Critical Theory of Jürgen Habermas* (Cambridge: MIT Press, 1978).

McCarthy, William, "'We Hoped the *Woman* Was Going to Appear': Repression, Desire, and Gender in Anna Letitia Barbauld's Early Poems," in Feldman and Kelley, eds., *Romantic Women Writers*, pp. 113–37.

"Why Anna Letitia Barbauld Refused to Head a Women's College: New Facts, New Story," *Nineteenth-Century Contexts* 23.3 (2001): 349–79.

McCracken, David, "Godwin's Literary Theory: The Alliance between Fiction and Political Philosophy," *Philological Quarterly* 49 (1970): 113–33.

McFarland, Thomas, *Coleridge and the Pantheist Tradition* (Oxford: Clarendon Press, 1969).

McGann, Jerome, *The Romantic Ideology* (University of Chicago Press, 1983).

McGrath, Patrick, ed., *Bristol in the Eighteenth Century* (Newton Abbott: David & Charles, 1972).

McKendrick, Neil, "Josiah Wedgwood: An Eighteenth-Century Entrepreneur in Salesmanship and Marketing Techniques," *Economic History Review* 12 (1959–60): 408–33.

McKusick, James C., *Coleridge's Philosophy of Language* (New Haven: Yale University Press, 1986).

McLachlan, Herbert, *English Education under the Test Acts: Being the History of the Nonconformist Academies 1662–1820* (Manchester University Press, 1931).

"Mary Priestley: A Woman of Character," in *Motion Toward Perfection: The Achievement of Joseph Priestley*, ed. A. Truman Schwartz and John G. McEvoy (Boston: Skinner House Books, 1989), pp. 251–64.

Warrington Academy: Its History and Influence (Manchester: The Chetham Society, 1943).

MacInnes, C. M., "Bristol and the Slave Trade," in McGrath, ed., *Bristol in the Eighteenth Century*, pp. 161–84.

Madden, Lionel, ed., *Robert Southey: The Critical Heritage* (London: Routledge, 1972).

Magnuson, Paul, *Reading Public Romanticism* (Princeton University Press, 1998).

Mandell, Laura, *Misogynous Economies: The Business of Literature in Eighteenth-Century Britain* (Lexington: University of Kentucky Press, 1999).

Marcy, Peter T., "Eighteenth Century Views of Bristol and Bristolians," in McGrath, ed., *Bristol in the Eighteenth Century*, pp. 11–40.

Marshall, Peter H., *William Godwin* (New Haven: Yale University Press, 1984).

Martin, Richard T., "Coleridge's Use of 'sermoni propriora,'" *The Wordsworth Circle* 3 (1972): 71–75.

Mee, Jon, *Romanticism, Enthusiasm, and Regulation: Poetics and the Policing of Culture in the Romantic Period* (Oxford University Press, 2003).

Mellor, Anne K., "Joanna Baillie and the Counter-Public Sphere," *Studies in Romanticism* 33.4 (1994): 559–67.

Messenger, Ann, *His and Hers: Essays in Restoration and Eighteenth-Century Literature* (Lexington: University Press of Kentucky, 1986).

Meyer, Eric, "'I know thee not, I loathe thy race': Romantic Orientalism in the Eye of the Other," *ELH* 58.3 (1991): 657–99.

Minchinton, Walter, "The Port of Bristol in the Eighteenth Century," in McGrath, ed., *Bristol in the Eighteenth Century*, pp. 127–60.

Mineka, Francis E., *The Dissidence of Dissent: The Monthly Repository, 1806–1838* (Chapel Hill: University of North Carolina Press, 1944).

Money, John, *Experience and Identity: Birmingham and the West Midlands 1760–1800* (Manchester University Press, 1977).

Montluzin, Emily Lorraine de, *The Anti-Jacobins, 1798–1800: The Early Contributors to the* Anti-Jacobin Review (New York: St. Martin's Press, 1988).

Moore, Catherine E., "'Ladies . . . Taking the Pen in Hand': Mrs. Barbauld's Criticism of Eighteenth-Century Women Novelists," in *Fetter'd or Free? British Women Novelists, 1670–1815*, ed. Mary Anne Schofield and Cecilia Macheski (Athens: Ohio University Press, 1986), pp. 383–97.

Morgan, Kenneth, *Bristol and the Atlantic Trade in the Eighteenth Century* (Cambridge University Press, 1993).

Morrow, John, *Coleridge's Political Thought: Property, Morality and the Limits of Traditional Discourse* (London: Macmillan, 1990).

Mullan, John, *Sentiment and Sociability: The Language of Feeling in the Eighteenth Century* (Oxford: Clarendon Press, 1988).

Mulrooney, Jonathan, "'Sounding on His Way': Coleridgean Religious Dissent and Hazlitt's Conversational Style," in *The Fountain Light: Studies in*

Romanticism and Religion In Honor of John L. Mahoney, ed. J. Robert Barth, S. J. (New York: Fordham University Press, 2002), pp. 176–92.

Mumby, Frank Arthur, *Publishing and Bookselling: A History from the Earliest Times to the Present Day* (London: Jonathan Cape, 1930).

Murray, A. Victor, "Doddridge and Education," in Nuttall, ed., *Philip Doddridge 1702–51: His Contribution to English Religion*, pp. 102–21.

Myers, Mitzi, "Godwin's Memoirs of Wollstonecraft: The Shaping of Self and Subject," *Studies in Romanticism* 20.3 (1981): 299–316.

"Reform or Ruin: 'A Revolution in Female Manners,'" *Studies in Eighteenth-Century Culture* 11 (1982): 199–216.

"Sensibility and the 'Walk of Reason': Mary Wollstonecraft's Literary Reviews as Cultural Critique," in Conger, ed., *Sensibility in Transformation*, pp. 120–44.

Myers, Sylvia Harcstark, *The Bluestocking Circle: Women, Friendship, and the Life of the Mind in Eighteenth-Century England* (Oxford: Clarendon Press, 1990).

Negt, Oskar, and Alexander Kluge, *Public Sphere and Experience: Toward an Analysis of the Bourgeois and Proletarian Public Sphere*, trans. Peter Labanyi, Jamie Owen Daniel, and Assenka Oksiloff (1972; Minneapolis: University of Minnesota Press, 1993).

Newlyn, Lucy, *Reading, Writing, and Romanticism: The Anxiety of Reception* (Oxford University Press, 2000).

Niebuhr, H. Richard, *The Social Sources of Denominationalism* (New York: Holt, 1929).

Nuttall, Geoffrey F., *Studies in English Dissent* (Weston Rhyn: Quinta Press, 2002).

Visible Saints: The Congregational Way 1640–1660 (Oxford: Basil Blackwell, 1957).

Nuttal, Geoffrey F., ed., *Philip Doddridge 1702–51: His Contribution to English Religion* (London: Independent Press, 1951).

O'Brien, P., *Warrington Academy, 1757–86: Its Predecessors and Successors* (Wigan: Owl Books, 1989).

Ousby, Ian, "'My Servant Caleb': Godwin's *Caleb Williams* and the Political Trials of the 1790s," *University of Toronto Quarterly* 44 (1974): 47–55.

Outhwaite, William, *Habermas: A Critical Introduction* (Stanford University Press, 1994).

Paley, Morton, *Apocalypse and Millennium in English Romantic Poetry* (Oxford: Clarendon Press, 1999).

Parke, Catherine, "What Kind of Heroine is Mary Wollstonecraft?" in Conger, ed., *Sensibility in Transformation*, pp. 103–19.

Parker, Irene, *Dissenting Academies in England: Their Rise and Progress and their Place among the Educational Systems of the Country* (Cambridge University Press, 1914).

Patton, Lewis, and Peter Mann, "Editor's Introduction," in *Lectures 1795: On Politics and Religion*, vol. 1 of *The Collected Works of Samuel Taylor Coleridge*, pp. xxiii–lxxx.

Peckham, Morse, *The Birth of Romanticism 1790–1815* (Greenwood: Penkeville, 1986).

Perkin, Michael, "William Eyres and the Warrington Press," in *Aspects of Printing From 1600*, ed. Robin Myers and Michael Harris (Oxford Polytechnic Press, 1987), pp. 69–89.

Philp, Mark, *Godwin's Political Justice* (London: Duckworth, 1986).

Pickering, Sam, "Mrs. Barbauld's *Hymns in Prose*: 'An Air-Blown Particle' of Romanticism?" *Southern Humanities Review* 92 (Spring 1975): 259–68.

Piper, H. W., "Coleridge and the Unitarian Consensus," in Gravil and Lefebure, eds., *The Coleridge Connection*, pp. 273–90.

Plank, Jeffrey, "John Aikin on Science and Poetry," *Studies in Burke* 18 (1977): 167–78.

Plomer, H. R., et al., *Dictionaries of the Printers and Booksellers Who Were at Work in England, Scotland and Ireland 1726–1775* (Ilkley: The Bibliographical Society, 1968).

Plumb, J. H., *The Growth of Political Stability in England: 1675–1725* (Baltimore: Penguin, 1967).

"The Public, Literature, and the Arts in the Eighteenth Century," in *The Emergence of Leisure*, ed. Michael R. Marrus (New York: Harper & Row, 1974), pp. 11–37.

Pocock, J. G. A., *Politics, Language, and Time; Essays on Political Thought and History* (New York: Atheneum, 1971).

Virtue, Commerce, and History: Essays on Political Thought and History, Chiefly in the Eighteenth Century (Cambridge University Press, 1985).

Porter, Dennis, "*Orientalism* and its Problems," in Williams and Chrisman, eds., *Colonial Discourse and Post-Colonial Theory: A Reader*, pp. 150–61.

Porter, Roy, "The Enlightenment in England," in *The Enlightenment in National Context*, ed. Roy Porter and Mikulas Teich (Cambridge University Press, 1981), pp. 1–18.

Postone, Moishe, Edward LiPuma, and Craig Calhoun, "Introduction: Bourdieu and Social Theory," in *Bourdieu: Critical Perspectives*, ed. Craig Calhoun et al. (University of Chicago Press, 1993), pp. 1–13.

Prest, Wilfrid, "Law, Lawyers and Rational Dissent," in Haakonssen, ed., *Enlightenment and Religion*, pp. 169–92.

Prickett, Stephen, *Romanticism and Religion: The Tradition of Coleridge and Wordsworth in the Victorian Church* (Cambridge University Press, 1976).

Priestman, Martin, *Romantic Atheism: Poetry and Freethought, 1780–1830* (Cambridge University Press, 1999).

Purton, Valerie, *A Coleridge Chronology* (London: Macmillan, 1993).

Radcliffe, Evan, "Godwin from 'Metaphysician' to Novelist: *Political Justice, Caleb Williams*, and the Tension between Philosophical Argument and Narrative," *Modern Philology* 97.4 (2000): 528–53.

Rajan, Tilottama, "Framing the Corpus: Godwin's 'Editing' of Wollstonecraft in 1798," *Studies in Romanticism* 39.4 (2000): 511–31.

"Wollstonecraft and Godwin: Reading the Secrets of the Political Novel," *Studies in Romanticism* 27.2 (1988): 221–51.

Rajan, Tilottama, and Julia M. Wright, eds., *Romanticism, History and the Possibilities of Genre: Re-Forming Literature, 1789–1837* (Cambridge University Press, 1998).

Reilly, Robin, *Josiah Wedgwood 1730–1795* (London: Macmillan, 1992).

Richey, Russell E., "Did the English Presbyterians Become Unitarian?" *Church History* 42 (1973): 58–72.

"The Origins of British Radicalism: The Changing Rationale for Dissent," *Eighteenth-Century Studies* 7 (1973–74): 179–92.

Ritchie, Anne Thackeray, *A Book of Sibyls* (London: Smith, Elder, & Co., 1883).

Rivers, Isabel, *The Defence of Truth through the Knowledge of Error: Philip Doddridge's Academy Lectures* (London: Dr. Williams's Trust, 2003).

"Dissenting and Methodist Books of Practical Divinity," in *Books and their Readers in Eighteenth-Century England*, ed. Isabel Rivers (New York: St. Martin's Press, 1982), pp. 127–64.

Reason, Grace, and Sentiment: A Study of the Language of Religion and Ethics in England, 1660–1780, vol. I, *Whichcote to Wesley* (Cambridge University Press, 1991), and vol. II, *Shaftesbury to Hume* (Cambridge University Press, 2000).

Robbins, Caroline, *The Eighteenth Century Commonwealthman* (Cambridge: Harvard University Press, 1959).

Rodgers, Betsy, *Georgian Chronicle: Mrs Barbauld and Her Family* (London: Methuen, 1958).

Roe, Nicholas, "Coleridge and John Thelwall: the Road to Nether Stowey," in Gravil and Lefebure, eds., *The Coleridge Connection*, pp. 60–80.

"Godwin's Integrity," *Durham University Journal* 85.54 (1993): 299–301.

"Pantisocracy and the Myth of the Poet," in Fulford, ed., *Romanticism and Millenarianism*, pp. 87–102.

The Politics of Nature: Wordsworth and Some Contemporaries (New York: St. Martin's Press, 1992).

Wordsworth and Coleridge: The Radical Years (Oxford: Clarendon Press, 1988).

Roper, Derek, *Reviewing before the* Edinburgh (Newark: University of Delaware Press, 1978).

Ross, Marlon, "Configurations of Feminine Reform: The Woman Writer and the Tradition of Dissent," in Wilson and Haefner, eds., *Re-Visioning Romanticism*, pp. 91–110.

The Contours of Masculine Desire: Romanticism and the Rise of Women's Poetry (Oxford University Press, 1989).

Rubinstein, W. D., *Men of Property* (New Brunswick: Rutgers University Press, 1981).

Rudé, George, *The Crowd in the French Revolution* (Oxford: Clarendon Press, 1959).

Paris and London in the Eighteenth Century: Studies in Popular Protest (New York: Viking Press, 1971).

Rupp, Gordon, *Religion in England 1688–1791* (Oxford: Clarendon Press, 1986).

Russell, Gillian, and Clara Tuite, eds., *Romantic Sociability: Social Networks and Literary Culture in Britain, 1770–1840* (Cambridge University Press, 2002).

Ryan, Robert M., *The Romantic Reformation: Religious Politics in English Literature, 1789–1824* (Cambridge University Press, 1997).

Said, Edward, *Orientalism* (New York: Vintage Books, 1978).

"Orientalism Reconsidered," in *Europe and Its Others*, ed. Francis Barker et al., 2 vols. (Colchester: University of Essex, 1985), i, pp. 14–27.

Schofield, R. E., *The Lunar Society of Birmingham: A Social History of Provincial Science and Industry in Eighteenth-Century England* (Oxford: Clarendon Press, 1963).

Schulz, Max F., *The Poetic Voices of Coleridge: A Study of His Desire for Spontaneity and Passion for Order* (Detroit: Wayne State University Press, 1963).

Scrivener, Michael, *Seditious Allegories: John Thelwall & Jacobin Writing* (University Park: Pennsylvania State University Press, 2001).

Seed, J., "Gentlemen Dissenters: The Social and Political Meanings of Rational Dissent in the 1770s and 1780s," *Historical Journal* 28 (1985): 299–325.

Sharafuddin, Mohammed, *Islam and Romantic Orientalism: Literary Encounters with the Orient* (London: I. B. Tauris, 1994).

Short, H. L., "Presbyterians Under a New Name," in *The English Presbyterians: From Elizabethan Puritanism to Modern Unitarianism* (London: George Allen, 1968), pp. 219–86.

Simmons, Clare, "'Useful and Wasteful Both': Southey's *Thalaba the Destroyer* and the Function of Annotation in the Romantic Oriental Poem," *Genre* 27 (Spring–Summer 1994): 83–104.

Simmons, Jack, *Southey* (New Haven: Yale University Press, 1948).

Smith, Olivia, *The Politics of Language 1791–1819* (Oxford: Clarendon Press, 1984).

Spector, Robert D., *Political Controversy: A Study in Eighteenth-Century Propaganda* (New York: Greenwood Press, 1992).

Stafford, W., "Dissenting Religion Translated into Politics," *History of Political Thought* 1.2 (1980): 279–99.

Stallybrass, Peter, and Allon White, *The Politics and Poetics of Transgression* (Ithaca: Cornell University Press, 1986).

Stanley, Brian, *The History of the Baptist Missionary Society 1792–1992* (Edinburgh: T&T Clark, 1992).

Stillinger, Jack, *Multiple Authorship and the Myth of Solitary Genius* (Oxford University Press, 1991).

Stone, Lawrence, *The Causes of the English Revolution, 1529–1642* (New York: Harper & Row, 1972).

The Family, Sex and Marriage in England, 1500–1800 (New York: Harper & Row, 1977).

Storey, Mark, "'A Hold upon Posterity': The Strange Case of Robert Southey," Inaugural lecture delivered on 20 February 1992 at the University of Birmingham (School of English, 1993).

Robert Southey: A Life (Oxford University Press, 1997).

Sullivan, Garrett A., Jr., "'A Story to Be Hastily Gobbled Up': *Caleb Williams* and Print Culture," *Studies in Romanticism* 32.3 (1993): 323–37.

Taylor, Barbara, "For the Love of God: Religion and the Erotic Imagination in Wollstonecraft's Feminism," in *Mary Wollstonecraft and 200 Years of Feminisms*, ed. Eileen Janes Yeo (London: Rivers Oram Press, 1997), pp. 15–35.

Mary Wollstonecraft and the Feminist Imagination (Cambridge University Press, 2003).

"The Religious Foundations of Mary Wollstonecraft's Feminism," in *The Cambridge Companion to Mary Wollstonecraft*, ed. Claudia L. Johnson (Cambridge University Press, 2002), pp. 99–118.

Thomas, Roger, "Philip Doddridge and Liberalism in Religion," in Nuttall, ed., *Philip Doddridge 1702–51: His Contribution to English Religion*, pp. 122–53.

Thompson, David M., ed., *Nonconformity in the Nineteenth Century* (London: Routledge, 1972).

Thompson, E. P., "18th Century English Society: Class Struggle without Class?" *Social History* 3 (May 1978): 133–65.

"Disenchantment or Default? A Lay Sermon," in *Power & Consciousness*, ed. Conor Cruise O'Brien and William Dean Vanech (University of London Press, 1969), pp. 149–81.

The Making of the English Working Class (New York: Pantheon Books, 1963).

Tompkins, J. M. S., *The Polite Marriage: Eighteenth-Century Essays* (Cambridge University Press, 1938).

Trevelyan, G. M., *Illustrated English Social History. Volume Three. The Eighteenth Century* (London: Longmans, 1951).

Trott, Nicola, "The Coleridge Circle and the 'Answer to Godwin,'" *Review of English Studies* 41.162 (1990): 212–29.

Tucker, Herbert F., "Southey the Epic-Headed," *Romanticism on the Net* 32–33 (November 2003–February 2004). 43 pars. 19 March 2005. <http://www.erudit.org/revue/ron/2003/v/n32–33/009263ar.html>.

Turner, Cheryl, *Living by the Pen: Women Writers in the Eighteenth Century* (London: Routledge, 1992).

Turner, William, *The Warrington Academy* (Warrington: Library and Museum Committee, 1957).

Tyacke, Nicholas, *Anti-Calvinists: The Rise of English Arminianism c. 1590–1640* (Oxford: Clarendon Press, 1987).

Tyson, Gerald P., *Joseph Johnson: A Liberal Publisher* (Iowa City: University of Iowa Press, 1979).

Uglow, Jenny, *The Lunar Men: Five Friends Whose Curiosity Changed the World* (New York: Farrar, Straus, and Giroux, 2002).

Walker, Gina Luria, "Mary Hays (1759–1843): An Enlightened Quest," in *Women, Gender and Enlightenment*, ed. Sarah Knott and Barbara Taylor (London: Palgrave, 2005), pp. 493–518.

Wang, Orrin N. C., "Romancing the Counter-Public Sphere: A Response to Romanticism and its Publics," *Studies in Romanticism* 33.4 (1994): 579–88.

Watson, George, *Coleridge the Poet* (New York: Barnes & Noble, 1966).

Watts, Michael R., *The Dissenters: From the Reformation to the French Revolution*, vol. I (Oxford: Clarendon Press, 1978) and *The Dissenters: The Expansion of Evangelical Nonconformity*, vol. II (Oxford: Clarendon Press, 1995).

Webb, R. K., "Price among the Unitarians," *Enlightenment and Dissent* 19 (2000): 147–70.

"The Unitarian Background," in *Truth, Liberty, Religion: Essays Celebrating Two Hundred Years of Manchester College*, ed. Barbara Smith (Oxford: Manchester College, 1986), pp. 1–30.

Weber, Max, *The Sociology of Religion* (Boston: Beacon Press, 1922).

The Theory of Social and Economic Organization, ed. Talcott Parsons, trans. A. M. Henderson and Talcott Parsons (New York: Free Press, 1947).

Wendling, Ronald C., *Coleridge's Progress to Christianity: Experience and Authority in Religious Faith* (Lewisburg: Bucknell University Press, 1995).

Werkmeister, Lucyle, *The London Daily Press, 1772–1792* (Lincoln: University of Nebraska, 1963).

A Newspaper History of England 1792–1793 (Lincoln: University of Nebraska Press, 1967).

Weston, Rowland, "Politics, Passion and the 'Puritan Temper': Godwin's Critique of Enlightenment Modernity," *Studies in Romanticism* 41.3 (2002): 445–70.

Whalley, George, "Coleridge and Southey in Bristol, 1795," *The Review of English Studies*, n.s., I (1950): 324–40.

Wharam, Alan, *The Treason Trials, 1794* (Leicester University Press, 1992).

White, Daniel E., "The 'Joineriana': Anna Barbauld's Prose, the Aikin Family Circle, and the Collaborative Production of the Dissenting Public Sphere," *Eighteenth-Century Studies* 32.4 (1999): 511–33.

Willey, Basil, "Coleridge and Religion," in Brett, ed., *S. T. Coleridge*, pp. 221–43.

Samuel Taylor Coleridge (New York: Norton, 1972).

Williams, Patrick, and Laura Chrisman, eds., *Colonial Discourse and Post-Colonial Theory: A Reader* (New York: Harvester Wheatsheaf, 1993).

Williams, Raymond, *Culture and Society 1780–1950* (New York: Columbia University Press, 1958).

The Long Revolution (New York: Columbia University Press, 1961).

Wilkie, Brian, *Romantic Poets and Epic Tradition* (Madison: University of Wisconsin Press, 1965).

Wilson, Bryan, *Patterns of Sectarianism: Organisation and Ideology in Social and Religious Movements* (London: Heineman, 1967).

Wilson, Carol Shiner, "Lost Needles, Tangled Threads: Stichery, Domesticity, and the Artistic Enterprise in Barbauld, Edgeworth, Taylor, and Lamb," in Wilson and Haefner, eds., *Re-Visioning Romanticism*, pp. 167–90.

Wilson, Carol Shiner, and Joel Haefner, eds., *Re-Visioning Romanticism: British Women Writers, 1776–1837* (Philadelphia: University of Pennsylvania Press, 1994).

Wood, Marcus, *Radical Satire and Print Culture, 1790–1822* (Oxford: Clarendon Press, 1994).

Woodcock, George, *William Godwin: A Biographical Study* (Montreal: Black Rose Books, 1989).

Woodmansee, Martha, "On the Author Effect: Recovering Collectivity," in Woodmansee and Jaszi, eds., *The Construction of Authorship*, pp. 15–28.

Woodmansee, Martha, and Peter Jaszi, eds., *The Construction of Authorship: Textual Appropriation in Law and Literature* (Durham: Duke University Press, 1994).

Woodring, Carl R., *Politics in English Romantic Poetry* (Cambridge: Harvard University Press, 1970).

Politics in the Poetry of Coleridge (Madison: University of Wisconsin Press, 1961).

Worrall, David, *Radical Culture: Discourse, Resistance and Surveillance, 1790–1820* (Detroit: Wayne State University Press, 1992).

Wykes, David L., "The Contribution of the Dissenting Academy to the Emergence of Rational Dissent," in Haakonssen, ed., *Enlightenment and Religion*, pp. 99–139.

"'A good discourse, well explained in 35 minutes': Unitarians and Preaching in the Early Nineteenth Century," *Transactions of the Unitarian Historical Society* 16.3 (1997): 173–90.

Wylie, Ian, "Coleridge and the Lunaticks," in Gravil and Lefebure, eds., *The Coleridge Connection*, pp. 25–40.

Yates, Gayle Graham, ed., *Harriet Martineau on Women* (New Brunswick: Rutgers University Press, 1985).

Zall, Paul M., "The Cool World of Samuel Taylor Coleridge: Mrs. Barbauld's Crew and the Building of a Mass Reading Class," *The Wordsworth Circle* 2 (Summer 1971): 74–79.

Index

abolitionism 9, 34, 159
Abrams, M. H. 2, 51, 139–40, 184, 193n, 219n
academies, *see* Dissenting academies
Act of Uniformity 8, 163, 192n
Adam, Robert 95, 96, 166, 226n
Adams, John 98
Addicott, Len 204n
Addington, Stephen 211n
Addison, Joseph 78, 104
Aikin, Anna, *see* Barbauld, Anna Letitia
Aikin, Arthur 72–3, 208n
Aikin, Charles 66
Aikin family 3, 11–12, 38, 67, 69, 70–2, 73,
    85–6, 92, 98, 128, 186, 187, 208n, 209n
Aikin, John, Jr. 11, 12, 23, 24, 39–40,
    66–7, 69, 70, 71–4, 193n, 208n
    *Address to the Dissenters of England on
    Their Late Defeat* 126
    and collaboration with Howard 72–3
    *Description of the Country from Thirty to Forty
    Miles round Manchester* 124–5, 198n
    "Epistle to Mr. Aikin" 72–3
    Evenings at Home 70–3, 74–5
    Miscellaneous Pieces in Prose 66, 73, 76–83
    *Spirit of the Constitution and that of the
    Church of England, Compared* 18–19
    Thoughts on Hospitals 72
    see also Aikin family; Barbauld,
        Anna Letitia, and collaboration
Aikin, John, Sr. 23, 30, 37, 50, 69–70, 98
Aikin, Lucy 69–70, 72, 74, 75–6, 200n
Aikin, Martha 66
Akenside, Mark 34, 139
Alcock, Nathan 166–7, 169
American War of Independence 20–1, 147
Andrews, Stuart 37, 139, 194n, 201n
Anglicans, *see* Church of England
Anne, Queen of England 9, 83
Annesley, Anne 204n
Annesley, Samuel 203–4n
Annesley, Susanna 204n

Anti-Jacobin 104, 168
apostasy 3, 14, 15, 90, 106, 130, 156, 166
Appleyard, J. A. 219n
Arianism 26, 70, 84, 122, 166, 198n, 205n
    and Barbauld 37, 38, 42, 69
    defined 189–90n
    and legal proscription 8
    and Presbyterianism 4, 20, 46, 92, 128, 190n
    and Price 39, 202n
    and Priestley 196n
    and Southey 155, 157–9, 162
    and Unitarianism 37–40, 190–1n
Arminianism 10, 25, 84, 94, 122, 197n, 205n
    and Barbauld 37, 42, 50, 69, 83
    defined 189n
    and Presbyterianism 4, 20, 46, 92, 128, 190n
    and Southey 155, 158–9
    and Unitarianism 38–40, 190n
Arius 163
Ashton, T. S. 195n, 198n
Ashworth, Caleb 24, 37, 38
Aspland, Robert 208n
Association for the Preservation of Liberty
    and Property against Republicans and
    Levellers 106
Athanasian Creed 9, 10
Athanasius 163
atheism 3–4, 93–4, 134, 146–7, 157–9,
    163, 166, 167
Attar, Farid ud-Din 228n
Augustine 158

Baillie, Joanna 39, 69
Bakhtin, Mikhail 12, 176–7, 216n
Bangorian controversy 18
Baptists 22, 39, 40, 119, 185, 188n
    General 10, 15, 37, 39, 40, 43, 96, 128
    and missionary movement 13, 153–4
    Missionary Society 153
    Particular 7, 13, 43, 46, 47, 92, 128,
        153, 165, 185

CAMBRIDGE STUDIES IN ROMANTICISM

General Editors

Marilyn Butler, University of Oxford
James Chandler, University of Chicago